Adventures in Transcendental Materialism

Speculative Realism

Series Editor: Graham Harman

Since its first appearance at a London colloquium in 2007, the Speculative Realism movement has taken continental philosophy by storm. Opposing the formerly ubiquitous modern dogma that philosophy can speak only of the human-world relation rather than the world itself, Speculative Realism defends the autonomy of the world from human access, but in a spirit of imaginative audacity.

Books available

Quentin Meillassoux: Philosophy in the Making by Graham Harman
Onto-Cartography: An Ontology of Machines and Media by Levi R. Bryant
Adventures in Transcendental Materialism: Dialogues with Contemporary Thinkers by Adrian Johnston
Form and Object: A Treatise on Things by Tristan Garcia, translated by Mark Allan Ohm and Jon Cogburn
The End of Phenomenology: Metaphysics and the New Realism by Tom Sparrow

Forthcoming series titles

Fields of Sense: A New Realist Ontology by Markus Gabriel
Romantic Realities: Speculative Realism and British Romanticism by Evan Gottlieb
After Quietism: Analytic Philosophies of Immanence and the New Metaphysics by Jon Cogburn
Quentin Meillassoux: Philosophy in the Making Second Edition by Graham Harman

Visit the Speculative Realism website at
www.euppublishing.com/series/specr

Adventures in Transcendental Materialism

Dialogues with Contemporary Thinkers

Adrian Johnston

EDINBURGH
University Press

© Adrian Johnston, 2014

Edinburgh University Press Ltd
The Tun – Holyrood Road
12 (2f) Jackson's Entry
Edinburgh EH8 8PJ
www.euppublishing.com

Typeset in 11/13 Adobe Sabon by
Servis Filmsetting Ltd, Stockport, Cheshire,
printed and bound in the United States of America

Reprinted 2014

A CIP record for this book is available from the British Library

ISBN 978 0 7486 7328 5 (hardback)
ISBN 978 0 7486 7329 2 (paperback)
ISBN 978 0 7486 7330 8 (webready PDF)
ISBN 978 0 7486 7331 5 (epub)

Contents

vi   Contents

Acknowledgments

Adventures in Transcendental Materialism, as its sub-title already signals, would not exist without the "general intellect" formed by a whole group of people I am honored and delighted to have as indispensable interlocutors. Among those "contemporary thinkers" I especially would like to thank are Alain Badiou, Frederick Beiser, Richard Boothby, Bruno Bosteels, Ray Brassier, Thomas Brockelman, Nathan Brown, Lorenzo Chiesa, Joan Copjec, Mladen Dolar, Thomas Eyers, Samir Haddad, Martin Hägglund, Peter Hallward, Davis Hankins, Graham Harman, Aaron Hodges, Thomas Johnston, Todd Kesselman, Richard G. Klein, Catherine Malabou, Kareen Malone, Tracy McNulty, Kelly Oliver, Knox Peden, Robert Pippin, Ed Pluth, Kenneth Reinhard, Jeremi Roth, Frank Ruda, Michael Shim, Gino Signoracci, Kristian Simcox, Daniel Lord Smail, Philippe Van Haute, Kathryn Wichelns, Slavoj Žižek, and Alenka Zupančič. These are some of the people from whom I have learned a great deal and who have profoundly shaped various aspects of the contents of this book.

I also would like to thank those involved with the institutions and events at which I had invaluable opportunities to present earlier versions of some of the material contained in *Adventures in Transcendental Materialism*: a preliminary draft of Chapter 5 at a "Theory Reading Group" conference at Cornell University (2007); a penultimate version of Chapter 6 as a keynote address at both "Real Objects or Material Subjects?: A Conference on Continental Metaphysics" organized and hosted by the Department of Philosophy at the University of Dundee (2010) as well as at another "Theory Reading Group" conference at Cornell University (2010); Chapter 8 at a roundtable at Cornell University (2008); Chapter 9 at a panel co-sponsored by the New School for Social Research, the City University of New York, and the National Psychological Association for Psychoanalysis (2012); and, Chapter 12 as a keynote address at the Annual Philosophy Student Conference at the University of New Mexico on "Drive, Desire, and Dissent: Philosophy at the Intersection of Politics and Psychoanalysis" (2012). Not only am I deeply grateful for the invitations and hospitality extended to me by the individuals who had hands in arranging these gatherings – I benefitted enormously from the stimulating conversations and critical feedback I enjoyed during my visits to these places. I hope my revisions and additions to the contents of this book begin to do some justice to these exchanges.

Furthermore, I am grateful to the editors and publishers who graciously have permitted earlier articles and essays to reappear here in modified form. These earlier pieces are: "Slavoj Žižek's Hegelian Reformation: Giving a Hearing to *The Parallax View*," *Diacritics: A Review of Contemporary Criticism*, vol. 37, no. 1, Spring 2007, pp. 3–20 (Chapter 5); "'Naturalism or Anti-naturalism? No, thanks – both are worse!': Science, Materialism, and Slavoj Žižek," *La Revue Internationale de Philosophie*, no. 261, 2012, special issue: "On Slavoj Žižek," pp. 321–46 (Chapter 6); "A Critique of Natural Economy: Quantum Physics with Žižek," *Žižek Now*, ed. Jamil Khader and Molly Rothenberg, Cambridge: Polity Press, 2013, pp. 103–20 (Chapter 7); "Life Terminable and Interminable: The Undead and the Afterlife of the Afterlife – A Friendly Disagreement with Martin Hägglund," *New Centennial Review*, vol. 9, no. 1, Spring 2009, special issue: "Living On: Of Martin Hägglund," ed. David E. Johnson, pp. 147–89 (Chapter 8); "The true Thing is the (w)hole: Freudian-Lacanian Psychoanalysis and Derridean Chronolibidinal Reading – Another Friendly Reply to Martin Hägglund," *Derrida Today*, 2013 (Chapter 9); "This Philosophy Which Is Not One: Jean-Claude Milner, Alain Badiou, and Lacanian Antiphilosophy," *S: Journal of the Jan Van Eyck Circle for Lacanian Ideology Critique*, no. 3, Spring 2010, special issue: "On Jean-Claude Milner," ed. Justin Clemens and Sigi Jöttkandt, pp. 137–58 (Chapter 10); "The Real Unconscious: A Friendly Reply to Catherine Malabou," *Theory @ Buffalo*, no. 16, 2012, special issue: "*Plastique*: Dynamics of Catherine Malabou," pp. 124–43 (Chapter 11); and, "Think Big: Toward a Grand Neuropolitics – or, Why I am not an immanent naturalist or vital materialist," *Essays on Neuroscience and Political Theory: Thinking the Body Politic*, ed. Frank Vander

Valk, New York: Routledge, 2012, pp. 156–77 (Chapter 12). Furthermore, the editors and readers of these pieces helped me clarify and refine the ideas elaborated in them.

Finally, I am immeasurably indebted to my family for their unwavering love and care. Kathryn and our son Ezra mean everything and more to me. I also am extremely grateful to Kathryn's and my sets of parents (Jerry and Anne Wichelns and Tom and Trish Johnston) for their loving support and concern.

Series Editor's Preface

Adrian Johnston is one of the most visible and influential younger figures in continental philosophy. With the present book, *Adventures in Transcendental Materialism*, his unique authorial voice resounds even more clearly than before. A trained Lacanian psychoanalyst and Professor of Philosophy at the University of New Mexico, Johnston is both a tireless writer and a charismatic public speaker. He is also the close collaborator of such European intellectual luminaries as Catherine Malabou and Slavoj Žižek. Johnston's work often has an almost magical effect on the young, who see in his combination of psychoanalysis, Leftist politics, German Idealist philosophy, and respect for the natural sciences the promise of a new future in philosophy.

Johnston's 2005 debut book, *Time Driven*,[1] expanded Freud's account of drives by identifying a conflict in the heart of the drives themselves. This first work drew heavily on Lacan, and was an important further contribution to molding continental philosophy with the insights of psychoanalysis. But Johnston's rise to public prominence can be linked most directly to his second and third books, in which he established himself as a peerless and insatiable interpreter of the philosophy of Žižek. In 2008, Johnston published the acclaimed *Žižek's Ontology*.[2] Against the frequent tendency to take Žižek for a witty philosophical observer of popular culture, Johnston energetically captured the serious ontology underlying Žižek's work: a specific fusion of Lacan with German Idealism that is not dissimilar to Johnston's own. This was followed in 2009 by *Badiou, Žižek, and Political Transformations*, in

[1] Adrian Johnston, *Time Driven: Metapsychology and the Splitting of the Drive*, Evanston: Northwestern University Press, 2005.
[2] Adrian Johnston, *Žižek's Ontology: A Transcendental Materialist Theory of Subjectivity*, Evanston: Northwestern University Press, 2008.

which Žižek was read in parallel with his older comrade-in-arms Alain Badiou, a duo that might be said to dominate European philosophy at present.[3] While demonstrating the close link between ontology and politics in these two thinkers, Johnston was frankly critical of the details of this link, which in his view has unfortunate political consequences. In 2013, Johnston followed up with two additional books. There was the long-awaited joint work with Malabou, *Self and Emotional Life*,[4] and the manifesto-like *Prolegomena to Any Future Materialism*.[5] That would make the present book his sixth unless the relentless Johnston, a veritable furnace of human energy, has already completed other works of which I am still unaware.

The title of *Adventures in Transcendental Materialism* tells us everything essential about the contents of the book. On the one hand, Johnston is an ardent materialist, proud of his debt to the Marxist tradition and lacking in all sympathy even for oblique flirtations with religion (see for example his blunt critique of Quentin Meillassoux's concept of the virtual God).[6] But the qualification of materialism as transcendental signals a distance from the old-school materialism in which particles of physical matter exist independently from the human mind. Johnston's combined debt to Lacan and German Idealism forbids him any appeal to such things-in-themselves, and hence the "matter" of materialism tends to become an obstacle internal to the subject itself rather than something lying outside it. (This much he shares with Žižek.) In turn, the word "adventures" refers to the organizational style of the book. Just as a pirate captain calls first on Jamaica, then Barbados, Surinam, Madagascar, and Ceylon, Johnston uses the present work to call on a variety of dead and living authors whose work is in some way close to his own: the German Idealists, Lacan, Žižek, Martin Hägglund, Jean-Claude Milner, Badiou, Malabou, William Connolly, and Jane Bennett.

All of these dialogues will be of interest to the reader, but three

[3] Adrian Johnston, *Badiou, Žižek, and Political Transformations: The Cadence of Change*, Evanston: Northwestern University Press, 2009.
[4] Adrian Johnston and Catherine Malabou, *Self and Emotional Life: Philosophy, Psychoanalysis, and Neuroscience*, New York: Columbia University Press, 2013.
[5] Adrian Johnston, *Prolegomena to Any Future Materialism: The Outcome of Contemporary French Philosophy*, Evanston: Northwestern University Press, 2013.
[6] Adrian Johnston, "Hume's Revenge: À Dieu, Meillassoux?," in Levi R. Bryant et al. (eds.), *The Speculative Turn: Continental Materialism and Realism*, Melbourne: Re.press, 2011.

in particular stand out as likely to make an especially lasting impression. Chapters 5 through 7 on Žižek may turn out to be the most significant of this book, since they show the greatest divergence so far between Johnston and the subject of two of his books. While Žižek has long paid serious attention to quantum physics in his work, Johnston finds this emphasis unconvincing, and recommends a turn to biology instead. In so doing, he also takes a distance from contemporary eliminativist approaches in the philosophy of mind. Chapters 8 and 9 show Johnston in friendly combat with the young Swedish philosopher Martin Hägglund of Yale University, whose recent writings on Derrida have sparked an uproar.[7] Precisely because Johnston and Hägglund have so much in common, their differences become especially striking. Finally, I would also call the reader's attention to the remarks in Chapter 12 on Jane Bennett and William Connolly. While Bennett's work has already entered continental philosophy through the admiring approval of the object-oriented ontologists, Connolly is only just beginning to enter the arena, despite his longstanding prominence in political theory. Johnston's closing chapter is among the first to import Connolly's ideas into continental thought.

Although Johnston is technically not a Speculative Realist, he is among the most prominent fellow travelers of the movement, being personally acquainted with its members and often engaged in friendly disagreement with them. For this reason, as well as the importance of Johnston's ideas themselves, *Adventures in Transcendental Materialism* is an important addition to the Speculative Realism series.

Graham Harman
Ankara
August 2013

---

[7] See Martin Hägglund, *Radical Atheism: Derrida and the Time of Life*, Stanford: Stanford University Press, 2008.

The task is to think the subject's emergence or becoming from the self-splitting of substance: the subject is not directly the Absolute, it emerges out of the self-blockage of substance, out of the impossibility of substance fully asserting itself as One.

Slavoj Žižek

To the memory of Robert and Thelma Cook,
with immense love, respect, and gratitude

Introduction

Reports From Philosophical Fronts: Exchanges with Contemporaries Past and Present

For philosophical thought particularly, the clashes and struggles arising from confrontations between partisans of different orientations are catalysts absolutely essential for this discipline's vivacity and development. However, not all such confrontations are productive in this way. Conflict-driven philosophical progress is best fueled by a mixture consisting of a finely balanced blend of fiercely stubborn adversarial advocacy and patient mutual understanding sustained by a background of respectful charity.

Over the past several years, I have gradually constructed and refined the position I label "transcendental materialism" within a context informed by a number of live fault lines of theoretical tensions. More precisely, these specific fault lines are rifts between stances (my own and those with which I engage) relating to each other in the above-described promising manner of combining argumentative ferocity with interpretive generosity. Whatever I might have to contribute to certain ongoing conversations in philosophy/theory today, I owe to a wonderfully motley ensemble, a sparklingly multifaceted Marxian "general intellect," of superb interlocutors and debating partners. Transcendental materialism has taken shape in fashions very much determined by its chosen significant others.

The chapters of this book contain, among other things, treatments of a number of living figures along lines informed by transcendental materialism. The current thinkers addressed here include, to provide a non-exhaustive list, Alain Badiou, Jane Bennett, William Connolly, Markus Gabriel, Iain Hamilton Grant, Martin Hägglund, Catherine Malabou, Jean-Claude Milner, Colette Soler, Slavoj Žižek, and Alenka Zupančič. Reflecting the invaluable historical sensibilities of the intellectual traditions of Continental Europe, these authors, as anyone familiar with

I

them knows, draw deeply and broadly from the history of ideas (philosophical, psychoanalytic, political) in the process of building their own bodies of concepts. Moreover, like all of the people just mentioned, I view the history of ideas (especially as regards philosophy and psychoanalysis) as not merely historical. That is to say, I am convinced that the canonical figures of philosophy and psychoanalysis represent rigorously formulated end-points of particular intellectual possibilities and trajectories, with these end-points continuing to remain viable options up through the present. Such proper names as Spinoza, Hume, Kant, Fichte, Schelling, Hegel, Marx, Freud, and Lacan name theoretical alternatives whose plausibility and enduring appeal are unlikely to disappear anytime soon in the foreseeable future. Hence, these members of the pantheon of the "mighty dead" are as much the contemporaries of transcendental materialism as are Badiou et al. (to refer back to the list at the start of this paragraph).

Through critical readings of these contemporaries past and present, I strive in this book to hone and advance transcendental materialism as a philosophical position with interdisciplinary links. I aim to illustrate herein how and why this theoretical framework of mine relies upon critical employments of resources drawn from German idealism, psychoanalysis, Marxism, and the life sciences. I draw contrasts and sharpen the distinctions between my fashions of working with these varied resources and those practiced by certain other contemporaneous theorists. In so doing, I underscore the differences these contrasts and distinctions make to an understanding of political, religious, and scientific issues central to our present socio-historical circumstances.

The four chapters constituting Part I ("No Illusions: Hegel, Lacan, and Transcendental Materialism") push off from what I call the "principle of no illusions," a thesis of transcendental materialism affirming its adamant opposition to mechanistic, reductive, or eliminative materialisms. More precisely, transcendental materialism, as a contemporary extension of historical and dialectical materialisms, crucially entails a principled refusal of recourse to such notions as epiphenomena and "folk psychology," notions signaling a dismissal of various entities and events as purely illusory *qua* causally inefficacious appearances, falsehoods, fantasies, fictions, unrealities, etc. Instead, in line with Hegelian-Marxian concrete/real abstractions (as well as Lacanian structures that "march in the streets"), my materialism is vehemently anti-reductive/eliminative for reasons similar to those furnished by Hegel, Marx, and Lacan, among others. Part I elaborates the arguments for this key aspect of transcendental materialism via an examination of criticisms of Spinoza's monistic substance metaphysics spelled out by Hume, Kant, and Hegel as being of continuing contemporary relevance to disputes about what materialism means today.

Chapter 1 ("The Latest System-Program of German Idealism: From Tübingen to Today") performs two tasks. First, it situates transcendental materialism in relation to the history of modernity beginning with the birth of modern science in the early seventeenth century. However, as this chapter's title and sub-title already indicate, the historical reference most emphasized by me here is the philosophical agenda of post-Fichtean German idealism initially forged in the 1790s – more specifically, that of the Tübingen trio of Hölderlin, Schelling, and Hegel (more than that of Novalis and Friedrich Schlegel as contemporaneous Romantic critics of Kant and Fichte). In several important senses, transcendental materialism involves a reactivation of suggestions voiced in the 1796 fragment "The Earliest System-Program of German Idealism" authored by one of these three Tübingen students (which one remaining a matter of disagreement amongst scholars). The second task executed in this chapter is a comparing and contrasting of transcendental materialism with the Žižek of 2012's *Less Than Nothing: Hegel and the Shadow of Dialectical Materialism* (as well as with Gabriel's Žižek-informed "transcendental ontology"). Žižek's work is the most influential inspiration for transcendental materialism. Furthermore, in his recent *magnum opus*, he articulates his own valuable clarifications regarding the defining essential characteristics of transcendental materialism. Chapter 1 also foreshadows the core issues around which revolve the three chapters of Part II ("Žižek: Dossier of an Ongoing Debate").

Chapter 2 ("For a Thoughtful Ontology: Hegel's Immanent Critique of Spinoza") exegetically reconstructs the multi-pronged Spinoza critique delineated by Hegel across the bulk of his corpus (but especially as formulated in his monumental *Science of Logic*). It does so in conjunction with sketches of Hume's, Kant's, and Schelling's critiques of Spinoza too (with Kant's critiques in particular informing Hegel's). I tie the Hegelian immanent (rather than external) critique of Spinozism to the insistence, from the preface to the *Phenomenology of Spirit*, on the requirement that substance must be thought also as subject (a stipulation central to transcendental materialism as well). Over the course of this reconstruction, I fight on behalf of this Hegel against Althusserian and Deleuzian Spinozist counter-offensives, doing so with an eye to the antagonism between neo-Spinozisms and neo-Hegelianisms seen as a fundamental battle front in today's ongoing struggles concerning the interrelated topics of materialism, realism, and the status of (modern) subjectivity.

Chapter 3 ("'Off with their thistleheads!': Against Neo-Spinozism") expands upon Chapter 2's defenses of Hegel *contra* the neo-Spinozists. Once again on the basis of the no-illusions principle as already explained and justified prior to this juncture, I argue against the structuralist and post-structuralist neo-Spinozisms of Althusser, Deleuze, and their followers as monochromatic world-views in which the negativity of autonomous subjects is indefensibly written off as an illusory epiphenomenon devoid of actual causal efficacy. Turning to "speculative realist" Grant's modified, updated rendition of Schellingian *Naturphilosophie* – Grant and I share convictions regarding the contemporary relevance of revisiting German idealism (including its long unfashionable philosophies of nature) in light of current philosophical controversies – I problematize this rendition on the basis of its Spinozist and Deleuzian tendencies to eclipse from view the speculative-dialectical distances Schelling, like Hegel, takes from Spinoza's monist ontology. Then, while still staying with a focus on recent and current varieties of neo-Spinozism, I address the life-scientific perspectives on these same matters offered by Antonio Damasio and Terrence Deacon. Damasio and Deacon end up advancing arguments against epiphenomenalism – I portray Spinozisms old and new as committed to treating subjectivity and a number of things associated with it as epiphenomenal – resonating with Marx's Hegel-indebted concept of real abstractions.

Chapter 4 ("'Lacan, our Hegel': Psychoanalysis, Dialectics, and Materialisms") shifts attention from Hegel to Lacan. As for Žižek, so too for me: Lacanian psychoanalysis is as important as Hegelian philosophy for transcendental materialism. Chapters 2 and 3 reread Hegel through the lens of the principle of no illusions. Accordingly, Chapter 4 applies this lens to Lacan (taking some of its leads from Žižek and Zupančič). Herein, I return to the Lacanian corpus so as to demonstrate how and why Lacan eventually arrives, in his later teachings, at a qualified endorsement of dialectical materialism. Additionally, and running with some of Zupančič's perspicuous insights, I seek to highlight the distinctive features of Lacan's realism (a realism steering between the poles of nominalism and metaphysical realism) as deeply relevant to contemporary controversies around speculative realism. Needless to say at this point, this simultaneously realist and materialist Lacan is a towering forefather of transcendental materialism (whether Žižek's or mine).

The three chapters constituting Part II are installments from a still-unfolding debate between Žižek and me. My transcendental materialist philosophical framework originated in a certain interpretation of Žižek's Lacanian appropriations of Kant and the post-Kantian German idealists Fichte, Schelling, and Hegel (as per my 2008 book *Žižek's Ontology: A Transcendental Materialist Theory of Subjectivity*). Since then, he and I have been arguing back and forth about what a contemporary materialism can and should be as well as how it ought to be positioned vis-à-vis both politics and science. The stakes of these exchanges include the relevance of Hegelianism to today's natural sciences, the history of Marxism's relations with these same disciplines, the importance (or lack thereof) of the life sciences especially for current philosophical and political thinking, and the status of human freedom within a thoroughly materialist *Weltanschauung*.

Chapter 5 ("Hegel's Luther: Žižek's Materialist Hegelianism") is organized around a close reading of Žižek's 2006 book *The Parallax View*, one of his most substantial philosophical works to date. I focus here on his dialectical materialist handling of the neurosciences; *The Parallax View* contains his most sustained engagement with these sciences thus far, which makes this book particularly important for me given my preoccupations. I contend in this chapter that my modified type of dialectical materialism accomplishes better than Žižek's type his attempted grounding of a dual philosophical-psychoanalytic model of subjectivity in the sciences of the brain.

Chapter 6 ("In Nature More Than Nature Itself: Žižek Between Naturalism and Supernaturalism") originally resulted from an exchange between me and Žižek in a special issue of the journal *Subjectivity*. In this chapter, I respond to his charges that my turns to biology risk naturalizing away key features of non-natural subjectivity *à la* German idealism and Lacanianism. The crux of this dispute concerns how close to or far from a life-science-based naturalism a materialist theory of the subject with allegiances to Kant, Hegel, Freud, and Lacan should be. I contend that materialism must be closer to naturalism than Žižek allows, while simultaneously insisting that the spontaneous naturalism of the cutting edge of the life sciences is not the semi-reductive paradigm Žižek believes it to be.

Chapter 7 ("Spirit is a Quark: Quantum Physics with Žižek"), following closely on the heels of the above, is a response to Žižek's reply to the contents of the preceding Chapter. *Contra* my anchoring of foundational aspects of transcendental materialism in biology and its branches (especially neuroscience, genetics, and evolutionary theory), Žižek pleads for basing a renewed materialism on dialectical interpretations of quantum physics. I respond not only by arguing for the greater relevance of biology with respect to envisioning human subjects – I also show how Žižek's recourse to physics violates the core principles of his own ontology and ends up inadvertently promoting a reductive monism at odds with his dialectical theories of subjectivity.

The five chapters constituting Part III ("Transcendental Materialism's Significant Others: Psychoanalysis, Science, and Religion"), as this Part's sub-title announces, explore the psychoanalytic, scientific, and religious dimensions and repercussions of transcendental materialism. This materialism draws extensively upon both Freudian-Lacanian analysis as well as the life sciences (two of its "significant others"). It does so aware of and interested in the politico-religious implications of materialist philosophy, analytic metapsychology, and modern science overall. In particular, I link transcendental materialism, faithful to its historical sources, to a radical leftist atheism (specifically, a both Marxist and psychoanalytic atheism) willing and able to do full materialist justice to phenomena otherwise pulling for an embrace of idealist spiritualism when the only alternatives are "contemplative" as non-dialectical materialisms (a situation described by Marx in the first of his "Theses on Feuerbach"). That is to say, transcendental materialism, in fidelity to Marxist historical and dialectical materialisms, aims to surpass mechanistic and eliminative scientistic philosophies while nonetheless avoiding relapses into the metaphysical visions of theosophical confabulating. Succinctly put, it aspires to be both non-reductive and yet stringently atheistic at the same time (the latter being a shared commitment between Marxism and Freudianism). In addition to my disciplinary significant others, I also engage with a whole host of my contemporaries throughout the chapters forming this last Part of *Adventures in Transcendental Materialism.*

Chapter 8 ("Life Terminable and Interminable: Hägglund and the Afterlife of the Afterlife") scrutinizes Hägglund's 2008 book *Radical Atheism: Derrida and the Time of Life.* Therein, Hägglund powerfully calls into question, from a Derridean standpoint, just how seriously strident and internally coherent the atheism of psychoanalysis really is when all is said and done. In response, I defend analytic atheism against Hägglund's criticisms of it and, in parallel, mount counter-attacks against his own Derrida-indebted position. What hangs in the balance of the disagreements between Hägglund and me is the question of what a thoroughly consistent philosophical critique of religion relying upon (among others) Freud and Lacan looks like in the end. Both of us also have an eye on recent attempts, in certain circles of Continentalists, to revive and/or update elements of traditional monotheistic religions (as per permutations of what has come to be known as "the post-secular turn").

Chapter 9 ("The true Thing is the (w)hole: Freudian-Lacanian Psychoanalysis and Hägglund's Chronolibidinal Reading") is a subsequent installment of my debate with Hägglund. It responds to texts of his appearing after *Radical Atheism,* especially his 2012 book *Dying for Time: Proust, Woolf, Nabokov* (texts in which Hägglund replies to the contents of the preceding chapter). In a manner connecting back with Part I, I redeploy Hegel's criticism of Schelling's excessive Spinozism – the former famously dismisses the Absolute of the latter's philosophies of nature and identity as a "night in which all cows are black" – against Hägglund's Derridean absolutizing of temporal finitude. I proceed to reveal how this absolutization motivates what arguably are misreadings of Freud and Lacan proposed by Hägglund. Then, I explain why my hybrid Freudian and Lacanian drive theory, as per my 2005 book *Time Driven: Metapsychology and the Splitting of the Drive* (itself critically addressed by Hägglund on several occasions), possesses the virtues of a temporality-concerned reinterpretation of atheistic psychoanalysis while avoiding the pitfalls of Derridean-Hägglundian radical atheist "chronolibidinalism."

Chapter 10 ("Antiphilosophy and Paraphilosophy: Milner, Badiou, and Antiphilosophical Lacanianism") takes up Badiou's notion/category of "antiphilosophy" as developed on the grounds of his recasting of the history of Western philosophy starting with the ancient Greek split between philosophy and sophistry. In a series of three consecutive unpublished seminars given between 1992 and 1995, Badiou addresses (one per academic year) three figures he identifies as the great antiphilosophers of the present age: Nietzsche, Wittgenstein, and Lacan. Motivated by my philosophical reliance upon Lacan, I contest Badiou's portrait of Lacan as an antiphilosopher, doing so with special focus on the former's 1994–95 seminar (albeit also drawing on his other published discussions of Lacan). In the process, I critically examine Milner's influential glosses on Lacan's complicated, vexed relations with philosophy (apropos these themes, Badiou and Milner have influenced such prominent Lacanians as Žižek, Soler, and François Regnault). I conclude by suggesting that Lacanianism is neither separable from nor identical with philosophy, defying capture by schematizations such as Badiou's opposition between the philosophical and the antiphilosophical.

Chapter 11 ("The Real Unconscious: Malabou, Soler, and Psychical Life After Lacan") defends Lacan along another front, one opened up by Malabou's critical appraisals of Freudian-Lacanian psychoanalysis. Malabou and I recently published a co-authored book entitled *Self and Emotional Life: Philosophy, Psychoanalysis, and Neuroscience*. Many of the themes and topics at the heart of *Adventures in Transcendental Materialism* (as already summarized here) are connected with the contents of *Self and Emotional Life*. In this chapter here, I continue my dialogue with Malabou, pushing our debate with each other beyond what is contained in our co-authored book. In sympathy with some of Soler's excellent work on Lacan (in her 2009 book *Lacan, l'inconscient réinventé* and 2011 book *Les affects lacaniens*), I rebut Malabou's depth-hermeneutic rendition of the unconscious as it figures in her neuroscience-inspired criticisms of psychoanalysis. Unlike Malabou, I see analysis as vindicated rather than undermined by the exponential progress made in the past several decades by empirical, experimental studies of the human central nervous system. For me, a novel Lacanian neuropsychoanalysis, constructed under the supervision of a transcendental materialist stance, is a real possibility for the twenty-first century. This chapter helps to explain this view.

Chapter 12 ("Toward a Grand Neuropolitics: Why I am Not an Immanent Naturalist or Vital Materialist"), bringing *Adventures* in *Transcendental Materialism* to a close, addresses the political theory duo of Connolly and Bennett. It focuses on the former's 2002 book *Neuropolitics: Thinking, Culture, Speed* and 2011 book *A World of Becoming* as well as the latter's 2010 book *Vibrant Matter: A Political Ecology of Things*. On first glance, Connolly's framework of "immanent naturalism" looks to be very similar to my transcendental materialism. However, there is a wide divide lurking here with major ramifications. Whereas Connolly's and Bennett's theoretical perspectives ultimately are rooted, in terms of the history of philosophy, in Spinoza's monistic ontology, my position is heavily reliant on the Hegel who is sharply critical of Spinoza for a number of important theoretical and practical reasons (with this twelfth and final chapter thus circling back to Part I above). Basically, this chapter pits the neo-Spinozism shared between Connolly's immanent naturalism and Bennett's "vital materialism" against the neo-Hegelianism of transcendental materialism. Given that Connolly and Bennett are motivated by interests in intervening with respect to environmental problems on the basis of their theories, I sketch out, with reference to ecology, the ethical, political, and practical differences resulting from this contrast between their Spinozism and my Hegelianism. Hence, this book closes by gesturing toward the contemporary significance of transcendental materialism not only for philosophy, but also for many of the socially shared circumstances and challenges characterizing the early twenty-first century.

Part I

No Illusions:
Hegel, Lacan, and
Transcendental Materialism

I

The Latest System-Program of German Idealism: From Tübingen to Today

Since the early seventeenth century of Francis Bacon, Galileo Galilei, and René Descartes, the relations between science and religion as well as mind and body have remained volatile sites of conflicts. The various controversies surrounding these relations are as alive and pressing now as at any point over the course of the past four centuries. Under the heading of "transcendental materialism," I seek to offer a new theoretical approach to these issues. Arming myself with resources provided by German idealism, Marxism, psychoanalysis, the life sciences, and contemporary philosophical developments, my aim is to formulate an account of subjectivity that, while both materialist and naturalist, nonetheless does full justice to human beings as irreducible to natural matter alone. At the same time, and in conformity with the sensibilities of my chosen historical sources, I adamantly oppose relapses into idealisms, dualisms, and spiritualisms.

But, what, exactly, is "transcendental materialism?" This is a name for a philosophical position indebted primarily to the speculative dialectics of G.W.F. Hegel and the historical materialism of Karl Marx and his followers. However, whereas certain versions of Hegelian-Marxian dialectical materialism tend to emphasize possible unifying syntheses of such apparent splits as that between mind and matter, transcendental materialism treats these splits as real and irreducible (while nevertheless depicting them as internally generated out of a single, sole plane of material being). As both Maoists and the young Alain Badiou would put it, this is the distinction between the Two becoming One (dialectical materialism) and the One becoming Two (transcendental materialism).[1] Or, with reference to emergentism as a set of theoretical frameworks in the life sciences, this is the difference between a somewhat weak and holistic/organicist emergentism versus a very strong and anti-holistic/organicist emergentism.

Along these lines, I am tempted to characterize transcendental materialism as an emergent dual-aspect monism, albeit with the significant qualification that these "aspects" and their ineradicable divisions (such as mind and matter, the asubjective and the subjective, and the natural and the more-than-natural) enjoy the heft of actual existence (rather than being, as they arguably are in Spinozistic dual-aspect monism, mere epiphenomena deprived of true ontological substantiality). My philosophical program is driven by the question: What sort of ontology of "first nature" (i.e., the one-and-only original reality of natural material substances) allows for the genesis of a "second nature" (i.e., autonomous subjects as epistemologically inexplicable and ontologically irreducible with reference to natural material substances alone) – a second nature immanently transcending first nature and requiring theorization in a manner that avoids the twin pitfalls of reductive/eliminative monisms and idealist/spiritualist dualisms? I strive to answer this question by combining inspirations from philosophy past and present with resources drawn from psychoanalysis and the sciences.

Slavoj Žižek, in his magisterial 2012 tome *Less Than Nothing: Hegel and the Shadow of Dialectical Materialism*, provides a clear and concise definition of transcendental materialism. With Quentin Meillassoux's "speculative" critique of "correlationism" (as anti-realist idealisms) in view,[2] he states:

> one can make out the contours of what can perhaps only be designated by the oxymoron 'transcendental materialism'…: all reality is transcendentally constituted, 'correlative' to a subjective position, and, to push this through to the end, the way out of this 'correlationist' circle is not to try to directly reach the In-itself, but to inscribe this transcendental correlation *into the Thing itself*. The path to the In-itself leads through the subjective gap, since the gap between For-us and In-itself is immanent to the In-itself: appearance is itself 'objective,' therein resides the truth of the realist problem of 'How can we pass from appearance For-us to reality In-itself?'[3]

Žižek soon adds – "The real difficulty is to think the subjective perspective as inscribed in 'reality' itself."[4] By sharp contrast with the Meillassoux of *After Finitude: An Essay on the Necessity of*

Contingency, who seeks to resuscitate the pre-Kantian epistemological question of how the subjective mind transcends itself so as to make direct knowing contact with the objective world, Žižek and I are preoccupied by the inverse problem: not how to escape from the idealist correlational circle so as to "touch the Real," but, rather, how this ideal circuit of subjectivity irrupts out of (and thereafter perturbs from within) the asubjective Real *an sich* of being *qua* being (*l'être en tant qu'être*).[5]

Throughout *Less Than Nothing*, Žižek advances a number of interlinked theses whose systematic cohesiveness is what I aim to capture with the label "transcendental materialism" as a sort of *point de capiton* for these theses (as per the sub-title of my 2008 book *Žižek's Ontology: A Transcendental Materialist Theory of Subjectivity*). The ultimate material condition of possibility for trans-material autonomous agency (*à la* the self-determining subject of transcendental idealism and its legacy) is, in hybrid Hegelian and Lacanian locution, the barring of the big Others of both *Natur und Geist*[6] ("we are free because there is a lack in the Other, because the substance out of which we grew and on which we rely is inconsistent, barred, failed, marked by an impossibility";[7] "the axiom of true materialism is not 'material reality is all there is,' but a double one: (1) there is nothing which is not material reality, (2) material reality is non-All"[8]). *Geist* as minded "spiritual" subjectivity, arising from natural substance thanks to this substance's "barred" status, is a desubstantialized negativity nonetheless immanent to substantial nature itself[9] ("*spirit is part of nature*"[10]). Furthermore, the irreducibility of such subjectivity is not merely an epistemological limit to humanity's explanatory powers, but an ontological fact mirrored by the disunity of the proliferating branches and sub-branches of knowledge and the perpetual elusiveness of a grand "Theory of Everything."[11] From this perspective, the existence of subjects testifies to the dialectical self-sundering character of substance as itself, given its auto-destructive character, not as solidly substantial as it is typically imagined to be.[12] More specifically, rendering the subject immanent to substance (as per Hegel's post-Spinozist project to think substance and subject together,[13] with the attendant "*absolute immanence of transcendence*"[14] in Hegelian philosophy) results in "an immanent de-naturalization of nature."[15] That is to say, "naturalizing" subjectivity affects not only images and ideas of it, but also those of nature in and of itself. This is because, by contrast

with garden-variety naturalisms that one-sidedly reduce away or
eliminate altogether any and every robust, full-blooded version
of more-than-natural subjectivity (treating it as either partially
or entirely illusory), transcendental materialist (quasi-)naturalism
refuses to water down or liquidate the denaturalized strangeness
of the subjects it forces the notion of nature to accommodate and,
in so doing, to undergo radical change as a notion.[16]

Despite being comrades-in-solidarity on these points, Žižek
and I indeed do diverge from each other in a number of respects.
To begin with, whereas he adamantly assigns quantum physics
pride of place as the alpha-and-omega scientific discipline on the
basis of which materialism today is to be rethought,[17] I consider
quantum physics by itself to be insufficient to serve as the sole or
ultimate referent in the natural sciences for a materialism engaging with these sciences (for more on this disagreement, see Part
II below). Particularly for any materialist theory of irreducible
subjectivity (such as furnished by versions of historical, dialectical,
or transcendental materialisms), biological, rather than quantum-
physical, explanatory resources are the most viable and plausible
bases on which to build such a theory (for several reasons, doing
so on the basis of the physics of the incredibly tiny is neither feasible nor defensible). The bodies out of which minded agents get
produced are, in many ways, very different from physical objects
of sizes smaller than cells, molecules, and even atoms.

Additionally, and related to the preceding, Žižek sides with
Hegel *contra* Marx apropos the latter's insistence that the origin
of (historical) dialectics resides in the brute corporeal positivity
of physical human labor.[18] This is another difference between
him and me.[19] Through his "quantum physics with Hegel (and
Lacan)," Žižek muses somewhat vaguely about a materialism
according to which various realities, including those of concern to
Marx's historical materialism, emerge out of a primal Void (such
as quantum vacuums), namely, the fundamental Nothingness of
an ostensibly materialist version of creation *ex nihilo*.[20] On the
more scientific side of things, I suspect that string theory, despite
its contentious status as armchair mathematical speculation in
relation to the discipline of physics as a modern empirical, experimental science, at least raises questions and casts doubts on some
of Žižek's quantum-physical associations linked to, for instance,
the figure of the Big Bang as an explosion of Everything out of
Nothing (in the field of string theory, Edward Witten, M-theory,

and the consequent possibility that the universe is itself part of a much larger multiverse challenge the notion of a *nihil* as the dark, empty backdrop out of which bursts the Big Bang).

Debates in and around physics aside, and turning to the more philosophical side here, I would defend Marx against Žižek's Hegel by making two claims in connection with the Darwinian life sciences (enthusiastically embraced by Marx and Friedrich Engels following the publication of Charles Darwin's *The Origin of Species* in 1859, an embrace consistent with and motivated by earlier aspects of Marxian materialism dating back to 1843–44[21]). First, as I observed above, an epistemological, if not also ontological, gulf separates the quantum-physical (to which Žižek relates Hegelian negativity) from the biological (to which Žižek relates Marxian positivity) such that the dialectics of the former (unlike the latter) by no means, even for the most committed physical reductionist or eliminativist, can account for the different subject-object dialectics operative at the levels of labor-driven human history. Second, at the significantly larger-than-quantum scales of the natural and human histories of evolution and phylogeny, dialectical-speculative negativities, rather than mysteriously and inexplicably pre-existing these histories in what could only be a spiritualist or supernatural mode, arguably are immanently generated by-products of material bodies and their kinetic processes (such as physical human labor *à la* Marx).[22] Apropos this second claim, Žižek's more Hegelian dialectics privileges the dynamic of the explosion of positivity out of negativity, whereas my comparatively more Marxian perspective focuses on the genesis of negativity out of positivity (to be more precise, the surfacing of the negativities characteristic of denaturalized, more-than-material subjects out of the positivities of natural matter[s]). One of my inspirations along these lines going against Žižek's Hegel-inspired criticisms of Marxist materialism is the later Georg Lukács of his unfinished project on *The Ontology of Social Being*.[23]

Lingering for a moment longer in the conceptual vicinity of the life sciences, Žižek, also in *Less Than Nothing*, displays a deep ambivalence concerning the topic of emergentism (something addressed mainly in biology, cognitive science, and Analytic philosophy of mind). On the one hand, he is critical of what he characterizes as "the obscurantism of 'emergent properties.'"[24] On the other hand, he invokes the idea of "downward causality" several times.[25] This idea is inseparable from the notion of emergence (specifically as per extremely strong versions of emergentism, in which emergent properties manage to achieve self-relating standings independent of their underlying material grounds) insofar as downward causation amounts to an emergent property coming to exert a reciprocal causal influence of its own on the ontological-physical base out of which it emerged. Although the negative side of Žižek's ambivalence makes him sound somewhat dismissive of emergentist models, his version of Hegel and appeals to downward causation oblige him to formulate a non-obscurantist variant of strong emergentism, which he has yet to do to date (this task preoccupies much of my ongoing work[26]). Transcendental materialism, as, in large part, an account of the emergence of self-determining, auto-reflexive transcendental subjectivity out of asubjective substance, also fairly could be depicted as a genetic, temporally elongated (meta-)transcendentalism.

Specifically as I conceive it, transcendental materialism starts with a decision to commit to an axiomatic positing of the real existence of subjects as transcendental, autonomous, and irreducible free agents of negativity nonetheless immanent/internal to the physical realities constituted by material bodies (in this respect, it can be viewed as a materialist recasting of the methodology and starting point of Fichteanism[27]). Its ontology of objective first nature is then reverse-engineered out of this commitment to there being an ineliminable facticity of subjective (as well as objective) second nature.[28] With this beginning and the focus on the subject-object dialectics between first and second natures it immediately entails, the human body as it features in biology, psychoanalysis, Hegel's philosophical anthropology, and Marxian-Engelsian historical and dialectical materialisms is by far the most important locus of intersection for the collisions and entanglements between the natural and the more-than-natural (as the denaturalized/non-natural *qua* cultural, social, etc.). Neither quantum physics *à la* Žižek nor pure mathematics *à la* Badiou can capture and adequately address this corporeal crossroads as the privileged place at which self-sundering substance becomes subject and being begins to think in and of itself.[29]

Panning back again to a wider historical perspective, philosophical materialism today, in the wake of the dialectical materialist orientation of the nineteenth and early twentieth centuries, still remains charged with an unfinished task: the rigorous construction of a rendition of human subjects as fully internal and immanent to the physical universe of the sciences of material nature. Non-dialectical materialisms (as "contemplative" *à la* the first of Marx's 1845 "Theses on Feuerbach"[30]), which have been around for as long as the perennial mind-body problem itself, enthusiastically help themselves to contentious (pseudo-)solutions of a reductive variety, unreservedly dissolving subjectivity into bodily matter in mechanical motion. The challenge for a contemporary materialism faithful to the anti-reductivism of the dialectical tradition is to preserve intact the reality of the subject while nonetheless avoiding relapses into idealisms, dualisms, or spiritualisms. Transcendental materialism aims to accomplish exactly such a feat.

Having briefly articulated these interlinked historical and philosophical characterizations of my position by way of a cursory introduction, I will proceed in what follows (specifically, in the chapters constituting Part I here), first, to state and unpack one of transcendental materialism's core axioms (all of which I enumerate and summarize elsewhere[31]) and, second, to link both this specific axiom and transcendental materialism more generally to two of my most significant sources of inspiration, namely, Hegel and Jacques Lacan. The axiom in question could be labeled "the principle of no illusions." The phrase "no illusions" is here endowed with several senses which will clearly come to light over the course of the ensuing elaborations.

For the time being and to begin with, the decision to commit to the no-illusions principle as philosophically axiomatic flows from faithfulness to Hegel's insistence that true, systematic philosophy avoids falling into any and every sort of "one-sidedness." That is to say, as per one of the several intended meanings of the dictum from the preface to the 1807 *Phenomenology of Spirit* according to which "The true is the whole" (*Das Wahre ist das Ganze*),[32] philosophies (or, more broadly, worldviews in general) fall into the nullifying untruth of self-induced dialectics when they opt to dismiss select features and facets of things as purely epiphenomenal, fictional, illusory, ineffective, unreal, and the like. Put differently, theoretical thought becomes lop-sided through utterly neglecting some dimensions in excessively favoring others. What is more, these imbalances inevitably result in the theories of such partial thinking being plagued by inconsistencies and impasses as symptoms of, in psychoanalytic terms, the returns of what is repressed by these theories' forms of one-sidedness (i.e., other sides left in the dark by lop-sidedness). In line with this Hegelian perspective, the principle of no illusions expresses a fundamental resolve not to explain away dismissively via reductions or eliminations (if not outright ignore altogether) anything as a mere illusion *qua* entirely ineffective epiphenomenon or completely unreal fiction.[33]

However, the no-illusions axiom of transcendental materialism by no means entails a monotone ontology in which everything is repeatedly said to be equally actual, situated on the same unidimensional surface of being. In other words, recognizing that everything possesses some degree of ontological gravity as a weight, however minimal, demanding acknowledgement by non-one-sided philosophy is not tantamount to endorsing an agenda of radically de-hierarchizing the inventory of real beings. Renouncing recourse to the concepts and categories of epiphenomenalism (such as that of "illusion" *qua* sterile unreality) does not automatically lead to endorsing a vision of all realities and existences as on a par with each other, as leveled down to a single stratum of ontological parity. A flattened out theoretical landscape of de-stratified entities and events is hardly an inevitable consequence following with automatic necessity from the principle of no illusions. Different degrees and kinds of real being consistently and unproblematically can be affirmed in tandem with the no-illusions axiom.

By marked contrast with so many varieties of neo-Spinozism, anti-humanism, structuralism/post-structuralism, deconstructionism, and similar theoretical brands and trends, transcendental materialism, consistent with its Hegelian and Lacanian roots, preserves the idea of subjectivity as philosophically central while nevertheless simultaneously repudiating the anti-realism of subjective idealisms (much of the background justification for this repudiation resides in Hegel's multi-pronged attack on Immanuel Kant's critical philosophy as transcendental idealism, something I will address in Chapter 2). In fact, as regards recent revivals of materialist and realist orientations in current Continental philosophical circles, I would go so far as to maintain that one of the primary antagonisms splitting materialism today from within is that between neo-Spinozist and neo-Hegelian tendencies, the former (incarnated by, for instance, Louis Althusser, Gilles Deleuze, and their various progeny) seeking to dissolve the figure of the subject and the latter (represented most notably by Žižek and Slovene Lacanianism[34]) to preserve it. Transcendental materialism's Hegel-inspired principle of no illusions obviously rules out writing off subjectivity as utterly illusory *qua* epiphe-nomenal, unreal, etc. – hence its opposition to all past and present denials of or eulogies for this subject in the veins of Spinozism, neo-Spinozism, and similar recent theoretical orientations. From this perspective, a cursory outline of the German idealist critical handlings of Spinoza's system (specifically, those of Hegel and F.W.J. Schelling) is warranted at this juncture.

Notes

1. Badiou 1976: 61–2; Badiou, Bellassen, and Mossot 1978: 44; Badiou 2009e, 14, 113–15.
2. Johnston 2011b: 92–113; Johnston, 2013i.
3. Žižek 2012: 906.
4. Ibid.: 907.
5. Ibid.: 131, 536–8, 611–12, 642–4, 646, 808–9, 905–7, 949.
6. Ibid.: 185, 263–6, 283–4, 960.
7. Ibid.: 263.
8. Ibid.: 742.
9. Ibid.: 185–6, 188, 459–61, 562.
10. Ibid.: 354.
11. Ibid.: 239.
12. Ibid.: 258, 261.
13. Hegel 1977c: 10.
14. Žižek 2012: 741.
15. Ibid.: 826.
16. Ibid.: 144–5.
17. Ibid.: 905–61.
18. Ibid.: 250–1.
19. Johnston 2011a; Hägglund, Johnston, and Žižek 2012.
20. Žižek 2012: 823.
21. Johnston 2011c: 141–82; Johnston 2013a: 103–36; Johnston 2013k; Johnston 2014.
22. Johnston 2012a: 23–52; Johnston 2013e; Johnston 2014.
23. Lukács 1978a: 5, 9, 61–2, 71, 113; Lukács 1978b: 5, 7–10, 31–2, 40, 45, 71–2, 87–8, 99–100, 103, 110; Lukács 1980: i–iv, 1–4, 9–10, 12–13, 20–4, 27, 34–5, 38–9, 42–6, 50, 54–5, 59–60, 67–8, 102–6, 135–6; Johnston 2015.
24. Žižek 2012: 467.
25. Ibid.: 726, 729, 732.
26. Johnston 2015.

27. Fichte 2005: 122; Henrich 2003: 240.
28. Johnston 2013j.
29. Johnston 2013i.
30. Marx 1977: 156.
31. Johnston 2013h.
32. Hegel 1970a: 24; Hegel 1977c: 11.
33. Longuenesse 1981: 14.
34. Žižek 2012: 374; Moder 2013: 182.

2

For a Thoughtful Ontology: Hegel's Immanent Critique of Spinoza

Near the end of the eighteenth century, while the *ancien régime* was being decapitated and its remnants liquidated in Revolutionary France, a new philosophical agenda was born in Tübingen. As is well known, German idealism in the wake of Kant, J.G. Fichte, and the controversies stirred up by F.H. Jacobi starting in the 1780s initially is animated by an ambition somehow to synthesize substance *à la* Spinozism with subjectivity *à la* Fichteanism.[1] What three students together in the Tübingen theological seminary, namely, Schelling, Hegel, and Friedrich Hölderlin, share in this vein is a desire to move beyond the anti-realist subjective idealisms of Kantian and Fichtean transcendentalisms without, for all that, anachronistically regressing back to the metaphysical dogmatisms decisively destroyed by Kant's critical "Copernican revolution."[2] Hölderlin's brief 1795 fragment "*Über Urtheil und Seyn*" ("On Judgment and Being")[3] as well as the lifelong endeavors of Schelling and Hegel (with their objective and absolute idealisms respectively) are the reflections of this youthful vision of a rapprochement between a monist ontology of the substantial and a transcendental theory of the subjective as radically autonomous. Another brief fragment from the immediate post-Tübingen period, "The Earliest System-Program of German Idealism" of 1796 (authored in all likelihood by either Hegel or Hölderlin), also can be read as announcing a project born out of a post-Kantian staging of a collision between Spinoza's and Fichte's philosophies.[4]

Likewise, I am inclined to label transcendental materialism "the latest system-program of German idealism" insofar as, partially through a materialist re-reading of German idealism informed by a number of post-Hegelian developments (in particular, Marxism, psychoanalysis, and the life sciences of the past several decades), it seeks to fuse monistic material being(s) and transcendent(al) subjects in a singular systematic fashion (admittedly, recasting Hegel's corpus especially in light of historical/dialectical material- isms and subsequent scientific developments apparently at odds with his commitments demands a sizable amount of interpretive labor in order to be executed in a satisfactory scholarly and philo- sophical manner – something I attempt elsewhere[5]). However, I diverge from the more Romantic side of German idealism repre- sented by Hölderlin, Schelling, and even a certain Hegel (the one who periodically toys with the picture of a vast cosmic organ- ism) in two interconnected ways. On the one hand, in solidarity with the Kant of the *Critique of Pure Reason* in particular, with his embrace of the disenchantment of nature brought about by modern science *à la* Bacon, Galileo, and Newton, as well as the Fichte who follows in this Kant's footsteps (not to mention the Marxist tradition later on), I resist and reject non/anti-scientific moves to "re-enchant" the material being of physical reality (a project of German Romanticism still pursued by some today, including Heideggerians and certain self-declared Hegelians).[6] On the other hand, I wholeheartedly concur with Hölderlin, Schelling, and Hegel (with the naturalized version of Spinozism informing their absolute idealisms) that the transcendental subject as per Kant's and Fichte's subjective idealisms can and must be rendered fully immanent (yet nonetheless irreducible) to a meta- transcendental substance (of a material nature, at least for me as a materialist), with the latter (i.e., meta-transcendental substance) as the asubjective being giving rise to the former (i.e., the transcen- dental subject) as a speculative identity-in-difference with this its ontological ground. However, an additional crucial caveat to this last point is requisite to note: By contrast with the idealists' ten- dencies to help themselves to floridly teleological language, I deny the existence of any preordained teleology whatsoever necessitat- ing and making inevitable the genesis of subject out of substance. Especially considering the aftermath of the Darwin-event postdat- ing the idealists, I treat this genesis (or geneses) as contingent, as an accident.

With the benefits of post-Newtonian, post-Darwinian, and post-Hebbian hindsight,[7] benefits obviously unavailable to the Tübingen trio and their illustrious immediate predecessors, I am confident that it is both possible and promising to reattempt a merger of "system" *à la* Spinoza and "freedom" *à la* Kant and Fichte (to employ the terms of Schelling's 1809 *Freiheitschrift*),[8] albeit to do so without ceding an inch of the modern scientific territory of desacralized, disenchanted material nature(s) to the irrationalist spiritualisms and superstitions of (neo-)Romantic mystical re-enchantments as regressions to a pre-modern, unscientific *Weltanschauung*. I believe this option, one simply not on the table at the end of the eighteenth and beginning of the nineteenth centuries, is feasible now because the natural sciences at the beginning of the twenty-first century do not automatically and necessarily entail a rigid, exceptionless determinism, namely, the vision of a single causal kingdom of universal heteronomy.[9] In connection with post-nineteenth-century natural science, it could be maintained that the neo-Humean skepticism leveled against Kant's critical philosophy by his contemporary Salomon Maimon[10] represents not an epistemological problematization of natural science as relying on the concept of causality analyzed in the first *Critique* but, instead, an ontological revelation of a lack of absolute, unqualified, iron-clad causal determinism within real material being itself.[11] Ontologizing Hume's problem of induction in the same manner that Hegel ontologizes Kant's "Transcendental Dialectic" is a key part of exorcizing Laplace's demon. These qualifications in this and the preceding paragraph to my labeling of transcendental materialism as the latest system-program of German idealism are far from minor or negligible.

Markus Gabriel, inspired similarly by a combination of German idealism and Žižekianism, proposes, under the heading of "transcendental ontology," a contemporary reactivation of the agendas motivating Schelling and Hegel. How is my transcendental materialism to be situated vis-à-vis Gabriel's transcendental ontology? Both positions share a commitment to combining a monist picture of being with a transcendental account of autonomous subjectivity in a style resembling the scheme hatched in late-eighteenth-century Tübingen to wed Spinoza and Fichte. Furthermore, as should be expected in connection with certain of his Hegelian allegiances, Gabriel subscribes to an outlook reflected in my no-illusions principle (as does Žižek too[12]).

However, as the different labels for our two stances already signal, Gabriel and I part company as regards materialism. The ontology of Gabriel's transcendental ontology, itself resulting mainly from the gesture of ontologizing Kantian and post-Kantian transcendental subjectivity, is a vision of being as a non-hierarchized, detotalized plurality of "fields of sense" defying grounding capture by any type of naturalism and/or science-allied materialism.[13] From my standpoint, one viewing classical German idealism with the benefit of hindsight provided by the immediately subsequent developments of historical and dialectical materialisms, Gabriel is still too proximate to subjective idealism and too distant from speculative dialectics: too proximate to subjective idealism in that the fields of sense into which being is parceled out in transcendental ontology seem to be modeled directly on the phenomenal spheres arising from Kantian and/or Fichtean ideal cognizing subjectivities; too distant from speculative dialectics in that transcendental ontology, in a one-way, lop-sided fashion, transforms the image of being after rendering thinking subjectivity immanent to it while, at the same time, not altering the image of thinking subjectivity in tandem with this gesture of immanentization. In a related vein, my materialist leanings incline me to see "fields of sense" as arising from embodied minded beings in ways at least partially explicable in natural-scientific (especially biological) terms. Similarly, Gabriel's transcendental ontology, from my perspective, is a realism about transcendental subjectivity in such a fashion as to be simultaneously an anti-realism about empirical reality (as objectively independent of subjectivity *qua* beyond, behind, or beneath subject-centered "fields of sense").

To return to German idealism itself, when Hegel, in the preface to the *Phenomenology*, dismisses the Schellingian philosophies of identity and nature as promoting an image of the Absolute as a "night in which all cows are black,"[14] part of what he is objecting to is Schelling's allegedly insufficient distance from Spinozism specifically.[15] This charge certainly sticks to many Schellingians of the time; it also arguably applies quite well to the young Schelling of the late 1790s and early 1800s. However, perhaps in response to Hegel's indictment, the more mature Schelling – in his *Lectures on the History of Philosophy*, Hegel concedes that the author of the 1809 *Freiheitschrift* displays a profound dialectical-speculative sophistication during a moment of his self-conducted philosophical education enacted on the public stage[16] – takes great pains to make explicit his differences with and distance from Spinoza. In fact, Hegel and the later Schelling articulate essentially the same criticisms of Spinoza's philosophy,[17] without either of them, in the wake of their split induced by Hegel's publication of the *Phenomenology*, directly acknowledging this convergence of views on the topic of Spinozism.

Several passages in Hegel's monumental *Science of Logic* furnish exemplary formulations of the complaints he directs toward Spinoza as expressed dissatisfactions with the latter's monist substance metaphysics that Schelling comes to share too. Immediately prior to the transition from "The Doctrine of Being" to "The Doctrine of Essence" (i.e., the first two of the three main divisions of Hegelian logic), Hegel says of Spinoza:

> Since absolute indifference (absolute Indifferenz) may seem to be the fundamental determination of Spinoza's *substance*, we may add that this is indeed the case in so far as in both every determination of being, like every further concrete differentiation of thought and extension and so forth, is posited as vanished (*als verschwunden gesetzt werden*). If we stop short at the abstraction [of substance] then it is a matter of complete indifference (*überhaupt gleichgültig*) what something looked like in reality before it was swallowed up in this abyss (*Abgrund*). But when substance is conceived as indifference (*Indifferenz*), it is tied up with the need for determining it and for taking this determining into consideration; it is not to remain Spinoza's substance, the sole determination of which is the negative one that everything is absorbed in it. With Spinoza, the moment of difference (*die Unterschied*) – attributes, thought and extension, then the modes too, the affections, and every other determination – is introduced quite empirically (*ganz empirisch*); it is intellect (*der Verstand*), itself a mode, which is the source of the differentiation. The relationship of the attributes to substance and to one another is not specified further than that they express the whole of substance, and their content, the order of things as extended and as thoughts, is the same. But by the determination of substance as indifference, the *difference* too, comes to be reflected on (*Reflexion*); whereas with Spinoza, the difference is an external (*äuberlicher*)... difference *only by implication* (*an sich*), now it is *posited* (gesetzt) as such.[18]

Hegel, summing up his objections, soon repeats his complaint that, with Spinoza, "substance is not determined as self-differentiating, not as subject" (*die Substanz nicht als das sich selbst Unterschiedende, nicht als Subjekt bestimmt*)[19] – and this contrary to the *Phenomenology*'s insistence on "grasping and expressing the True, not only as *Substance*, but equally as *Subject*" (*das Wahre nicht als* Substanz, *sondern ebensosehr als* Subjekt *aufzufassen und auszudrücken*),[20] an insistence he sticks to right up through his 1831 Berlin *Lectures on Logic*.[21] Further on in the *Science of Logic* (as well as in the *Encyclopedia Logic*[22] and *Philosophy of Mind*[23]), this complaint is again rearticulated – "substance lacks the principle of *personality* (der Persönlichkeit)."[24]

In the first two sentences of the above block quotation, Spinoza's monistic metaphysics clearly is being depicted as a "night in which all cows are black" (*à la* the dismissal of a certain Schellingianism in the *Phenomenology*), namely, as an indeterminate "abyss" into whose flat, uniform blackness everything is abandoned to mere "vanishing."[25] Such an "abstraction" fails to do philosophical justice to the multicolored and multifaceted differentiations of manifest revealed reality, treating these differentiations as insubstantial epiphenomena with no real being relative to the lone One-All of God/Nature as substance; they are "posited as vanished" in the Spinozist worldview, left to be "swallowed up" by an undifferentiated, monochromatic ontological darkness.[26] The associative link between Spinoza and Schelling is further strengthened by Hegel's repeated employment of the word "*Indifferenz*"; an allusion to the early Schelling's philosophies of nature and identity, with their Absolute as the "point of indifference,"[27] undoubtedly is intended here.

The remainder of the preceding lengthy quotation from the *Science of Logic* succinctly elaborates an immanent critique of Spinozism, showing how this philosophical framework self-subvertingly dialecticizes itself.[28] The key to this critical maneuver is Hegel's observation that Spinoza (or anyone else speculating along similar monist lines) at least has to determine substance, even if this amounts to the most minimal of determinations of substance as nothing more than indeterminate *qua* devoid of distinguishable attributes, modes, and so on[29] ("But when substance is conceived as indifference [*Indifferenz*], it is tied up with the need for determining it and for taking this determining into consideration"). Through the reflective intuiting (as "*Reflexion*") of God/Nature by Spinoza's "intellect" – Hegel's use of "*der Verstand*" (as per *Verstand* [understanding] *qua* distinct from *Vernunft* [reason]) to translate the latter should be heard with the full range of multiple resonances this German term has in the Hegelian system – a supplementary difference is added to the indifference of substance, namely, the difference between the being of substance itself and the thinking of this being. That is to say, in Hegelian locution, substance cannot be thought without the "also" of subjectivity as reflective cognition (i.e., the *Phenomenology*'s "substance also as subject").[30]

However, since Spinoza's substance admits no differences (as determinations, distinctions, etc.), a destabilizing dialectical contradiction arises for his system in that he cannot escape philosophical reliance upon, at a minimum, the difference between substantial being and subjective thinking ("it is not to remain Spinoza's substance, the sole determination of which is the negative one that everything is absorbed in it"). In other words, his substance is negated as pure indifference by the very intellectual intuiting of it as supposed pure indifference ("But by the determination of substance as indifference, the *difference* too, comes to be reflected on [*Reflexion*]"). This is because such intuiting, in the language of Spinoza himself, must be performed by a mode (i.e., intellectual intuition) of an attribute (i.e., thinking) of this substance, a mode somehow or other distinguished from substance per se in and of itself (insofar as this mode is not entirely "absorbed in" substance without remainder or trace).[31]

Spinoza obviously is aware that existence, at least as he and other human beings experience it, is not registered as the infinite, indivisible, homogeneous Whole of a single divine-yet-also-natural Being – hence his inclusion of attributes and modes in his philosophical discourse, concepts designating the differences, determinations, and distinctions familiar to human subjects in their experiences of what they take to be the world of humdrum, normal reality. But, as Hegel points out, "With Spinoza, the moment of difference (*die Unterschied*) – attributes, thought and extension, then the modes too, the affections, and every other determination – is introduced quite empirically (*ganz empirisch*)"[32] (subsequently in the *Science of Logic*, Hegel combines the charges of externality and empiricism). Three fundamental critical claims are compressed into this statement. First, Spinoza allegedly defines and depicts attributes, modes, and the like (i.e., instances of differences, by contrast with the allegedly perfect self-sameness of presumably homogeneous substance in and of itself) on the basis of nothing more than empirical examination of everyday experience; a descriptive phenomenology of quotidian phenomena, instead of rationalist-type deductive proofs à la the "geometric method" (*more geometrico*) of the *Ethics*, justifies the inclusion of everything other than seamlessly undifferentiated substance alone (and this despite Spinoza deceptively dressing up this disavowed phenomenology in the trappings of mathematical-style argumentative systematicity).[33] Of course, Hegel repeatedly criticizes both Spinoza and Schelling for practicing a dry, mechanical, and rigid formalism suitable for the lifeless *Verstand* of mathematics but entirely unsuited for the living *Vernunft* of speculative philosophy.[34] Second, with Spinoza himself being a (partially) finite entity situated in a world divided up between thinking, extension, and their various permutations, his (intellectual) intuition of the infinite, indivisible One-All of God/Nature is a reflection internal to and arising from the world of differences. Third, the Spinozist system therefore utterly lacks, even judged by its own methodological standards for theoretical systematicity, a properly philosophical (rather than simply empirical) account of the very position from which this system itself is constructed (not to mention, as underscored by Fichte,[35] Schelling,[36] and Hegel,[37] its general failure to explain how and why substance takes the trouble to fragment itself into and refract itself through the multitude of different finite appearances of seemingly individuated thinking and extended beings – hence Hegel's recurrent accusation that Spinoza proceeds initially from attributes and modes to substance without ever providing a systematic philosophical delineation of the inverse logical and/or genetic movement wherein attributes and modes proceed from substance in the first place as itself supposedly primary[38]). From the subsequent vantage point of Marx's first, and quite dialectical-speculative, thesis on Feuerbach (to refer to it once again), Spinoza's philosophy shares with those of the eighteenth-century French materialists he inspires the defect of being purely and strictly contemplative. In his *Lectures on the Philosophy of Religion*, Hegel already draws this exact connection of culpability between "Spinoza's nature" (i.e., the closed, deterministic Whole of subjectless substance) and "the matter and nature of the materialists and naturalists" (as Spinoza's heirs).[39]

As per Hegel's characteristic "hands off" dialectical procedure of stepping back so as to allow other figures and positions to unfold their inner resources up to the point of inadvertently undermining themselves of their own accord (i.e., "doing violence to themselves at their own hands"),[40] he notes, in the earlier block quotation from the *Science of Logic*, that, "whereas with Spinoza, the difference is an external (*äuberlicher*) . . . difference *only by implication* (*an sich*), now it is *posited* (*gesetzt*) as such." Put differently, Hegel is asserting that his critique of Spinoza is an immanent one in which what is implicitly (*"by implication"*) already there in Spinozism (i.e., its dialectically self-subverting "in itself" [*an sich*]) is merely made explicit (i.e., *"posited* [*gesetzt*] as such"). To paraphrase Jacobi's most famous gripe about Kant's critical transcendental idealism (concerning the notorious thing-in-itself [*Ding an sich*]),[41] for Hegel, without "the moment of difference (*die Unterschied*)" (i.e., attributes, modes, and so on) one cannot enter into Spinoza's philosophy, but, with it, one cannot remain within the parameters of this same philosophy (as one of sheer indifference). Hegel reiterates all of these indictments later in the *Science of Logic*.[42]

The *Science of Logic*'s subsequent critical revisitation of Spinozism, situated in a remark on "The Philosophy of Spinoza and Leibniz" in the third and final section ("Actuality" [*Die Wirklichkeit*]) of "The Doctrine of Essence," repeats some of the content already covered immediately above. However, Hegel does introduce some new twists to his critique here, two of which are relevant in relation to my purposes in the present context. The first of these has to do with the role of negation in Spinoza's and Hegel's respective systems[43]:

> *Determinateness is negation* (die Bestimmtheit ist Negation) – is the absolute principle of Spinoza's philosophy; this true and simple (*wahrhafte und einfache*) insight establishes the absolute unity of substance. But Spinoza stops short at *negation* as *determinateness* or quality; he does not advance to a cognition of negation as absolute, that is, *self-negating, negation* (sich negierender Negation); thus *his substance does not itself contain the absolute form*, and cognition of it is not an immanent cognition (*immanentes Erkennen*). True, substance is the absolute unity of *thought* and being or extension; therefore it contains thought itself, but only in its *unity* with extension, that is, not as *separating* itself from extension, hence in general not as a determinative and formative activity (*Bestimmen und Formieren*), nor as a movement which returns into and begins from itself (*die zurückkehrende und aus sich selbst anfangende Bewegung*).[44]

Hegel rarely, if ever, offers merely external criticisms, namely, shrill, dogmatic objections in which others' positions ultimately are confrontationally and narcissistically criticized simply and solely for nothing more than the sin of not being one's own. The above observations regarding negation are no exception. In other words, despite possible appearances to the contrary, they do not rest upon an unproductive side-by-side juxtaposition in which two independent and incompatible conceptions of negativity (i.e., a Spinozist versus a Hegelian one) are externally compared and contrasted. Instead, Hegel's real underlying point is once more that a dialectical-speculative engagement with Spinozism reveals it to rely implicitly upon something which nonetheless it cannot explicitly avow and accommodate within the strict confines of its own systematic parameters (here, "self-negating negation" à la the dialectical-speculative "negation of negation" that is not the straightforward double-negation of classical, bivalent logic).[45]

To unpack the preceding quotation in detail, Hegel starts by endorsing the Spinozist dictum according to which *omnis determinatio est negatio* (any reader of him knows just how important this proposition is for Hegel's own philosophical apparatus). But, Hegel intends to go on to make the point that Spinoza neither should nor can, as he nevertheless does, limit negation to its relationship with determination exclusively in the sense of differentiation and individuation as themselves compatible all the same with the radical monism of infinite substance as the one-and-only single Totality. Now, Spinoza's intellectual intuition is a mode of the attribute of thinking, hence a determination which, as such, is what it is in its differentiated and individuated identity by not being everything else (as per "all determination is negation"). And yet, in Spinoza's own philosophy, this mode is simultaneously the privileged finite node within the infinite network wherein the infinite network as a whole is reflected and encompassed. Thereby, in Hegel's language, substance becomes subject, the infinite achieves reflexive self-consciousness in and through a finite moment of itself. In this dynamic, intellectual intuition as a mode of the attribute of thinking is a specific determination-*qua*-negation that self-reflexively negates (as a second negation, a negation of negation, added to the first negation of its monism-compatible determinism) its particularity as a finite determination. Intellectual intuition must perform this dialectical-speculative double-negation so as to think, as Spinoza-the-philosopher indeed thinks, both all determinations (itself included) as well as the infinite ontological ground of all determinations irreducible to any particular finite determination (i.e., the One-All of substance).[46] Although failing to acknowledge and explain what he actually does, Spinoza nonetheless demonstrates and performs the power of thinking to separate and distance itself from being (as un/pre-thinking) so as to be capable of capturing in thoughts both this being and itself as a sublating (*als Aufhebung*) identity-in-difference (i.e., unity of unity and disunity) with respect to this same being.[47] That is to say, Spinoza unavowedly presupposes thinking subjectivity as a dual epistemological and ontological transcendence-in-immanence in relation to substance without being willing and able avowedly to posit this subjectivity as such.

Hegel thus turns against Spinoza the very insight into the true nature of the infinite the former takes from the latter. From a Hegelian perspective, Spinoza's greatest breakthrough arguably is his realization of the mutual exclusivity between infinitude and transcendence (i.e., what is transcendent cannot be infinite and vice versa). If something stands separately over and above other things, then this something is limited, namely, rendered finite by whatever subsists beyond/outside its own transcendent sphere; inversely but correlatively, if something is genuinely (instead of spuriously) infinite, it neither is external to anything else nor is anything else external to it. Hence, the true (rather than specious) infinite directly and necessarily entails strict immanence insofar as it fundamentally excludes any and every transcendence. According to Hegel's immanent critique of Spinoza's rationalist substance metaphysics (with the latter's radical monism inextricably intertwined with these musings on the infinite), what Spinoza rightly prohibits for the infinity of God/Nature as the One-All of ultimate Being he implicitly and wrongly, judged even by his own ideas and standards, permits for the reflective position of intellectual intuition as external reflection. In other words, with Spinozism being a contemplative metaphysics in Marx's precise sense of this adjective, Spinoza's epistemological subject is surreptitiously and illegitimately granted a tacit transcendence vis-à-vis the otherwise exemptionless universality of ontological immanence as required under the strictures of a consistent, consequent thinking of authentic infinitude. Succinctly stated, the Spinozist ban on complete, unqualified transcendence, as a ban brooking no exceptions, must apply to the subjective as well as the divine.

Therefore, referring back to the prior block quotation from the *Science of Logic*, Hegel reaches the verdict regarding Spinoza that "*his substance does not itself contain the absolute form, and cognition of it is not an immanent cognition (immanentes Erkennen).*" Put differently, a supposedly absolute substance that does not include within itself, in an explicitly explained fashion, the philosophical subject that reflects upon it is not really absolute (as infinite, omnipresent, all-embracing, and so on) – and this insofar as such a substance thereby is left lacking a non-negligible part of the reality related to it (i.e., the part through which this substance becomes self-reflectively cognizant of itself).[48] Similarly, when Hegel, in the same passage, remarks that the attribute of thinking (of which intellectual intuition is a mode) is not properly conceived of by the author of the *Ethics* "as a determinative and formative activity (*Bestimmen und Formieren*)" – of course, in Hegel's parlance, this is presupposed (as "in itself") without being posited (as "in and for itself" [*an und für sich*]) by Spinoza[49] – this reiterates a now-familiar charge: The kinetic process of the thinking subject endowing substantial being with a definite determination and form (as, in this instance, God/Nature *qua* the infinite One-All of substance) impermissibly drops out of and is unreflected by the resulting static object of this thus-determined/formed picture of substantial being.[50] Likewise, Hegel's phrase "*Bestimmen und Formieren*" hints at a dialectical dynamic between substance and subject in which the latter defies being quickly and easily dismissed as a mere epiphenomenon, as nothing more than an ineffective appearance, attribute, fantasy, fiction, illusion, mode, etc.

To paraphrase an earlier-quoted Hegel, the true infinite/Absolute is the whole, a totality including subject as well as substance, namely, a subject immanent to substance as demanded by a systematic monism of the genuinely infinite (i.e., the very type of ontology to which Spinoza himself avowedly is committed).[51] Additionally, this Hegelian line of criticism, summarized thusly, even hints that the Tübingen-born version of the shotgun marriage between Spinoza and Kant/Fichte (i.e., "the earliest system-program of German idealism" shared by Schelling, Hölderlin, and Hegel and also arrived at by the later Fichte of 1804 and after[52]) is more an *Aufhebung* of Spinoza's own philosophy than a forceful imposition from without. This perhaps licenses hearing yet another resonance in the later Hegel's well-known statement, from his Berlin *Lectures on the History of Philosophy*, that "thought must begin by placing itself at the standpoint of Spinozism; to be a follower of Spinoza is the essential commencement of all Philosophy"[53] (I also strongly suspect that this declaration about philosophy's beginnings is a rejoinder to Jacobi's claim that all rigorously consequent philosophizing ends in Spinozism). If to follow Spinoza can mean to be faithful to "what is in Spinozism more than Spinozism itself" (as Lacan might put it), to be true to Spinozism's "extimate" *an und für sich* (to resort to another bit of Lacanese), through immanent critique, then Hegel, from Tübingen to Berlin, indeed counts as "a follower of Spinoza."[54]

But, to conclude from this, as do Althusser and his student Pierre Macherey,[55] that Spinoza already anticipates and answers Hegel's immanent critique in advance is to confuse and falsely conflate two very distinct levels: on the one side (that of Hegel's "in itself"), that which is implicitly presupposed without accompanying supporting argumentation; on the other side (that of Hegel's "in and for itself"), that which indeed is explicitly posited with accompanying supporting argumentation. Moreover, this very "thing" implicit in Spinozism made explicit by Hegelianism is that which Spinozism is unable to accommodate within its systematic parameters – at the same time, this system is made possible by and relies upon this its unavowable presupposition – and that which Althusserianism is unwilling to accommodate: in a word, subjectivity. I even am tempted to suggest that those defending Spinoza against Hegel sometimes mistake Hegelian for Spinozist ideas due to the ever-so-close immanence of Hegel's critique, anachronistically crediting Spinozism *an sich* with insights that arise *an und für sich* only in and through Hegelianism.[56]

The second additional critical twist added in the later discussion of Spinoza in the *Science of Logic* has to do with Spinozism's particular form of one-sidedness. Hegel notes that "The one-sidedness of a philosophical principle is usually countered by its opposite one-sidedness and totality, as in all of them, is usually present as a *dispersed completeness*."[57] This observation alludes to central features of Hegel's manner of relating his philosophy to the history of philosophy as a whole; it calls to mind the Hegelian system as a speculative sublation of the dialectics generated within and between its one-sided historical predecessors. That said, Hegel, in this specific context, has in view the relationship between Spinoza and Gottfried Wilhelm Leibniz. In particular, on the plane of rationalist substance metaphysics, he sees Leibniz's monadological ontology as the diametrically opposed counter-thrust to Spinoza's intellectual image of substantial being as a seamlessly consistent fullness of unified ontological homogeneity. With Leibnizian monadology, being is parceled out instead into a teeming multitude of entirely separate and absolutely self-enclosed "formal atoms" (i.e., non-physical "monads"). As pictures of substance, the contrast could not be sharper and more extreme: Spinoza's continuous and indivisible One versus Leibniz's discrete and divided Many. With their shared rationalism, Hegel portrays the substance metaphysics of Spinoza and Leibniz as two poles of complementary-but-contradictory one-sidedness.[58]

Before Hegel, the British empiricist David Hume similarly plays off Spinoza and Leibniz against each other. In the fifth section of the first book of *A Treatise of Human Nature* – this section, entitled "Of the Immateriality of the Soul," immediately precedes (and is closely related to) the famous analysis of personal identity in the following sixth section[59] – Hume takes up the topic of the "soul" as metaphysical principle or essence of individuated personhood. Such an entity is traditionally defined and characterized as a supersensible substance underlying the manifest and accessible dimensions of the familiar everyday self. But, according to Hume's empiricism, there is no epistemologically justifiable and defensible way of knowing whether or not substantial being, as supersensible, is, in fact, divided up into individual units in such a fashion as to contain metaphysical correlates paired with sensible-as-experiential empirical selves. In short, there is no way of really knowing if substance does or does not harbor souls within itself. For Leibniz, whose monadology is bound up with a Christian theosophical worldview, metaphysical substance indeed is dispersed into a plurality of individuated units (i.e., monads as indivisible formal atoms), some of which are souls corresponding to persons (as per traditional Christianity). However, for Hume, with his anti-rationalist epistemology, Spinoza's non-Christian metaphysics, in which substance is not individuated and, therefore, is devoid of souls as singular supersensible selves, is no less (and no more) plausible than Leibniz's ostensibly intellectually intuited *Weltanschauung*. These rationalists' mutually exclusive systems, in which two seemingly equal degrees of intense certainty about substance(s) are pitted directly against each other, arguably cancel out each other, leaving the question of whether or not there are "immaterial souls" unresolved.[60]

Hume's handling of Spinoza and Leibniz exemplifies certain aspects of his empiricism integral to Kant's critical philosophy. The Kantian critique of rationalism via the "Transcendental Dialectic" (particularly the "Antinomies of Pure Reason") clearly is foreshadowed by this Hume. What is more, Hegel, as should go without saying, is well aware of Hume's profound influence on Kant.[61] Of course, Kant, with his comparatively greater empiricist sympathies, draws the conclusion from this that the sorts of substances as noumenal referents aimed at by Spinozist and Leibnizian intellectual intuitions are epistemologically inaccessible and philosophically out-of-bounds things-in-themselves. In Kant's eyes, the particular dialectics of pure reason enacted and exemplified by the Spinoza-Leibniz couple reveal rationalist substance metaphysics as a whole to be futile and illusory, immanently generating insurmountable contradictions. Insofar as the noumenal Real is assumed by Kant to be free of contradictions, these deadlocks and impasses bear witness to the impossibility of transcending the limits of possible phenomenal experience so as to touch directly this thinkable-but-not-knowable Real through pure reason as intellectual intuition.

As seen above, Hegel appears to adopt Hume's and Kant's similar responses to the antinomic antagonisms pitting the substance metaphysics of Spinoza and Leibniz against each other. So, what, if anything, distinguishes Hegel's response to these two early-modern Continental rationalists? There indeed is a major difference here, and it has everything to do with the contrast between, on the one hand, Hume's empiricist skepticism as well as Kant's transcendental idealism and, on the other hand, Hegel's absolute idealism. For Hegel, whereas subjective idealism (such as the transcendental sort of his immediate predecessors) is diametrically opposed to robust realism, absolute idealism is anything but anti-realist. That is to say, to interpret Hegel's philosophy as an anti-realism in any standard, traditional sense is to misinterpret it as a subjective (including macro-subjective *qua* panpsychical) idealism.[62] I have made this case in detail on a prior occasion.[63] Moreover, anyone who believes German idealism overall to be an aggressively anti-realist movement/orientation would do well to read Frederick Beiser's meticulous and massive study *German Idealism: The Struggle Against Subjectivism, 1781–1801*.[64] Beiser persuasively demonstrates that idealism as per the German idealist program, starting with Kant and Fichte, is not the opposite of realism *tout court*. Quite the contrary: From the *Critique of Pure Reason* (with its "empirical realism" and "Refutation of Idealism"[65]) onward, these idealists, unlike, say, Bishop Berkeley, "struggle against subjectivism" by highlighting and insisting upon necessary and universal features of intersubjectively valid, spatially extended objective reality. The admittedly thin, minimalist sense of realism *à la* the Kant of the B-version of the first *Critique* maintains the reality of universal constraints on minds as parameters irreducible to individual subjects, which already is enough to capture much of what is desired by many of those espousing realist views; of course, Schelling and Hegel especially go much further down realist paths in their breaks with the subjective (and intersubjective) idealisms of Kantian and Fichtean transcendentalisms. Furthermore, as long maintained in the Marxist tradition (by Engels[66] and V.I. Lenin,[67] among others), the true opposite of idealism is materialism – and this insofar as a number of variants of realism are perfectly compatible with anti-materialist idealism (such as the realisms of Kant and, arguably, Fichte too). The proper name "Plato" is enough to make this point: The metaphysical realist position he establishes at the dawn of Western philosophy is robustly realist and, at the same time, virulently opposed to any and every variant of materialism. Excluding vitalisms, panpsychisms, and similar sorts of stances, being a materialist entails being a realist, although the opposite certainly is not the case.

Directly related to the preceding, a "Remark" (*Anmerkung*) on "Idealism" (*Der Idealismus*) closing the second chapter ("Determinate Being" [*Das Dasein*]) of the first book of the *Science of Logic* unambiguously stipulates that the opposite of absolute idealism is not realism, but, instead, finitism.[68] Long before Meillassoux (who indeed is avowedly influenced by the German idealists), Hegel is obsessed with pursuing what comes "after finitude." In Hegel's logical framework, this path beyond the finite unfolds through the immanent critical deabsolutizing, at the end of "The Doctrine of Being," of "determinate being" (a dialectic leading on to "The Doctrine of Essence" and "The Doctrine of the Notion"). It is no coincidence at all that Hegel issues his "Remark on Idealism" on the heels of a chapter handling determinate being, namely, the manner of existence of purportedly immediate, particularized thises, thats, and others.[69] Absolutizing such being would be tantamount to making finite things, conceived of as wholly self-standing and completely independent individual beings, sufficient unto themselves as the unmediated alpha-and-omega constituents of the ultimate true Real *überhaupt*. Hegel, by objecting to a finitist worldview of this kind (through his usual procedure of showing how it spontaneously self-sublates in inadvertently but inevitably inflicting fatal dialectical damage on itself of its own accord), does not in the least cancel out objective reality as the actual, factual existence of asubjective entities and events. Contrary to the disinformation of propagandistic myths, he does not negate and replace the latter with an implausibly insane metaphysics of an inflated God-like mega-Mind, a ridiculously puffed up *Geist* as a gargantuan cosmic macro-Subject always-already having devoured the entire universe without leaving any leftovers whatsoever. Similarly, a casual glance at the opening of the *Philosophy of Nature* (the first part of the more-than-logical *Realphilosophie* of *Natur und Geist* and the significant middle third of Hegel's system as per the *Encyclopedia*) reveals to the reader that Hegel rejects Kant's pivotal anti-realist thesis regarding the strict ideality of space and time in the "Transcendental Aesthetic,"[70] with Hegelian *Naturphilosophie* (and the *Realphilosophie* in its entirety) pushing off from a foundational conception of space and time as objectively real instead of subjectively ideal.[71]

However, again contrary to yet another popular myth, Hegel's not-anti-realist absolute idealism is resolutely post-, rather than pre-, Kantian. Hegel unreservedly accepts that Kant's critical-transcendental turn breaks the history of philosophy in two (to use a Nietzschean turn of phrase) – more specifically, that the "Transcendental Dialectic" of the first *Critique* in particular sounds the death knell of old-fashioned substance metaphysics (such as practiced by Spinoza and Leibniz) especially.[72] Admittedly, Hegel repeatedly purports to reveal that what he labels the "subjective idealism"[73] of transcendentalism *à la* Kant (and Fichte), like all other non-Hegelian theoretical positions, inevitably succumbs to self-subversion via its own internally generated dialectical contradictions, imploding under the weight of these inner antagonisms and conflicts lying within its heart. In line with many of his predecessors and contemporaries, he construes Kant as relying upon a dogmatic two-worlds metaphysics at odds with the spirit, if not also the letter, of the very critical philosophy Kant himself founds. Such Kantian notions as that of a "limit" between phenomenal and noumenal realms as well as that of *das Ding an sich* are widely dismissed by the German idealists, Hegel included, as pre-Kantian residues compromising the systematic consistency of the critical-transcendental apparatus. Hegel's distinctive dialectical approach aims to uncover how these notions upon which Kant rests dissolve themselves, autonomously inducing their own destabilization and collapse.[74] But, from Hegel's vantage point, the immanent (self-)critique of the Kantian critical philosophy as lop-sidedly subjectivist by no means licenses the anachronism of a regression back to any type of pre-Kantian transcendental realism (whether associated with metaphysical rationalism, materialist empiricism, or whatever else along these lines). In short, Hegel, as is to be expected of the philosopher of the *Aufhebung*, strives to sublate (*qua* preserve and elevate while negating and destroying) Kant's transcendental idealism.

Without getting bogged down too much in the task of rehearsing yet again the highly fraught and incredibly complicated Kant-Hegel relationship so decisive for the past two centuries of Western philosophy, suffice it for now to state that the post-Kantian realism of Hegel's absolute idealism is grounded, in part, on the problematization of Kant's gestures of attempting to establish an uncrossable boundary demarcating what is potentially knowable (i.e., the "limits of possible experience" within which phenomenal objects appear) and, in addition, hypothesizing, on the other side of this boundary, a Beyond of beings unknowable in principle (i.e., things-in-themselves as essentially and eternally evading the grip of concepts). If these Kantian gestures undo themselves, as Hegel's (immanent) critique maintains, then the realm of the conceptual is no longer finite in the sense of bounded vis-à-vis another realm forever out of its reach, namely, the thinkable-but-not-knowable noumenal domain of things-in-themselves.

Nevertheless, the consequent Hegelian infinitude of the concept does not signify the completed, exhaustive conceptual digestion of non/extra-conceptual reality. Focusing on Kant's *Ding an sich*, Hegel's specific manner of doing away with this thing's "in itself" dimension in no way signals the intention to push forward with the attempted absorption-without-remainder of everything real into the ideal spiritual cobwebs of micro- and/or macro-subjectivities. The conceptual is "infinite" for Hegel only in the sense of not being rendered finite through being limited in principle by anything intrinsically unknowable, by supposed things-in-themselves presumed to be insurmountably refractory to the advances of knowing. In still other words, Hegelian knowing is "absolute" strictly insofar as there is nothing that by some eternal nature absolutely eludes the possibility of being grasped conceptually, no timeless "x" of an utterly ineffable *je ne sais quoi* as non-subjective being externally opposing and limiting subjective cognition (with

Kantian transcendental idealism's rigid dualism of phenomenal objects-as-appearances and noumenal things-in-themselves being, from Hegel's perspective, the latest and most sophisticated version of this insistence on the inherent finitude of knowledge due to unchanging limits maintained by ineliminable unknowns).

The crucial caveat not to be missed is that none of this is equivalent to claiming that everything always-already has been grasped conceptually. Put differently, concluding that there is no *apriori* limitation permanently imposing a finite status on knowledge as bounded by an unknowable transcendent Outside (i.e., the noumenal Beyond of things-in-themselves) is not the same as asserting that the actual process of knowing ever was, is, or will be completed in the form of a definitively accomplished totality of decisively established "absolute knowledge." In Hegelian philosophy, the verb of kinetic knowing is absolute/infinite, while the noun of static knowledge, in whatever shape at whatever moment in its historical development, nevertheless is not.[75] Knowing is not checked in principle by anything eternally and intrinsically unknowable (epitomized here by *das Ding an sich*). But, this does not entail that conceptually mediated knowing therefore ever achieves full penetration into and saturation of the extra/non-subjective being(s) of the realities of both nature as well as the trans-subjective dimensions of *Geist* (with these realities being dealt with in Hegel's *Realphilosophie* as distinct from his logical apparatus). Succinctly rearticulated once more, the infinitude/absoluteness of knowledge is, for Hegel, a principle of potentiality rather than a fact of actuality.

The preceding responses to commonplace, widespread misreadings of Hegel as an intoxicated spiritualist anti-realist nonetheless imply a feature of Hegelian thought further provoking and encouraging these very same misreadings. Before proceeding further, I must identify this feature and explain why, in truth, it does not support those who accuse Hegel of being a grandiose macro-subjective idealist. The Hegelian immanent critical dismantling of Kantian transcendental idealism's alleged dogmatic dependence on a two-worlds metaphysics – again, Hegel's repudiation of subjectivist anti-realism is post-Kantian, arrived at by passing through (rather than simply bypassing) Kant – implies that the extra/non-subjective Real is not extra/non-conceptual in terms of its own mind-independent architectures and trajectories.[76] This Real, despite being extra/non-subjective as transcending the confines of first-person conscious and self-conscious mindedness (i.e., the cognitions, emotions, and motivations of sentient and sapient individuals), is "conceptual" in the precise-yet-broadened Hegelian sense of consisting of structures and dynamics allowing, at least in principle, for being apprehended by "concepts" in the narrower sense of mental mappings by human thinkers. If all two-worlds metaphysics of the kind epitomized by Kant's subjective idealism (with its limits of possible experience and unknowable things-in-themselves) ultimately self-destruct, as Hegel maintains, then mutually mirroring isomorphisms between the logics of the *an sich* objective Real and the *für sich* subjective Ideal are, at a minimum, always possible. That is to say, in the absence of a forever epistemologically inaccessible dimension (such as a noumenal realm *à la* Kant), the in-principle infinite knowability of the extra/non-subjective Real implies that it itself, in its very being as mobile ensembles of spatio-temporal entities and events ontologically distinguishable from the being of thinking, is not absolutely different-in-kind from the concepts and logics operative in the minds of cognizing beings as knowers. In fact, instances of actual Hegelian knowing involve two-way reflections into each other of the "concepts" and "logics" of the Real and those of the Ideal (the latter being concepts and logics according to more familiar, non-Hegelian definitions and characterizations).

Those inclined to indict Hegel for some sort of subjective idealism likely would latch onto this post-Kantian expansion and generalization of the conceptual/logical to cover the Real of being as well as the Ideal of thinking as proving Hegelianism culpable of being a panpsychism. However, this verdict relies upon an illegitimate conflation of panlogism with panpsychism. Hegel indeed might be guilty of a certain variety of panlogism – and this insofar as one of the upshots of his Kant critique is that the organization and functioning of objective realities beyond subjects' concepts and logics, as knowable realities capable of being captured by these subjects, are organized and function in "conceptual"/"logical" ways (taking "conceptual"/"logical" in Hegel's broadened senses). To be knowable in and through subjects' thoughts, asubjective things must not be wholly alien and completely foreign to the forms and contents of thoughts. Therefore, if the forms and contents of the subjective thoughts of things known are logical and conceptual, then the dynamics and structures of these things themselves are similarly somehow logical and conceptual too. This might very well be panlogism of a particular (post-Kantian) type. But, non-dogmatically reasoning via a critical assessment of Kant's transcendentalism that the architectures and trajectories of the extra/non-subjective Real are not different-in-kind from those of the subjective Ideal (i.e., the mindedness of sentient and sapient thinking knowers) is hardly tantamount to positing that everything in existence (in particular, non-human existences) really is minded as aware, conscious, etc.[77] Hegel's panlogism is far from hypothesizing anything panpsychical, since ascribing knowability to something by no means entails attributing knowledge of itself (through reflective/reflexive self-awareness/consciousness) to this same something. As further exculpatory evidence in this case, Hegel tends to depict minded human subjects as exceptional points at which substantial being uniquely achieves a cognizance of itself. Such subjects are the exception rather than, as in panpsychism, the universal rule.

To return to the topic of Hume's and Kant's critical responses to the clash between Spinozist and Leibnizian versions of rationalist substance metaphysics, Hegel's stance on this issue with respect to the more empiricist side of transcendental idealism is nuanced and multifaceted. To begin with, given that Hume takes up this matter in connection with the disputed notion of the soul, it should be noted that Hegel greatly appreciates the post-Humean assault mounted by Kant in "The Paralogisms of Pure Reason" on Cartesian-style "rationalist psychology" (i.e., non-empirical discourses about the soul *qua* Kantian "psychological idea of reason" in which the "I" of first-person subjectivity is spoken of as if it were a stable metaphysical thing, a reified object-referent of an *apriori* philosophical psychology).[78] Leibniz's reaction against the, as it were, soullessness of Spinoza's ontology is clearly to be situated as an instance of the Cartesianism targeted by the first *Critique*'s "Paralogisms." Hegel agrees with Kant that "spiritual" (*als geistige*) subjects are not to be grounded upon the inertness of the objectified substantiality of a special sort of soul-stuff, not to be reduced to fixed and frozen metaphysical entities. However, consistent with his above-glossed departure from Kant's limits of possible experience and related things-in-themselves, Hegel disagrees with what he portrays as the Kantian move of preserving the old soul of rational psychology in the modified guise of a peculiar type of *Ding an sich*, namely, as a thinkable-but-unknowable noumenal self hiding behind or beneath the manifest dialectical conflicts strikingly put on display in the "Paralogisms."

A fundamental difference between Kant and Hegel is directly related to the immediately preceding. This has to do with their respective conceptions of the implications of dialectics. Of course, the basic intention of Kant's lengthy "Transcendental Dialectic" (including the "Paralogisms" and "Antinomies") is to hammer home the thesis that human knowers, contrary to the vast bulk of the Western metaphysical tradition, have no true epistemological access to such supposed transcendent beings as the soul, the world, and God, namely, the three ideas of reason: the psychological, the cosmological, and the theological (as illusory noumenal referents inevitably posited due to the "interest of reason" as a mental faculty in completing, totalizing, or unifying the finite regions of phenomenal experience). Kant brings to light various dialectics afflicting pre-Kantian philosophical discussions of the soul, the world, and God. The *Critique of Pure Reason* makes the case for interpreting these deadlocks and impasses in the history of philosophy (i.e., the contradictions and antagonisms arising within and between metaphysicians' non-empirical treatments of the psychological, the cosmological, and the theological) as interminable and insurmountable – thus suggesting that a resolution on terms other than those of the metaphysicians of the past is desirable, possible, and, in truth, requisite (this resolution being nothing other than Kant's proffered Copernican revolution).

With its intra-systemic links to the "Transcendental Aesthetic" (with this section's insistence on the pure ideality of time and space) and the rest of the theoretical edifice of the first *Critique* (especially its load-bearing notions of the noumenal-phenomenal distinction, the limits of possible experience, and the thing-in-itself), the "Transcendental Dialectic" is employed by Kant in the service of arguing for a subjective idealism (at loggerheads with, among other alternate options, a realist materialism). His arguments involving dialectics betray an assumption, arguably a dogmatic one at odds with his own critical epistemology, that being-beyond-knowing (i.e., noumenal things-in-themselves on the nether side of the limits of possible experience) is free of anything and everything dialectical. That is to say, the demonstrative power of the "Transcendental Dialectic" depends upon the presumption that the supersensible Real of being(s) *an sich*, whatever else it might be, is consistent with itself and fully cohesive on its own, devoid of dialectical contradictions. If this is so, then revealing the metaphysics of the soul, the world, and God to be burdened by irremovable contradictions is to prove that the knowing subject has no knowledge of such asubjective, supersensible entities.

With respect to Kant's critique of discourses about the soul in the "Paralogisms" and elsewhere (as itself foreshadowed by Hume's objections to this notion as it features in the various versions of seventeenth-century rationalist substance metaphysics), Hegel implicitly takes up the contradiction between the ontologies of Spinoza and Leibniz as indicative of the really contradictory character of subjectivity in and for itself, with the real dialectics of the subject involving unity and disunity, continuity and discontinuity, immediacy and mediation, and other oscillating opposites too. And, with reference to the "Antinomies" of the "Transcendental Dialectic," Hegel alleges that Kant is wrong to limit such contradictions to only four; Hegelian philosophy, as dialectical-speculative, obviously is invested in the thesis that a thriving multitude of antinomic contradictions (well in excess of four) are constitutive of being(s) *an sich*, including the existence of the soul-like subject.[79] Furthermore, Hegel's admiration for Kant's redeployment of the previously neglected art of dialectics as per ancient (rather than modern) skepticism is tempered by his dismay that Kant limits dialectics to being subjectively ideal and not (also) objectively real (a limitation relying upon the dogmatic presupposition that the Real is self-consistent and free of contradictions).[80]

This lament regarding the anti-realism *qua* subjective idealism of Kant's brand of (transcendental) dialectics is expressed by Hegel's repeated indictments of the Kantian "tenderness for the things of this world."[81] As he puts it in the *Science of Logic*, "It shows an excessive tenderness for the world to remove contradiction from it and then to transfer the contradiction to spirit, to reason, where it is allowed to remain unresolved."[82] Or, as he reiterates this in his *Lectures on the History of Philosophy*, "Kant shows . . . too much tenderness for things: it would be a pity, he thinks, if they contradicted themselves. But that mind, which is far higher, should be a contradiction – that is not a pity at all."[83] Therefore, from a Hegelian perspective on Hume's and Kant's skeptical and critical assessments of the Spinoza-versus-Leibniz tug-of-war over the soul as supposed seat of subjectivity, Humean empiricism and Kantian transcendentalism are far from cruel enough to the souls of the rationalist substance metaphysicians of the previous century. To be more precise, insofar as, one, Hume leaves the supposed seat of subjectivity alone once introspection results in skeptical agnosticism regarding its existence and, two, Kant hypothesizes an at-one-with-itself noumenal "I" as a self-consistent thinking *Ding an sich* untouched by its own intra-subjective contradictions (as antinomies, paralogisms, etc.), both Hume and Kant avoid making the Hegelian move of quite un-tenderly identifying antagonisms, oppositions, and so on as integral epistemological and ontological structures of the subject *an und für sich* (with this move paving the way for, among other things, Lacan's psychoanalytic barring/ splitting of subjectivity).

Before I rejoin certain current discussions and debates in what is soon to follow (in Chapters 3 and 4), the relevance of the preceding revisitation of modern philosophical history for today can be summed up with a now-clichéd (but no less true) warning from, of all people, Edmund Burke: Those who do not know history are doomed to repeat it (of course, this is especially ironic given the sharp contrast between the German idealists' sympathies and Burke's antipathy toward the French Revolution). Forgetting or repudiating the legacies of Kant and Hegel eventuates only in lax indulgences in the quaint hobby of playing at antiquated reenactments of pre-Kantian metaphysical squabbles, with the original battles themselves, as already demonstrated at detailed length in the "Transcendental Dialectic," being essentially fruitless due to their unwinnable, interminable natures. As approximately 2,000 years of pre-critical Western philosophy amply revealed by the end of the eighteenth century, these stalemates (i.e., those of metaphysical and/or transcendental realism) are foregone conclusions. They are preordained argumentative cul-de-sacs always-already mapped out in advance by dialectical logics delineated by Kant and Hegel and inevitably coming into force as soon as the critical stance and its positive legacy is ignored. No amount of fashionable new jargon (whether that of "speculative realism" as an overall orientation or so-called "new materialisms") can conceal these simultaneously both historical and philosophical facts. Hence, as instances of an anachronistic regression to a pre-Kantian position, contemporary permutations of Spinozism, with their interrelated rejections of subjectivity and epistemologically un- or under-justified intellectual intuitions into the purported fundaments of ontology, are just as vulnerable to, for instance, Leibnizian, Humean, Kantian, and (most importantly here) Hegelian contestations as Spinoza's philosophy itself. By contrast, a neo/post-

Hegelian ontology including within itself a neither reductive nor eliminative theory of non-epiphenomenal subjectivity – and, as I showed above, this ontology also is post- rather than merely anti-Spinozist in that it results from Hegel's own immanent critique of Spinozism – circumvents and makes progress beyond these sterile old dead-ends. Not all history bears well being repeated, however knowingly or not.

Notes

1. Beiser 2005: 71–4.
2. Kant 1965: Bxvi–xvii [22].
3. Hölderlin 1972: 515–16.
4. Hegel 2002a: 110–12; Henrich 2003: 93–8, 100–1.
5. Johnston 2012c: 103–57; Johnston 2014; Johnston 2015.
6. Johnston 2011d: 71–91; Johnston 2014.
7. Johnston 2008c: 27–49; Johnston 2013i.
8. Schelling 1936: 3, 7, 9.
9. Johnston 2011e: 159–79; Johnston 2011d: 71–91; Johnston 2013e; Johnston 2013f; Johnston 2013i; Johnston 2014.
10. Maimon 2010: 37–8, 42–3.
11. Johnston 2013i; Johnston 2014.
12. Žižek 2012: 4, 141, 143–5, 395.
13. Gabriel 2011: viii–ix, xii, xiv–xv, xix–xxii, xxiv–xxix, xxxi, 1, 3, 51, 54, 60, 71, 76, 82, 86, 92–3, 96, 98.
14. Hegel 1977c: 9.
15. Hegel 1955: 268–9; Hegel 1984a: 225–6.
16. Hegel 1955: 513–15.
17. Schelling 1936: 10–11, 13–14, 16–19, 23–4; Schelling 1994c: 214; Schelling 2000: 104–5; Schelling 1994a: 64–75; Schelling 2007: 126; Hegel 1977c: 10–13; Hegel 1991c: §151 [226–7]; Hegel 1970b: §359 [385–6]; Hegel 1971b: §415 [156]; Hegel 1955: 257–61, 263–4, 268–9, 280, 287–9.
18. Hegel 1969b: 454–5; Hegel 1969a: 382–3.
19. Hegel 1969b: 455; Hegel 1969a: 383.
20. Hegel 1970a: 23; Hegel 1977c: 10.
21. Hegel 2008: 212, 227.
22. Hegel 1991b: 8.
23. Hegel 1971b: §573 [309–10].
24. Hegel 1969c: 195; Hegel 1969a: 537.
25. Hegel 1969a: 538; Hegel 1955: 260–1, 288–9.

26. Hegel 1984a: 376–8; Hegel 1987: 95, 727; Della Rocca 2012: 17, 22.
27. Schelling 1988: 45–7; Schelling 2004: 40, 87, 117, 186, 219–22; Schelling 1978: 207–12; Schelling 1984: 120, 142, 159, 164, 166, 176–7, 188–9, 201–2, 221; Schelling 1966: 76–7, 122–3; Schelling 1994b: 190–2.
28. Moyar 2012: 204–7.
29. Henrich 2010a: 143–4.
30. Hegel 1984a: 370.
31. Doz 1987: 138.
32. Hegel 1969a: 537–8.
33. Vaysse 1994: 279.
34. Hegel 1977a: 105–6; Hegel 1991c: §229 [298], §231 [299–300]; Hegel 1969a: 537; Hegel 1955: 263–4, 268–9, 282–3, 285; Beiser 2005: 91; Vater 2012: 174; Hindrichs 2012: 223–4.
35. Fichte 2005: 41; Vaysse 1994: 72–3, 80, 90.
36. Vaysse 1994: 152.
37. Ibid.: 279.
38. Hegel 1969a: 537; Hegel 1970b: §359 [385–6]; Hegel 1971b: §389 [31]; Hegel 1955: 260–1, 264, 268–9, 288–9; Hegel 2008: 113, 166; Doz 1987: 137–8; Beiser 2005: 64–5, 92–3; Houlgate 2006: 163, 370.
39. Hegel 1987: 106.
40. Hegel 1977c: 9, 15–17, 31–3, 35–6, 49, 51–4; Hegel 1969a: 27–8, 31–2, 36–40, 43–4, 53, 55–6; Hegel 1991a: §2 [26], §3 [29–30], §31 [60].
41. Jacobi 1994: 336.
42. Hegel 1969a: 536–9.
43. Theunissen 1980: 156–8.
44. Hegel 1969c: 195; Hegel 1969a: 536–7.
45. Doz 1987: 135.
46. Hegel 1955: 287–9.
47. Moder 2013: 146–7.
48. Hegel 1991c: §50 [97]; Hegel 1984a: 254; Henrich 2010b: 220; Houlgate 2006: 136.
49. Hegel 1955: 285.
50. Vaysse 1994: 250–1, 253–7, 269, 279–80.
51. Hegel 1955: 257–8; Henrich 2003: 289.
52. Fichte 1976: 25–7, 31–2, 35–7; Henrich 2003: 273.
53. Hegel 1955: 257; Beiser 2005: 58–60.
54. Hegel 1971b: §415 [156]; Vaysse 1994: 277; Houlgate 2006: 434–5.

55. Althusser 1976: 134–5; Macherey 1990: 11–12, 17, 248, 259–60.

56. Moder 2013: 30.

57. Hegel 1969a: 539.

58. Hegel 1969a: 539–40; Hegel 1991c: §151 [226]; Hegel 1955: 289–90.

59. Hume 1969: 299–311.

60. Ibid.: 280–99.

61. Hegel 1977b: 69, 154; Hegel 1991c: §39 [80], §40 [80–1]; Hegel 1955: 374.

62. Westphal 1989: x, 1, 7, 100–4, 140–5; Maker 1998: 3–5, 14–15.

63. Johnston 2012c: 103–57.

64. Beiser 2002: 1–14.

65. Kant 1965: B274–9 [244–7], A374–7 [348–50].

66. Engels 1941: 31.

67. Lenin 1972: 22–3, 33–4, 95, 106, 128–9, 140–2, 145, 167, 188–9, 191, 232, 321, 344, 407–13, 416–17, 431, 434.

68. Hegel 1969a: 154–6.

69. Hegel 1969b: 172–3; Hegel 1969a: 111.

70. Kant 1965: A27–8/B43–4 [72], A35–6/B52–3 [78], B69–71 [88–9].

71. Hegel 1970b: §253–4 [28–30], §257–8 [33–6].

72. Hegel 1969a: 190; Hegel 1991c: §41 [82], §48 [91–2]; Hegel 1955: 450; Hegel 2008: 30–1; Hegel 1984c: 277, 281.

73. Hegel 1969a: 489; Hegel 1991c: §42 [86], §45 [88–9]; Hegel 2008: 37.

74. Hegel 1977b: 76–7; Hegel 1969a: 132, 134–6, 490–1; Hegel 1991c: §44 [87], §60 [105–6]; Hegel 2008: 37–8; Hegel 1984d: 498–9; Johnston 2008d: 133–42.

75. Johnston 2008d: 15, 130–1, 235–6.

76. Hyppolite 1997: 3–5, 7–8.

77. Ibid.: 58–9.

78. Hegel 1969a: 223–4, 775–80; Hegel 1991c: §47 [90–1]; Hegel 2008: 40.

79. Hegel 1969a: 190–3; Hegel 1991c: §48 [92–3]; Hegel 2008: 41–4.

80. Hegel 1969a: 831–3; Hegel 1991c: §48 [91–2].

81. Hegel 1991c: §48 [92].

82. Hegel 1969a: 237.

83. Hegel 1955: 451.

3

"Off with their thistleheads!": Against Neo-Spinozism

In relatively recent European intellectual history, Hegel's philosophy, especially its logic, has been reinterpreted as a powerful precursor of mid-twentieth-century anti-humanism, itself closely associated with permutations of structuralism and its aftermath. Jean Hyppolite's *Logic and Existence*, so influential for Deleuze and those of his generation in French philosophy, is the paradigmatic example of this arguably anachronistic reading of Hegel's corpus.[1] This reading is motivated, in part, by a reaction against and desire to counter-balance Alexandre Kojève's preceding and equally anachronistic introduction of Hegel into twentieth-century France, during the 1930s, via an existentialist and quasi-Marxist interpretation indefensibly favoring the *Phenomenology of Spirit* (over the *Science of Logic*) as itself a sort of humanist philosophical anthropology. Although Hyppolite portrays Hegel's Spinoza critique in an approving light,[2] this Hegelian non/post-Spinozism is, of course, not shared by structuralist Althusserianism or poststructuralist Deleuzianism, both quite favorably inclined toward Spinoza's philosophy. Nonetheless, Althusser and Deleuze definitely are solidary with the anti-humanism coloring Hyppolite's structuralist rendition of Hegelian logic.

In an 1808 letter to his personal friend and professional protector Friedrich Immanuel Niethammer, Hegel complains about "those thistleheads the Spinozists" who "in general view man as a portion of seawater sealed off in a bottle floating adrift in the ocean."[3] As regards Hyppolite's above-mentioned structuralism-inspired rereading of the Hegelian system, this complaint is a reminder that one must distinguish between anti-humanism and anti-subjectivism. Although Hyppolite evinces awareness of this difference, his structuralist and post-structuralist neo-Spinozist contemporaries seem to conflate the two, operating as though an anti-humanist program requires dissolving any and every figure of subjectivity tracing its lineage back to the post-Cartesian modernity of, among others, Hegel himself. However, Hegel's radical, unflinching assault on all forms of finitude and finite understanding (*Verstand*) as prematurely and one-sidedly elevated to an absolute standing likewise would entail rejecting "humanism" as defined and derided in post-war France (hence Hyppolite's ability to justify and carry off his particular exegesis). Nonetheless – and, this signals that the forced choice between either repudiating humanism or embracing subjectivity is a false dilemma – Hegel almost certainly would level against Althusserian and Deleuzian neo-Spinozisms objections to their subject-squelching stances along the exact same lines as his above-summarized immanent critique of Spinoza himself (see Chapter 2). These more historically proximate and still-influential "thistleheads" view humans as nothing more than mere portions of such "oceans" as a "process-without-a-subject" or a "pre-individual, impersonal virtual," bodies of water as uniformly dark as the night in which all cows are black.

The intellectual milieu of the early-twenty-first-century present hardly is lacking in neo-Spinozists. Variants of "post-humanism" and so-called "new materialism" are advocated from a number of quarters. In philosophy, politics, science, and other fields, references to Spinoza and appeals to Spinozist notions have become increasingly frequent and fashionable. Contemporary authors such as, to name just a few, Macherey, Jane Bennett, William Connolly, Manuel DeLanda, Elizabeth Grosz, and Michael Hardt and Antonio Negri all are, to varying degrees and in different manners, representative of this revival of Spinozism in today's multidisciplinary theoretical landscape. These authors' revivals often are inflected by additions of elements (ones consistent with the absolutely flat immanent ontology of Spinozistic monism) drawn from Schelling, Henri Bergson, Maurice Merleau-Ponty, Althusser, and/or Deleuze, among others. Admittedly, those joining the big tent of neo-Spinozism do so in the name of any number of distinct reasons, be these, for instance, metaphysical, phenomenological, (quasi-)Marxist, feminist, democratic, multicultural, ecological, or (ostensibly) biological. Nonetheless, adherents to Spinozism, whether in the early nineteenth century of Hegel or nowadays and whatever their differences, are united in their common cause to liquidate *Cogito*-like subjectivity *à la* Descartes, Kant, Fichte, and Hegel. Equivocating between the subject of humanism and the modern subject *überhaupt*, this motley coalition of modernity's discontents blames such a subject for a daunting, dizzying array of theoretical and practical problems plaguing humanity. They lend their voices to the chanting of mantras straining to conjure away this awful "x." However updated the terminology, the refrain remains the same over the centuries: *Hen kai pan* (Ἐν καὶ Πᾶν).

In the present context, Iain Hamilton Grant's efforts to resuscitate Schelling and *Naturphilosophie* deserve and promise to repay some attention. Although his 2006 book *Philosophies of Nature After Schelling* contains ample detailed investigations into Schelling's texts and their reception backed up by a substantial amount of painstakingly careful scholarship, this is not a work of intellectual/philosophical history exclusively. As the word "after" in its title signals at the get-go, Grant is interested in reviving the legacy of Schellingian *Naturphilosophie* in the contemporary conjuncture, thereby deliberately and avowedly opting to view it through the lenses of post-Schellingian hindsight.[4]

Coming after Schelling, the philosopher who seems most profoundly to shape Grant's reconstruction of Schelling's philosophy (or philosophies) of nature is none other than Deleuze. As a glance at the index of *Philosophies of Nature After Schelling* quickly reveals, Deleuze's name indeed is peppered throughout the book. But, even when not explicitly named, Deleuzianism manifestly is the omnipresent theoretical master-matrix undergirding Grant's endeavors. How so? To begin with, Grant rejects both Hegel's derisive accusation that Schelling self-indulgently underwent his philosophical education publicly in print as well as those strains of Schelling scholarship likewise reading his itinerary as a discontinuous series of incompatible and incomplete "systems" (of whatever number, depending on which scholar is doing the counting). Instead, Grant's proposal is that specific ideas of "Identity" and "Nature" function as consistent red threads running uninterrupted throughout the entire span of Schelling's philosophical career even after he moves past the youthful periods in his development of the philosophies of identity and nature per se.[5] Despite the chronological sweep of this proposal in relation to the Schellingian *oeuvre* in its entirety, Grant generally limits his interpretive coverage of Schelling's writings to the first decade between 1794 and 1804. Hence, the later Schelling (for instance, of the 1809 *Freiheitschrift*) insisting on his dialectical-speculative (and more than just Spinozist) credentials[6] (maybe provoked into doing so by the potent sting of Hegel's *Phenomenology of Spirit*) does not feature centrally in *Philosophies of Nature After Schelling*. Given Deleuze's virulent anti-Hegelianism, the absence of a more dialectical-speculative Schelling (i.e., a post-1809, middle-period Schelling) from Grant's book perhaps should not come as a surprise to readers.

Weirdly, Grant refers to Spinozism only once, in the context of critically discussing Fichte.[7] This is strange because both Schelling and Deleuze, Grant's two key sources of inspiration, obviously engage with and rely upon Spinoza extensively. Nonetheless, insofar as Deleuze's recasting of the rapport between the modalities of possibility and actuality via his notion of the virtual involves reactivating Spinoza's *Verstand*-type distinction between *natura naturans* and *natura naturata*, the Schelling of *Philosophies of Nature After Schelling* is doubly anachronistic: not only, through a deliberate anachronism on Grant's part, retrojectively Deleuzian, but also projectively more Spinozist than he defensibly can be claimed to be. As I noted much earlier here (see Chapter 2), Schelling, soon after 1804, begins distancing himself from Spinozism, articulating criticisms of it very much in line with those spelled out by Hegel. This shift away from pre/non-dialectical Spinozism in Schelling's thinking, postdating the initial period of his trajectory focused on by Grant, problematizes Grant's assertion that his reconstruction of Schelling the philosopher of nature and identity of the decade 1794–1804 does fundamental justice to the full stretch of Schelling's evolution unfolding over the course of the subsequent fifty years of his life.

In fact, Grant's Schelling appears to be quite guilty of Hegel's charge of insufficiently dialectical Spinozism (*à la* the night in which all cows are black). This Schelling's culpability of dissipating all differences and determinations in the dark abyss of Nature-with-a-capital-N as a primal One-All is testified to by three main aspects of Grant's interpretation. First, Grant debatably reads Schelling and Schellingianism as essentially non/anti-, instead of ambivalently post-, Kantian[8] (a reading open to challenge through, for example, an appreciation of the German Romantics' immanent, rather than external, critiquings of Kantianism in which the young Schelling of interest to Grant participates). Therefore, Grant's "realist" Schellingian *Naturphilosophie* rejects and ignores the critical revolution with the stylistic flourish of a defiant gesture of abruptly thumbing its nose at Kant (although, admittedly, this gesture is tempered and qualified by Grant's occasional indications that Schellingianism is more of a post-Kantian geneticization and/ or naturalization of Kant[9]). Thus, this realism is as much regressively pre-Kantian as non/anti-Kantian. By not being arrived at through a post-Kantian path laid out via an immanent critique of the critical philosophy, the Schellingianism of *Philosophies of Nature After Schelling* is closer to the early-modern rationalist metaphysics of Spinoza than to the late-modern, post-critical systems of the German idealists themselves (Schelling arguably included). Hence, this realism is a throwback to the sort of metaphysical worldviews mercilessly scrutinized by the "all-destroyer" (as per Moses Mendelssohn) in the *Critique of Pure Reason*, with its "Transcendental Dialectic" marking a black-and-white boundary line between early and late modernity. In the current theoretical conjuncture, one of the important stakes hanging in the balance in both the struggles between neo-Spinozism and neo-Hegelianism as well as the clashes around "speculative realism" is the question of whether or not it is possible or defensible to step out from under the long shadows cast by Kant's critical philosophy and revive pre-Kantian styles of metaphysical speculation, with their intellectual intuitions into the supposed absoluteness of being(s) *an sich*.

The second piece of evidence bearing witness to an excessively Spinozist *qua* monochromatic ontology is that Grant's Schelling propounds a *Naturphilosophie* in which distinctions between multiple levels and layers of nature (such as the mechanical, the chemical, and the organic) are in danger of being reduced away or eliminated altogether. Grant repeatedly objects to any partitioning of the organic and the inorganic in particular. In place of an emergentist-type dialectical-speculative identity-in-difference between nature's multiple strata, Grant opts to (over)emphasize the seamless continuity and unity of all things both living and non-living.[10] He one-sidedly envisions Nature as a cosmic Totality such that discrepancies between the realms of astrophysics, geology, evolution, etc. are rendered negligible as ultimately unreal epiphenomena with no true ontological standing. If this is not the straightforward pre-nineteenth-century Spinozism ruthlessly criticized by Kant and his idealist successors, then what is?

The third Spinozist black mark besmirching Grant's brand of Schellingian *Naturphilosophie* is nothing other than the *Ur*-distinction forming the very foundation of *Philosophies of Nature After Schelling* in its entirety. A posited difference between productivity and products is absolutely fundamental to Grant. He constantly elaborates variations of this difference throughout his book.[11] Probably as a result of his Deleuzianism, Grant, like Deleuze, basically redeploys the Spinozist non/anti-dialectical contrast between *natura naturans* (i.e., productivity) and *natura naturata* (i.e., products). According this too neat-and-clean contrast, the empirical and experimental natural sciences begin and end with references to the actual, ontic bodies and movements of already-constituted *natura naturata*. By contrast, Grant situates his Schellingian-Deleuzian (and crypto-Spinozistic) *Naturphilosophie* at a separate, non-empirical level, that of Nature as *natura naturans*, namely, a virtual, ontological creative power of constitution functioning as a single, homogeneous, and ultimate transcendental possibility condition for *natura naturata* as its created (by-) products. Like Spinoza's God-Nature and Althusser's History as process, the only subject in Grant's framework is the mega-Subject of a dynamic universal Whole, a divine One-All transcendent vis-à-vis its creations. Not only is this *Weltanschauung* completely exposed to exactly the same criticisms Hegel hurls with deadly effectiveness against Spinoza and the early Schelling – if this counts as the naturalism of a philosophy of nature with any relationship whatsoever, however distant and tenuous, to the natural sciences, then the label "naturalism" loses all meaning. Insofar as naturalism, in recent philosophical history up through today, designates positions not without their connections to materialism and empirical science, rationalist *apriori* intellectual intuitions into an infinite and indivisible sovereign creator absolutely separate as over-and-above its creations signal fidelity to a type of position at the antipodes of naturalism as characterized by professional philosophers: theosophical, obscurantist pantheism/panpsychism.

The time has come for a circling back to the anti-epiphenomenalist principle of no illusions as an axiomatic thesis of transcendental materialism (see Chapter 1). Neo-Spinozisms, to the extent that they remain faithful to their historical origin in Spinoza himself as their chosen authoritative source, inevitably involve some degree of reliance upon epiphenomenalism. In the original Spinozist system, differentiated attributes and modes are epiphenomena as de-ontologized appearances; solely the one undifferentiated Substance behind or beneath the many attributes and modes is ontologically real. Likewise, for neo-Spinozists, individuated, sapient subjects seemingly irreducible to and indissoluble within the flatly monistic expanse of a lone "plane of immanence" also are epiphenomenal. *Cogito*-like transcendental subjectivity resists full absorption without remainder within a trans-individual, exhaustively interconnected web of whatever sort (envisionings of this saturated Network-of-networks vary, depending on the particular permutation of neo-Spinozism in question). As such, it automatically gets written off by neo-Spinozists as a mere illusion, an unreality often associated in these dismissals with any number of insidious, pernicious ideologies.

In the conclusion ("The Unbearable Lightness of Being Free") to *Žižek's Ontology* (2008), I lay out a number of arguments against epiphenomenalism drawing on philosophy (especially Kant's practical philosophy), psychoanalysis, and neurobiology (particularly the Lacanian neuro-psychoanalysis of François Ansermet).[12] I wish here briefly to extend and embellish upon certain of these arguments through a couple of more recent references. World-renowned neuroscientist Antonio Damasio, despite his enthusiasm for Spinozism in 2003's *Looking for Spinoza: Joy, Sorrow, and the Feeling Brain*, curtly dismisses the plausibility of epiphenomenalism in his most recent book, 2010's *Self Comes to Mind: Constructing the Conscious Brain*, thus:

> Conscious deliberation, under the guidance of a robust self built on an organized autobiography and a defined identity, is a major consequence of consciousness, precisely the kind of achievement that gives the lie to the notion that consciousness is a useless epiphenomenon, a decoration without which brains would run the life-management business just as effectively and without the hassle. We cannot run our kind of life, in the physical and social environments that have become the human habitat, without reflective, conscious deliberation. But it is also the case that the products of conscious deliberation are significantly limited by a large array of nonconscious biases, some biologically set, some culturally acquired, and that the nonconscious control of action is also an issue to contend with.[13]

Whatever Damasio's degree of awareness of the tensions between his Spinozism and his anti-epiphenomenalism, he clearly insists here that subjective mindedness shapes and guides cognition and comportment by the human organism as itself internal to and interacting with the material world. As such, the mental subject cannot be demoted to the meager (non-)standing of an epiphenomenon *qua* causally inefficacious fantasy, fiction, etc. But, as the last sentence of the preceding block quotation rightly stipulates, anti-epiphenomenalism does not and should not rule out a range of mitigations and checks on the powers of reflective deliberation and sapient mindedness more generally.

Even more recently, biological anthropologist Terrence Deacon (Chair of the Department of Anthropology and affiliated with the Helen Wills Neuroscience Institute and the Cognitive Science Program at the University of California, Berkeley), in his 2012 book *Incomplete Nature: How Mind Emerged from Matter*, independently makes several arguments also made in the conclusion to *Žižek's Ontology* (I address Deacon's book at greater length elsewhere[14]). On the second page of his almost 600-page tome, Deacon, speaking precisely of the types of structures and phenomena targeted for reduction or elimination by monistic reductivists and eliminativists, contends, "even this property of being a pretender to significance will make a physical difference in the world if it somehow influences how you might think or act."[15] Much later in the book, in a sub-section entitled "Evolution's Answer to Nominalism," he expands upon this important observation in some detail. By this juncture in his study, Deacon is talking about what he dubs "teleodynamics" defined as "A form of dynamical organization exhibiting end-directedness and consequence-organized features"[16] (i.e., the distinctive, characteristic configurations of sentient and/or sapient organisms as teleologically driven living beings internally generated out of non-teleological natural processes). Several of his remarks warrant quoting. To begin with, apropos the ancient, perennial debate between metaphysical realists and nominalists, Deacon maintains:

> there is a sense in which the emergence of teleodynamics has significantly augmented this efficacy of generals; and with the evolution of the teleodynamics of brains, this mode of causality has even begun to approach a quasi-Platonic abstract form of causal influence. Ironically, the structure of the nominalistic argument for the epiphenomenality of general types provides the essential clue for making sense of this augmented notion of causal realism. This is because both living and mental processes do indeed break up the physical uniqueness of physical processes into similarity classes, due to the way they ignore details that are not relevant to the teleodynamic processes they potentially impact. But this simplification *has* causal consequences.[17]

He continues:

> Seeing this clustering by simplification as necessitating epiphenom-
> enality turns out to be both right and wrong at the same time. It is
> right when it comes to providing a reliable predictor of causal proper-
> ties that are present irrespective of organism discernment. It is wrong,
> however, when one includes organism agency as a causal factor.[18]

Deacon's solution to the conflict between metaphysical realism
and nominalism is to draw a level distinction such that each side
has its appropriate domains of both ontological and epistemological jurisdiction. On the level of the purely inorganic as inanimate
matter devoid of any trace of sentience or agential purposiveness
(as per physics, chemistry, and similar scientific disciplines and
sub-disciplines dealing with the non-living material universe),
nominalism, arguably the spontaneous philosophy of scientism
(to paraphrase Althusser), indeed is the best framing worldview.
But, on the levels of life, sentience, and especially sapience (as per
biology as well as both the social sciences and humanities), living
beings' powers of abstraction problematize strict nominalism – and
this because the resulting abstractions influence and steer actions
realized in the actual physical world within which organisms are
included as members (i.e., Deacon's "organism agency as a causal
factor"). Particularly in the case of human beings, the symbolic-
linguistic groupings of unique spatio-temporal individuals into
general categories, concepts, predicates, sets, and the like (i.e.,
"naming" *à la* nominalism as the means by which particulars are
subsumed under universals, with the latter as Deacon's "similar-
ity classes") are integral to and inseparable from the mind's sense
of overall reality itself.[19] These symbol- and language-facilitated
falsifications of the nominalist "truth" of the pure uniqueness
of each and every spatio-temporal individual themselves become
true as causally efficacious via mind-molded behavior operative in
and through the spatio-temporal reality of the non-living material
world. As Deacon points out, "physical responses, perceptions,
and mental categories aren't merely passive reflections on the
world . . . the mere resemblance of an object to a perceptual class
can be what causes that object to be modified in a particular way
by an animal or person."[20]

Although mindedness appears to the most committed, hard-
nosed nominalists (whether reductivists or eliminativists) to be

illusory (i.e., epiphenomenal as fantasmatic, fictional, unreal, etc.), this appearance itself is illusory. Even when the mental construct motivating a given instance of behavior is as false *qua* otherworldly fantastic as can be imagined – this also holds for mindedness *tout court* – insofar as it gets translated into this-worldly action generating material effects, it cannot be dismissed even by the most die-hard scientistic types as entirely epiphenomenal (i.e., illusory as causally inefficacious – for instance, one does not have to be a practicing psychoanalyst to know that fantasies can have very real consequences). In other words, although the structures and phenomena of minded beings as intentional agents are "absential" in Deacon's sense (i.e., of an order other than the presence of here-and-now matter in motion as the only reality acknowledged and recognized by positivist sciences and scientisms), the natural sciences themselves must become "absentialist" in order to take account of and do justice to such far-from-epiphenomenal realities.[21]

Deacon himself quickly proceeds to focus on the sapience actualized by human brains specifically. With respect to the causally efficacious power of metaphysical-realism-style abstractions (i.e., what Deacon dubs "causal realism"), he states:

> Brains have elaborated this causal realism to an extreme, and minds capable of symbolic references can literally bring even the most Platonic of conceptions of abstract forms into the realm of causal particulars. To list some extreme but familiar examples, a highly abstract concept like artistic beauty can be the cause of the production of vastly many chiseled marble analogues of the human female form; a concept like justice can determine the restriction of movement of diverse individuals deemed criminal because of only vaguely related behaviors each has produced; and a concept like money can mediate the organization of the vastly complex flows of materials and energy, objects and people, from place to place within a continent. These abstract generals unquestionably have both specific and general physical consequences. So human minds can literally transform arbitrarily created abstract general features into causally efficacious specific physical events.[22]

Serendipitously, certain of Deacon's examples here provide bridges back to key philosophical precursors of his absential realism of more-than-material (final) causes (as cases of teleodynamics). Of course, the choices of beauty and justice cannot but call to mind the Platonic origins of Western philosophy as a whole. But, the quite heterodox version of a highly qualified metaphysical realism advanced by Deacon in his parallel compromise with nominalism is closer to Hegel's and Marx's related handlings of abstractions. For a Hegelian, the notion of the concrete apart from the abstract (or, in Deacon's scheme, the nominalist's particulars apart from the metaphysical realist's universals) is itself the height of abstraction. Countless remarks by Hegel about beauty and justice/goodness (as well as truth) convey this thesis that concrete particulars in such domains as art, ethics, politics, and the myriad branches of knowledges are what they are, as "singular"/"individual" (*einzeln*) in Hegel's technical sense of being simultaneously neither-nor/both-and particular and universal, only in and through their dialectical-speculative relations with abstract universals.[23]

Similarly, Marxian "real abstractions," epitomized by commodity fetishism[24] and the real becoming-abstract of labor through capitalist industrialization[25] (as well as the virtual realities of capital itself *überhaupt*), are not unrelated to this aspect of Hegelian philosophy. Moreover, perhaps fortuitously (or, alternately, maybe with a subtle knowing nod to Marx), Deacon mentions in the passage quoted immediately above how "a concept like money can mediate the organization of the vastly complex flows of materials and energy, objects and people, from place to place." For attentive, careful Marxist critics of ideologies, it always must be taken into account that the nitty-gritty materialities of social realities both infrastructural and superstructural are suffused with the real effects of mediating abstractions in the forms of beliefs, doctrines, errors, ideas, illusions, mistakes, and so on. Especially through the Marxist historical materialist uptake of Hegelian dialectics, "false consciousness," to the extent that it indeed has actual causal repercussions in social reality, is, in certain fashions, more true than what is (pre)supposed to be objectively true as independent of such consciousness. When seeming "distortions" become part of the very field they distort, there no longer is a real field apart from the distortions since the real field now includes within itself the distortions as aspects of its *an sich* existence. In this situation (i.e., the topsy-turvy "inverted worlds" of human realities), the "distortion," as the skewed perspective mistaking fiction for fact, is the very notion of a non-distorted field.

Lacan, like Deacon after him, takes up this same Hegelian-Marxian line of thought.[26] I will address Lacan's appropriations of dialectical materialism and real abstractions below (see Chapter 4). However, before turning sustained attention to the Lacanian background behind transcendental materialism, I need to say a few more things about anti-epiphenomenalism and real abstractions à la Hegel and Marx. A stubbornly resistant partisan of reductive or eliminative materialistic-scientistic nominalism might promptly retort that the neurological and evolutionary-genetic underpinnings of human mindedness and everything this brings with it remain where the explanatory buck stops as the causal alpha-and-omega of subjective and social abstract (epi)phenomena. He/she could maintain that, however many intermediary links in chains of causes and effects consist of mental and cultural constructs, the ultimate first and/or final causes of all this are of a physical nature entirely explicable by the modern natural sciences in their present-best positivist, presentist (as non-absentialist in Deacon's sense) incarnations.

Arguably, neuroplasticity and epigenetics in particular have severely problematized these sorts of reductivist and eliminativist stances. Insofar as both of these biological facts entail the consequence that the brain and body of the human organism are shaped by and shot through with more-than-biological (i.e., cultural, historical, linguistic, social, etc.) mediating influences, purportedly satisfactory and complete explanations of humans that simply begin and end with appeals to what is presumed to be raw, natural, bare biology alone are highly contentious. Nonetheless, with reference to the phylogeny-ontogeny couplet, reductivists and eliminativists could, for instance, fall back to a phylogenetic position, defending their views by moving to encompass the more-than-biological ontogenetics of neuroplasticity and epigenetics within a larger temporal arc in which fully biological forces and factors hold undisputed sway (vulgar evolutionary psychologies exemplify this kind of position).

Therefore, advocates of non-reductive, post-dialectical, and science-informed materialisms cannot confine themselves solely to the spheres of ontogeny. Incursions into the realms of phylogeny are mandatory. In the absence of such measures, real abstractions are open to being redescribed as mere pseudo-causes *qua* secondary ontogenetic outgrowths of causally ultimate natural grounds. Minds and subjects likewise are open to being redescribed as phylogenetically epiphenomenal, even if not ontogenetically so – in other words, as on long leashes (even if not short ones) held firmly in the grasp of Nature-with-a-capital-N as a phylogenetic Prime Mover with its inviolable laws written in the codes of DNA.[27] When all is said and done, a non-reductive, post-dialectical, and science-informed materialism, including its materialist theory of non-epiphenomenal subjectivity, must demonstrate nature to be underdetermining and self-sundering on phylogenetic as well as ontogenetic levels: underdetermining, namely, not the still-influential Newtonian-era *Weltanschauung* of a seamless plane of all-powerful universal necessity dictated strictly by efficient causes; self-sundering, namely, giving rise out of itself to movements of (auto-)denaturalization eventually achieving full independ-ence vis-à-vis natural material grounds – with these movements therefore being strongly emergent, more-than-natural structures and phenomena endowed with efficacious powers of downward causation exerted on the physical and biological bodies of nature itself.[28]

I turn now to Lacan as another indispensable, invaluable source of inspiration for transcendental materialism. In line with the principle of no illusions as spelled out in the preceding, Lacanian theory contributes much to arguments against epiphenomenal-ism and to arguments for real abstractions – not to mention its controversial and anti-neo-Spinozist fidelity to modern concep-tions of subjectivity, namely, its untimely refusal to repudiate the *Cogito*-like subject. However, discerning these contributions and appropriating them as resources requires appreciating hitherto underappreciated facets of Lacan's *oeuvre*. Not only is Lacan, despite certain widespread impressions to the contrary, situated in the lineage of post-Hegelian historical and dialectical materialism – he is far from being, as per orthodox, textbook Lacanianism, a rigid, unflinching anti-naturalist (as I elsewhere already have argued at detailed length[29]). Furthermore, he is an especially radical realist, going so far as to espouse a realism of the non-phenomenal in additional to the (epi)phenomenal; put differently, the negatives of impossibilities unrepresentable but nonetheless influential within the representational economies of subjects both conscious and unconscious (i.e., points situated in the Lacanian register of the Real) are causally efficacious (non-)beings in addi-tion to the positives of the experiential and ideational contents of minded life (i.e., constituents of Lacanian reality as both Imaginary and Symbolic).[30] This ultra-realism of the non-existent also can be thought of as an extreme extension of Deaconian absentialism *avant la lettre*.[31] The next chapter scrutinizes the unfamiliar figure of a materialist, realist, and quasi-naturalist Lacan who engages in informative delicate balancing acts between transcendental idealism and historical/dialectical materialism. As Germans sometimes like to observe, most philosophical discussions over the past two centuries sooner or later boil down to the basic question, "Kant *oder* Hegel?"

Notes

1. Hyppolite 1997: 11, 18–20, 34–5, 41–2, 73–4, 107–8, 179, 187–9; Deleuze 1997: 191–5.
2. Hyppolite 1997: 58–9, 106, 138, 150.
3. Hegel 1984b: 180–1.
4. Grant 2008: vii, 2, 8–9.
5. Ibid.: 3–4.
6. Schelling 1936: 13–14, 16–18.
7. Grant 2008: 90.
8. Ibid.: 5–6, 59–61.
9. Ibid.: x-xi, 2, 29, 37–8, 158, 189.
10. Ibid.: 10–11, 16–18, 164.
11. Ibid.: 8, 28–9, 36, 42–5, 53–5, 68–9, 77, 108–10, 137–8, 142–6, 149–50, 162, 168–71, 173, 180, 197.
12. Johnston 2008d: 269–87.
13. Damasio 2010: 271–2.
14. Johnston 2013f.
15. Deacon 2012: 2.
16. Ibid.: 552.
17. Ibid.: 481–2.
18. Ibid.: 482.
19. Ibid.: 482.
20. Ibid.: 482.
21. Ibid.: 2–3, 547; Johnston 2013f.
22. Deacon 2012: 483.
23. Hegel 1969a: 600–22; Hegel 1991c: §164 [241–2], §212 [286].
24. Marx 1990: 163–77.
25. Marx 1993: 104–5.
26. Johnston 2012a: 23–52; Johnston 2013f.
27. Johnston 2011e: 159–79; Johnston 2013i; Johnston 2013e.

28. Johnston 2013e; Johnston 2013i; Johnston 2014.
29. Johnston 2011e: 159–79; Johnston 2012a: 23–52; Johnston 2013e.
30. Johnston 2012a: 23–52; Johnston 2013f.
31. Johnston 2012a: 23–52; Johnston 2013f.

4

"Lacan, our Hegel": Psychoanalysis, Dialectics, and Materialisms

In Reality More Than Reality Itself – Zupančič, Žižek, and a Materialist Lacanianism

In his 1982 *Theory of the Subject*, Badiou proclaims that "Lacan . . . is our Hegel."[1] Badiou's reading of him in this set of seminars artfully and compellingly situates Lacanian analysis in the lineage of Hegelian dialectics from Hegel through Marxism, up to and including Maoism. Distinguishing between different dialectical dynamics in different periods of Lacan's thinking – Badiou herein proposes an early version of the now-standard distinction between the middle Lacan of the Symbolic and the late Lacan of the Real[2] – he evinces a preference for the later Lacanianism centered around the Real in conjunction with this rapprochement between Hegel's leftist legacy and Freudian psychoanalysis as carried forward by Lacan. This Badiou can be identified as a powerful precursor of the version of Lacanian theory pioneered by Žižek and the Slovenian School.

A recent article by Alenka Zupančič elaborating a Lacanian critique of Meillassoux's speculative materialism, entitled "Realism in Psychoanalysis,"[3] footnotes a passage from Lacan's eighteenth seminar (*D'un discours qui ne serait pas du semblant* [1971]) as evidence for Lacan being both a realist and a dialectical materialist.[4] In *Less Than Nothing*, Žižek quotes this same passage (in a chapter section entitled "Why Lacan Is Not a Nominalist"), crediting Zupančič with having pointed it out to him.[5] The remarks in question, from the January 20, 1971 session of this seminar, run as follows (the translations are Žižek's):

> If there is something I am, it is clear that I am not a nominalist. What I want to say is that my starting point is not that the name is something

65

like a nameplate which attaches itself, just like that, onto the real. And one has to choose. If one is a nominalist, one has to renounce completely dialectical materialism, so that, all in all, I evidently reject the nominalist tradition which is effectively the only danger of idealism which can arise in a discourse like mine. The point is not to be a realist in the sense in which one was a realist in Medieval times, in the sense of the realism of the universals; the point is to emphasize that our discourse, our scientific discourse, can only find the real.[6]

Lacan continues:

The articulation, and I mean the algebraic articulation, of the semblant – and because of this we are only dealing with letters – and its effects, this is the only apparatus which enables us to designate what is real. What is real is what opens up a hole in this semblant, in this articulated semblant which is the scientific discourse. The scientific discourse progresses without even worrying if it is a discourse of semblance or not. All that matters is that its network, its texture, its *lattice*, as one is used to say, makes the right holes appear at the right place. The only reference reached by its deductions is the impossible. This impossible is the real. In physics, we aim at something which is real with the help of the discursive apparatus which, in its crispness, encounters the limits of its consistency.[7]

Before unpacking Zupančič's and Žižek's interpretations of Lacan's statements here, situating these statements in the larger context of this 1971 seminar as a whole promises to be helpful. Such contextualizing will bring out into sharper relief how and why Lacan performs his specific *Aufhebung* of the opposition between metaphysical realism and nominalism with an eye to modern science especially (and Freudian psychoanalysis as an heir to the legacy of scientific modernity). Of course, Hegel repeatedly sublates this same opposition too.

In particular, the opening session of *Seminar XVIII* (January 13, 1971, the week prior to the second session from which the preceding quotations are taken) contains a series of claims setting up the crucial supports for Lacan's dialectical anti-nominalism as spelled out the following week. Therein, he stipulates that the discursive realities inhabited by (and inhabiting) speaking beings (*parlêtres*) constitute a "*désunivers*," namely, a detotalized, disunified multiplicity multiplying without set limits – and this by contrast with the universe as One-All (i.e., "uni-").[8] He then goes on to declare that "the truth is only a half-saying" (*la vérité n'est qu'à mi-dire*).[9] Soon after this declaration, it is added that "for discourse, there is no fact, if I can speak thusly, there is only a fact from the fact of saying it. The stated fact is entirely a fact of discourse."[10] What do these theses mean? And, how do they fit together?

Beginning with the last assertion immediately above, Lacan's insistence on the strictly discursive status of "facts" makes him sound utterly guilty of propagating a non-dialectical, anti-realist, socio-symbolic constructivism (as per Badiou's accusation, also voiced in *Theory of the Subject*, that Lacan sometimes traffics in "*idéalinguisterie*"[11]). However, Lacan nonetheless is not culpable of this. Understanding his innocence requires taking into consideration, as indispensable parts of the background of his 1971 talk of *discours*, both analysis as theory and practice as well as Lacan's then-new account of the four discourses (of the "master," "university," "hysteric," and "analyst") first delineated in the seventeenth seminar of 1969–70 (*The Other Side of Psychoanalysis*).

Within the four walls of the analytic consulting room, the analyst, listening to the analysand, is not (or, at least, should not be) concerned with truth-as-correspondence, namely, with whether what the patient says matches up with and accurately reflects in the forms of linguistic representations extra-analytic states of affairs in the world outside the analyst's office. If psychical, rather than empirical, reality is what is truly of interest in analysis, with the unconscious as its fundamental "object" of investigation, then correspondences between, on the one hand, the analysand's words and, on the other hand, the entities and events of empirical reality off the couch are secondary, if not negligible, issues. Instead, as the analytic sessions go by and the analysand unfurls an ever-growing web of associations through the textual tapestry-in-formation of his/her free associations, the analyst listens attentively for cross-resonating consistencies, as well as inconsistencies, in the analysand's monologue. The truths of the unconscious and psychical reality, as the types at stake in analysis, have to do with truth-as-coherence (in this case, [in] coherence amongst the myriad statements spoken on the couch by the patient) rather than truth-as-correspondence (with extra-psychical reality). More precisely, given the interpretive orientation of analysis toward slips of the tongue and related sorts of phenomena, it might be more accurate to talk here of truth-as-

incoherence, with the unconscious speaking through moments of
inconsistency, incompetence, and contradiction surfacing within
the flow of speech. This analytic focus on coherence within psychical reality rather than correspondence with empirical reality, a
focus dictated by the quite specific aims of analytic practice, by no
means entails an extreme idealist as anti-realist denial of the extra-
psychical existence of empirical reality. Lacan certainly does not
commit himself to negating beings beyond the speaking subject on
the couch, namely, things outside the consulting room.

Furthermore, a "discourse" (*discours*) in Lacan's precise sense is
a kind of "social link" (*lien social*).[12] That is to say, the discourses
of the master, university, hysteric, and analyst embody four different permutations of how socio-symbolic beings (i.e., speaking
subjects) can be and are positioned in relations with each other.
And, of course, these various sorts of social links come into play
in clinical analyses too. According to the theory of the four discourses, each of them involves four positions (filled in differently
in each discourse): those of "agent," "other," "product," and
"truth." Without delving into specifics for the time being, suffice it
to note at this juncture that every discourse as social link involves
the structure of an "agent-other" rapport. Hence, with reference
to Lacan's above-quoted 1971 assertion about the discursive
status of facts, several clarifications now are possible on the basis
of these brief reminders regarding his concept of discourse.

To begin with, Lacan understands "facts" not as asubjective
states of affairs in the extra-mental world (he does not in the least
ridiculously deny that there are such states of affairs) but as propositions and judgments stated in language claiming that something
is the case, that such-and-such holds as "true." Considering that
Lacan is an analyst whose teachings are first and foremost about
analysis, an analytic approach to facts as discursive phenomena –
and, once more, one must keep in mind that a Lacanian discourse
structurally contains a social link between an agent and an other
addressed by this agent – is attentive not so much to whether given
facts are true at the level of correspondence with empirical reality
(recalling again the analyst's methodical preoccupation with truth
as psychical-subjective [in]coherence). Instead, this approach is
attentive precisely to such questions as: Why are you stating this
fact right now? Why are you stating this fact to me right now?
What investment do you have in this fact being true, and being
true to me as well as you? How does affirming the truth of this

fact fit with other things you have (or have not) said? In this sense, saying the truth as stating a fact is a "half-saying" (*mi-dire*), as Lacan stresses in the same context of the opening session of the eighteenth seminar in which he emphasizes the discursive nature of facts. This is because of these yet-to-be-answered questions that immediately arise and proliferate, for an analytically attuned ear, with each stating of a fact. Moreover, the "universe of discourse" constructed over the course of an analysis-in-process is a "*désunivers*" because each new discursive fact added to the already articulated network of discourse expands and retroactively modifies (via the *Nachträglichkeit* of *après-coup*) this network, decompleting and recompleting it in an open-ended structural dynamic moving within and between both linear and non-linear temporalities. Whatever else they might be, facts are argumentative-inferential moves (i.e., "reasons" *à la* Robert Brandom's inferentialism) made by subjects (*qua* agents as per Lacan's discourse theory) engaged in and by discourses in which others (and Others) necessarily figure too. Apropos the Lacanian clinic, the preceding underscores that analytic interpretation, even when dealing with supposed "facts," must not deviate from its focus on the speaking subject's transferences to Symbolic, Imaginary, and Real others and Others (with transferences and their accompanying fantasy-templates configuring social links between the subject and its addressees).

Although Lacan, in this same January 13, 1971 seminar session, insists that he is not a philosopher comically trying to cover "everything" with his pronouncements,[13] he still, as is usual for him, theoretically ventures well beyond the circumscribed domain of analytic practice alone. But, before I shed some light on these wider-ranging theoretical forays (having to do primarily with modern science), I should make a few additional remarks regarding the more clinical-practical upshots of Lacan's claims. Despite the explanatory virtues and merits of the above-employed distinction between truth-as-correspondence and truth-as-coherence, Lacan soon, in the first two sessions of *Seminar XVIII*, destabilizes and problematizes this distinction both practically and theoretically. In the opening session and promptly following his earlier-quoted statements, he presents the Oedipus myth as illustrating that, in psychoanalysis, truth has the future anterior (i.e., the "will have been" tense) status of a self-fulfilling prophecy[14] (as is common knowledge, in Sophocles' *Oedipus Rex*, the oracle's true warnings about the tragic events-to-come are precisely what drive Oedipus down his fateful path). Analysis shows how words, thoughts, and fantasies (all involving signifier-like psychical *Vorstellungen*), although semblances, are not mere semblances as inconsequential fictions. Like Hegelian-Marxian real abstractions (and the related no-illusions principle of transcendental materialism), the semblants of psychoanalysis are not epiphenomenal since they are causally efficacious, quite palpably shaping the vicissitudes of subjects' life histories. These signifying materials have a lot of say in determining one's *à venir*. Going through an analysis involves, among many other experiences, appreciating just how concretely actual and causally efficacious abstract phenomena can be and are. The coherence truths of intra-psychical reality tend to become the correspondence truths of extra-psychical reality. As Lacan puts it, semblants intrude into the real, signifiers fall into the realm of signifieds.[15]

Still in the opening session of the eighteenth seminar and on the heels of the reference to Oedipus just mentioned, Lacan establishes a chain of equivalence between three of his better-known one-liners, all beginning with "*Il n'y a pas*": There is no metalanguage; There is no Other of the Other; There is no truth about the truth.[16] I can provide here a few quick indications regarding some of the practical-clinical implications of these statements. Analytic patients often believe that certain of their utterances and behaviors are performed, so to speak, in parentheses. Of course, analysands interact with their analysts off the couch too, however brief these windows are: on the "fringes" of sessions (i.e., the times of meeting the analyst before getting on the couch, dealing with the analyst right after the "official" couch portion of the session is over, settling bills, confirming upcoming session schedules, simply saying "Goodbye," etc.), over the phone between sessions, or even if and when analyst and analysand accidentally bump into each other at some public place. Moreover, during the couch portions of analytic sessions themselves, patients sometimes signal in any number of ways their desire that something they have said or are about to say is to be bracketed off from the rest of their free-associational monologues, to be heard and understood by their analysts as separate from and unrelated to what the patients themselves intend to offer up for their analysts' interpretive consideration. In short, through viewing these kinds of instances of speech and conduct as situated above and apart from the signifying materials of the analysis proper, analysands believe, in their defensiveness against being analyzed (what Lacan would call their "passion for ignorance"[17]), that they are able occasionally to have recourse in their relations with their analysts to a meta-level beyond analysis, namely, that they can take periodic refuge from being analyzed and interpreted by their analysts when interacting with the latter. One of the meanings of Lacan's "there is no meta-language" – non-Lacanian analytic practitioners certainly would agree with this – is that this perspective of analysands is defensive self-deception on their part. Any clinician worth his/her salt knows that, precisely because patients let their guards down when under the impression that they are speaking and acting, as it were, "off the record," everything, including "parenthetical" material, is to be analyzed.

Similarly, quotidian individuals (and many who are analysands too) are prone to consider certain phenomena in their lives (such as their dreams, daydreams, mistakes, jokes, fantasies, and the like) as trivial froth and fringe, as mere, meta-level window dressing of no real importance or significance. Beginning with Freud's work of the 1890s, culminating in the early *magnum opera The Interpretation of Dreams* (1900), *The Psychopathology of Everyday Life* (1901), and *Jokes and Their Relation to the Unconscious* (1905), analysis is founded on a categorical rejection of the view that these phenomena are "meta(-languages)" in this sense. This rejection not only is captured by and reflected in the principle of no illusions – the reciprocal, back-and-forth influences running between intra- and extra-psychical realities blurs, without totally dissolving, the distinction between truth-as-correspondence and truth-as-coherence.

Clinically speaking, Lacan's denial of there being an "Other of the Other" can be understood in several fashions. Patients both neurotic and psychotic often evince convictions that certain inaccessible authorities and powers lie hidden behind the courses of their lives (the invisible hands of Fate, God, Society, etc.), that impersonal transcendent guarantees underpin and necessitate their ways of living, and that the ultimate meaning and purpose of their individual, institutional, and/or historical existences somehow is vouched for somewhere. Through transference, the analyst him/her-self also becomes a representative standing in for Analysis as such, for objectively true Absolute Knowledge of the unconscious in general and the analysand's unconscious in particular. All of these articles of faith posit some second-order big Other as a repository of authority, power, and/or knowledge. As working to analyze away such things as fate neuroses, paranoid delusions, and transference neuroses, analysis operates according to the dictum that "there is no Other of the Other."

The topic of *vérité à la* Lacan, like that of truth overall, is too huge for me to address adequately in passing. Nevertheless, apropos analytic practice, suffice it for now to connect Lacan's "there is no truth about the truth" with his opposition to portrayals of psychoanalysis as any sort of depth-psychological hermeneutics. For Lacan, the "subjective destitution" experienced at the end of a genuinely completed analysis is associated with the analysand confronting the unembellished contingency and meaninglessness of the destinal truths of his/her unconscious, the brutal, idiotic facticity of the nodal points forming the "extimate" core of the analysand's subjectivity. By sharp contrast with Jungian or other approaches, Freudian-Lacanian analysis attributes no quasi-religious "deep meanings" to what its interpretive procedures uncover. Such profound rhymes and reasons would be truths about the truths of the unconscious, which Freud and Lacan pointedly eschew.

However, shifting from a practical-clinical to a theoretical-philosophical angle is requisite for solidly grasping the knot conjoining Lacan's three "*il n'y a pas*" claims in the opening session of *Seminar XVIII* in connection with, first, the other assertions from this same session quoted by me even earlier above, as well as, second, some other related remarks I will be quoting soon below. In this first session of the eighteenth seminar, Lacan also identifies his "semblance" (*semblant*) with "the signifier in itself" (*le signifiant en lui-même*)[18] and insists that this semblance "is not the semblance of another thing" (*n'est pas semblant d'autre chose*).[19] In other words, the Lacanian signifier (unlike the Saussurian one as bound up with a signified so as to form a meaningful sign) is not a unit of resemblance vis-à-vis something else it is intended to reflect representationally. Lacan deliberately opts to speak of "semblance" rather than "resemblance." Another way to put this would be to say that signifiers in Lacan's sense here are not to be taken as meta-level redoublings of any sort of supposed first-order real(ity). These signifiers are a real unto themselves (or in themselves as *an sich* [*en lui-même*]). They are not epiphenomenal or illusory abstract idealities with respect to concrete realities. Moreover, as I noted a short while ago, signifiers and their coherences with each other can become parts of (i.e., "fall into") the register of the objective signifieds with which they presumably are intended to correspond (as "resemblances" *qua* representational reflections). Similarly, when Lacan, in the second session of *Seminar XVIII* (January 20), maintains that "Truth is not the contrary of semblance" (*La vérité n'est pas le contraire du semblant*),[20] this stresses several points all at once (points both clinical and philosophical). As formations of the unconscious, the truths of concern to analysis are themselves "semblances" (i.e., the ideational representations and signifiers [*Vorstellungen*] of fantasies and the like). These very semblances become "true" *qua* real as causally efficacious forces and factors integrally shaping subjects' lived existences, regardless of whether or not these subjects have had any dealings with analysis. Also, in such theoretical/ intellectual fields as psychoanalysis and the sciences of modernity, semblances as abstract formalizations and models are absolutely necessary for, so to speak, hitting the bull's-eye of the Real and pinning down the truth.

Still in the same session of the eighteenth seminar (January 13, 1971), Lacan, as I just foreshadowed, turns his attention to modern science in addition to psychoanalysis per se. Therein, he states that "the discourse of science . . . started very specifically from the considerations of semblances" (*le discours de la science . . . est parti très spécialement de la considération de semblants*).[21] In connection with this statement, he later, in the third session of February 10, argues that contemporary science, despite the dethroning of Newton at the start of the twentieth century, remains, in a certain manner, decidedly Newtonian.[22] In this context and elsewhere, one must bear in mind that Lacan adheres to Alexandre Koyré's Galileo-centric narrative about the essence of modern scientificity, as established during its early-seventeenth-century birth, consisting in the mathematization of nature (a narrative problematically downplaying the empiricist methodology forged by Galileo's contemporary Francis Bacon in the latter's 1620 *New Organon*).[23]

That said, the Newtonianism Lacan alleges is intrinsic to modern science *tout court*, including post-Newtonian physics, is the Galilean method of formal modeling as the privileged route of access to the material Real *an sich*. Empirically observed reality presents, as per nominalism, always-unique spatio-temporal particulars, namely, entities and events as absolutely singular thises, thats, and others. But, as per scientific method, abstraction from these particulars through the construction, on the basis of carefully gathered empirical observations, of ideal mathematical models of the phenomena under investigation is an underlying possibility condition for both the initial designing of experiments as well as subsequent interpreting of their results. Such formalized abstractions, couched in the language of mathematics (as algorithms, equations, formulas, and the like), establish virtual baselines against which deviations from the hypothetical, ideal models can be registered and measured. A key interpretive question invariably is whether or not a model can, with compatible supplementary information, accommodate and account for whatever deviations from it are recorded. If so, then the model has a chance to be promoted from tentative hypothesis to less-tentative theory (with this step also involving an intra-discursive, coherentist cross-checking of the hypothesis-become-theory with other already-established theories in the same scientific field). If not, then these deviations become problematic anomalies for the model, forcing it to be revised or scrapped altogether.

With reference to the title of Lacan's twenty-first seminar (*Les non-dupes errent* [1973–74]), an unbending nominalist would be, scientifically speaking, a non-dupe who errs. Put differently, as regards the post-Baconian, post-Galilean sciences of modernity, affirming only absolutely unique spatio-temporal particulars as true *qua* concrete and real – this would be to reject all generalizing abstractions and idealizations from these particulars as false *qua* illusory and unreal – would be to "err" by refusing to be "duped" by the hypothetical virtual realities of formal models. Through this refusal, the uncompromising nominalist would deprive him/her-self of the very possibility of arriving at the truths of the modern natural sciences (i.e., their experimentally tested theories and laws) insofar as these disciplines rely on modeling as integral to scientific method itself. Exclusively through the ideal detours of the abstractions of formal fictions is one able to arrive at the actual facts of the material Real *an und für sich* (as in Lacan's gloss on the Oedipus myth mentioned previously, such truths arrived at thereby are generated by a process akin to a self-fulfilling prophecy). The nominalist who tries to bypass this fictional mediation so as to seize this factual Real directly is doomed to miss it. However, especially given the empirical component to all of the above, Lacan's stress on this Newtonianism as inherent to modern science hardly amounts to an endorsement of metaphysical realism, with its strong links to anti-empiricist rationalism. All of this also is articulated by Lacan in the passages from the session of the eighteenth seminar (January 20, 1971) referred to by both Zupančič and Žižek.

Returning again to Lacan's earlier-quoted statement that "The stated fact is entirely a fact of discourse" (from the opening session of *Seminar XVIII*), this thesis is related to his philosophy of science as much as to his positions apropos psychoanalysis as a clinical practice. In the *New Organon*, the founding document of modern scientific method, Bacon emphasizes again and again that his new approach to gaining knowledge of the real world is not a matter of placing the human mind in a purely passive and receptive position vis-à-vis this world. Instead of being a mere "mirror of nature," the Baconian-minded natural scientist is an engaged agent of *praxis* applying a procedure and exercising a discipline so as actively to intervene in nature and, through intervening thusly, constitute and extract true facts about nature itself (a point deeply appreciated by Kant,[24] Schelling,[25] and Hegel,[26] among others). That is to say, for Bacon as an inaugurator of scientific modernity, subjective activity (as methodically guided) is an indispensable condition of possibility for objective knowledge, for generating and confirming factual truths about asubjective objects in and of themselves.[27] In conjunction with Lacan's above-glossed underscoring of Newtonian-style modeling as also pivotal to making possible the empirical modern and contemporary sciences as experimental – these models are couched in the artificial formal languages of mathematics and symbolic logic – his assertion about the discursive nature of facts is scientifically as well as psychoanalytically cogent. Moreover, given that, as I explained a while ago, a *"discours"* à la the Lacan of this later period of his teachings is a "social link" and, hence, is not strictly linguistic (i.e., not limited to the structures and phenomena of natural languages per se), a discourse in this precise Lacanian sense encompasses under its broad heading socio-symbolically mediated practices,[28] including those of the natural sciences as reliant on a coordination between formal modeling and experimental activity (in *Seminar VIII* [1960–61], Lacan even knots together three declarations of "In the beginning was...": the Word [*le Verbe*], the Act/Deed [*Tat*], and *Praxis*[29]).

To further tie together the bundle of Lacan's seemingly disparate remarks quoted by me throughout this chapter thus far, discourses and their facts, in line with a post-Hegelian immanentism, do not stand in complete separateness over-and-above their ostensible corresponding referents (in the case of natural science, these being natural objects and processes). As fully immanent to nature itself, the open-ended socio-historical unfolding of the sciences de/in-completes the material universe of which this unfolding is an internal member and inhering constituent, making it a not-All (*pas tout*) "*désunivers*" – and this through repeatedly and perpetually adding, via its signifier-mediated practices, supplementary facts and truths to the thereby mutating and expanding expanse of the one-and-only Real. Or, there being no meta-language also means that language is no meta, namely, in this context, that the languages and language-facilitated activities of the natural sciences are not entirely ontologically transcendent (i.e., meta) vis-à-vis nature (addressing nominalism again in *Seminar XXII* [1974–75], Lacan refers to Saul Kripke's account of names in *Naming and Necessity* to drive home this point from *Seminar XVIII*[30]). Additionally and relatedly, apropos there being "no truth about the truth" and "no Other of the Other," the disenchanted, desacralized infinite universe of modern science (the same universe in which psychoanalysis as both a metapsychological theory and clinical practice comes to be and operates) is a meaningless material Real of brute, contingent facticities not in the least bit underwritten by any more profound reality of meaningfulness as a deeper truth/Other beyond, behind, or beneath the superficial, stupid immanence of senseless material being(s).[31]

However, the immediately preceding is best illustrated and appreciated through the examples furnished by scientifically based technology (as already signaled by Lacan with his neologistic talk of the "alethosphere" of "lathouses" in *Seminar XVII* [1969–70][32]). Such gadgets, instruments, tools, and toys, whose production is enabled by scientific knowledge, are quite literal materializations in the lone register of physical existence of the discourses and facts of the sciences, putting the "real" in the real abstractions of these disciplines. Technologies are incarnations of scientific signifiers falling into, and thereby transforming, the plane of signifieds. Like Hegel before him and Deacon after him (see Chapters 2 and 3), Lacan, on these grounds, refuses to take either side in the traditional dispute between nominalism and metaphysical realism.

With this framing of the later Lacan in place, referring back to Zupančič's and Žižek's readings of Lacan's pronouncements (from the second session of *Seminar XVIII*) on dialectical materialism and the nominalism-realism debate now is appropriate. Zupančič, citing the second session of the eighteenth seminar specifically, notes that, for Lacan, "The true materialism . . . can only be a *dialectical materialism*."[33] Such a Lacanian dialectical materialism: "is not grounded in the primacy of matter nor in matter as first principle, but in the notion of conflict, of split, and of the 'parallax of the real' produced in it. In other words, the fundamental axiom of materialism is not 'matter is all' or 'matter is primary,' but relates rather to the primacy of a cut."[34] This "cut" can be equated with the incisions made in the Real by the Symbolic, namely, the descent of signifiers (as ideational formations, real abstractions, formal models, etc. however "realistic" or "unrealistic" by the standards of truth-as-correspondence) in which they slice into and become parts of signi-fied beings. In an essay whose main agenda is a Lacanian critique of Meillassoux's brand of (non-dialectical) realism, Zupančič's focus is on a Real permeated by the effects of the Symbolic as a result of materialist dialectics in which the concrete and the abstract, the sub-jective and the objective, and the like dance, get entangled, reverse positions, and thoroughly interpenetrate each other (without, for all that, becoming utterly indistinct from one another). She spells out the upshot of this focus a few pages after the prior quotation:

If the subject of the unconscious is the subject of (modern) science, this is precisely insofar as it is essentially linked to the field in which discourse has consequences. Without the latter there is no subject, and certainly no subject of the unconscious. This is how one should under-stand Lacan's statement that the subject is the 'answer of the real,' *la réponse du réel*. Which is something else than to say that it is an effect of discourse or discursively constituted. The subject, or the uncon-scious, are not the effects of language, let alone linguistic entities, they belong to the field of the real, that is to the field that only emerges with language, but which is not itself language, nor is reducible to it (say as its performative creation); the real is defined by the fact that language has consequences in it. And we could perhaps say: if science creates and operates in the field where discourse has consequences, psychoa-nalysis is the science of this singular field, of the surprising ways in which these consequences work, and of the peculiar ontological status of the objects of this field.[35]

For dialectical materialism, Lacanian or otherwise, the sort of realism advocated by Meillassoux is dangerously close to what Marx, in his "Theses on Feuerbach," critically diagnoses as the pre-dialectical "contemplative" standpoint. As Zupančič brilliantly illuminates, the sole way to avoid contemplation and its shortcomings both epistemological and ontological is, following Lacan, to embrace, so to speak, a realism of the signifier (as transcendental materialism does too with its axiomatic no-illusions principle). Only thereby can one account for the fact that symbolico-linguistically mediated structures and phenomena indeed do take on lives of their own, coming to be as real as anything presumed to be entirely asubjective *qua* immediately *an sich*.

Resonating with Hegel's dialectics of universality and particularity and Marx's real abstractions (both of which undermine and move beyond the impasse between nominalism and metaphysical realism), Lacanian dialectical materialism *à la* Zupančič rightly recognizes that responsibly taking the full measure of signifiers' impacts on the surface of thereby cratered signifieds in no way automatically amounts to conceding an inch to the idealisms of the so-called "linguistic turn," social constructivisms, pragmatist relativisms, and similar anti-realisms. If anything, contemplative realism, just like contemplative materialism, already harbors or is at risk of inadvertently endorsing an anti-realist subjective idealism precisely through its failure to include subjects and their discourses/languages (including the subjects contemplatively constructing a realist discourse/language) in its realist picture of the world. This exclusion, however principled or not, is tantamount to insinuating that contemplation stands on a transcendent meta-level above whatever is material/real, thus implicitly making contemplation something immaterial/ideal (as is explicitly done by traditional idealisms as anti-materialist and/or anti-realist).[36]

Žižek most lucidly elaborates his interpretation of the same Lacan referred to by Zupančič not so much in the place in *Less Than Nothing* where he quotes from *Seminar XVIII* and credits Zupančič with alerting him to this material. Instead, somewhat earlier in this 2012 book, his glosses on select moments in Lacan's deservedly famous eleventh seminar clearly and compellingly bring to the fore what is under discussion here. Žižek zeroes in on one line in particular from *Seminar XI*: "*Le tableau, certes, est dans mon œil. Mais moi, je suis dans le tableau*"[37] ("The picture is certainly in my eye. But me, I am in the picture" – Alan Sheridan's

English translation mistakenly renders the second sentence as the contradictory statement "But I am not in the picture"[38]). Just prior to quoting this line, Žižek declares, "the move from Kant to Hegel has to be accomplished, the move from transcendental constitution to the dialectical self-inclusion of the subject into substance"[39] (i.e., the move from the transcendental to the speculative, as per his tripartite distinction between the metaphysical, the transcendental, and the speculative drawn much earlier in *Less Than Nothing*[40]). After quoting it, Žižek adds:

> The picture is in my eye: as the transcendental subject I am the always already given horizon of all reality, but, at the same time, I myself am in the picture: I exist only through my counterpoint or counterpart in the very picture constituted by me; I as it were have to fall into my own picture, into the universe whose frame I constitute, in the same way that, in the Christian Incarnation, the creator God falls into his own creation.[41]

He continues:

> From the transcendental standpoint, such an inclusion of the subject into its own *perceptum* can only be thought as the transcendental subject's constitution of itself as an element of (constituted) reality: I constitute 'myself' as an inner-worldly entity, the 'human person' that is 'me,' with a set of positive ontic properties, etc. But the self-inclusion of the transcendental I itself into the field of its own *perceptum* is non-sensical from the transcendental standpoint: the transcendental I is the a priori frame of reality which, for that very reason, is exempted from it. For Lacan, however, such a self-referential inclusion is precisely what happens with the *objet petit a*: the very transcendental I, $, is 'inscribed into the picture' as its point of impossibility.[42]

The transcendentalism being referred to here is that of Kant and the early Fichte. This is a subjective idealism in which the minded "I" makes possible the sphere of its experience (*Erfahrung*) as the only reality to which it has valid and genuine epistemological access. However, as Žižek explains, such transcendental subjectivity, for Kantian and early Fichtean transcendental idealism, cannot appear (to itself) as one phenomenal object among others within this same sphere of experience it makes possible (like Ludwig Wittgenstein's eye that by nature necessarily cannot see itself

within its own visual field[43]). The verso of the activity of constituting is barred by a level distinction from showing up on the side of
the recto of the passivity of the thus-constituted.

Žižek's thesis here is that the later Fichte, Schelling, Hegel,
and Lacan all share in common the project of sublating this level
distinction through a proper *Aufhebung* in which, as such, key
aspects of the differences between the transcendental and the
ontic/empirical are preserved even while being problematized too
– and this through the gesture of rendering transcendental subjectivity fully immanent to its others (whether as the Absolute, God,
nature, substance, and/or experience, depending on the figure
performing this gesture). As a consequence of being thereby folded
into each other, both the transcendental and the non-transcenden-
tal are reciprocally modified. Before proceeding further, I must
point out a potentially misleading aspect of the first of the two
block quotations in the prior paragraph. Particularly as reinforced
through the comparison between Lacan's "I am in the picture"
and the act of creation by the Christian God, Žižek is at risk of
erroneously suggesting that the subject of a post-Kantian (and
post-early-Fichtean) transcendentalism enjoys logical and/or temporal priority as an "x" that pre-exists and/or can be isolated from
what it contributes to making possible (thus reintroducing the very
non-dialectical level distinction being dialectically sublated). But,
just a couple of paragraphs later, Žižek rearticulates himself such
that this misleading aspect is corrected:

> the task is to think the subject's emergence or becoming from the
> self-splitting of substance: the subject is not directly the Absolute, it
> emerges out of the self-blockage of substance, out of the impossibil-
> ity of substance fully asserting itself as One. Hegel's position here is
> unique: the subject is the operator of the Absolute's (self-)finitization,
> and to 'conceive the Absolute not only as Substance, but also as
> Subject' means to conceive the Absolute as failed, marked by an inher-
> ent impossibility. Or, to borrow terms from one interpretation of
> quantum physics: the Hegelian Absolute is *diffracted*, splintered by
> an inherent – virtual/real – impossibility/obstacle. The key turning
> point in the path toward Hegel is Fichte: the late Fichte was struggling
> with the right problem resolved later by Hegel. After radicalizing
> the Kantian transcendental subject into the self-positing 'absolute
> I,' Fichte then struggled till the end of his life with how to limit this
> absolute I, how to think the primacy of the trans-subjective absolute

('God') over the I without falling back into a pre-critical 'dogmatism.'
(This problem is first outlined in Hölderlin's famous system-fragment.)
Frederick Beiser is right to point out that the basic problem of all post-
Kantian German Idealism is how to limit subjectivity: Fichte's attempt
to think a trans-subjective Absolute is based on a correct insight, but
he is unable to accomplish his task successfully; later, Schelling and
Hegel offer two different ways out of this Fichtean deadlock.[44]

In this passage, Žižek rectifies his account of this common thread
arguably conjoining the post-Kantian idealists and Lacan. For
both German idealism (especially that of Schelling and Hegel) and
Lacanian psychoanalysis, transcendental-type subjectivity genetically emerges out of a substantial, asubjective ground before or
beneath it (and not, as per Žižek's above-noted comparison of
Lacanianism and Christianity, the other way around).

Sticking with a focus on Lacan in relation to the preceding (I
already have covered much of the German idealist ground surveyed
by Žižek in the immediately prior block quotation [see Chapters 2
and 3]), a number of other moments in Lacan's eleventh seminar
related to his "I am in the picture" remark can be reinterpreted
in light of Žižek's and Zupančič's Lacanian dialectical materialism. To begin with, Lacan therein evinces a bit of evasiveness in
response to Jacques-Alain Miller inquiring about his ontology.[45]
Furthermore, he seems rapidly to rattle off a series of conflicting
statements in this context: "I ought to have obtained from him
to begin with a more specific definition of what he means by the
term ontology"[46] (this hints that Lacan might have an ontology, at
least as per a certain characterization of it); "when speaking of this
gap one is dealing with an ontological function"[47] (this appears
to affirm that, with his *manque-à-être* [i.e., "this gap"], he indeed
intervenes at the level of matters ontological); "The gap of the
unconscious may be said to be *pre-ontological*"[48] (with this claim
and the questions it raises about exactly what "pre-ontology" is
and how it is positioned with respect to ontology, doubts suddenly arises as to whether Lacan really is admitting to having an
ontology); "the unconscious . . . does not lend itself to ontology"[49]
(insofar as psychoanalysis is centered on the unconscious, he now
seems to be indicating that he, as an analytic thinker, is not in the
business of putting forward ontologies); "the unconscious . . . is
neither being, nor non-being, but the unrealized"[50] (the waters are
thoroughly muddied at this juncture, with it being quite difficult to

discern if and how the "pre-ontological unrealized" relates to one or more possible definitions of ontology). However, reexamining several relevant utterances elsewhere in *Seminar XI* in the light provided by both Žižek and Zupančič will help cut through this tangled thicket of apparent inconsistencies.

At the start of the session of February 12, 1964 (entitled by Miller "Tuché and Automaton"), Lacan admits that, "at first sight, psycho-analysis seems to lead in the direction of idealism."[51] From his comments that promptly follow, it is clear that Lacan specifically has in mind extreme forms of subjective idealism flirting with or even outright embracing solipsism (as he puts it, idealisms according to which "*Life is a dream*"[52]). He vehemently rejects the idea that analysis is in any way invested in the project of portraying psychical subjectivity as a solipsistic prison-house in which nothing not mediated/constituted by this subjectivity can exist and function; on this occasion, he points to the Real of the subjectively unmasterable *tuché*.[53] Without getting myself bogged down in unpacking the details of Lacan's Real as *tuché* in the present context (something I do on a separate occasion[54]), suffice it for now to underscore that, if nothing else, Lacan refuses the subjective idealist maneuver of one-sidedly reducing being to thinking, substance to subject.

In the subsequent session of the eleventh seminar (February 19, 1964), Lacan again addresses the topic of ontology, this time directly in relation to his discussions "Of the Gaze as *Objet Petit a*" (the set of 1964 seminar sessions also containing the line "I am in the picture"). Just after observing that "I see only from one point, but in my existence I am looked at from all sides"[55] (this already signals that "I am in the picture"), he states:

> of course, I have my ontology – why not? – like everyone else, however naïve or elaborate it may be. But, certainly, what I try to outline in my discourse – which, although it reinterprets that of Freud, is nevertheless centered essentially on the particularity of the experience it describes – makes no claim to cover the entire field of experience. Even this between-the-two that opens up for us the apprehension of the unconscious is of concern to us only in as much as it is designated for us, through the instructions Freud left us, as that of which the subject has to take possession. I will only add that the maintenance of this aspect of Freudianism, which is often described as naturalism, seems to be indispensable, for it is one of the few attempts, if

not the only one, to embody psychical reality without substantifying it.[56]

Later in *Seminar XI*, Lacan, in this same vein, warns against anything that would "over-substantify the unconscious" (*trop substantiver l'inconscient*).[57] The first sentence of the above quotation indicates that, in Lacan's view, it is impossible to avoid having an ontology, if only a tacit, spontaneous one (in *Less Than Nothing*, Žižek likewise maintains that "one cannot avoid ontology"[58]). Even if unintentionally, this observation places Lacan directly in line with Kant's German idealist critics. For the latter, the critical epistemology of transcendental idealism, arguably attempting to be, as post-metaphysical, a theory of knowledge without a corresponding theory of being, nonetheless must of necessity unavowedly rely upon a dogmatic ontology (i.e., the two-worlds metaphysics of phenomenal objects-as-appearances and noumenal things-in-themselves). The post-Kantian idealists, each in his own way, face up to the unavoidability of ontology in connection with epistemology, elaborating their idealisms as post-critical immanent critiques of Kant's critical transcendental idealism.

The second sentence of the preceding block quotation resonates with some of Lacan's characterizations of philosophical ontologies elsewhere.[59] Insofar as ontology *à la* philosophy purports to "cover everything" as the fundamental theory of being *überhaupt*, Lacan does not indulge himself in its pursuit (i.e., he "makes no claim to cover the entire field of experience"). Instead, if he admits to engaging in reflections not without ontological ramifications, these would add up, at most, to a regional ontology restricted to the fields disclosed in and through Freudian analysis. Additionally, Lacan, despite his reputation for being fiercely hostile to any and every naturalistic perspective (I have problematized this commonplace picture of him on other occasions[60]), here alludes to his solidarity with a specifically Freudian naturalism in which "nature" is not "substantified." If, following Žižek's and Zupančič's readings, Lacan is a dialectical materialist to be viewed as furthering the German idealist project to think, in Hegel's words, substance also as subject (and vice versa), then the desubstantialization of substance alluded to in the eleventh seminar is linked to the move of rendering psychical subjectivity an immanent and internal part of substance itself.

Hegelian and Marxian Things – Lacan's Realist Dialectical Materialism

I now will carry forward the preceding explorations of Lacan's interlinked realism and dialectical materialism through a close reading of one of the most relevant single moments in his teachings as regards these topics: the eighteenth session of *Seminar XVI* (*D'un Autre à l'autre* [1968–69]), a session delivered on April 30, 1969 and entitled by Miller "Inside Outside" (*Dedans Dehors*). Other instances in which Lacan discusses realism and/or historical and dialectical materialisms will be addressed by me in the course of this close reading, woven into the interpretation of this 1969 seminar session. In conjunction with the prior exegetical labor I have performed here, this examination will help bring into sharper relief, among other things, Lacan's debts to Marx's materialist appropriation and redeployment of the legacy of German idealism as transmitted to him (Marx) primarily by Hegel.

At the start of the previous academic year, during the opening session of the fifteenth seminar (*L'acte psychanalytique* [1967–68]), Lacan vehemently denies in any way endorsing the (subjective) idealist belief according to which no independent reality pre-exists (conscious) subjectivity.[61] However, he distinguishes "reality" (*réalité*) from "knowledge" (*savoir*) and, in turn, distinguishes the latter from "knowledge" as acquaintance/familiarity (i.e., *connaissance* as distinct from *savoir*).[62] Although, in a realist gesture, Lacan unhesitatingly affirms that "*la réalité est antérieure à la connaissance*," with "*connaissance*" being a function depending on the first-person experience of a conscious mind, he gives pause for hesitant thought apropos whether knowledge as *savoir* does or does not inhere in the very being of the Real in and of itself, linking this question to the examples of "*savoir-vivre*" and "*savoir-faire*."[63] With these related phrases' ties to an Aristotelian-style notion of *phronēsis* (φρόνησις), Lacan seems to be hinting at the issue of whether subjects, phylogenetically and/or ontogenetically, fabricate socio-symbolic second natures that can and do "fall into" asubjective "first nature." My earlier unpackings of the eleventh and eighteenth seminars suggest that, in his dialectical materialism, he indeed posits a dynamic of the becoming-Real of the Symbolic.

In the second session of *Seminar XVI*, and following closely along the lines both of remarks made at the beginning of *Seminar*

XV as well as of the non-idealist emphasis on the discursive status of (scientific) facts in *Seminar XVIII* (as I explained above), Lacan stresses the difference between the physical Real of nature and the scientific discipline of physics that speaks to this Real.[64] Making this differentiation is not, Lacan insists, tantamount to putting forward an "idealist postulate."[65] He does not dispute that nature in itself is already there prior to the *connaissance* of physicists and even the *savoir* of physics.[66] Physics itself is described as a "discourse" (*discours*) that "has consequences" for nature.[67] In her essay on psychoanalytic *contra* speculative realism (the latter as per Meillassoux), Zupančič quotes this portion of the sixteenth seminar immediately before meticulously tracing out, through a focus on the eighteenth seminar, the path of Lacan's dialectical materialism as moving between and beyond the old ontological dispute between metaphysical realism and nominalism.[68] In particular, the causal efficacy, vis-à-vis nature and via technologies, of the Symbolic signifiers of both theoretical and applied physics in relation to natural substance *an sich* amounts to the becoming-spatio-temporally-real (as the spatio-temporal particulars of nominalism) of the ideal generalizations (as the universals of metaphysical realism) essential to natural science as distinct from nature per se. The real abstractions of idealized models and universal equations/formulas make possible both the experimental testing of *savoir* as well as the technical applications of *savoir-faire*. Any realist ontology failing to include these considerations and qualifications is incomplete in the same way as non-dialectical contemplative materialisms.

Turning now to the eighteenth session of *Seminar XVI* (April 30, 1969), Lacan begins this session addressing himself particularly to those in his audience who perhaps are philosophers and, as such, might be interested in echoes of the perennial idealism-versus-realism struggle they understandably detect in and around his discourse.[69] Both at the start of this meeting and later on during it, Lacan describes this long-standing philosophical problem as not so much solved as allowed to fall by the wayside over the course of historical time. As reinforced by his subsequent references to Bishop Berkeley in this same seminar session,[70] he maintains that subjectivist (or even solipsistic) idealisms are impossible to refute intra-philosophically.[71] Instead, this type of radical anti-realism simply ends up being repudiated by "common sense."[72]

However, in addition to repudiation by common sense, what

Lacan characterizes as the idealist "mythology of representation" came to be philosophically challenged (although not refuted) by another "mythology," namely, that of "ideology" as per its critique (without mentioning this by name, Lacan clearly has in mind here historical materialism à la Marx and Engels).[73] He quickly proceeds to ask whether the anti-idealism of historical materialism's theory of ideology is sufficiently realist, especially since its dialectical "real" (réel), including the infrastructural and superstructural dimensions of societies, is something "we consider . . . ourselves in the state of transforming."[74] That is to say, according to Marxism, the real(ity) underlying and conditioning ideologies is not just natural as purely asubjective and immediate, but also socio-historical as created and maintained by the collective activities (i.e., praxes) of subjects past and present. Put in Hegelian parlance, one of the questions raised by Lacan's remarks is whether "objective spirit" (or, for Lacan, the trans-individual big Others of symbolic orders) is, in terms of the old realism-versus-idealism battle, real or ideal. One reason why this is a genuine question is that the peculiar réel targeted by Hegel's objective spirit, Marx's ideology critique, and Lacan's symbolic order has a strange in-between ontological status as neither straightforwardly objective (as given, natural, unmediated, etc.) nor wholly subjective (as intra-mental).

Still reflecting on Marxist historical materialism, Lacan promptly points to a related but somewhat different line of inquiry – "The question is thus of knowing if, somewhere, this knowledge in progress is or is not already there."[75] The fact that Lacan soon proceeds to take up the topic of science on the heels of suggesting this query strongly hints that he is interrogating historical materialism on the basis of Marxist claims that it is the first true science of history in the strictest of senses of "science" (earlier in the sixteenth seminar, Lacan's gestures at Althusser's Marx as a structuralist avant la lettre similarly imply this,[76] with Lacan, Althusser, and others frequently linking structuralism to certain conceptions of scientificity). In what amounts to an implicit critique of Althusserian structuralist Marxism as "scientific" (as well as of "scientific socialism" tout court), Lacan, again in the April 30, 1969 session of Seminar XVI, articulates a chain of equivalences between the notion of knowledge (savoir) always-already there in the Real, the subject supposed to know (sujet supposé savoir), and theism.[77] He thereby implies, as charged by others both before and after him, that "scientific" Marxist historical materialists (claiming to be subjects supposed to know the inherent objective logic of History in and of itself), whether those of Second International economism, Stalinist "diamat," or Althusserian structuralism, unavowedly rely upon a dogmatic faith in the providence of a (pseudo-)secular theodicy, despite their official atheism.

Lacan refers both to Newton's religious views as "the theological envelope of the first steps of our science"[78] (i.e., the modern sciences of nature) and to Einstein's insistence that God does not play games with dice.[79] He does so in order to propose that natural scientists themselves (in addition to certain Marxists), however consciously or (if they are consciously secular or atheistic) unconsciously, are really believers in God, if only as the Cartesian-style trustworthy guarantor of a stable, structured reality able to be accurately mirrored by the fixed formulas of natural science (i.e., God/Nature as the big Other of a subject supposed to know and vouch for the knowledge always-already there in the Real).[80] But, admittedly, Lacan's talk of the Newtonian "theological envelope of the first steps of our science" indicates that he is not categorically critical without qualifications of the religious historical bases of the sciences. Instead, he seems to allude to a dialectical vision according to which theism historically makes possible modern science, which in turn makes possible a radical atheism specific to modernity.

At this juncture, an extended detour running through a number of Lacan's various references to Marx peppered throughout his corpus is appropriate (after which I will pick back up the thread of the eighteenth session of *Seminar XVI*). In fact, in order adequately to appreciate his intertwined relations to both realism and historical/dialectical materialism, this detour is necessary. To begin with, Lacan repeatedly heaps the highest praise he has to offer on Marx. Near the very end of the 1946 *écrit* "Presentation on Psychical Causality," he declares:

> You have heard me lovingly refer to Descartes and Hegel ... It is rather fashionable these days to 'go beyond' the classical philosophers. I could just as easily have started with the admirable dialogue in the *Parmenides*. For neither Socrates nor Descartes, nor Marx, nor Freud, can be 'gone beyond,' insofar as they carried out their research with the passion to unveil that has an object: truth.[81]

Later, in the seventh seminar (*The Ethics of Psychoanalysis* [1959–60]), he echoes this declaration – "One never goes beyond Descartes, Kant, Marx, Hegel and a few others because they mark a line of inquiry, a true orientation. One never goes beyond Freud either."[82] For Lacan, this is the most illustrious company possible in which to include Marx. Subsequently, in *Seminar XVII*, he states that "What is characteristic of the two of them, Freud and Marx, is that they don't bullshit."[83] On other occasions, he compares Marx and Freud as being of equal importance.[84] Coming from Lacan, all of this is high praise indeed.

Near the end of the essay "*L'étourdit*" (1972/73), Lacan briefly indicates in passing that he is as materialist as Marx himself.[85] Elsewhere, in his earlier intervention "Responses to Students of Philosophy Concerning the Object of Psychoanalysis" (1966), he provides a more detailed sense of what he might have in mind as justifying this comparison. These remarks are worth unpacking at some length. Lacan begins:

> in order to avoid any misunderstanding, note that I maintain that psychoanalysis does not have the slightest right to interpret revolutionary practice . . . but that on the contrary, revolutionary theory would do well to hold itself responsible for leaving empty the function of truth as cause (*la vérité comme cause*), when therein lies, nevertheless, the first supposition of its own effectiveness.[86]

Although in, for example, the sixteenth seminar, it sounds as though Lacan flirts with insinuating that analysis indeed has a "right to interpret revolutionary practice" when he asserts that Marxist historical materialism presupposes a theory of *jouissance*,[87] he here insists that it should refrain from doing so. That said, the key to decoding the quotation above is the notion of "truth as cause" (*la vérité comme cause*). Obviously, the very idea of a cause is necessarily connected to the idea of an effect; a cause is, by definition, something that brings about an effect, thereby being a cause through enjoying causal efficacy. To cut a long story short – I will substantiate and elucidate this further in what follows shortly – *la vérité comme cause* designates, for Lacan, the real causal efficacy specifically of signifiers in their material dimensions. Put in terms made familiar by the preceding discussions here, "truth as cause" points to the dialectical materialist dynamic through which Symbolic signifiers fall into Real signifieds, through which abstractions have concrete consequences.

Lacan's immediately ensuing remarks reinforce this interpretation. He goes on to add: "It is a matter of calling into question the category of dialectical materialism, and it is a matter of common knowledge that Marxists are not very adept at doing it, even though they are, on the whole, Aristotelians, which is already not too bad."[88] Lacan continues:

> Only my theory of language (*langage*) as structure of the unconscious can be said to be implied by Marxism, if, that is, you are not more demanding than the material implication with which our most recent logic is satisfied, that is, that my theory of language is true (*vraie*) whatever be the adequacy of Marxism, and that it is needed by it, whatever be the defect that it leaves Marxism with.[89]

In the first of these two quotations, Lacan seems to be boasting that he can provide a more thorough and satisfying rethinking of dialectical materialism than the Marxists themselves. In the second quotation, Lacan has recourse to "material implication" precisely as per conditional claims in classical, bivalent formal logic: "$p \rightarrow q$" (i.e., "if antecedent 'p' is the case, then consequent 'q' is the case"). A conditional "$p \rightarrow q$" claim is false only when the antecedent "p" is the case (i.e., true) but the consequent "q" is not the case (i.e., false). Contrary to certain versions of (sub-logical) common sense, a conditional "$p \rightarrow q$" claim is true even in the instance in which the antecedent "p" is not the case (i.e., false) but the consequent "q" is the case (i.e., true). Hence, Lacan here posits the following "material implication": If Marxist dialectical materialism is true, then the Lacanian theory of language as structure of the unconscious is also true. But, as he underlines through reference to the truth-values of conditional claims, even if Marxism is false, then both this conditional claim as a whole and his theory as its consequent remain true. He also hints that Marxism might have to change itself in order to accommodate this theory of language it allegedly entails ("it is needed by it, whatever be the defect that it leaves Marxism with").[90]

On the heels of this in "Responses to Students of Philosophy," Lacan then endorses Joseph Stalin's remarks on linguistics in which the latter dismisses Comrade Marr's idea that language itself is superstructural in the Marxist sense.[91] In Lacan's eyes, this "situates" Stalin "far above the logical positivist"[92] – and this presumably insofar as Marrism and logical positivism both focus on language as a supposed second-order transcendence, whether as a Marrist superstructure or a logical positivist meta-language. Two interesting sentences follow here: "The least you can accord me concerning my theory of language is, should it interest you, that it is materialist"[93]; and, "The signifier is matter transcending itself in language" (*Le signifiant, c'est la matière qui se transcende en langage*).[94] Of course, Lacan has in mind his doctrine of the material (rather than meaningful) signifier as a Saussurian recasting of unconscious "primary process" mentation as per Freud, a doctrine consistently held to throughout the various phases and stages of his teachings[95] (and on which I have commented elsewhere[96]). Furthermore, in the context of this invocation of aspects of Marxism, Lacan obviously is identifying himself specifically as some kind of a dialectical materialist, an identification reinforced by his anti-reductivist notion of a more-than-material transcendence nonetheless immanent to materiality ("*Le signifiant, c'est la matière qui se transcende en langage*").

At this point, one thing that safely can be said regarding Lacan's dialectical materialism is that it involves the movements of signifiers falling back into (if they ever really left to begin with) the ontological grounds from which they originally arose. Thus, these signifiers are integral participants in the thereby auto-disruptive dynamics of being as a stratum of restless, unstable, self-sundering substances. In fact, Lacan re-reads the relationship between Hegel and Marx on this basis. In "On the Subject Who Is Finally in Question" (from the same year, 1966, as "Responses to Students of Philosophy"), Lacan, right before mentioning Marx by name, alludes to him (implicitly along the lines of Althusser *circa* 1965[97]) as the founder of the Freudian analytic concept of the "symptom" as the truth that speaks (i.e., *la Chose freudienne*, with its "*Moi, la vérité, je parle*" [Me, the truth, I speak][98]) in, through, and as a "gap" (*faille*) of "knowledge" (*savoir*).[99] As is well known, Lacan subsequently repeats this crediting of Marx as the "inventor" of the symptom *à la* Freud.[100]

Apropos Hegel *avec* Marx, Lacan plays off Marx's "truth" (*vérité*) against Hegel's "knowledge" (*savoir*), with the former purportedly throwing monkey wrenches in the latter's *savoir absolu* of world history, including the ruses of historical reason's tricky twists and turns (Lacan, in line with many others, clearly judges

Hegel guilty of believing in the God-like big Other of a *Weltgeist* as a mega-Subject whose intentional sufficient reasons are the final causes as rational *teloi* of a single, unified History-as-theodicy). Marx's truth is the symptom of Hegel's absolute knowledge of the cunning of reason-in-history, "whose fine order it manages to disturb."[101] Speaking of Marx's materialist "inversion" of Hegel's absolute idealism, Lacan states:

> a part of the reversal of Hegel that he carries out is constituted by the return (which is a materialist return, precisely insofar as it gives it figure and body) of the question of truth. The latter actually forces itself upon us, I would go so far as to say, not by taking up the thread of the ruse of reason, a subtle form with which Hegel sends it packing, but by upsetting these ruses (read Marx's political writings) which are merely dressed up with reason...[102]

He promptly adds that this truth-knowledge couplet is "the crux ... of philosophy as such."[103] Lacan's rendition of Marx's inversion of Hegel (or, more precisely, what Marx and Lacan inaccurately associate with the name "Hegel") implies that this inversion proceeds through two moments: First, Marx's truths initially show up as symptoms *qua* anomalies, holes, snags, etc. in the narrative texture of Hegel's knowledge; second, these symptoms, with the benefit of hindsight, reveal *après-coup* that these apparent exceptions *à la* Marx to the ostensible cunning of reason *à la* Hegel are the actual rule (as in the actual rule of Hegelian *Wirklichkeit*), namely, the real ruses of history's zigs and zags. In this second Marxian-Lacanian moment, it allegedly can be seen that Hegel's *List der Vernunft* is an upside-down version of the distinction between what is an exception and what is a rule in history, a version "merely dressed up with reason" – meaning that, when it comes to the true cunning of history, "Hegel sends it packing."

Soon after the preceding in "On the Subject Who Is Finally in Question," Lacan, as on other occasions, draws a connection between Marx and Freud apropos the topic of the symptom. In both its Marxian and Freudian versions, and in stark contrast to the medical notion designated by the same word, a symptom is not a (Saussurian) "sign" involving something akin to the relationship between smoke and fire (this is the example Lacan employs here).[104] Symptoms, instead of being superficial effects of underlying causes as these symptoms' profound truths, "*are* truth, being made of the same wood from which truth is made, if we posit materialistically that truth is what is instated on the basis of the signifying chain."[105] The transcendence of depth vis-à-vis surface in the medical model of a symptom as a known effect of a true cause yet to be known is here replaced by a conception of a symptom as transcendent-while-immanent – more precisely, as itself a true cause internal to (and woven of the same cloth as) the known planes it perturbs and problematizes from within as a foreign body *qua* intimate externality (i.e., extimacy). For Lacan, Marx's inversion of Hegel entails rereading what the latter would treat, along the lines of symptoms in medicine, as secondary surface effects of a deeper historical dynamic (i.e., cunning reason-in-history); Marxism reinterprets these symptoms as themselves this very historical dynamic incarnate, with no positing of hidden profundities beneath them (such as Hegel's *List der Vernunft*). Similarly, according to Lacan's version of Freudian analysis, analytic symptoms, just like the other formations of unconscious primary-process thinking of which they too are products, are ultimately knots of meaningless material signifiers (i.e., "signifying chains" as per Lacan's materialism of the signifier).[106] That is to say, an analytic symptom is not the meta-level sign of a secret subterranean meaning as its first-order grounding truth. Rather, a symptom is this contingent, meaningless truth itself directly embodied and manifestly on display "out there," being misrecognized for what it really is insofar as it is misinterpreted as a sign of profound depths of (pre)supposed significance.

Before further scrutinizing Lacan's invocations of Marx, I feel compelled to point out in passing a stunning irony to the specific sort of anti-Hegelianism indulged in by Lacan in this context presently under discussion. In fact, no better illustration can be found of Žižek's observation that Lacan, on the one hand, is Hegelian where he does not think to mention Hegel as at all relevant and, on the other hand, is hardly Hegelian in those places where he indeed does mention Hegel (with these references usually reflecting either Kojève's philosophical anthropology blending Marxist and existentialist influences or grotesque caricatures of Hegel widespread in twentieth-century France).[107] When speaking of truth, Hegel sometimes emphasizes that it necessarily, by its own nature, reveals itself; part of its power is to shine through no matter what, to display itself in spite of anything and everything that might otherwise threaten to obscure it in impenetrable darkness.[108] If purported truth lacks this potency, it is not truly true. *Contra* Lacan's construal of the *List der Vernunft*, Hegelian truth, whether as historical *Wirklichkeit* or whatever else, is never a transcendent, meta-level depth hidden beneath manifest existences.

In his *écrit* "The Freudian Thing" (1955), Lacan, much like Voltaire with (dis)respect to Leibniz, mocks Hegel's cunning of reason.[109] But, the very section of this text in which the mockery occurs, entitled "The Thing Speaks of Itself" and containing the famous line "*Moi, la vérité, je parle,*" ironically presents, unbeknownst to Lacan, a quite Hegelian characterization of truth as too powerful not to make itself heard, not to thrust itself forward into the light of visible day. One of the central messages of this *écrit* (again, a very Hegelian one) is that the secret of *la Chose freudienne* as unconscious truth is that there is no secret (a point also underscored by the story of the *trompe l'œil* painting competition between Zeuxis and Parrhasios recounted in *Seminar XI*[110] – "if one wishes to deceive a man, what one presents to him is the painting of a veil, that is to say, something that incites him to ask what is behind it"[111]). Reinforcing this message palpably at odds with vulgar visions of Freudian analysis as a depth-psychological hermeneutics in search of eclipsed meanings, Lacan's prosopopeia of "The Thing Speaks of Itself" has *la Chose comme vérité* repeatedly emphasizing that it openly talks and talks directly about itself ("Men, listen, I am telling you the secret,"[112] "I am now publicly announcing the fact,"[113] etc.).

In the section of "The Freudian Thing" in which "The Thing Speaks of Itself," Lacan draws attention to the pioneering period of Freud's first discoveries founding psychoanalysis proper. These discoveries are conveyed mainly in such works as *The Interpretation of Dreams* (1900), *The Psychopathology of Everyday Life* (1901), and *Jokes and Their Relation to the Unconscious* (1905), with Lacan's analytic adversaries in the tradition of ego psychology neglecting the early Freud in favor of the later period inaugurated by *The Ego and the Id* (1923) through its introduction of the "second topography" (or, as the ego psychologists call it, the "structural model"). For Lacan, a crucial lesson of the myriad examples of dreams, parapraxes, and jokes analyzed in detail by the early Freud of 1900 to 1905 is that, as Freud himself puts it in his contemporaneous "Fragment of an Analysis of a Case of Hysteria" (1901/05), "He that has eyes to see and ears to hear may convince himself that no mortal can keep a secret. If his lips are silent, he chatters with his finger-tips; betrayal oozes out of him at every pore."[114] Efforts to repress truths always are just partially successful at best, with the repressed inevitably returning to manifest itself somehow or other, if only through the seemingly marginal phenomena (i.e., dreams, jokes, and parapraxes) providing Freud with the initial grist for his analytic mill (such phenomena also include the conversion symptoms and psychosomatic suffering characteristic of hysteria à la Dora, namely, Lacan's "power of truth . . . in our very flesh"[115]).

Lacan goes so far as to indicate that even the most apparently and overtly resistant conduct – illustrations of this could be, for instance, analysands who, at least from time to time, refuse to talk, avoid free associating, and/or lie to and deliberately try to deceive their analysts – still cannot but, when all is said and done, be revelatory of the true Thing (i.e., the *parlêtre* as the speaking subject-being of the unconscious) that repeatedly has its say even in and through this very same conduct struggling to silence or falsify it.[116] As an aside, I cannot resist the temptation of highlighting an especially intense peak of irony apropos Lacan's relationship to Hegel here: In "The Freudian Thing," a "Hegelian Thing" (specifically, Hegel's depiction of truth as necessarily disclosed due to its inherent, essential potency as true) succeeds at articulating itself precisely in and through the very statements in which Lacan takes himself to be advancing an anti-Hegelian idea of *vérité* – with this *Chose hégélienne* thereby functioning in relation to Lacan's speech exactly like Lacan's *Chose freudienne* in relation to the speech of speaking subjectivity in general. That noted, even if an analysand deliberately invents "false" content for his/her analyst's aural consumption (for example, fake dreams, fabricated childhood memories, concocted extra-analytic social scenarios, and the like), these conveyed artificial fictions still end up betraying the unconscious truths they are meant to stifle and conceal. The analysand's choices of intentionally misleading materials themselves can and should lead an attentive analyst "with ears to hear" to interpretations hitting the bull's-eyes of truths that speak even in and through the lies that strain in vain to oppose and obscure them. In analysis, lies are always, as it were, "true lies," tellings of truths in the guise of lies; attempts not to tell the truth still amount to at least half-telling it (à la Lacan's *mi-dire*).[117] This is part of what Lacan is getting at when he opens his 1974 television appearance

with the lines, "I always speak the truth. Not the whole truth..."
(*Je dis toujours la vérité: pas toute*).[118]

In "The Freudian Thing," the section "The Thing Speaks of Itself" closes with *la Chose comme vérité* addressing its post-Freudian pursuers, namely, non-Lacanian analysts as Freud's hunting dogs who turn on their master when they finally come upon this Thing as their supposed prey[119] (paraphrasing Jean-Paul Sartre, one might say that, by Lacan's estimation, every non-Lacanian analyst is a dog). *La Chose* proclaims to them, "Now that you are already lost, I belie myself, I defy you, I slip away: you say that I am being defensive."[120] A subsequent section of this same *écrit* is entitled "Resistance to the Resisters."[121] In Lacan's prosopopeia, the hounds are analysts who permit themselves recourse to an approach relying upon a distinction between, on the one hand, the superficial resistances of defense mechanisms and, on the other hand, the unconscious depths purportedly covered over by these defensive layers envisioned as being closer to the "surface" of consciousness. According to Lacan's consciously Freudian (and unconsciously Hegelian) conception of truth, defenses against the unconscious still are revelatory of it despite themselves. However, treating them, in the fashion of many non-Lacanian analysts past and present, as resistances blocking analytic progress is to ignore this truth about Freudian truth, imagining instead that defensiveness could be so powerfully effective as to muzzle and censor altogether the speaking subjectivity of the unconscious. The section title "Resistance to the Resisters" hence has two meanings: First, analysts who label certain instances of their analysands' speech, silences, and actions "resistances," thereby neglecting to analyze these instances as also expressive of the unconscious as a Thing that speaks (speaking even in and through defenses), are the ones who resist the unconscious in their refusal to analyze its perhaps more challenging displays and outbursts; second, these analysts, as themselves "resisters" against the truths of the unconscious, should be resisted through a "return to Freud."

Having taken this detour through "The Freudian Thing," I still need to touch upon a few more aspects of Lacan's perspective on the Hegel-Marx rapport (as illuminating his specific variant of dialectical materialism) before circumnavigating back to the treatment of the conflict between idealism and realism in the eighteenth session of *Seminar XVI* (which I began unpacking earlier here). In the sole opening session of his aborted seminar on *The Names-of-the-Father* (November 20, 1963), Lacan at one point claims that it was "through" (*via*) Marx that the "Hegelian dialectic . . . entered into the world" (*la dialectique hégélienne . . . est entrée dans le monde*).[122] Arguably, Lacan's dialectical materialist path between nominalism and metaphysical realism, with its notion of the becoming-Real of the Symbolic as signifiers falling into their signifieds, allows him to maintain that the Marx epitomized by the famous eleventh thesis on Feuerbach extracts from Hegel's speculative dialectics what thereby becomes a set of socio-politically efficacious real abstractions "changing the world," with these abstractions partially remaking this world in their own image. Lacan explicitly suggests that even if dialectical speculation as per Hegel is not true in its initial versions within Hegel's texts, it goes on to become true through the causal efficacy it achieves in and through Marxism.[123]

Subsequently, in the *écrit* "Science and Truth" (originally given on December 1, 1965 as the opening session of the thirteenth seminar on *The Object of Psychoanalysis* [1965–66]), Lacan seems to complicate and further nuance this train of thought. He does so in connection with a line from Lenin's 1913 essay "The Three Sources and Three Component Parts of Marxism" – "The Marxist doctrine is omnipotent because it is true."[124] Lacan remarks:

> In writing that 'Marx's theory is omnipotent because it is true,' Lenin says nothing of the enormity of the question his speech raises: If one assumes the truth of materialism in its two guises – dialectic and history, which are, in fact, one and the same – to be mute, how could theorizing this increase its power? To answer with proletarian consciousness and the action of Marxist politicos seems inadequate to me.[125]

Lacan immediately adds, "The separation of powers is at least announced in Marxism, the truth as cause being distinguished from knowledge put into operation" (*la vérité comme cause au savoir mis en exercise*).[126] This reference to Lenin recurs in both the fourteenth and sixteenth seminars, with the former recurrence involving Lacan associating this moment in "Science and Truth" with his "*Moi, la vérité, je parle*" in "The Freudian Thing."[127]

In the above-quoted lines from "Science and Truth," Lacan, in a move controversial within Marxist circles at least, equates historical with dialectical materialism. As my prior examinations of such later seminars as the sixteenth and eighteenth in conjunction with Zupančič's and Žižek's coverage of similar terrain already indicates, Lacan's (dialectical) materialism allows him to engage with and move amidst a wide range of philosophical, social, and scientific fields – and this along lines similar to those of the expanded version of Marx's materialist approaches to political economy pioneered by Engels. Lacan implies that Marx's historical materialism already is, in itself, a dialectical materialism.

I believe that the keys to decoding Lacan's reaction to Lenin in "Science and Truth" (1965) are to be found in his roughly contemporaneous "Responses to Students of Philosophy" (1966) – more specifically, the passages from the latter text quoted and commented upon by me a short while ago here. In both interventions, Lacan employs the phrase "truth as cause." In "Responses to Students of Philosophy" he insists, as seen, on the importance of maintaining a dialectical materialism "leaving empty the function of truth as cause, when therein lies, nevertheless, the first supposition of its own effectiveness" (i.e., the practical effectiveness of dialectical materialism as a revolutionary theory à la Marxism). In "Science and Truth," he hints that his materialism of signifiers as themselves true causal powers *qua* real abstractions[128] (i.e., what he calls "my theory of language" in "Responses to Students of Philosophy") arguably fills in the explanatory gap within Marxist materialisms epitomized by Lenin's failure to ask and answer the riddle of the causal efficacy of theorizations. This dovetails with his subsequent 1966 assertion that "my theory of language is true whatever be the adequacy of Marxism, and . . . it is needed by it, whatever be the defect that it leaves Marxism with." Moreover, when, in "Science and Truth," he observes that "The separation of powers is at least announced in Marxism, the truth as cause being distinguished from knowledge put into operation," this indicates that a Lacanian dialectical materialism of the signifier allows for the possibility of an indefinite number of signifiers becoming causally efficacious (not just those of traditional Marxism-Leninism – for instance, Lacan's handlings of science and technology portray these domains as bearing witness to this same type of causal efficacy that is neither nominalist nor metaphysically realist). This possibility of materially real causal efficacy (i.e., *la vérité comme cause*) is hence itself an "empty" place of potentiality, although particular instances of theorizing force certain signifiers (for example, "E = mc^2" or "Workers of the world unite!") rather than others to enter the world, fall into their signifieds, and thereby become a singular "*savoir mis en exercice*," whether this *savoir* be Hegelian, Marxian, scientific, technological, or whatever else. Furthermore, in distinguishing the emptiness of *la vérité comme cause* from *savoir* – the latter does not preexist the former as the fullness of the knowledge in the Real of a subject supposed to know as big Other (whether the God of Descartes and Newton or the secular theodicies of certain versions of Hegelianism and Marxism) – Lacan, along with the Marxism he credits as exhibiting an awareness of this distinction, strives toward a thoroughly atheistic dialectical materialism (unlike theistic strains of it, such as the strong messianism of Stalin's pseudo-secular doctrine of diamat contrasting sharply with, for instance, Walter Benjamin's "*weak* messianic power"[129]).

Having reached a better understanding of Lacan's dialectical materialism, I want now to return to my already-underway close reading of the April 30, 1969 session of the sixteenth seminar (as might be recalled, this detour exploring how Lacan construes the Hegel-Marx relationship pushed off from reflections on Marxism and modern science in this same seminar session). What remains for me briefly to unpack from this session of *Seminar XVI* concerns specifically a non-idealist historical account of the genesis of (subjective) idealism. Lacan therein proceeds to claim that a peculiar "representation of representation" constitutes the "secret knot" of anti-realist, anti-materialist idealism.[130] This model of how the mind models things is based, Lacan asserts, on vision as a real material sense, as a physical faculty of perception[131] (an assertion also made in *Seminar XIII*[132]). More precisely, he puts forward the artificially constructed contraption of the optical black box as the historically privileged basis for the representation of the representing (idealist) subject as itself a reflecting interior separated by a surface from a representationally reflected exterior[133] (it would not be difficult to imagine a Marxist historical materialist analysis of the science and technology of optics readily compatible with Lacan's observations). Not only, Lacan alleges, does Bishop Berkeley as a borderline solipsist tacitly rely on this ocular-centric representation of representation[134] – so too does Freud, as shown by certain of his models of the psychical apparatus as well as concepts such as "projection."[135] In an implicitly historical materialist gesture, Lacan insists on calling into question and casting into doubt idealist reliance upon such optical models, even if and when the figure doing the relying is Freud himself.[136] However, in resonance with Zupančič's rendition of a Lacanian realism, Lacan here signals that the "real" (*réel*) of his realism is an "outside" (*dehors*) of the Other, namely, a real suffused with and saturated by the signifiers of symbolic orders (i.e., big Others).[137]

Both before and after this eighteenth session of *Seminar XVI*, Lacan occasionally says a number of additional things about realism and idealism in relation to Freudian psychoanalysis over and above those I already have mentioned. In *Seminar VI* (*Desire and Its Interpretation* [1958–59]), the transcendent subjectivity of anti-realist idealism is demoted to the status of a mere presupposition projected by both the enunciating subject him/her-self as well as his/her interlocutors beyond, behind, or beneath the fragmentary multitude of enunciated chains of signifiers (as signifiers of demands in Lacan's precise technical sense of "demand").[138] Hence, in this context, the speaking subject *qua* $, as a (pre)supposition, would be a precursor of the subject supposed to know introduced in 1964.

In *Seminar VII*, Lacan emphasizes that Freud is no subjective idealist insofar as his Real(ity) is not a tamed and domesticated construction of and in psychical subjectivity itself.[139] This 1959 pronouncement is echoed later in, among other places, the sixteenth seminar (specifically, in a session of it other than that of April 30, 1969).[140] Also elsewhere in *Seminar XVI* (specifically, in the thirteenth session of March 5, 1969), Lacan gestures at a realist quasi-naturalism of *jouissance* (what he dubs a "nativism" of signifier-mediated drives) according to which this core concept of his mature metapsychology of the libidinal economy is the second nature of an asubjective Real formed through the penetration of signifying structures and dynamics into the it/id (*ça*).[141] The seventh seminar already begins paving the way for this Freud-inspired realist quasi-naturalism subsequently alluded to by Lacan in 1969. At the end of this seminar's ninth session (January 27, 1960), he declares, "the *Trieb* can in no way be limited to a psychological notion. It is an absolutely fundamental ontological notion."[142]

Onto-topology – Dupes Who Do Not Err

But, exactly what sort of ontology, if any, results from a Freudian-Lacanian metapsychology of the libidinal economy? In *Seminar*

XIV, Lacan not only anchors what arguably amounts to his quasi-naturalist realism in a "materialism" of the body – he vehemently posits that "there is no *jouissance* except for that of the body" (*il n'y a de jouissance que du corps*)[143] – he also proposes therein that this psychoanalytic anchoring in what I would label a "corpo-Real" is not vulnerable to the temptations of formalist dematerializations as non-materialist idealizations hinted at by advances in mathematized physics as a natural science[144] (temptations alarming Lenin in his 1908 response to philosophical appropriations of the then-fresh revolutionary upheavals in physics[145]). Likewise, at the same moment during the fourteenth seminar, Lacan once again walks a fine ontological line between nominalism and metaphysical realism, maintaining that even the (Symbolic) Other (as a seeming metaphysical reality) ultimately is nothing more than a multitude of bodies[146] – despite, for all that, not being nominalistically reducible to nothing more than the aggregate of a mass of atomized material individuals.

Subsequently in Lacan's teachings, the range of analytic libidinal concepts mobilized against idealisms is broadened. In *Seminar XIX* (*...ou pire* [1971–72]), Lacan, although taking his distance from philosophy as allegedly a paradigmatic form of "university discourse"[147] (as per his theory of the four discourses forged a couple of years prior), once more mentions idealism-versus-realism so as to underscore that he self-identifies as a realist ("*je me classe parmi les réalistes*").[148] However, his is a realism of fantasies and *lalangue* in addition to *jouissance* too.[149] *Seminar XXI* similarly invokes a "materialism of writing,"[150] perhaps as a dialectical materialism of the dupes who do not err through nominalism, reductivism, epiphenomenalism, and the like. Both *lalangue* and "writing," in this 1970s-era context, are notions resting on Lacan's doctrine of the material (rather than meaningful) signifier in its graphic and/or acoustic embodiments. Apropos *lalangue*, Lacan, when cautiously self-identifying as a realist in *Seminar XIX*, indicates that the primary-process-style unconscious mentation adhering to the meaningless materiality of intra-psychical *Vorstellungen* subverts idealism on its home terrain; it does so by suggesting that cognizing subjectivity is itself buffeted from within by the mental processes of senseless signifiers spontaneously enchaining themselves in an idiotic, asubjective activity of a thinking different-in-kind from, yet profoundly affecting, conscious thought.[151] In this instance, Lacan's materialist realism is extimate vis-à-vis the subjectivity of subjective idealism. In line with Freud's Copernican revolution, this subject is no longer master in its own house insofar as the language of thought is partially transubstantiated by psychoanalysis into the intimate externality, the foreign body, of a contingent, nonsensical material Real (as *lalangue*, writing, letters, and so on as per the late Lacan).

During this same period of his teaching (i.e., the 1970s as its final decade), Lacan, as is well known, increasingly relies in his theorizations upon resources drawn from topology as the mathematical science of continuously transformable surfaces. I am convinced that a significant link conjoins Lacan's turns to topology with his allegiance to a realist, quasi-naturalist dialectical materialism (an allegiance arguably testified to by a number of his pronouncements unpacked at length by me in the preceding). But, in what does this link consist? Quite a while ago here, in the course of my examination of *Seminar XVIII* prompted by Zupančič and Žižek, I proposed reading Lacan's thesis according to which "There is no meta-language" as entailing, among other of its implications, the proposition that "Language is no meta." This proposition can be rearticulated as: Speaking being (*parlêtre*) is also being speaks (*ça parle*). One should bear in mind, as I highlighted above, that Lacan bases whatever ontology he could be said to advance on aspects of the it/id (*ça*) as the base of the libidinal economy. And, reinforcing the link between the *parlêtre* and *ça parle*, Lacan sometimes plays with the homophony between Freud's German *Es* (*ça*/id) and "S" as the first letter of the subject (*sujet*), with the latter specifically as the speaking subject of the unconscious (*ça parle*).[152]

However, Lacan, as both consciously extending dialectical materialism as well as unconsciously carrying forward Hegel's and Schelling's German idealist "system-program," is certainly not to be mistaken for a proponent of the absolutely flat, featureless immanentism of a (neo-)Spinozist monism. In hybrid Hegelian-Lacanian parlance, thinking the subject *qua parlêtre* also as substance *qua ça* (*parle*) and vice versa involves the dialectical-speculative notion of the substantial immanence of the subjective transcendence of substantial immanence itself (i.e., the subject-*qua*-$ as a transcendence-in-immanence, as both continuous and discontinuous with substance-*qua*-S). The late Lacan's focus on topology arguably assists him in conceiving of a plane of immanence internally differentiating itself, as self-sundering and auto-dividing, into a multitude of curves, folds, holes, interiors, and warpings. These twists and turns represent the structures and dynamics of subjects as dialectical-speculative identities-in-differences vis-à-vis the single, sole surface of their lone plane of immanence.

In *Seminar XXIII* (*Le sinthome* [1975–76]), Lacan depicts his topologized rendition of analysis as resulting in "the first philosophy that it appears to me supports itself."[153] I would recommend that this remark be interpreted in tandem with the whole preceding reconstruction of what arguably amounts to Lacan's realist dialectical materialism. Like the Marx of the "Theses on Feuerbach," Lacan embraces a materialist immanentism without, for all that, inadvertently offering encouragement to idealist reactions through painting the unsatisfying monochromatic old pictures of mechanistic and/or reductive Spinozist naturalisms, with their notorious "night in which all cows are black." As a speculative immanentism leaving open space for irreducible transcendences-in-immanence, Lacan's dialectical materialism, like Marx's, "supports itself" in that it rests on no totally transcendent meta-levels as extrinsic supports, whether these be explicitly posited (as in subjective idealisms) or implicitly presupposed (as in contemplative *qua* non-dialectical materialisms).

A materialist realism of *jouissance* tethers the libidinal subject to the physical body, thereby de-idealizing subjectivity and heavily qualifying whatever transcendence it may be said to achieve with respect to its corporeal grounds. This results in the hypothesis that subject-formation involves a partial transcendence of things bodily, with this partial quality amounting to incomplete and uneven denaturalization. And, referring back to *Seminar XIX* as cited by me a short while ago, a materialist realism of *lalangue/* writing not only supplements that of *jouissance* by blocking any risk of crude naturalist reductivism connected with the latter – it also both subverts from within the ostensibly immaterial thinking subject of subjective idealism as well as implies an incarnate dialectic operative between the "nature" of human organisms and the "nurture" of the socio-symbolic orders surrounding them. A materialist realism of fantasies (also mentioned by Lacan in the nineteenth seminar) points in the direction of an anti-nominalist theory of real abstractions in line with the principle of no illusions (as spelled out earlier by me). Overall, as a heterodox dialectical materialist tacitly in line with Marx and, hence, implicitly opposed to purely contemplative/transcendent stances, Lacan ups the ante for partisans of realist positions through insisting that such partisans exclude nothing whatsoever from their ontological inventories, including themselves as thinking/knowing subjects and even the most apparently "unreal" structures and phenomena. To once again resort to now-familiar Hegelian locution, Lacanianism insists upon conceiving of subjects also as substances (as the verso of the recto formed by the famous injunction pronounced early on in the preface to the *Phenomenology of Spirit*).

Each of these dimensions of Lacan's thinking informs my transcendental materialism. I share his dialectical sensibilities according to which the denaturalized subject-as-*parlêtre* ($) and "natural" substance-as-*ça* (S) induce mutual modifications in each other as a result of the former being rendered immanent (and yet nonetheless irreducible) to the latter.[154] I also share his adamant opposition to variations of what can be labeled as reductivism and epiphenomenalism. For both a proper Lacanianism as well as transcendental materialism, those who believe that "illusions" are just illusions (i.e., causally inefficacious fictions, unrealities, etc.) and nothing more are the non-dupes who err (*les non-dupes errent*). A Lacanian transcendental materialist has no illusions about illusions.

Notes

1. Badiou 2009e: 132.
2. Badiou 2009e: 132–3; Johnston 2009a: 119–22.
3. Zupančič 2011: 29–48.
4. Ibid.: 36–7.
5. Žižek 2012: 780.
6. *SXVIII*: 28.
7. Ibid.: 28.
8. Ibid.: 12.
9. Ibid.: 12.
10. Ibid.: 12.
11. Badiou 1982: 204; Johnston 2009a: 120–3.
12. *SXIX: ...ou pire*: 1/12/72, 5/4/72, 6/21/72; *SXX*: 17, 30, 54; *SXXI*: 12/11/73, 1/15/74, 4/9/74, 5/21/74.
13. *SXVIII*: 12.
14. Ibid.: 14.
15. *SIII*: 258–70; Žižek 2012: 586–7.

16. *SXVIII*: 14.
17. *SI*: 271, 277–8; *SXX*: 121.
18. *SXVIII*: 14.
19. Ibid.: 18.
20. Ibid.: 26.
21. Ibid.: 15.
22. Ibid.: 42–3.
23. Koyré 1958: 99, 278; Johnston 2013i; Johnston 2013f.
24. Kant 1965: Bii [4], Bxii–xiv [19–21].
25. Schelling 1966: 80–1, 120, 128–9.
26. Hegel 1977c: 147–53; Hegel 1955: 175–7.
27. Bacon 2000: 9–11, 33.
28. Balmès 2007: 57.
29. *SVIII*: 12.
30. *SXXII*: 3/11/75.
31. *SI*: 147; *SVII*: 122; Johnston 2013i.
32. *SXVII*: 162, 187.
33. Zupančič 2011: 36.
34. Ibid.: 36–7.
35. Ibid.: 43–4.
36. Johnston 2009a: 122–4.
37. *SXI* [Fr.]: 89.
38. *SXI*: 96.
39. Žižek 2012: 706.
40. Ibid.: 144–5.
41. Ibid.: 706.
42. Ibid.: 707.
43. Wittgenstein 1961: 5.632–5.633 [117].
44. Žižek 2012: 707–8.
45. *SXI*: 29–30, 134.
46. Ibid.: 29.
47. Ibid.: 29.
48. Ibid.: 29.
49. Ibid.: 29.
50. Ibid.: 30.
51. Ibid.: 53.
52. Ibid.: 53.
53. Ibid.: 53–4.
54. Johnston 2005c: 37, 40–3, 204–6.
55. *SXI*: 72.
56. Ibid.: 72.

57. *SXI* [Fr.]: 122; *SXI*: 134.
58. Žižek 2012: 195.
59. *SXIX: ...ou pire*: 6/21/72; *SXX*: 30–1.
60. Johnston 2011e: 159–79; Johnston 2012a: 23–52; Johnston 2013e.
61. *SXV*: 11/15/67.
62. Ibid.: 11/15/67.
63. Ibid.: 11/15/67.
64. *SXVI*: 33.
65. Ibid.: 33.
66. Ibid.: 33.
67. Ibid.: 33.
68. Zupančič 2011: 36.
69. *SXVI*: 279.
70. Ibid.: 282, 285–6, 290.
71. Ibid.: 279, 285–6.
72. Ibid.: 279.
73. Ibid.: 279–80.
74. Ibid.: 280.
75. Ibid.: 280.
76. Ibid.: 16–17, 21, 30.
77. *SXVI*: 280–1; Balmès 2007: 27–30.
78. *SXVI*: 283.
79. Ibid.: 280–1.
80. Lacan 2001f: 329–39; Lacan 2001g: 376–7; Balmès 2007: 23–4, 27–32.
81. Lacan 2006e: 157.
82. *SVII*: 206.
83. *SXVII*: 71.
84. Lacan 2006j: 368; *SXIV*: 2/22/67.
85. Lacan 2001i: 494.
86. Lacan 2001c: 208; Lacan 1990c: 111.
87. *SXVI*: 103.
88. Lacan 1990c: 111.
89. Lacan 2001c: 208; Lacan 1990c: 111–12.
90. Lacan 1990c: 112.
91. Stalin 1972a: 5–9, 25; Stalin 1972b: 33–5; Lacan 2006i: 344.
92. Lacan 1990c: 112.
93. Ibid.: 112.
94. Lacan 2001c: 209; Lacan 1990c: 112.
95. Lacan 2006g: 248; Lacan 2006l: 496; Lacan 2001a: 137–8; Lacan

2001b: 199; Lacan 1970: 187; *SI*: 244; *SII*: 82; *SIII*: 32; *SIX*: 1/10/62; *SXIV*: 2/1/67, 5/10/67.

96. Johnston 2008d: 85–90; Johnston 2009a: 122–4; Johnston 2007b: 9.

97. Althusser 2009a: 28–9; Althusser 2009b: 95, 130, 213; Althusser 1996: 170–2.

98. Lacan 2006i: 334–63.

99. Lacan 1966a: 234; Lacan 2006f: 194.

100. *SXIV*: 5/10/67; *SXVIII*: 24, 164; *SXIX: Le savoir du psychanalyste*: 12/2/71; *SXIX: ...ou pire*: 1/19/72; *SXXII*: 1/21/75, 2/18/75; *SXXVII*: 3/18/80.

101. Lacan 2006f: 194.

102. Ibid.: 194.

103. Ibid.: 194.

104. Lacan 2006f: 194–5; Lacan 2006i: 348.

105. Lacan 2006f: 195.

106. Lacan 1990a: 10.

107. Žižek 2005: 26–37.

108. Hegel 1977c: 44; Hegel 1991c: §6 [29–30]; Hegel 1991a: 20–3.

109. Lacan 2006i: 341–2.

110. *SXI*: 103, 111–12.

111. Ibid.: 112.

112. Lacan 2006i: 340.

113. Ibid.: 341.

114. *SE* 7: 77–8.

115. Lacan 2006i: 337–8.

116. Ibid.: 341–2.

117. *SXVII*: 51, 103.

118. Lacan 1973: 9; Lacan 1990a: 3.

119. Lacan 2006i: 342–3, 362–3.

120. Ibid.: 342.

121. Ibid.: 348–9.

122. Lacan 2005b: 74; Lacan 1990b: 84.

123. Lacan 1990b: 83–4.

124. Lenin 1975: 640.

125. Lacan 2006q: 738.

126. Lacan 1966b: 869; Lacan 2006q: 738.

127. *SXIV*: 4/19/67; *SXVI*: 172–3.

128. Lacan 2006q: 743.

129. Stalin 1940: 13, 40–1, 43–4; Benjamin 1969: 253–4, 262, 264; Johnston 2009a: xiv-xvi.

130. *SXVI*: 282.
131. Ibid.: 283.
132. *SXIII*: 5/4/66.
133. *SXVI*: 283–4.
134. Ibid.: 286.
135. Ibid.: 284, 286–8.
136. Ibid.: 284, 286–8.
137. Ibid.: 291.
138. *SVI*: 11/19/58.
139. *SVII*: 30–1.
140. *SXVI*: 194.
141. Ibid.: 212, 214.
142. *SVII*: 127.
143. *SXIV*: 5/31/67.
144. Ibid.: 5/31/67.
145. Lenin 1972: 309–14, 318, 340, 342, 377–8.
146. *SXIV*: 5/31/67.
147. *SXIX*: ...*ou pire*: 3/8/72.
148. Ibid.: 3/8/72.
149. Ibid.: 3/8/72.
150. *SXXI*: 4/9/74.
151. *SXIX*: ...*ou pire*: 3/8/72.
152. *SIII*: 14, 296–7; *SIV*: 44, 46, 49–50; *SVI*: 5/20/59; Lacan 2006i: 347–8.
153. *SXXIII*: 144–5.
154. Johnston 2013i.

Part II

Žižek: Dossier of an Ongoing Debate

5

Hegel's Luther:
Žižek's Materialist Hegelianism

The three chapters (5, 6, and 7) of Part II here are installments of a continuing, long-running exchange between Žižek and me. Žižek's substantial (and still-growing) body of work is the principle living source of inspiration for transcendental materialism. As I noted in the Introduction above, I coined the very phrase "transcendental materialism" (in my 2008 book *Žižek's Ontology*) specifically to characterize Žižekian philosophy insofar as it is constructed around a core formed through a precise, particular fusion of German idealism and Lacanian theory. More recently, Žižek, in his 2012 *magnum opus Less Than Nothing*, approvingly adopts the label as his own (see Chapter 1). However, he and I, despite sharing so much in common intellectually, have come to disagree with each other about a number of important points related to what transcendental materialism is as well as what it can and should be. These differences have to do with, among other topics: how materialism is related to naturalism; which natural sciences ought to be the privileged partners of materialism today; how to interpret transcendental materialism's indebtedness to Marxist historical/dialectical materialisms, including the controversial matter of a "dialectics of nature"; the status and place of autonomous subjectivity in a materialist ontology; and, the political and religious implications of a proper (transcendental) materialism. My thinking past and present on these and other subjects is intimately bound up with Žižek's ideas about these shared concerns. Therefore, the following tour (in Part II) through our still-unfolding conversations is crucial to this book as a whole. Of contemporary thinkers in dialogue with whom I have arrived at the position I call "transcendental materialism," Žižek is by far the most important and influential for me.

Near the end of a two-hour presentation at Calvin College in

Grand Rapids, Michigan on November 10, 2006, Žižek confesses that, in terms of his dearest intellectual ambitions nearest to his heart, "my secret dream is to be Hegel's Luther."[1] This confession comes approximately just seven months after the publication of *The Parallax View*, a text described by him at this time as a new *magnum opus*. There are ample justifications within this 2006 book to license retroactively rereading it through the lens of Žižek's subsequent public admission that he now is preoccupied with rescuing Hegel from the numerous misinterpretations to which this giant of German idealism (who casts such a long shadow over the Continental European philosophical tradition) has been subjected repeatedly over the past 200 years of the history of post-Hegelian philosophy (a rescue operation carried out at even greater length in his more recent tome *Less Than Nothing*). *The Parallax View*, at certain points explicitly and in other places implicitly, can be seen as centered on an effort to confront aggressively the various received versions of Hegel widely accepted as official and orthodox exegetical renditions. The motif of the "parallax gap," elaborated in a plethora of guises throughout this work, condenses and reflects the axiomatic theses of what could be called Žižek's Hegelian reformation.

The critical assessment of *The Parallax View* I will offer in what follows seeks to go straight to its theoretical heart by highlighting a single line of argumentation running through the full span of this text's different moments and phases. Žižek's own Hegelian-style conceptions of truth (as fiercely partisan rather than calmly neutral) and universality (as immanently concrete rather than transcendently abstract) validate such an interpretive approach[2] – *"universal Truth is accessible only from a partial engaged subjective position."*[3] Deliberately extracting particular conceptual constellations and forcing them to link up with each other according to the plan of a certain directed philosophical agenda promises to be much more revealing of the essential features of Žižekian thought than an attempt to survey comprehensively the sum total of the content covered in this major piece of his philosophical corpus.

The specific argumentative thread I will isolate in this context is the extended engagement with the terrain covered by cognitive science and the neurosciences. *The Parallax View* contains Žižek's broadest and deepest reflections on life-scientific renditions of human mindedness articulated by him to date. As becomes apparent in the rest of Part II, two of the main bones of contention between Žižek and me concern, first, how to position philosophical materialism with respect to a naturalism informed by biology and, second, how to interpret things biological in relation both to philosophy (specifically, a materialist one with a dialectical as non-reductive/eliminative theory of subjectivity) as well as to the other natural sciences (especially physics). Hence, given the importance of biology in the exchanges between Žižek and me apropos the interlinked topics of materialism, naturalism, and the sciences, zooming in on the discussions of neurobiology in *The Parallax View* is an important first move for me to make here.

Apart from the task of denouncing falsifying popular pictures of Hegel, one of Žižek's other driving ambitions in *The Parallax View* is the desire to formulate a fundamental ontology appropriate to the theory of subjectivity mapped out over the course of his entire intellectual itinerary (a theory informed by Kant and post-Kantian German idealism combined with Lacanian psychoanalytic metapsychology). And, herein, the articulation of such an ontology appropriately gets entangled, via reflections on the nature of the brain, with the latest instantiations of the perennial philosophical problem of the relationship between mind and body. Žižek grants that the central nervous system is, in at least several undeniable and important senses, the material, corporeal ground of the subject, the bodily being without which there cannot be the *parlêtre* (speaking being). But, in the spirit of Schelling and Hegel, the fashions in which Žižek attempts to tie together systematically a materialist ontology with an account of more-than-material subjectivity illuminate a normally obscured and ignored set of implied consequences flowing from the gesture of dissolving hard-and-fast dualist distinctions between body and mind, nature and spirit.

The philosophical engagement with the neurosciences over the past few decades, an engagement almost completely monopolized by the Anglo-American Analytic philosophical tradition and neglected by the Continental European philosophical tradition with an equal amount of completeness, has emphasized (to put this in the vernacular of German idealism) the naturalization of spirit resulting from the collapse of any strict nature-spirit dichotomy. The materialisms promoted by those Analytic philosophers amenable to grounding the mental on the neuronal simply assume that the outcome of folding mind and matter into each other is a becoming-material of the mind, namely, a naturalization of the spirit (i.e., the mind comes to resemble the brain conceived of as just another part of the physical world as depicted by the cause-and-effect laws posited by the natural sciences at larger-scale levels above the quantum domain). This is one way of describing the essentially reductive orientation of those mainstream material-isms developed thus far in conjunction with certain philosophical interpretations of the neurosciences. Described differently, the reductive assumption here is that rendering mind immanent to matter requires, to greater or lesser degrees, de-mentalizing the mind so as to materialize it in conformity with the image of matter (and, more generally, the material universe) as an integrated web of mechanisms held together and made exhaustively consistent with itself through the basic governing force of efficient causality. The discussions of materialism and the mind-body problem in Analytic philosophy seem to remain stuck with visions of mate-riality not much different from those underlying the pre-Kantian early modern perspectives of, among others, Hobbes, Boyle, and Locke.

What presumptively fails to be asked in all this is the question of whether the common proto-conceptual pictures of material being tacitly informing theoretical reflections on such matters can and should remain unchanged once the outdated, inflexible binary oppositions between nature and spirit or body and mind are desta-bilized critically. Whereas Analytic philosophers generally take it for granted that passing through the fires of this destabilization yields a straightforwardly naturalized spirit as its reduced product, Žižek, inspired by the German idealists, takes seriously the possi-bility that, at least as a correlative-yet-inverse set of consequences, folding mind and matter into each other (also) results in a (partial) spiritualization of nature (but, for Žižek, these consequences defi-nitely are not to be depicted in the guise of some sort of crude pan-psychism). Žižek's materialist ontology, particularly as elaborated in *The Parallax View* (and, more recently, *Less Than Nothing*), is motivated, to a significant extent, by the question of how basic proto-philosophical images of materiality must be transformed in the aftermath of the gesture of rendering the subject and its structures as fully immanent to material being. Žižek is convinced that (in Hegel's vocabulary) including the apparently immaterial subject (i.e., mind or spirit) within apparently material substance (i.e., matter or body) cannot leave substance untouched and unal-tered in the process. The unavoidable philosophical price to be paid for naturalizing human beings is the accompanying denaturalization of nature.[4]

Prior to tackling his take on the mind-body problem, Žižek's Hegelianism in *The Parallax View* (with which he introduces the dialectical subtleties of post-Kantian late modernity into conversations about the brain) ought to be examined. On first glance, the term "parallax," as deployed by Žižek, seems to involve a return to Kant because, in connection with this term, select contradictions and incompatibilities are elevated to the status of insurmountable absolutes. Insofar as Žižekian parallax splits are characterized as ruptures between incommensurable dimensions, as rifts between strata prohibiting any reconciliation or translation of these separated strata on the placid plane of a third sublating medium, it appears that Kantian-style antinomies are presented here as brute metaphysical facts indigestible by the Hegelian *Aufhebung* (or anything else akin to it). However, early on in *The Parallax View*, Žižek warns that the assertion of the existence of these parallax gaps is not tantamount to a "Kantian revenge over Hegel."[5] Instead, this assertion allegedly leads to a revivification of Hegelian philosophy as the most supremely subtle incarnation of "dialectical materialism."[6] Žižek's Hegel is the exact opposite of what he usually is conceived to be – not an idealist metaphysician of the all-consuming conceptual synthesis of a thereby totalized reality, but, instead, a materialist thinker of (in Lacanese) a not-All Real shot through with antagonisms, cracks, fissures, and tensions.[7] Apropos Kant, this peculiar reincarnation of Hegel further radicalizes (rather than overcomes) the parallax gaps posited within the critical-transcendental framework[8] (a radicalization in which Kantian epistemological contradictions and impasses are ontologized[9]). What is more – and, this is a point not to be missed – whereas Kantian transcendental idealism treats the subjectively mediated structures (including various dichotomous splits found therein) which it analyzes as inexplicable givens, Žižek's Hegel-inspired ontology purports to be able to get back behind these structures so as to explain their very emergence in the first place, both historically and materially.

Before delving deeper into the essential features of Žižek's Hegelian dialectical materialism, it should be asked: Why is exhuming the corpus of an allegedly materialist Hegel important, especially today? Žižek depicts the current intellectual situation as one in which a false forced choice between either "mechanical materialism" (i.e., a reductive approach in which material being is treated as nothing more than an aggregate of physical bodies bumping and grinding against each other) or "idealist obscurantism" (i.e., a reaction against mechanical materialism that insists upon the existence of a sharp dehiscence between the physical and the metaphysical) is repeatedly presented in diverse forms of packaging.[10] Despite cutting-edge work in the contemporary sciences appearing to vindicate after-the-fact the intuitions contained in the philosophies of nature delineated by the early nineteenth-century German idealists, these sciences and the majority of those who claim to represent them have tended to turn a blind eye to the theoretical resources contained in the writings of, among others, Schelling and Hegel (this is unsurprising, given that twentieth-century Anglo-American Analytic philosophy arises, in part, as a reaction against nineteenth-century British Hegelianism). Throughout *The Parallax View*, Žižek, departing from the work of others engaged with the natural sciences (especially cognitive neuroscience) who either gesture in the direction of or strive to develop more sophisticated materialist theoretical frameworks (such as Damasio, Daniel Dennett, Joseph LeDoux, Malabou, Thomas Metzinger, and Francisco Varela), aims to show not only that today's sciences would be better able to express their insights if equipped with the concepts and terminology of a dialectical materialism formulated in dialogue with German idealism – Žižek's thesis goes one step further: The natural sciences cannot even properly come to recognize and realize their true results if their fashions of self-understanding continue to remain mired in the ill-framed debates staged between, on the one hand, varieties of materialism whose notions of matter are no more sophisticated than seventeenth-century conceptions of "corporeal substance" moved solely by the mechanisms of efficient causes, and, on the other hand, equally unsophisticated varieties of idealism interminably stuck reactively combating such materialisms (an impasse already described with elegant brevity by Marx in the first of his "Theses on Feuerbach"). Among its many advantages, Žižekian dialectical materialism promises to move beyond the recurrent disputes between materialist reductionists and idealist anti-reductionists that have grown so sterile and unproductive.

Žižek specifies that what he calls "dialectical materialism" is a philosophical orientation centered on the question/problem of *"how, from within the flat order of positive being, the very gap between thought and being, the negativity of thought, emerges*"[11] (and he claims that this is Hegel's fundamental concern too,[12] a thesis reiterated in *Less Than Nothing*[13]). What makes Žižek's materialism specifically dialectical, on his account, is its ability to elucidate the material genesis of more-than-material phenomena and structures. Along these very lines, in the introduction to *The Parallax View*, he refers to a process of "transcendental genesis,"[14] namely, the immanent emergence of configurations that, following this emergence, thereafter remain irreducibly transcendent in relation to the immanence out of which they emerged (although, of course, a dialectic of oscillating reciprocal modifications between material immanence and more-than-material transcendence takes shape in the wake of the "generation"[15] of this split).

Succinctly stated, Žižek, as a self-proclaimed dialectical materialist, is an emergent dual-aspect monist. As is well known, Spinoza is a dual-aspect monist insofar as he asserts, ontologically speaking, that there is one (and only one) substance (i.e., "God"/"Nature"), although this single totality of being necessarily appears refracted into distinct, disparate attributes (in particular, the attributes of thinking and extension). Both Schelling and Hegel (and, by implication, Žižek too) are troubled by the absence of any explanation on Spinoza's part of how and why the monistic One comes to be refracted into the disparate appearances of a dualistic Two[16] (of course, Spinoza is a major point of reference for Hegel given Spinoza's importance in Kantian and post-Kantian intellectual circles at the time; and Žižek frequently engages with contemporary manifestations of Spinozism as advanced by, most notably, Deleuze and his progeny). Moreover, not only does a Spinozistic substance metaphysics lack such an explanation – it also runs the risk of licensing reductionist stances according to which anything other than the ontological One-All is dismissible as merely illusory or epiphenomenal in relation to this ultimately homogeneous substratum. The Žižekian Hegel (or, alternately, the Hegelian Žižek) promotes a non-reductive materialism in the form of a monism of the not-All One, a materialist ontology of the ground of being as a self-sundering substance fracturing itself from within so as to produce parallax splits between irreconcilable layers and tiers of existence.[17]

However, insofar as the word "dialectical" nowadays tends vaguely to connote hazy notions of integration and synthesis (arguably due to widespread confusion as regards Hegel's quite precise distinction between dialectics and speculation as two sides or moments of reason *als Vernunft*[18]), it does not seem entirely appropriate for Žižek to describe his monism of the not-All One as a materialism that is recognizably dialectical. Instead, Žižek's tethering of so-called dialectical materialism to an ontology of a self-sundering substance internally generating parallax-style antinomies and oppositions seems more like a sort of genetic transcendentalism, a theory centered on the model of a trajectory involving the immanent genesis of the thereafter-transcendent (i.e., an emergentist supplement to Kantian transcendental idealism). One could call this, as I have done, "transcendental materialism," defined as a doctrine based on the thesis that materiality manufactures out of itself that which comes to detach from and achieve independence in relation to it.[19] If Kant's transcendental subject amounts to the set of conditions of possibility for the constitution and cognizance of phenomenal reality, then Žižek's emergent dual-aspect monism (with its delineations of the dynamics through which transcendentally conditioned phenomenal realities arise from material being) attempts to identify the conditions of possibility for these Kantian conditions of possibility. Put differently, Žižekian dialectical materialism also could be described, with respect to Kant, as a materialist meta-transcendentalism proposed as the "real" basis for idealist transcendentalism.[20]

And yet, in the face of the danger of possible misinterpretations, the decision to christen the fundamental philosophical position espoused in *The Parallax View* "dialectical materialism" is part of Žižek's Hegelian reformation, his protracted effort, as I characterized it above, to reinterpret Hegel as a thinker of discordant material inconsistency rather than harmonious ideational consistency. Although this might initially strike the ear as a heterodox Hegel, Žižek insists throughout his extensive *oeuvre* that his is really the sole orthodox Hegel. This is quite reminiscent of Lacan's (in)famous "return to Freud." Žižek's "return to Hegel" is likewise an interpretive stance involving the assertion that the standard construal of the orthodox-heterodox distinction needs to be reversed given the inaccurate bastardizations essential to the supposedly orthodox renditions of the original source in question. Like the Lacanian Freud, the heterodox appearance of the Žižekian Hegel arises from its notable contrasts with the enshrined vulgar distortions widely accepted as faithful depictions.

In the course of elaborating the foundational thesis of Žižekian dialectical materialism stating that the materiality of a not-All One gives rise to a series of conflicting, irreconcilable Twos (as more-than-material dimensions and dynamics), *The Parallax View* runs through a dizzying array of distinctions, all of which are treated as parallax pairs (i.e., as seemingly insurmountable oppositions between mutually exclusive poles/positions): being and thought,[21] positivity and negativity,[22] the temporal and the eternal,[23] immanence and transcendence,[24] particularity and universality,[25] substance and subject,[26] is and ought,[27] the ontological and the evental,[28] essence and appearance,[29] the neuronal and the mental,[30] the finite and the infinite,[31] and the Pre-Symbolic and the Symbolic.[32] With each of these pairs of terms, the question recurrently posed by Žižek is: How does the latter term emerge out of the former term? And, the basic, general model being constructed here stipulates that once a second plane is produced by a first plane – this amounts to the genesis of a trans-ontological dualistic Two out of an ontological monistic One – the resulting split between these planes becomes an ineradicable gap, an ineliminable dehiscence permanently resistant to any and every gesture aimed at its dissolution. Moreover, the thus-produced second plane, according to Žižek, achieves a self-relating autonomy with respect to its thereby transcended originary ground or source (as a substantial base/foundation giving rise to desubstantialized appearances and processes). In short, the effect comes to outgrow its cause.

The underlying logic of the theoretical matrix elaborated by Žižek in *The Parallax View* can better be clarified and evaluated by fleshing it out through paying carefully selective attention to just a few of the concepts and distinctions I mentioned in the immediately preceding paragraph. In particular, examining in greater detail Žižek's recasting of philosophical notions of materiality vis-à-vis the natural sciences (especially cognitive neuroscience) will help both to illuminate what is essential to Žižekian dialectical materialism as well as to illustrate why such a materialism is timely and important. Building on arguments deployed in many of his previous texts,[33] Žižek insists that the images of matter informing familiar, standard varieties of and perspectives on materialism reduce materiality to being nothing more than the stable solidity of bodily density. This type of mindless matter is envisioned as exhaustively determined by the physical laws of nature vouched for by the perceived authority of the natural sciences. Faced with the ostensibly unanalyzable existence of this supposedly foundational type of matter, one tends to be pushed into either absolutely affirming its ultimate status (with all the reductive implications entailed by such an affirmation) or categorically rejecting it as primary with an equal degree of absoluteness (precisely so as to avoid the reductive implications entailed by affirming its ultimate status). That is to say, one is pressured into choosing between either the reductionism of a monistic mechanistic materialism or the anti-reductionism of a dualistic spiritualist idealism. Given the manners in which matter is represented by the picture-thinking of theorists still clinging to terribly outdated images of the material Real, the false dichotomy of this hackneyed, tired either/or alternative inevitably foists itself upon theoretical reflection again and again. In *The Parallax View*, Žižek seeks nothing less than an exit out of this stale, sterile cul-de-sac, an escape from the see-sawing of this unproductive, go-nowhere philosophical rut.

The key to such an exit consists of Žižek's contemporary reformulation of Hegel's 1807 injunction to conceive of substance also as subject.[34] In relation to what is at stake in this injunction, Žižek presents a forced choice of his own – "either subjectivity is an illusion, or reality is *in itself* (not only epistemologically) not-All"[35] (a proposition reiterated verbatim in *Less Than Nothing*[36]). In other words, one must decide between a "closed" ontology of asubjective material being – both mechanistic materialism and its rebellious-yet-reactive idealist shadow orbit around this option – and an "open" ontology positing a form of materiality that is more and other than the stupid, solid stuff of traditional philosophical imaginings of matter. Relatively early in *The Parallax View*, Žižek appeals, in the context of a discussion of the rapport between the ontological and the evental, to a notion of being as shot-through with holes and voids; rather than existing as a smooth, uninterrupted fullness consistent with itself in its homogeneity, the ontological harbors the actual discontinuities of (and potential disruptions arising from) vacant spaces internal to itself (with some of these spaces becoming the fault lines of discrepancies and rifts surfacing within being). From the perspective of what Žižek identifies as "the materialist standpoint," there dwells, within the "constellation of Being," a "minimally 'empty' distance between . . . beings."[37] This perforation of being provides the minimal opening needed for the introduction of the psychoanalytic motif of conflict into ontology itself,[38] an introduction interfering with the general penchant of thought to conceive of being as a harmonious organic cosmos at one with itself – with this move being utterly central to Žižek's endeavors. A little over twenty pages later, in association with the issue of the distinction between idealism and materialism, he starts to draw out the consequences of re-imagining matter as porous and broken-up rather than as an impenetrable heftiness: "for the materialist, the 'openness' goes all the way down, that is, necessity is not the underlying universal law that secretly regulates the chaotic interplay of appearances – it is the 'All' itself which is non-All, inconsistent, marked by an irreducible contingency."[39] The materialism of which Žižek speaks here is, of course, his own version of it. Invoking a Žižekian distinction I cited previously, what both "mechanical materialism" and "idealist obscurantism" share in common – this link firmly shackles these two positions to each other, establishing an agreement underlying and organizing their more superficial disagreements – is a consensus stipulating that materiality is, when all is said and done, really just the corporeal substance of, say, Galileo or Newton (i.e., physical objects blindly obeying the clockwork automaton embodied in the cause-and-effect laws of nature as formulated at the level of seventeenth- and eighteenth-century science). From the perspective of *The Parallax View*, a curious time lag plagues current philosophical consciousness: Although aware of momentous developments in the historical march of the natural sciences from the beginning of the twentieth century onward (especially developments connected to quantum physics and the neurosciences), today's predominant collective theoretical imagination, as expressed in continuing disputes between varieties of materialism and idealism that seemingly have not digested certain recent scientific discoveries, remains stuck with representations of matter that pre-date the twentieth century. For Žižek, certain crucial aspects of the sciences of the twentieth century accomplish, so to speak, a desubstantialization of substance[40] (*à la*, for instance, string theory's grounding of physical reality on ephemeral vibrating strands of energy captured solely through the intangible abstractions of branches of mathematics operating well beyond the limitations and confines of crude imaginative picture-thinking). This desubstantialization of substance makes possible a conception of materiality as open and contingent – in other words, as something quite distinct from the closed and necessary tangible stuff of old.

Parallel to the insistence that (in Hegel's parlance) substance is also subject (i.e., material being, as incomplete and inconsistent, contains within itself the potentials for the creative genesis of modes of subjectivity exceeding this same ontological foundation), Žižek's dialectical materialism conversely-but-correlatively proclaims that subject is (also) substance. Žižek declares, "a truly radical materialism is by definition nonreductionist: far from claiming that 'everything is matter,' it confers upon 'immaterial' phenomena a specific positive nonbeing."[41] In fact, as can be seen clearly at this juncture, Žižekian materialism is non-reductive in two distinct senses: First, it depicts material being as an auto-rupturing absence of cosmic-organic wholeness prone to produce immanently out of itself precisely those parallax-style splits supporting trans-ontological, more-than-material subjectivities; second, these thus-produced subjective structures acquire a being of their own in the form of a certain type of incarnate existence (examples of this special sort of dematerialized matter integral to the constitution of subjectivity include Schelling's "bodily spirituality"[42] and the strange "materiality" of the signifiers spoken of by Lacan[43]).

The Parallax View is the first text in which Žižek devotes time to a sustained treatment of the perennial philosophical problem of the mind-body rapport as informed by recent work in the neurosciences. Moreover, this recently opened theoretical front dealing with disciplines rarely addressed directly by those interested in German idealism and/or Lacanian psychoanalysis promises to be a fruitful testing ground for Žižekian dialectical materialism. As regards the positioning of the neuronal and the mental with respect to each other, Žižek speculatively ponders whether "the emergence of *thought* is the ultimate Event."[44] By "Event," he is alluding, of course, to Badiou's notion of the evental as distinct from the ontological.[45] In this precise context, Žižek is suggesting that, like the irruption of the event out of being, the emergence of the mental (i.e., "thought"), although arising from within the neuronal, nonetheless comes to break away from being determined by the electro-chemical inner workings of the wrinkled matter of the central nervous system (and, connected with the brain, the evolutionary-genetic factors shaping the human body as a whole). This is to claim that the mental phenomena of thought achieve a relatively separate existence apart from the material corporeality serving as the thus-exceeded ontological underbelly of these same phenomena. From this contention, Žižek then proceeds to elucidate that particular dimension of the theoretically vexing mind-body relation brought to a heightened degree of visible prominence through the lens of his philosophical-psychoanalytic brand of dialectical materialism:

> Consciousness is 'phenomenal' in contrast to 'real' brain processes, but therein lies the true (Hegelian) problem: not how to get from phenomenal experience to reality, but how and why phenomenal experience emerges/explodes in the midst of 'blind'/wordless reality. There must be a non-All, a gap, a hole, in reality itself, filled in by phenomenal experience.[46]

The issue identified here as distinct from "the true (Hegelian) problem" is, as is common knowledge, a classic question of epistemology (i.e., the traditional problem of the mind's access to an extra-mental world). In addition, this very question motivates Kant to initiate the "Copernican revolution" of his critical-transcendental turn as launched right at the start of the *Critique of Pure Reason*.[47] However, in terms of the rapport between the neuronal and the mental, what interests Žižek instead is the occurrence of the genesis of the latter out of the former (subsequently in *The Parallax View*, he again describes this genesis as explosive, as an "ontological explosion"[48]). In this vein, if one reasonably grants that the brain is, at a minimum, a necessary condition for the mind, one is prompted, as Žižek's reflections indicate, to wonder what kind of matter can and does give rise to something that then, once arisen, seems to carve a chasm of inexplicable irreducibility between itself and its originary material ground/source. Phrased differently, if mind is, at least partially, an effect of brain, what is the ontological nature and status of a cause capable of causing such an effect (i.e., an effect appearing to establish an unbridgeable divide between itself and its supposed prior cause)?

Žižek begins answering this question through discussing the notions of body and selfhood as associated with the problematic of the connection between the neuronal and the mental. Starting with the example of "reality" as bio-material existence, he asserts: "At the level of reality, there are only bodies interacting; 'life proper' emerges at the minimally 'ideal' level, as an immaterial event which provides the form of unity of the living body as the 'same' in the incessant changing of its material components."[49] At first, these remarks perhaps sound slightly like an endorsement of a sort of nominalism combining Heraclitus (everything that exists is in a constant state of flux) with Hobbes (only the singular things of corporeal substance really exist). However, the Hegelian Žižek is certainly neither a nominalist nor a metaphysical realist (and, obviously, his materialism is definitely distinct from that espoused in the *Leviathan* of 1651). The ideality of immaterial events spoken of here is something neither physical nor non-physical, a more-than-material dimension that, despite Žižek's avowedly materialist ontology, is not without its proper ontological status (including an ability to generate "effects in the Real,"[50] to affect the very material beings giving rise to this dematerialized dimension[51] – moreover, one would do well here to recall Lacan's many elaborations concerning the materialities specific to signifiers and structures). All of this becomes clearer when, two pages after the statement just quoted, he shifts from talking about "life" (as the impersonal identity of an organism, an "ideal" identity amounting to more than the sum of the organism's "real" parts) to discussing selfhood (as the personal identity of a subject):

> Here we encounter the minimum of 'idealism' which defines the notion of Self: a Self is precisely an entity without any substantial density, without any hard kernel that would guarantee its consistency. If we penetrate the surface of an organism, and look deeper and deeper into it, we never encounter some central controlling element that would be its Self, secretly pulling the strings of its organs. The consistency of the Self is thus purely virtual; it is as if it were an Inside which appears only when viewed from the Outside, on the interface-screen – the moment we penetrate the interface and endeavor to grasp the Self 'substantially,' as it is 'in itself,' it disappears like sand between our fingers. Thus materialist reductionists who claim that 'there really is no self' are right, but they nonetheless miss the point. At the level of material reality (inclusive of the psychological reality of 'inner experience'), there is in effect no Self: the Self is not the 'inner kernel' of an organism, but a surface-effect. A 'true' human Self functions, in a sense, like a computer screen: what is 'behind' it is nothing but a network of 'selfless' neuronal machinery . . . in the opposition between the corporeal-material process and the pure 'sterile' appearance, subject is appearance itself, brought to its self-reflection; it is *something that exists only insofar as it appears to itself.* This is why it is wrong to search behind the appearance for the 'true core' of subjectivity: behind it there is, precisely, nothing, just a meaningless natural mechanism with no 'depth' to it.[52]

As he summarizes this train of thought later, "there is no 'true substance' of the Self beneath its self-appearance . . . the Self 'is' its own appearing-to-itself."[53] These reflections on the status of selfhood provide an opportunity both for clarifying, through precise concretization, the essential dimensions of Žižekian dialectical materialism as well as for distinguishing this theoretical position from superficially similar stances. Apropos the relationship between the reality of material bodies and the ideality of more-than-material identities, this specific variety of dialectical materialism maintains that there are two things to be explained here: one, the emergence or production of (to employ a Schellingian distinction informing Žižek's position) the Ideal (in Žižek's more Lacanian terms, the Imaginary-Symbolic dimension involving both the subject and subjectification[54]) out of the Real (in this instance, material being as a tension-plagued not-whole, as heterogeneous and inconsistent); two, the becoming-autonomous (as Hegel would put it, the achievement of a self-relating "for itself" mode of existence) of this thus-generated dimension of more-than-material ideality. The first part of this account identifies Žižek as a materialist. The second part indicates the non-reductive nature of this materialism. And, in the vein of this second part, Žižek, speaking of the vectors through which subjective freedom arises, proposes that understanding the becoming-autonomous of more-than-material ideality hinges on answering the question, *How can appearance exert a causality of its own?*[55] Normally, the word "appearance" involves the notion of a superficial manifestation entirely dependent for its being on the corresponding that-which-appears (for example, if the mental is deemed an appearance of the neuronal, this would seem to entail a reductive materialism according to which the mind is epiphenomenal with respect to the brain). However, Žižek's non-reductive dialectical materialism, as coupled with a type of emergentism, posits that apparently epiphenomenal appearances cease to be epiphenomenal if and when (as happens with human beings) these appearances begin to interact on the basis of logics internal to the "ideal" field of appearance itself. In other words, epiphenomena allegedly can no longer be said to be epiphenomena once an intra-ideal set of cross-resonances is established between appearances themselves after these appearances have arisen from the ground of "real" materiality[56] (an ontological ground partially broken with precisely through the establishment of autonomous logics of self-relating between appearances at more-than-material levels of existence).[57]

One might want to pause at this point so as briefly to consider how all of this is compatible with Žižek's adamantly avowed Lacanianism. Does Lacanian theory not generally treat the body as a passive receptacle or surface for receiving the images and signifiers inscribed onto it by virtue of its insertion into the mediating milieu of Imaginary-Symbolic reality? Is not the material of raw human flesh, in Lacan's picture, a mere bearer of or support for extra-corporeal constructions arranged by the representative instantiations of the big Other? Although the ontogenetic dynamics of subjectification temporally unfolding within the registers of the Imaginary and the Symbolic do indeed involve, according to Lacan, processes in which the body of the individual is stamped with marks and traits originating from an outside beyond this body, these processes themselves could not take place in the first place, would not even be possible to begin with, were it not for human corporeality being such that this fleshly materiality is already open to the alterity of externally impressed inscriptions. What needs to be grasped here is the receptivity of the endogenous with respect to the exogenous (to resort to the vocabulary of the early Freud).

In *The Parallax View*, Žižek reminds readers of the central role language, with its marks and traits, enjoys in the Lacanian depiction of subjectivity. According to the Žižekian rendition of Lacan, the linguistic signifiers of the symbolic order, as a big Other, conjure into existence a subject that is neither the bodily being of an organism nor the meaningful stories of some sort of recognizable, humanized personal identity (in relation to this topic, Žižek refers to Damasio's distinction between the "core self" and the "autobiographical self,"[58] rightfully arguing that the Lacanian subject is neither the moment-to-moment physiological reality of the core self nor the continuous, coherent ideational-narrative content of the autobiographical self).[59] Symbolic signifiers supposedly, as Žižek has it, bore holes and hollow out spaces within the positive plenitude of being, creating the nothingness he persistently identifies as subjectivity proper (as opposed to the subjectifying selfhood of the ego and its coordinates of identification).[60] As Žižek stipulates, this is not to claim that the Lacanian subject is itself reducible to the signifying chains representing (or, more accurately, misrepresenting) this anonymous, faceless "x"[61] (although, nonetheless, this subject would not exist without the tension established between it, as a locus of enunciation [i.e.,

Lacan's "subject of enunciation"], and the utterances in which this enunciator is alienated and alienates itself [i.e., Lacan's "subject of the utterance"][62]). He explains:

> we should take Lacan's term 'subject of the signifier' literally: there is, of course, no substantial signified content which guarantees the unity of the I; at this level, the subject is multiple, dispersed, and so forth – its unity is guaranteed only by the self-referential symbolic act, that is, 'I' is a purely performative entity, it is the one who says 'I.' This is the mystery of the subject's 'self-positing,' explored by Fichte: of course, when I say 'I,' I do not create any new content, I merely designate myself, the person who is uttering the phrase. This self-designation nonetheless gives rise to ('posits') an X which is not the 'real' flesh-and-blood person uttering it, but, precisely and merely, the pure Void of self-referential designation (the Lacanian 'subject of the enunciation'): 'I' am not directly my body, or even the content of my mind; 'I' am, rather, that X which has all these features as its properties. The Lacanian subject is thus the 'subject of the signifier' – not in the sense of being reducible to one of the signifiers in the signifying chain ('I' is not directly the signifier I, since, in this case, a computer or another machine writing 'I' would be a subject), but in a much more precise sense: when I say 'I' – when I designate 'myself' as 'I' – this very act of signifying adds something to the 'real flesh-and-blood entity' (inclusive of the content of its mental states, desires, attitudes) thus designated, and the subject is that X which is added to the designated content by means of the act of its self-referential designation. It is therefore misleading to say that the unity of the I is 'a mere fiction' beneath which there is the multitude of inconsistent mental processes: the point is that this fiction gives rise to 'effects in the Real,' that is to say, it acts as a necessary presupposition to a series of 'real' acts.[63]

As Žižek subsequently puts it in a footnote, language functions, in this case, in the capacity of "a machine of 'abstraction.'"[64] More specifically, the avatars of subjectivity furnished by the Symbolic big Other (in particular, proper names, as per Saul Kripke's "rigid designators," and personal pronouns, as per Emile Benveniste's "linguistic shifters"[65]) generate a subjective "One" (or, as the young Jacques-Alain Miller contends vis-à-vis Frege, zero[66]), namely, a contentless void devoid of anchoring in either the body or, for that matter, the rest of the language that gave birth to this void through the always fateful collision of bodies and languages.

Additionally – this is crucial to note in order to avoid understandable misunderstandings – the abstraction of which Žižek speaks here is a precise theoretical notion tied into a common thread running through three of Žižek's favorite thinkers: Hegel (in terms of his claim that the idea of a concrete reality existing apart from conceptual abstractions is itself the height of conceptual abstraction), Marx (in terms of his concept of "real abstraction" indebted to the preceding Hegelian claim), and Lacan (in terms of his rebuttals of the May 1968 slogan protesting that "structures do not march in the streets"). In all three of its instances (Hegelian, Marxian, and Lacanian), the fundamental thesis as regards the notion of abstraction is that abstractions (such as, in Žižek's discussion glossed by me above, the abstractions constitutive of subjectivity as such) do not remain ineffectively removed from the particularities of the nitty-gritty concreteness of actual, factual existence. To paraphrase Lacan, these abstractions have legs – or, as Žižek phrases it, they have (to quote this phrase once again) "effects in the Real." The material Real itself comes to be perturbed by the fictions it secretes.

With respect to the issue of the mind-body problem, this has important repercussions insofar as it provides a potent argument against epiphenomenalism. Mind (including, for present purposes, the dimensions of the subject) cannot be demoted to the status of pure epiphenomenon, as asserted by reductive mechanistic materialists. Why not? Even if dematerialized subjectivity, engendered by, among other things, the intervention of the signifiers of symbolic orders, is "illusory," it is an illusion that nonetheless really steers cognition and comportment[67] (along similar lines, Alenka Zupančič refers to "the Real of an illusion"[68]) – and, hence, thanks to certain other variables (most notably, neuroplasticity, about which I will say more below), this fiction partially remakes reality in its own image (with this dynamic process involving a materiality that is "plastic" as per Malabou's conceptualizations of plasticity[69]). Expressing this line of thought in a vaguely Hegelian style, the "true" reality of material being (as substance) passes into the "false" illusions of more-than-material non-being (as subject). But, through a movement of reciprocal dialectical modification, these illusions then pass back into their respective reality, becoming integral parts of it; and, at this stage, they no longer can be called illusions in the quotidian sense of the word (i.e., false, fictional [epi]phenomena). The only further qualification to be added here, in light of Žižek's hitching of his dialectical materialism to the motif of parallax splits, is that this movement of reciprocal dialectical modification is interminable to the extent that it forever fails to close the gap opened up within the material Real through the initiation of processes of subjectification and the ensuing advent of subjectivity proper as $.

However, to return to a point I made several paragraphs earlier, this entire Lacanian-Žižekian theory of the subject, measured according to the standards of Žižek's own dialectical materialist position, requires something more to be philosophically satisfying. As an emergent dual-aspect monist, Žižek must go one explanatory step further by discerning the prior conditions of possibility for the event of the advent of subjectivity out of materiality. Unsatisfied with treating this event as a miraculous transubstantiation of the otherwise inert material density of the all-too-human individual body, a Žižekian dialectical materialist believes in the necessity of theoretically tracing the genesis of subject out of substance and, in tandem with this, refuses to associate the emergence of subjectivity with anything resembling the inexplicable abracadabra of, say, grace. Žižek himself notes that only thus can one remain a materialist and avoid backsliding into idealism – "idealism posits an ideal Event which cannot be accounted for in terms of its material (pre)conditions, while the materialist wager is that we *can* get 'behind' the event and explore how Event explodes out of the gap in/of the order of Being."[70] Briefly returning again to Lacan, there indeed are various moments in Lacan's corpus (ranging from the early *écrits* on the mirror stage and psychical causality to the late seminars of the 1970s[71]) when he acknowledges, with varying degrees of directness, the importance for his theory of subjectivity of delineating the material-ontological conditions of possibility for the surfacing of the subject.[72] Through a backwards glance informed by Žižek's parallax perspective, it can be seen that Lacan's model of subject-formation must ask and answer a crucial question: What makes Real bodies receptive to being overwritten by features of Imaginary-Symbolic realities? Posed in less overtly Lacanian language, what, in the nature of human corporeal materiality, inclines this nature in the direction of trajectories of denaturalization? What sort of being paves the path of its own eventual effacing?

A plethora of significant lines of speculation potentially could be pursued in response to these questions. Lacan himself sketches the contours of several distinct replies to such queries (replies not to be spelled out in extensive detail here in the midst of a reading of Žižek's *The Parallax View*). In addition to Lacan's ways of raising and wrestling with this issue of the material conditions of possibility (at the level of the body) for the emergence of the more-than-material (at the level of selfhood and subjectivity), Žižek, drawing on certain other authors (in particular, Dennett, LeDoux, and Malabou), mobilizes the resources of contemporary cognitive neuroscience:

> Where . . . do we find traces of Hegelian themes in the new brain sciences? The three approaches to human intelligence – digital, computer-modeled; the neurobiological study of brain; the evolutionary approach – seem to form a kind of Hegelian triad: in the model of the human mind as a computing (data-processing) machine we get a purely formal symbolic machine; the biological brain studies proper focus on the 'piece of meat,' the immediate material support of human intelligence, the organ in which 'thought resides'; finally, the evolutionary approach analyzes the rise of human intelligence as part of a complex socio-biological process of interaction between humans and their environment within a shared life-world. Surprisingly, the most 'reductionist' approach, that of the brain sciences, is the most dialectical, emphasizing the infinite plasticity of the brain – that is the point of Catherine Malabou's provocative Hegelian reading of the brain sciences, which starts by applying to the brain Marx's well-known dictum about history: *people make their own brain, but they do not know it*. What she has in mind is something very precise and well-grounded in scientific results: the radical *plasticity* of the human brain. This plasticity is displayed in three main modes: plasticity of development, of modulation, and of reparation. Our brain is a historical product, it develops in interaction with the environment, through human praxis. This development is not prescribed in advance by our genes; what genes do is precisely the opposite: they account for the structure of the brain, which is open to plasticity . . . Vulgar materialism and idealism join forces against this plasticity: idealism, to prove that the brain is just matter, a relay machine which has to be animated from outside, not the site of activity; materialism, to sustain its mechanical determinist vision of reality. This explains the strange belief which, although it is now empirically refuted, persists: the brain, in contrast to other organs, does not grow and regenerate; its cells just gradually die out. This view ignores the fact that our mind does

not only reflect the world, it is part of a transformative exchange with the world, it 'reflects' the possibilities of transformation, it sees the world through possible 'projects,' and this transformation is also self-transformation, this exchange also modifies the brain as the biological 'site' of the mind.[73]

Not only is the empirical fact of neuroplasticity pregnant with philosophical-theoretical ramifications that have yet to be fully explored and utilized in discussions of the relations between materiality and subjectivity – this fact, approached by Žižek for the first time in *The Parallax View*, helps to concretize key aspects of his Hegel-inspired ontology and corresponding theory of the subject. The plastic nature of the brain – as Dennett and LeDoux accurately observe with regard to this plasticity, human beings are designed by nature to have re-designable natures, that is, at a larger level, biologically determined to be free (as undetermined) in a sense beyond biology[74] – is the paradigmatic incarnation of Žižek's ontological notion of material being as a permeable, porous openness (rather than as a closed density or causally saturated heaviness). In this vein, he maintains that "the only way effectively to account for the status of (self-)consciousness is to assert the ontological incompleteness of 'reality' itself: there is 'reality' only insofar as there is an ontological gap, a crack, in its very heart"[75] (an assertion recurring in various guises and permutations throughout *Less Than Nothing*[76]). These fissures fragmenting being from within are characterized by Žižek in a number of ways in different places. However, neuroplasticity here tangibly signifies the essential essencelessness or groundless ground of human nature, the natural mandate that seems to be missing right down to the bare bones of corporeality itself.[77] This plasticity, in its oscillations between the making and unmaking of an indefinite number of structures and phenomena, is nothing other than the embodied epitome of the new image of matter underpinning Žižekian dialectical materialist ontology.[78]

And yet, ontological openness alone, whether specifically as human neuroplasticity or generally as being's lack of integrated organic wholeness, is a necessary but not, by itself, sufficient condition for Žižek's correlative accounts of the initiation of processes of subjectification and the ensuing genesis of subjectivity.[79] Psychoanalysis is quite relevant here. Of course, as I already noted, Žižek opens up ontology, creating breathing room for subjects, by injecting the Freudian motif of conflict – for the later Freud in particular, with his dual-drive model, unsynthesized and irreconcilable divisions and ruptures are to be found within the bedrock of the very libidinal-material heart of human existence – into the nucleus of being itself. But, more than this is required to extract subject from substance; an ontology of material being as shot-through with cracks, gaps, and splits merely establishes the preconditions for the possibility of such an extraction as the absence of prohibiting conditions foreclosing this potentiality (i.e., no stifling ontological closure smothers in advance subjects-to-come). As argued by me elsewhere, three other ingredients must be added to Žižekian ontological openness – these three are complexity, affectivity, and temporality (the second and the third receiving sustained attention in Freudian-Lacanian psychoanalysis) – in order for his ontology and theory of subjectivity to come together in a systematic fashion. Summarized much too quickly, the material being of Žižek's ontology, so as to give rise to something other than itself, must: first, harbor degrees of extreme complexity in terms of the relations between its fragmented features capable of canceling out, through the generation of loophole-producing short-circuits, any over-riding pressure of "natural" default determinism as traditionally associated with standard, pre-dialectical versions of materialism; second, put into circulation forces of affectivity that prompt excessive investments in and attachments to specific elements of subjectification subsisting within the conflict-ridden spheres of extant existence; third, at the level of temporality, unfold along temporally elongated trajectories of subjectification in which a series of select features of material being displace each other in a sequence of struggles driven by antagonistic tensions within the self-short-circuiting complexity of substance-as-potential-subject. This third dimension eventually brings to light the silhouette of the Lacanian-Žižekian subject-as-void, the emptied "x" emerging from the successive implosions of identification transpiring as moments of the processes of subjectification to which the volatile not-All of being gives rise.[80]

Žižek hints that *The Parallax View* is a book meant to function as a systematizing encapsulation of the core components of his philosophical outlook. And yet, certain readers might experience a feeling of frustration in their attempts to discern the systematic unity supposedly underlying and tying together the wide-ranging discussions of the vast amount of diverse content contained in this text (analyses of philosophy, psychoanalysis, neuroscience, literature, film, politics, and so on – namely, the typical Žižekian smorgasbord of topics). Turning to another roughly contemporaneous reference he makes to Hegel (apart from the one cited at the very beginning of this chapter) promises to help shed light on Žižek's understanding of what would count as systematicity. In a May 2006 interview broadcast on French radio, he comments on one of the features of his work for which he has become famous: his extensive use of examples drawn from numerous areas, including a plethora of bits plucked from contemporary popular culture's entertainment industries. Whereas Žižek elsewhere appears to favor presenting these examples as just that (i.e., handy illustrations for rendering more easily legible theoretical concepts already established prior to their application to the examples in question), here, in this radio interview, he maintains that both Hegel and himself operate in a particular dialectical fashion in their methodical navigations of the interplay between empirical-historical instances and philosophical-theoretical concepts. More specifically, Žižek claims that, as a good Hegelian, he lets the form of the concept emerge from the content of the instance. And, he proceeds to insist that, in a way, an example's inherent conceptual richness is always richer than the concepts distilled out of the example by the reflective consciousness of a philosopher[81] (thus also providing a justification for his reexaminations of select examples reiterated throughout his writings insofar as the example requires repeated theoretical parsing in order for its implicit multifaceted significance to be made explicit).

Is this the method employed in *The Parallax View*? If so, how can a conceptually coherent philosophical-theoretical system arise out of an approach that tarries with a seemingly fragmented, heterogeneous multitude of disparate empirical-historical instances? Some people might be tempted to throw up their hands and deny the very possibility of anything systematic arising in this fashion. Others might go even further, accusing Žižek of pulling a cheap-and-easy trick through which, via the notion of parallax gaps as splits of incommensurability, he attempts to construct a system around his failure to be systematic (in other words, to appeal to Hegel in making a virtue out of this failure by hastily ontologizing his own intellectual inconsistencies, remaking being in the image of his idiosyncratic incoherence). A final return to Lacan, however, permits giving *The Parallax View* a much more sympathetic hearing (specifically by listening to Žižek with something akin to the ear of the psychoanalyst), a hearing this work genuinely deserves. As is well known, Lacan's strange style, the difficulty of the ways in which he conveys his teachings in both spoken and written formats, is part of his pedagogical technique in the training of aspiring future psychoanalysts; his articulations about the theory and practice of analysis, in order to be properly appreciated, must be interpretively approached by his audience in a manner roughly resembling how one, as an analyst, listens to an analysand's free associations. In short, Lacan tries to force his students to engage in analysis even while learning about analysis.

The texts of Lacan and Žižek sometimes seem to wander along a winding road strewn with *non sequiturs* and heading in a less-than-clear direction. But, as with even the most chaotic and disorganized associations of someone on the couch, there is invariably an integrated logic/pattern to be detected in what superficially sounds not to be systematically organized. Simply put, for psychoanalysis, there is always method to the madness. Giving *The Parallax View* a hearing according to the theoretical criteria and parameters Žižek himself establishes therein – this Hegelian-style hearing (i.e., evaluating a position according to its own standards) obviously must include Lacanian considerations – allows one to hear a recurrent refrain, a line of argumentation surfacing many times in this text with an almost obsessive insistence. This refrain is nothing other than the revivification of Hegel's frequently misunderstood emergent dual-aspect monism in the form of an ontology of the not-All One, a materialism of self-sundering substance generating out of itself structures of subjectivity coming to break with this substantial ground in their achieving a self-relating, trans-ontological autonomy. Žižek consistently seeks to trace trajectories involving the immanent material genesis of thereafter more-than-material modes of transcendence. His labors and struggles in *The Parallax View* are oriented around the incredibly ambitious endeavor to assimilate, without simply liquidating, transcendental idealism (i.e., the Kantian position animating the subsequent history of European philosophy up through the present, a history that justifiably could be described by a paraphrase of the title of Freud's 1930 masterpiece as "transcendental idealism and its discontents") within the framework of a position that is both dialectical and materialist. The title of the first section of the foreword to the 2002 second edition of *For they know not what they do* speaks of "The Hard Road to Dialectical Materialism"; and, the introduction to *The Parallax View* is entitled "Dialectical Materialism at the Gates." Perhaps what makes this such a difficult path to pursue, a path guaranteed to run up against powerful resistances, is that it begins only with the absolute renunciation of faith in every figuration of the big Other whatsoever (including the deterministic authority of nature enshrined in the vulgar mechanistic materialism of contemporary scientism). The burden that must be borne by each traveler walking this "hard road" is the unbearable lightness of the absence of any and every One-All.

It would be appropriate at this juncture to step back so as to situate my debate with Žižek (especially as it unfolds in Chapters 6 and 7 below) within the arc of the wider historical narrative articulated by this book (particularly as I elaborate it in Part I above). In my view, the power and originality of Žižek's contributions to contemporary thought are rooted primarily in his fashions of retrieving and reinterpreting the inexhaustibly rich resources of the German idealist tradition with the benefits of hindsight furnished by Marxism, psychoanalysis, the sciences, and recent developments in late-twentieth/early-twenty-first-century philosophy. A broadly similar set of positions (which I gather under the terminological umbrella of "transcendental materialism") striking careful balances between freedom and determinism as well as naturalism and anti-naturalism result for both of us from folding in precise manners this shared ensemble of philosophical/theoretical orientations into each other. On this common basis, we both are preoccupied with constructing something new resembling the "Spinozism of freedom" of the post-Fichtean German idealists (see Chapters 1 and 2), albeit doing so in ways exquisitely responsive to crucial, indispensable post-idealist insights pertaining to, among other topics, history, materialism(s), the unconscious, sexuality, nature, affects, and various (over)determining trans-individual, trans-subjective forces and factors. However, as the rest of Part II to follow will show, Žižek and I disagree with each other to varying degrees as regards nearly every element of transcendental materialism mentioned in the immediately preceding sentences; our construals and redeployments of the figures and disciplines forming our overlapping constellations of references often diverge from each other, sometimes dramatically. The next two chapters will explore some of these differences between us (and their consequences).

Notes

1. Žižek 2007b.
2. Žižek 2012: 226.
3. Žižek 2006a: 35.
4. Johnston 2008d: 241; Žižek 2012: 373, 416, 441, 826.
5. Žižek 2006a: 4.
6. Ibid.: 4.
7. Žižek 2002a: 67, 217; Žižek 1993: 19; Žižek 1999a: 60; Žižek 2004b: 60; Johnston 2008d: 126–7.
8. Žižek 1999a: 55, 84–5, 86, 113; Žižek 2002a: xcvi; Žižek 2006a: 25.
9. Johnston 2008d: 15, 129–30.
10. Žižek 2006a: 4.
11. Ibid.: 6.
12. Ibid.: 29.
13. Žižek 2012: 31–9, 131, 642–4, 646–7.
14. Žižek 2006a: 7.
15. Ibid.: 406.
16. Schelling 1994a: 71–2; Hegel 1977c: 10–13.
17. Žižek 2006a: 36.
18. Hegel 1991c: §79–82 [125–33].
19. Johnston 2008d: xxiii–xxiv, 61, 74, 81, 209, 228–9, 274–5, 284.
20. Johnston 2006: 50–1; Johnston 2008d: xxv, 71, 108–9, 273.
21. Žižek 2006a: 6.
22. Ibid.: 6.
23. Ibid.: 31.
24. Ibid.: 36.
25. Ibid.: 41.
26. Ibid.: 42.
27. Ibid.: 49.
28. Ibid.: 56.
29. Ibid.: 106–7.
30. Ibid.: 178, 197, 210–11.
31. Ibid.: 273–4.
32. Ibid.: 390.
33. Žižek 1996b: 227, 230–1; Žižek 2004b: 24–5.
34. Žižek 2006a: 42.
35. Ibid.: 168.
36. Žižek 2012: 725.

37. Žižek 2006a: 56.
38. Johnston 2013i.
39. Žižek 2006a: 79.
40. Ibid.: 165, 239, 407.
41. Ibid.: 168.
42. Schelling 1994c: 237; Schelling 2002: 39–40; Žižek 1996b: 3–4, 112, 152; Žižek 1997a: 46, 60–1; Žižek 1997b: 136; Žižek 1999b: 73; Žižek 2004b: 75.
43. Lacan 2006g: 248; Lacan 2006l: 496; Lacan 2001a: 137–8; Lacan 2001b: 199; Lacan 2001d: 224; Lacan 1970: 187; *SI*: 244; *SII*: 82; *SIII*: 32; *SIX*: 1/10/62; *SXIV*: 2/1/67, 5/10/67; *SXVI*: 88–90.
44. Žižek 2006a: 178.
45. Badiou 2005: 173; Badiou 2006c: 253.
46. Žižek 2006a: 197.
47. Kant 1965: Bxvi–xvii [22].
48. Žižek 2006a: 210–11.
49. Ibid.: 204.
50. Ibid.: 245.
51. Žižek 2012: 4, 96–7, 721–2, 726–7.
52. Žižek 2006a: 206.
53. Ibid.: 217.
54. Žižek 1999a: 159–60, 183.
55. Žižek 2006a: 206.
56. Johnston 2007a; Johnston 2008d: 283–4.
57. Žižek 2012: 143, 186, 188–9, 595–7, 707–8, 726–7, 729.
58. Damasio 1999: 172–5, 224–5.
59. Žižek 2006a: 226–7.
60. Žižek 1989: 195; Žižek 1993: 39, 245–6; Žižek 1996b: 124, 160; Žižek 1999a: 196–7.
61. Žižek 2012: 65, 414, 729–30.
62. *SXI*: 139–40, 207–8, 218, 236; Lacan 2001i: 449, 452–3.
63. Žižek 2006a: 244–5.
64. Ibid.: 414–15.
65. Kripke 1972: 48–9, 52–3, 57–8; Benveniste 1971: 226; Johnston 2008d: 214–15, 217–20, 285.
66. Miller 1977/1978: 32–4.
67. Johnston 2007a; Johnston 2008d: 281–4.
68. Zupančič 2001: 141–2; Zupančič 2002: 52.
69. Malabou 2004: 15–17, 22; Malabou 2005: 8–9, 73–4, 192–3.
70. Žižek 2006a: 166.

71. Lacan 2006c: 78; Lacan 2006e: 144; *SVIII*: 410; *SXXIII*: 12; *SXXIV*: 5/17/77.
72. Johnston 2006: 34–6; Johnston 2012a: 23–52.
73. Žižek 2006a: 208–9.
74. Dennett 2003: 90–1, 93; LeDoux 2002: 8–9; Žižek 2006a: 213–14.
75. Žižek 2006a: 242.
76. Žižek 2012: 12–13, 15–16, 185, 211–13, 239, 263–4, 282–4, 378–80, 386, 389–90, 399–400, 416, 473.
77. Johnston 2008d: 106–11, 114–15, 172–3, 200, 205, 208.
78. Malabou 2004: 127, 141, 146–7, 159, 161–4.
79. Johnston 2013i; Johnston 2014.
80. Johnston 2008d: 222–3, 231–2.
81. Žižek 2006b.

6

In Nature More Than Nature Itself: Žižek Between Naturalism and Supernaturalism

Nobody has done more to revive the fortunes of materialism today than Žižek. Through innovative, heterodox interweavings of what could be dubbed, in Leninist fashion, the three sources of Žižekianism (i.e., German idealist philosophies, Marxist political theory, and Freudian-Lacanian psychoanalysis),[1] Žižek aims to articulate an account of the irreducible subject compatible with the basis provided by a non-eliminative materialist ontology. To be more precise, what I have dubbed his "transcendental materialism" seeks to delineate how the negativity of *Cogito*-like subjectivity (especially in its related Kantian, Schellingian, Hegelian, and Lacanian manifestations) is internally generated out of material being.[2] He insists that this materialism, the one true version, must be founded upon a certain interpretation of Lacan's dictum declaring that "the big Other does not exist" ("*le grand Autre n'existe pas*"), an interpretation according to which the ultimate *Grund* hypothesized at the level of ontology should be envisioned as a lone inconsistent immanence riddled with gaps and deprived of the wholeness provided by such Others as the theological idea of God or the cosmological idea of Nature-with-a-capital-N (i.e., the monistic One-All of a seamless tapestry of entities and events bound together by mechanical relations of efficient causality).[3] The absence of such unity within being, a unity which would be a stifling, subject-squelching closure, is what permits the material genesis of more-than-material subjects; that is to say, this lack of underlying cohesion, as a "barred Real," is a contingent ontological condition of possibility for the emergence of trans-ontological subjectivity.[4] As Žižek reiterates recently, "the basic axiom of today's materialism is for me the *ontological incompleteness of reality.*"[5] He goes on to propose in the same text that "a true materialism not only asserts that only material reality 'really exists,' but has to assume all the consequences of what Lacan called the nonexistence of the big Other."[6] All of this is part of his solution to a philosophically significant problem he poses: "What ontology does freedom imply?"[7]

Žižek's parallel ontology and theory of subjectivity (the former being reverse-engineered out of the latter[8]) raise a series of interesting, concatenated questions crucial to the future of materialism in contemporary theory: To begin with, what sort of material is posited by Žižek as the groundless ground of not-whole being? What connection, if any, is there between this material and notions of nature associated with various versions of naturalism? Assuming that there indeed is some manner of relation between Žižekian ontologically primary "matter" (however ephemerally disappearing[9]) and what is imprecisely referred to as "nature" – in other words, this is to presume that, as Lacan would put it, materialism is "not without" (pas sans)[10] its naturalism – what can and should the relationship be between materialist philosophy and the empirical, experimental sciences of nature? Asked differently, how, if at all, ought philosophical and scientific materialisms to affect each other in terms of both their conceptual contents and methodological procedures? Supposing they rightfully affect each other, what obligations and constraints do theoretical materialism and the sciences place upon one another? Specifically, is a materialist philosophy responsible to and limited by the natural sciences? Even more specifically, is a materialist account of subjects, in whatever might be the ways, somehow answerable to the life sciences (in particular, evolutionary and neurobiological studies of human beings)?

These queries, orbiting around the significant core matter of the rapport between theoretical and empirical materialisms, are at the very heart of an ongoing debate between Žižek and myself, at least as I see it. This debate began with an article of mine (entitled "The Misfeeling of What Happens: Slavoj Žižek, Antonio Damasio, and a Materialist Account of Affects"[11]) in an issue of the journal *Subjectivity* devoted to Žižek's work and his response to this contribution, among others, in the same journal issue.[12] The present chapter is my reply to his response, a reply guided by the questions enumerated in the preceding paragraph. In the course of directly addressing Žižek's objections, I will refer to several other of his contemporaneous texts in which remarks relevant to this debate surface, including his contributions to the books *The Monstrosity of Christ: Paradox or Dialectic?* and *Mythology, Madness and Laughter: Subjectivity in German Idealism* (given both the need for brevity as well as the fact that I have engaged with his pre-2009 writings in great detail on prior occasions, I will not spend time in what follows on lengthy analyses of his earlier discussions of materialism).

In order properly to frame this reply to Žižek, a rapid sketch of its contextual backdrop is necessary. The article "The Misfeeling of What Happens" was extracted from my half of a book manuscript Catherine Malabou and I finished writing together not too long ago, entitled *Self and Emotional Life: Philosophy, Psychoanalysis, and Neuroscience* (Žižek mentions Malabou in his response to me, and, as will be seen subsequently, her corpus illuminates important facets of the terrain at stake here). This article consisted, in part, of an assessment of Žižek's Lacan-inspired criticisms of Damasio's neuroscientific depictions of affective life laid out in the fourth chapter of *The Parallax View*. Succinctly stated, the verdict of this assessment was that Damasio is not nearly so guilty of being quite as un-psychoanalytic, so at odds with analytic thinking, as Žižek charges him with being. In establishing this case *contra* Žižek, I attempted to show that discoveries alighted upon in the overlapping fields of affective neuroscience and evolutionary biology offer invaluable components for a materialist account of subjectivity faithful to the essential tenets of Freudian-Lacanian theory. While granting the correctness and perspicacity of many of Žižek's indictments (in which Damasio's fellow brain investigator LeDoux, and the neurosciences as a whole, come under carefully directed fire), I argued there, as elsewhere, that a truly materialist psychoanalytic metapsychology is obligated to reconcile itself with select findings of the life sciences (of course, this reconciliation should be dialectical, involving mutual modifications between these disciplines, albeit without any formal, dogmatic determination in advance of the delicate calibration of what is likely to be the usually uneven balance between the theoretical and empirical dimensions of this dialectic in the ongoing pursuit of its unfolding).

As a number of his interventions reveal (not only *The Parallax View*, but also such books as *The Indivisible Remainder: An Essay on Schelling and Related Matters* [1996] and *Organs without Bodies: On Deleuze and Consequences* [2004]), Žižek is hardly averse or unsympathetic to attempts at a rapprochement between psychoanalysis and the sciences. Nonetheless, I alleged in "The

Misfeeling of What Happens" that his critical treatments of the life sciences in *The Parallax View* (as well as in 2008's *In Defense of Lost Causes*) rely, at certain moments, on a sharp dichotomy between the natural and the anti-natural that these sciences have undermined empirically over the course of the past several decades[13] and that psychoanalytic metapsychology ought not to invoke theoretically (in other texts, I even try to demonstrate that Lacan himself, contrary to accepted exegetical consensus, does not subscribe to any standard type of anti-naturalism predicated upon a clear-cut contrast of nature versus anti-nature [*antiphusis, contre-nature*] and dictating unqualified hostility to biology and its branches[14]). Departing from the Žižekian critique of Damasian affective neuroscience, I pled for something I have been struggling to outline preliminarily and programmatically in recent years, that is, an alternate hybrid analytic-scientific vision of human subjectivity as depending upon and arising from a multitude of constitutive temporal-material strata running the full-spectrum gamut from the natural to the non-natural and sandwiched together as a collage of conflicting layers-in-tension.[15] This vision resonates indirectly or directly with a diverse array of references, ranging from, for instance, Althusser's Marxist (and, to a lesser extent, psychoanalytic) picture of a plurality of (historical) times bound up with "relatively autonomous" (social) structures[16] to contemporary neuroscientific characterizations of the evolved brain as a "kludge," a barely functional hodge-podge jumble of out-of-synch disparate modules.[17] Apropos Althusser, it is worth briefly noting that the materialist perspective informing this intervention is closer to that of Mao, as compared with other inheritors of Marx's legacy, in fashions that take a measure of distance from a certain Althusserian "theoreticist" conception of Marxist materialism (in that Althusserians wrongly might accuse the approach to interfacing the philosophical and the scientific adopted by me here as flirting with what the Althusser of the mid-1960s condemns as empiricist "pragmatism"[18]). Incidentally, it is also worth speculating in passing that historical and dialectical materialist handlings of the infrastructure-superstructure distinction at the level of the macrocosm of societies by such different thinkers as Gramsci, Mao, Sartre, and Althusser might harbor the potential to shed much-needed light on the microcosm of the perennial mind-body problem. But, this is a speculation for another time.

Before presenting and responding to Žižek's replies to me, I feel compelled to highlight an aspect of the place from which I respond here. Already in *Žižek's Ontology*, I detected and problematized instances when Žižek appears to deviate from his own version of materialism, a materialism resting on Lacan's "*le grand Autre n'existe pas*" as a central ontological principle (whether this Other be God, Nature, History, Society, or whatever else along these capitalized lines[19]). Of special relevance to the debate hopefully to be advanced productively by the present chapter are my hesitations with respect to his occasional talk of there being, in addition to the two dimensions of nature and culture, some sort of un-derived third vector (whether labeled the "night of the world," the "death drive," the "vanishing mediator," etc.) as the root-source of what comes to be subjectivity proper in and for itself ($).[20] On my view as first expressed in *Žižek's Ontology*, a view to be further clarified and sharpened below, Žižek's periodic summonings of a mysterious neither-natural-nor-cultural force, as an arguably under- or un-explained supplement to his ontology, are both incompatible with an authentically materialist materialism as well as superfluous considering his Lacanian renditions of nature and culture as equally "barred" Others (as inconsistent, conflict-ridden, and so on). In these disagreements, I find my situation to involve being caught between two Žižeks, as it were. However accurate, justifiable, or not, I experience myself as a voice speaking on behalf of a systematic Žižek and against another Žižek who strays from his own best philosophical insights, instead of as a critic intervening from a position purely external to Žižek's body of thought. As a Lacanian, he hopefully will not object in principle to having his subjectivity split.

Žižek launches his rebuttal of my article "The Misfeeling of What Happens" by vehemently asserting that any notion of the unconscious able to be extrapolated from Damasio's reflections would have to exclude key features of the Freudian-Lacanian psychoanalytic unconscious. On the Freudian hand, the Damasian unconscious leaves no room for anything "beyond the pleasure principle," namely, the infamous *Todestrieb* so dear to Žižek's heart. On the Lacanian hand, the non-conscious layers of Damasio's embodied mind allegedly lack, in their theoretical descriptions provided by him, the mediators of the big Other as symbolic order.[21] Žižek also repeats a Lacanian line integral to his critique of Damasio in *The Parallax View* (contained in a section entitled "Emotions Lie, or, Where Damasio Is Wrong"), maintaining that "for Freud, emotions cheat, with the exception of anxiety"[22] (both the general psychoanalytic issue of unconscious affects and Lacan's specific interpretation of Freud's metapsychology of affective life are reassessed in my half of the book with Malabou,[23] so the comparison of Freudian-Lacanian with Damasian portraits of things affective will be left to the side in this context here). As he notes in fairness, I too acknowledge a number of contrasts between the analytic and neuroscientific unconsciouses.[24] Indeed, although I sought to narrow the rift Žižek sees yawning between, on the one side, Freud and Lacan, and, on the other side, Damasio and LeDoux, I want to underscore that I in no way intended to close it altogether. For instance, I concur that the death drive or an equivalent is not explicitly integrated into Damasio's picture, although I drew attention to sites within the Damasian apparatus where there are receptive (albeit unexploited) openings for distinctively psychoanalytic concepts, such as the *Todestrieb*, that can and should be inserted at those precise loci.[25] I am less ready to grant that Damasio's and LeDoux's conceptions of everything other than self-conscious awareness are utterly devoid of acknowledgements of the influences stemming from what Lacan christens the "symbolic order." Both Damasio and LeDoux recognize and discuss the role of linguistic mediation in the phenomena they study[26] (of course, Lacan's and Žižek's multivalent uses of the phrase "big Other" refer to much more than just language, so it must immediately be conceded that certain aspects of this Other do not find expression in affective neuroscience *à la* the two researchers currently under consideration).

Comparing and contrasting Freud, Lacan, Damasio, and LeDoux aside, Žižek adds on the heels of the above that "I tend to agree with Catherine Malabou that the neuronal unconscious and the Freudian unconscious are not only different, but incompatible."[27] However, Žižek's agreement with Malabou on this topic ends here and goes no further.[28] For him, to affirm the split of incommensurability between the analytic and neuroscientific versions of the unconscious is also to affirm the autonomy of the former vis-à-vis the latter, or even the former's right to correct the latter without being reciprocally corrected by the latter in turn (i.e., the status of the analytic unconscious as a theoretical object is more or less independent of the empirical findings of the neurosciences). For her, this same affirmation dictates the opposite, namely, the task of thoroughly transforming (perhaps as far as immanently negating) psychoanalysis under the influence of contemporary neurobiological investigations (i.e., the independence of the analytic unconscious as a theoretical object is emphatically denied).[29] Observing the profound disagreement beneath the façade of consensus between Žižek and Malabou provides an opportunity for me to highlight, as intimated earlier, that I take a stance in-between these two poles. From this dialectical perspective, Freudian-Lacanian metapsychology, to varying extents depending on the specific concepts concerned therein, is "relatively autonomous" (to resort once again to a handy but tricky Marxist turn of phrase) in relation to the sciences. And yet, this variable-degree independence is far from exempting psychoanalysis, especially if it is of a sincere materialist bent, from a duty to be "plastic" (in Malabou's precise sense as a combination of firmness and flexibility[30]) in connection with these other disciplines. Additionally, the shape of this plasticity always should be determined concretely in each instance of a potential point of convergence and/or conflict between the analytic and the scientific (i.e., in a non-*apriori* fashion).

Žižek proceeds to claim that, "For Johnston, the 'denaturalization' of the human animal which takes place when the human animal is caught in the network of the symbolic order should not be conceived as a radical break with nature."[31] A lot hinges on how one construes the phrase "radical break." Insofar as Žižek and I share a notion of subjectivity extrapolated from a merging of German idealism and Lacanian theory, we both are against any kind of crude, reductive conflation of the category of the subject with the register of the merely natural and corporeal (as is Malabou also[32]). Nonetheless, I would contend (and, on my reading, so too would the more consistently materialist side of Žižek I appeal to in this debate) that a fully rational and atheistic/secular materialism requires a satisfactory account of how, to put it in Hegelese, subject surfaces out of substance alone.[33] This account would identify what the material possibility conditions are within the physical being of "nature" for the internal production out of itself of structures and phenomena (with which subjects are inextricably intertwined) that eventually achieve, through naturally catalyzed processes of denaturalization, a type of transcendence-in-immanence[34] as a self-relating dynamic in which non-natural causalities come to function within natural-material milieus.[35] Hence, for me, the emergence and self-founding of the subject-as-$ indeed marks a "break with nature."

Whether this break is "radical" depends on what Žižek means by this adjective. Given my insistence that the negativity of non-natural subjectivity remains susceptible to being buffeted and perturbed (or, as Malabou's ontology of traumatic accidents has it, disrupted or destroyed) by the natural ground from which it originally arises and with which it ruptures, perhaps my conception of the break of denaturalization is not radical enough in Žižek's eyes. However, too radical a rendering of this break between the natural and the non-natural, a rendering wherein the subject accomplishes an absolutely total and final subtraction from bio-material being and thereby closes in upon itself at the apex of a perfectly completed movement of denaturalization, would be unacceptable in light of Žižek's commitment to psychoanalysis (so too would be his non-genetic picture of autonomous subjectivity set against the ontogenetic models of subject-formation ineliminable from Freudian-Lacanian metapsychology). This is because he wishes to capture as essential to his picture of subjectivity the sorts of dysfunctionalities so familiar in analysis. Not only is there now ample empirical scientific evidence that many uniquely human dysfunctions, even though their modes of being psychically subjectified are anything but prescribed beforehand by exclusively biological variables, have their sources in the sub-optimal, evolutionarily slapped-together anatomy of the less-than-completely-coordinated central nervous system (i.e., the kludge-like brain) – from the vantage point of strictly theoretical musings, it seems probable that an excessively radical break with nature as corporeal substance(s) would yield a subject much too smoothly functional for Žižekian psychoanalytic sensibilities.[36] An insistence on denaturalization as not-too-radical, as uneven, partial, incomplete, failed, etc. is more likely to be conducive to the construction of a solidly materialist theory of the subject incorporating characteristics of psychical subjectivity at the center of the psychoanalytic depiction of the "human condition."

Žižek's ensuing employments of Kant's *Anthropology from a Pragmatic Point of View* and Hegel's *The Philosophy of History* in his criticisms are quite revelatory in relation to the issues presently at stake. As regards Kant, Žižek redeploys his interpretation of a note to §82 (in "Book Three: The Faculty of Desire") of the *Anthropology*, a note wherein infants are said to display an innate "passion" (*Leidenschaft*) for freedom.[37] Diagnosing what is "missing" from what he describes as my "vision of the archaic natural substance which is gradually, but never completely, civilized, 'mediated' by the symbolic order," he proceeds, with reference to Kant, to state:

> We find the first indication of this third dimension – neither nature nor culture – already in Kant, for whom discipline and education do not directly work on our animal nature, forging it into human individuality: as Kant points out, animals cannot be properly educated since their behavior is already predestined by their instincts. What this means is that, paradoxically, in order to be educated into freedom (*qua* moral autonomy and self-responsibility), *I already have to be free* in a much more radical – 'noumenal,' monstrous even – sense. The Freudian name for this monstrous freedom, of course, is death drive. It is interesting to note how philosophical narratives of the 'birth of man' are always compelled to presuppose a moment in human (pre) history when (what will become) man is no longer a mere animal and simultaneously not yet a 'being of language,' bound by symbolic Law; a moment of thoroughly 'perverted,' 'denaturalized,' 'derailed' nature which is not yet culture. In his anthropological writings, Kant emphasized that the human animal needs disciplinary pressure in order to tame an uncanny 'unruliness' which seems to be inherent to human nature – a wild, unconstrained propensity to insist stubbornly on one's own will, cost what it may. It is on account of this 'unruliness' that the human animal needs a Master to discipline him: discipline targets this 'unruliness,' not the animal nature in man.[38]

This paragraph appears verbatim in Žižek's contemporaneous essay "Discipline between Two Freedoms – Madness and Habit in German Idealism,"[39] followed by some further specifications regarding Kantian discipline.[40] Subsequently, in his sequel essay in the same volume (a piece entitled "Fichte's Laughter"), Žižek speaks of Hegel as having "no need for a third element."[41] And yet, this ardently self-professed Hegelian materialist seems to reach for what he himself, appealing to the authority of Kant-the-idealist, labels a "third dimension" (at this moment, one wonders whether, in the shadows, there might be a very un-Žižekian argument akin to Italian then-Marxist Lucio Colletti's contention that Marxism is led away from its materialism by relying on the dialectics of Hegelian idealism instead of the purportedly materialist "rational kernel" of the non-metaphysical anti-dogmatism in the critical transcendental idealism much maligned by ostensibly misguided Marxists, from Engels onward, preferring Hegel to Kant[42]).

My initial response to the Žižek of the passage quoted immediately above is simple: Put in the form of a naïve question, from where does this enigmatic neither-natural-nor-cultural third stratum come? Even if, sticking with Kant's example of babies, one quite contentiously insists that this untamed excess of impassioned (proto-)autonomy is, at the ontogenetic level of individual subject-formation, something intrinsic and hard-wired, that merely pushes the question back to the phylogenetic level without answering it. One is left to wonder what the cause or origin is for this magical kernel of free negativity, this "mysterious flame" (to borrow the title of a book by Colin McGinn advocating a "new mysterianism," deservedly criticized by Žižek,[43] which preaches that the mind-body problem, construed as an entirely epistemic difficulty, is inherently insoluble in that the mental cannot convincingly be derived theoretically from the material due to purportedly unsurpassable limits imposed by an inbuilt human "cognitive closure"[44]). From whence does Žižek's noumenal monstrosity arise if not nature as an inconsistent, Other-less physical universe: God, soul, *res cogitans*, the Absolute self-positing I, the hazy vapors of a ghostly *Geist*...?[45] I would rather my materialism fall flat than be three-dimensional in this non-materialist manner. This materialism, which is as much that of another Žižek (the Hegelian-materialist philosopher of transcendental materialism) as it is mine, rests solely on the two dimensions of a barred Real (i.e., what I have taken to naming a "weak nature,"[46] having nothing whatsoever to do with coincidental postmodern bandyings of this adjective, as internally divided and self-sundering material substance) and an equally barred Symbolic (i.e., the Lacanian-Žižekian inconsistent Others of culture and related structures).[47] Anything more than these two dimensions, any Third, is a derivative, emergent by-product of the natural and/or cultural – and not an inexplicable given always-already there (following the Lacan of the second sentence of the *écrit* on the mirror stage, a Cartesian- or Fichtean-style I is to be eschewed as a non-genetic first principle, although this is not tantamount to a rejection *tout court* of *Cogito*-like subjectivity[48]).

To put my cards on the table in terms of making explicit my philosophically ground-zero axioms, decisions, and intuitions, I am enough of a naturalist – mine is a non-reductive naturalism of

an auto-denaturalizing nature, hence really neither a strict naturalism nor anti-naturalism – to wager that an avoidance or refusal
of an explanation for the natural/material genesis of non-natural/
more-than-material beings and happenings (such as Lacan's $-as-
parlêtre alluded to by Žižek's phrase "being of language") is, as
the Lenin of *Materialism and Empirio-Criticism* would warn, a
dangerous concession cracking open the door to the irrationalities
of obscurantist idealisms, spiritualisms, and theisms. In a pre-
publication draft version of his debate with the backward-looking
theologian John Milbank in *The Monstrosity of Christ*, Žižek
declares that "the 'theological turn' of postmodernity is one of
THE figures of the enemy for me." If so, he should be warier
of the ways in which he encourages, however unintentionally,
attempts to appropriate his work by fanatical advocates of a terribly traditional religiosity deludedly romanticizing the wretched
darkness of medieval pre-modernity (regardless of this profound
conservatism being trendily repackaged in the flashy guises of
"radical orthodoxy" or any variant of "post-secularism" in
Continental philosophical circles, including an oxymoronic "theological materialism").

A few additional remarks warrant formulating before inquiring into the justness and accuracy of Žižek's reading of the Kant
of the *Anthropology*. In the wake of mobilizing the Hegel of *The
Philosophy of History*, portrayed as agreeing with the Kantian
insistence on freedom as something "in nature more than nature
itself" (to paraphrase Lacan[49]) – the role of Hegel's philosophy
in this discussion will be taken up after an examination of Kant's
Anthropology – Žižek cites some reflections by Jonathan Lear on
sexuality as situated between animal naturalness and human non-
naturalness.[50] Elsewhere, he likewise expresses approval of Lear's
recasting of the Freudian death drive[51] (with Žižek's recourse
to the latter notion clearly being crucial to our exchange). This
recasting proposes that the Freudian word "*Todestrieb*," although
naming a hypostatization mistakenly performed by Freud himself,
is a concept-term not for a positive thing, but for the negativity
of the pleasure principle's disruptive malfunctioning, its constitutive inability always and invariably to assert its intra-psychical
hegemonic dominance (in *Time Driven*, I similarly suggest that
Freud's problem-plagued death drive is best salvaged and recon-
structed as designating a discord built into the metapsychological
architecture of any and every drive [*Trieb*], more specifically, an

antagonistic temporal split between a repetitive "axis of iteration" [the source and pressure of a drive] and a repetition-thwarting "axis of alteration" [the aim and object of a drive][52]). That is to say, according to Lear and the Žižek who sides with him,[53] there is only the dysfunctional pleasure principle, and nothing more; in other words, there is not a second, deeper counter-principle externally opposing this lone principle. Once again enacting the gesture of playing off one Žižek against another, I am inclined to pit the Žižek who endorses Lear's thesis apropos the death drive against the Žižek who appears precisely to succumb to the temptation of hypostatization for which Lear rebukes Freud, namely, treating the *Todestrieb* as a substantial "third dimension" that is perplexingly neither natural nor cultural. By contrast, for both me and the Žižek who appropriates the Learian death drive, there actually exist nothing more than the two dimensions of nature and culture, plus the insubstantial negativity (i.e., not a positive third thing) of the conflicts within and between, but still immanent to, these two dimensions. What is more, in Schellingian language agreeable to us, I would add that, for a materialism not without its carefully qualified (quasi-)naturalism, the *Urgrund* (as also an *Ungrund*)[54] of a weak nature (exemplified in this context by Lear's sub-optimal pleasure principle minus the Other of a more profound, underlying meta-law such as the hypostatized version of the *Todestrieb*) is the ultimate baseless base of autonomous subjectivity, whether ontogenetically and/or phylogenetically.[55] Lumping together allusions to the eclectic set of Paul Churchland, Douglas Hofstadter, and Badiou, this non-reductive materialism is a self-eliminative one (in the sense of natural materiality as auto-negating *qua* canceling of its own dictates) in which the "I" is a "strange loop" (or loophole[56]) ensconced within a nature from which has been "subtracted" this nature's fantasized strength (i.e., its hallucinated deterministic rule as an inescapable, all-powerful tyrant). Through this approach, the "I" of autonomous subjectivity is not added to nature as some sort of supplementary super-nature, but arrived at instead through withdrawing things traditionally misattributed to nature.

What about *Anthropology from a Pragmatic Point of View*? The least one can state is that the letter of Kant's text is ambiguous enough to render Žižek's presentation of it in his response to me contestable, although admittedly defensible (a related Kantian essay, his "Speculative Beginning of Human History" of 1786, touches upon these same ambiguities[57]). On the one hand, Kant overtly claims that the passions for freedom and sex are innate ("*natürlichen*," rather than "acquired" [*erworbenen*]) to human nature.[58] This detail goes against the grain of Žižek's reading, in that the *Leidenschaft für Freiheit* is counted amongst those features which humans are endowed with by nature, instead of this being bequeathed to them by a neither-natural-nor-cultural (I am tempted uncharitably to employ the adjective "super-natural") "x." On the other hand, two additional details testify in favor of the interpretation upon which Žižek relies. First, in the footnote referring to the example of infants, Kant describes this always-already present sense of autonomy as "a vague idea (or an analogous representation)" ("*einer dunkelen Idee [oder dieser analogen Vorstellung]*")[59] – in Kant's philosophical universe, an innate *Idee* or *Vorstellung* suggests something different from a naturally instinctual animal impulse – that "evolves together with the animal nature" ("*sich mit der Tierheit zugleich entwickele*")[60] as developmentally parallel-yet-distinct from this nature. Second, in a move Žižek mirrors in his above-mentioned reference to Lear on sexuality, Kant goes on to stipulate that human passion, including those innate ones for freedom and sex, cannot be conflated with rudimentary animal inclination (*Reigung*).[61] As does Lear regarding sexuality (and Fichte regarding the not-I, for that matter), Kant deploys an argument whose basic structural logic is that whatever is dis-identified with as other than the same or the self (passion as apparently animalistic inclination, or Fichte's non-me and Lear's seemingly natural sexuality) can manifest itself as such only in and through its mediated constitution within the framework of scaffolding established by the same or the self (understanding [*Verstand*] and reason [*Vernunft*], or the Fichtean I and the Learian denaturalized, peculiarly-human psyche). In short, the other-than-human can be what it is not as an *an sich*, but solely thanks to being a correlate of already-there humanity. Without pushing the *Anthropology* itself on the tensions internal to its proclamations, suffice it for now to say that while the facets of it amenable to the Žižek replying to me are not problematic for an idealist like Kant (or Fichte), they ought to be deeply troubling for a materialist. When Žižek qualifies the death drive as "meta-physical,"[62] maybe he should be taken more literally than he might mean to be.

Curiously, in his subsequent recourse to Hegel's *The Philosophy of History*, Žižek winds up, despite his adamant recurrent self-identifications as a dyed-in-the-wool Hegelian, wielding the earlier-glossed Kantian-Fichtean-Learian logic to counter both Hegel and me (Colletti again comes to mind at this juncture). In the beginning of Žižek's turn to Hegel here, it sounds as though he has this post-Kantian German idealist merely reiterating what he imputes to Kant apropos there allegedly being something more-than-natural inherent and internal to human nature itself (specifically, the zero-level void of a monstrous, perverse excess of enflamed free will operative from the get-go).[63] However, three Hegel scholars whose work Žižek greatly admires – these three are Gérard Lebrun (his 1972 *La patience du Concept: Essai sur le Discours hégélien* is one of Žižek's favorite books on Hegel), Malabou (with her *The Future of Hegel: Plasticity, Temporality and Dialectic*), and Robert Pippin (his 1989 *Hegel's Idealism: The Satisfactions of Self-Consciousness* lends crucial support to Žižek's depiction of the Kant-Hegel relationship[64]) – all would take issue with attributing to Hegel a Kantian-style anti-naturalism according to which an underived supernatural surplus originally dwells within nature as an inherent potential transcendentally responsible for the effective existence of an utterly non-natural, autonomous subject.[65] What is more, even within the passages from the "Introduction" to *The Philosophy of History* Žižek cites, Hegel is unambiguous in his racist references to African "savages": They are spoken of as "natural man in his completely wild and untamed state" (*"natürlichen Menschen in seiner ganzen Wildheit und Unbändigkeit"*),[66] as hopelessly submerged in the violent stasis of a pre-historical "Natural condition" (*"Naturzustand"*).[67] Hence, they are not depicted by Hegel in quite the same guise as Žižek's Kant of the *Anthropology* characterizes human babies. Moreover, Hegel would be loathe to allow for insinuations risking an equivocation between this sort of "state of nature" and freedom proper.

But, something very interesting comes to light if one provisionally entertains Žižek's reading of Hegel's *The Philosophy of History* in conjunction with particular statements to be found within the pages of this text's "Introduction." Therein, Hegel remarks that "Spirit is at war with itself" (*"So ist der Geist in ihm selbst sich entgegen"*).[68] For the version of psychoanalytically influenced Žižekian materialism I defend in many other places (and defend on this occasion against what I perceive as momentary non-materialist deviations on the part of Žižek himself), nature too (i.e., the not-All material universe of physical beings) could be described as "at war with itself." As Zupančič observes, "a crucial lesson of materialism ... refers to the inconsistencies and contradictions of matter itself."[69] Prior to this observation, she notes in her study of comedy that "comedy's frequent reduction of man to (his) nature makes a further comic point about nature itself: nature is far from being as 'natural' as we might think, but is itself driven by countless contradictions and discrepancies."[70] Her point is pertinent in this setting too, and she elegantly articulates an idea shared by her, me,[71] Žižek, Lear,[72] and, for instance, the cognitivist philosopher of mind Metzinger.[73] All five of us generally agree that naturalizing human beings entails a reciprocal denaturalization of natural being – and this because the effort to render the strangenesses of subjectivity immanent to nature forces a radical recasting of fundamental, proto-theoretical images and ideas of nature itself (that is, if, as per a not-entirely-anti-naturalist materialism, nature is taken to be both the wellspring and enveloping environs of human subjects, containing such beings, these *parlêtres*, as internal to itself). So, in blending Hegel's ethnocentric comments about the undomesticated volatility of natural-as-ahistorical Africa with Žižek's loose appropriation of Hegelian nature as per *The Philosophy of History*, one arrives at the following synthesis: Nature itself, "red in tooth and claw," is an anarchic battlefield lacking harmony, stability, wholeness, and so on; in other words, it is anything but a cosmic unity of synchronized spheres placidly co-existing with one another. For a dialectical tradition running from Hegel through Marx, Freud, Mao, and up to Žižek (himself avowedly influenced by these predecessors), conflictual heterogeneity, instead of peaceful homogeneity, is to be discovered even within the most basic substrates of material being.[74]

Hegel himself voices some fascinatingly suggestive pronouncements about nature in *The Philosophy of History*. In its "Introduction," he asserts, "Mere nature is too weak to keep its genera and species pure, when conflicting with alien elementary influences" ("*Die Ohnmacht der Natur vermag ihre allgemeinen Klassen und Gattungen nicht gegen andere elementarische Momente festzuhalten*")[75] (in his compressed outline of the *Encyclopedia* project, Hegel talks similarly about the "weakness of the concept" exhibited by the chaotic proliferating of earthly life bursting forth out of the fecund soil of nature[76]). He later goes on to say, in the paragraph opening the treatment of the "Geographical Basis of History," that:

> Nature should not be rated too high nor too low ... awakening consciousness takes its rise surrounded by natural influences alone (*nur in der Natur*), and every development of it is the reflection of Spirit back upon itself in opposition to the immediate, unreflected character of mere nature. Nature is therefore one element in this antithetic abstracting process; Nature is the first standpoint from which man can gain freedom within himself, and this liberation must not be rendered difficult by natural obstructions. Nature, as contrasted with Spirit, is a quantitative mass, whose power must not be so great as to make its single force omnipotent (*allmächtig*).[77]

Without the time to do anything close to exegetical justice to Hegel's philosophy, these lines are quoted here in order to claim Hegel as a precursor of my Žižek-inspired materialism of a weak nature (elsewhere, I go into much greater detail with respect to *die Ohnmacht der Natur* in Hegel's *Naturphilosophie*[78]). Likewise, the Žižek with whom I do not disagree can be seen characteristically wearing a Hegelian badge with fierce pride at various moments in his contemporary writings, such as when he states, "*spirit is part of nature*, and can occur/arise only through a monstrous self-affliction (distortion, *derangement*) of nature,"[79] and, "what is 'Spirit' at its most elementary? The 'wound' of nature."[80] As both Pippin (as cited earlier) and Žižek[81] justly maintain, Hegelian Spirit is not a substantial, noun-like thing akin to the Cartesian *res cogitans* as a positivized being, entity, or object. Rather, *Geist* is a kinetic, verb-like process. Moreover, this non-substantial dynamism of negativity, as a movement of denaturalization giving rise to complex subject-beings whose complexity escapes and disrupts control by the laws and mechanisms of natural materialities, is entirely immanent to nature itself[82] – with the latter thus being envisioned in Hegelian philosophy as an internally self-sundering substance set against itself ("*selbst sich entgegen*").

What Hegel terms the "impotence" or "weakness" of the natural provides, as a contingent material condition of possibility, the cracks and fissures of elbow room for the immanent transcendence of nature by Spirit as more-than-material autonomous subjectivity still embedded in, but not governed by, its physical ground(s). And, even if, measured against the standards of post-Baconian scientific method, Hegel was presciently right for the wrong speculative reasons, he nevertheless was right. To take just one set of cutting-edge scientific sub-domains among others, non-reductive versions of evolutionary psychology and meme theory (put forward by such thinkers as Richard Dawkins,[83] Susan Blackmore,[84] Dennett,[85] and Keith Stanovich[86]) share in common an unconscious Hegelianism in the form of an underlying dialectical thesis to the effect that, to lean on Stanovich's language in particular, humans are nature-created Frankensteins who can and do rebel against their creator, a creator without sufficient power either to forestall this rebellion in advance or quash it after its outburst so as to rein these disobedient offspring back under the yoke of defied old authority. The sciences themselves are beginning to show that such incarnations of the notion of nature as evolution and genes are, as Hegel would put it, too weak, too powerless (*ohnmächtig*), to dictate the course of lives with an unwavering iron fist.[87] Human subjects are living proof that this imagined omnipotent big Other, this idol, of an outdated, bankrupt, and scientifically falsified scientism has, in fact, clay feet.

In the closing sentences of his reply to my piece "The Misfeeling of What Happens," Žižek, after the above-mentioned invocation of Lear on sexuality, corrects both Hegel and me. He contends:

> from the Freudian standpoint, Hegel has to be immanently criticized here: it is not just that sexuality is the animal substance which is then 'sublated' into civilized modes and rituals, gentrified, disciplined, etc. – the excess itself of sexuality which threatens to explode the 'civilized' constraints, sexuality as unconditional Passion, is the result of Culture ... In this way, the civilization/culture retroactively posits/transforms its own natural presuppositions: culture retroactively 'denaturalizes' nature itself, and this is what Freud called the Id, libido. So, back to Johnston, this retroactive excess of de-naturalized nature is missing in the image he proposes of a gradual cultural 'mediation' of nature.[88]

I am not necessarily committed to a gradualist perspective as regards emergent denaturalization (if anything, I am more inclined in the direction of a "punctuated equilibrium" model *à la* Niles Eldredge and Stephen Jay Gould[89] – as LeDoux hints, evolution does not exclude revolution[90]). Anyhow, that aside, with reference to the third session of Lacan's fourth seminar, a session entitled by

Miller "The Signifier and the Holy Spirit,"[91] Žižek articulates this same line of thought in a separate text:

> the Holy Ghost stands for the symbolic order as that which cancels (or, rather, suspends) the entire domain of 'life' – lived experience, the libidinal flux, the wealth of emotions, or, to put it in Kant's terms, the 'pathological': when we locate ourselves within the Holy Ghost, we are transubstantiated, we enter another life beyond the biological one.[92]

Žižek's recourse to blatantly religious language in this specific vein (including Kant's thinly sublimated, barely secularized version of such language) arguably is no accident or coincidence. Another of the intuitions informing my overall position can be conveyed as the thesis that, especially on the terrain of ideology, the Enlightenment tension between the materialism of (or shaped by) science and the idealism of religion (as theology, spiritualism, etc.) continues to face us as a "point" in Badiou's precise sense as per *Logics of Worlds*.[93] That is to say, confronted side-by-side, the *Weltanschauungen* of scientificity and religiosity contain, in however concealed or obfuscated a state, a fundamental and unavoidable either/or choice between mutually exclusive commitments (this assertion being faithfully in line with Engels, Lenin, and Freud, among others). In my view, the Žižek who conjures up an occult "x" to account for there being free subjects (and, in so doing, who relies upon a still-Christian Kant more than anyone else) is forced to embrace flagrantly theological terminology. By contrast, I insist, in fidelity to another, systematically materialist Žižek, the one portrayed in *Žižek's Ontology*, that no such mysterious Third can or should be posited; this sort of Third is ideologically risky in addition to being theoretically gratuitous. Going a step further, I would even venture to propose that, echoing Churchill's overused one-liner, psychoanalysis and the physical sciences are the worst bases for philosophical materialism and leftist ideology critique except for all those others tried from time to time.

Before concluding this chapter, I have three responses to Žižek's critique of Hegel and me, apart from my answer to his question "Is it still possible to be a Hegelian today?" (my answer being that this really is possible for both him and me to a much greater extent than the Žižek of this specific back-and-forth between us seems to admit). First, it is unclear to me whether his non-Hegelian and purportedly Freudian (Freud's engagements with biology render this appeal to authority dubitable[94]) conception of the "cultural 'mediation' of nature" is epistemological, ontological, or both. I suspect that, given his general philosophical leanings as well as recent textual evidence,[95] Žižek intends to claim that the retroactive denaturalization of nature is ontological, namely, an *après-coup* "transubstantiation" that, as it were, goes all the way down, permeating and saturating nature through and through.

If Žižek's intention is indeed to posit a real cultural-symbolic mediation of nature in which the latter, in its material actuality, is thoroughly and exhaustively digested by the former, then this leads into my second response to him. Pointing back to a query asked at the outset of this chapter, Žižek's indictments of me within the parameters of a discussion in which the rapport between philosophical materialism and the physical sciences (especially the life sciences) is under dispute raise the issue of whether or not the theoretical ought to be constrained methodologically by the empirical. Žižek speaks as though all of the above could be adjudicated without leaving the philosopher's armchair. But, wording my objection to this in a Hegelian style, the history of philosophy, in its development in tandem with other disciplines and practices, bears witness to a dynamic within which the mobile line of division between the empirical and the theoretical is a distinction internal to the empirical itself. Put differently, problems previously able to be posed only at the level of the philosophical/ theoretical often come to be grasped in time as properly posed at the level of the scientific/empirical. As already stated in "The Misfeeling of What Happens," I am convinced that the question of whether or not denaturalization, so to speak, hits rock bottom without remainder is, for a materialism not without its naturalism, both a genuine question as well as one that can and should admit empirical adjudication as an indispensable ingredient in the process of its attempted resolution.[96]

My third response to Žižek is that the Kantian-Fichtean logic informing his replies to me brings him into proximity with a type of anti-naturalist idealism he himself has been appropriately careful to avoid in other instances.[97] As he stipulates in *Tarrying with the Negative* (one of his very best philosophical works), "simply because the opposition between nature and culture is always-already culturally overdetermined, i.e., that no particular element can be isolated as 'pure nature,' does not mean that 'everything is culture.' 'Nature' qua Real remains the unfathomable X which resists cultural 'gentrification.'"[98] Although I have reservations with respect to the supposed unfathomability of this "x," I enthusiastically endorse the rest of the content of this quotation and want to remind Žižek of it. I would tack on that, as hypothesized in "The Misfeeling of What Happens," it is less problematic and more plausible for the kind of materialist ontology I think is most valid and legitimate to speculate that the real genesis of autonomous subjectivity, of the *parlêtre*-as-$, splits the material ground of its being into both the first Real of a nature undigested by cultural mediation and the second Real of a nature mediated by culture (this second Real being exemplified by the notions of nature and sexuality Žižek employs as examples against me). Žižek's own subtle and detailed delineations of the Lacanian register of the Real encourage such a move to be made (particularly his valuable distinction between the "Real-as-presupposed" and the "Real-as-posed").[99] In short, I refuse what I see as a false dichotomy, a specious forced choice. As in psychoanalytic interpretation as linked to the crucial analytic concept of overdetermination, when one is faced with the choice between "this or that," the right answer, an answer refusing one of the key premises of the question itself, frequently is "Yes, please!" (i.e., it is not one or the other, but both).

The Žižek with whom I feel the deepest solidarity is alive and well today. Recently, he proclaims:

> to be an actual naturalist is not to subscribe to necessary fiction, but to really believe in materialism. It is . . . not enough to insist that Kant and Hegel have to teach us something about the realm of normativity which takes place in the wider domain of the realm of nature. It is, on the contrary, important to re-appropriate German Idealism to a fuller extent. If discourse, representation, mind, or thought in general cannot consistently be opposed to the substantial real which is supposed to be given beforehand, independent of the existence of concept-mongering creatures, then we have to bite the bullet of idealism: *we need a concept of the world or the real which is capable of accounting for the replication of reality within itself.*[100]

Along related lines, he declares in a contemporaneous text that "we are subjects only through a monstrous bodily distortion."[101] In resonance with these remarks of Žižek's (ones subsequently

echoed in *Less Than Nothing*[102]), the transcendental materialism of a weak nature I advocate, itself profoundly marked by his
interlinked ontology and theory of the subject, gestures at a vision
of nature as itself monstrous, as self-distorting (insofar as explaining the emergence out of nature of humans as deranged monsters
rebelling against nature requires a much weirder picture of nature
than standard, traditional species of naturalism usually offer).
This vision has no need (nor does Žižek, despite his reaction to
me) for imagining the presence of a supernatural excess/surplus as
a neither-natural-nor-cultural third power miraculously sparking
the *ex nihilo* irruption of peculiarly human subjectivities running
amok down paths of denaturalization. Self-sundering natural-
material substance is auto-disruptive enough to account for these
explosions of unrest, of the restlessness of negativity. Where I
perhaps go further than Žižek, beyond laboring to revivify German
idealism, is in the amount of explanatory jurisdiction I grant to the
empirical sciences (particularly biology and its offshoots, given my
interests) in the struggle to construct a truly contemporary materialism with both philosophical and political ramifications.

Not only do I wholeheartedly second Žižek's cry to "repeat
Lenin"[103] – for theoretical in addition to political materialism, I
think the moment is ripe to call for repeating Engels[104] (as well
as the Mao of "On Contradiction"[105]). *Contra* Lukács' still-
prevailing condemnatory verdict on any "dialectics of nature,"[106]
one quite convincingly could maintain that the main flaw of Engels'
efforts to conquer the territories of the sciences and claim them on
behalf of Marxist materialism is that these efforts were ahead of
their time, that the sciences of his era were not yet ready to receive
these aggressive overtures. But, starting with such mid-twentieth-
century scientific breakthroughs as Donald O. Hebb's research on
the psycho-physiological mechanisms of learning,[107] the biological
sciences have managed to "weaken" empirically their image of
(human) nature (in the precise sense of natural weakness I specified previously). Through this self-induced weakening, empirical,
experimental studies of the living material foundations of humanity have given us, in forms like neuroplasticity and epigenetics,
the wiggle room we need and want for a materialist ontology of
freedom (such as that desired by Žižek). These scientists are falling
into our hands through the cunning of their own reason.

Colletti identifies the Italian Renaissance thinker Giovanni Pico
della Mirandola as an ancestral precursor of Marx in terms of the

foundations of the latter's idea of human beings as "generic"[108] (i.e., as natureless by nature, born faceless and taking on plastic visages via the labor-mediated, historicizing subject-object dialectic). Agamben also refers to Pico della Mirandola,[109] similarly recognizing the radicality of this Renaissance author's humanism (as a humanism of anonymous humanity, akin to what Žižek detects in Descartes' *Cogito*[110]) announced in his 1486 oration "On the Dignity of Man"[111] (in relation to Sartre, Badiou, despite what he owes to Althusser and structuralism, recognizes in a Sartrean humanism[112] resonating with Colletti's Renaissance-indebted Marx a radicalism allowing it to converge with such an opposite as the anti-humanism of Foucault[113]). In the nineteenth century, aspects of German romanticism, Marxism (specifically, Marx's analyses of industrial mechanization), and existentialism herald subsequent critiques of post-Galilean scientificity as limited, nihilistic, and vulgar vis-à-vis the multifaceted richness of lived human experience. By the twentieth century, the majority of Continental philosophers, with such odd bedfellows as Husserl, Lukács, Heidegger, Sartre, and Adorno to the fore, become suspicious of, if not utterly hostile to, the empirical, experimental sciences of modernity. Both mathematized science generally and the life sciences specifically come to be viewed as lamentably reductive and objectifying; from this perspective, a perspective shared by a number of figures on both the right and left sides of the political spectrum, these disciplines are seen as incorrigibly complicit with a range of afflictions plaguing modern societies and their inhabitants. In defiance of European philosophy's long-standing, deeply entrenched aversion to the "hard sciences" perceived as diametrically opposed, inassimilable adversaries, the hour has arrived for philosophical materialism to storm the gates of these sciences. Whether the scientists themselves are aware of it or not, their fields have been primed by them to receive the inscription of a portrait of human subjectivity whose first glimmerings already are to be glimpsed in a fifteenth-century ode inaugurating Renaissance humanism. The life sciences are no longer the enemy of the dignity Pico della Mirandola lyrically and lavishly praises. However wittingly or unwittingly, they have become its ally, the very ground for a scientifically informed materialism incorporating the radical humanism (maybe even superhumanism) of Sartrean-style atheist existentialism. Both humanists and materialists have every reason to be unshakably confident. The future definitely is ours.

Notes

1. Johnston 2013j.
2. Johnston 2008d: xxiii–xxvi, 16, 74, 77, 81, 208–9, 236, 269–87; Johnston 2009a: 79; Johnston 2007b: 3–20; Žižek 2012: 144–5, 197, 906–7.
3. Johnston 2008d: 208; Žižek 2012: 11–13, 15–16, 185, 263–4, 282–4, 378–9, 473, 712; Balmès 1999: 106–7.
4. Johnston 2008d: xxv, 65–6, 77–9, 92–3, 106–16, 168–80.
5. Žižek 2009c: 240.
6. Ibid.: 287.
7. Žižek 2009b: 82.
8. Johnston 2013j.
9. Žižek 2011c: 406–8.
10. *SVI*: 2/11/59; *SIX*: 4/4/62; *SX*: 105.
11. Johnston 2010b: 76–100.
12. Žižek 2010b: 102–5.
13. Rogers 2001: 2–3, 5, 20, 23–4, 47–8, 68, 97–8; Ansermet 2002: 377–8, 383; LeDoux 2002: 2–3, 5, 9, 12, 20, 66–7, 91, 296; Solms and Turnbull 2002: 218, 220–2; Damasio 2003: 162–4, 173–4; Changeux 2004: 32–3, 207–8; Libet 2004: 5; Jablonka and Lamb 2005: 1–2, 5–7, 58–60, 62–5, 67, 72–5, 77–8, 109–11, 144–5, 160–1, 166, 176, 189, 191, 193, 204–5, 220–3, 226, 238, 285–6, 319, 344, 372, 378–80; Kandel 2005a: 21; Kandel 2005b: 41–3, 47; Kandel 2005c: 150; Ansermet and Magistretti 2007: xvi, 8, 10, 239.
14. Johnston 2006: 34–55; Johnston 2007b: 14; Johnston 2008b: 166–88; Johnston 2008d: 270–3; Johnston 2011e: 159–79; Johnston 2012b: 105–21; Johnston 2012a: 23–52; Johnston 2013d: 73–210; Johnston 2013i.
15. Johnston 2005c: xxxi–xxxii, 340; Johnston 2008d: 260–1; Johnston 2011e: 159–79; Johnston 2013d: 162–84.
16. Althusser 2009b: 106–8, 110–12, 114–21.
17. Linden 2007: 2–3, 5–7, 21–4, 26, 245–6; Marcus 2008: 6–16, 161–3; Varela, Thompson, and Rosch 1991: 106–7; Damasio 1999: 331; LeDoux 1996: 105; LeDoux 2002: 31; Panksepp 1998: 147; Johnston 2013d: 175–8.
18. Althusser 2009a: 61–2; Althusser 2005a: 14–15; Althusser 2005b: 170–1; Althusser 2003: 185–6.
19. Balmès 1999: 122–3.
20. Johnston 2008d: 188–90.

21. Žižek 2010b: 102.
22. Ibid.: 102.
23. Johnston 2013d: 73–210.
24. Žižek 2010b: 102.
25. Johnston 2010b: 76–100.
26. Damasio 1994: 130, 185, 187–8; Damasio 1999: 218–19, 222; Damasio 2003: 72; LeDoux 2002: 197–8, 203–4; Johnston 2013d: 185–210.
27. Žižek 2010b: 102.
28. Žižek 2008a: 9–29.
29. Malabou 2007: 59–60, 85, 338–9; Malabou 2009d: 33, 75–7, 83–4; Malabou 2013b: 211–24.
30. Malabou 2005: 8–9, 73–4, 192–3; Malabou 2008: 5–6, 8, 12, 17, 29–30, 71–2; Malabou 2010: 8–9, 59.
31. Žižek 2010b: 102.
32. Malabou 2009a: 9–10; Malabou 2009b: 213–18, 227–8; Malabou 2009c: 229–31, 233, 235–7.
33. Johnston 2008d: 165–7, 171–4; Johnston 2007b: 4–7, 9–12, 16–17.
34. Zupančič 2008: 53–4.
35. Johnston 2008c: 39.
36. Johnston 2010b: 96–7.
37. Kant 1978: 176; Žižek 1997c: 237; Johnston 2008d: 180–1.
38. Žižek 2010b: 103.
39. Žižek 2009d: 96–7.
40. Ibid.: 98.
41. Žižek 2009e: 127.
42. Colletti 1979: 59–60, 90–4, 103, 118–22, 192, 213–16.
43. Žižek 2004b: 134–5; Žižek 2006a: 217.
44. McGinn 1999: 43–6, 68–76, 101, 104, 197.
45. Johnston 2012b: 119.
46. Johnston 2008b: 182–88; Johnston 2011e: 159–79.
47. Johnston 2008d: 122, 169–71, 180, 208–9, 234, 236, 272, 285–7; Johnston 2007b: 18–19.
48. Lacan 2006c: 75; Johnston 2008d: 53–4.
49. SXI: 268.
50. Žižek 2010b: 104–5; Lear 2005: 19, 75.
51. Lear 1990: 13–14, 146; Lear 2000: 80–1, 84–5; Žižek 2003: 70–1; Johnston 2008d: 186–7; Johnston 2011e: 159–60.
52. Johnston 2005c: 123–54, 175–83, 237, 330–1, 368–9.
53. Žižek 2008a: 19.

54. Johnston 2008d: 109–10, 120–2.
55. Johnston 2011e: 159–79.
56. Johnston 2008d: 112–13, 167–76, 186–7, 195–6, 208, 236.
57. Kant 1983: 49–51; Johnston 2005c: 333–5, 340–1.
58. Kant 1917: 267–8; Kant 1978: 175; Johnston 2008d: 180–1.
59. Kant 1917: 269; Kant 1978: 176.
60. Kant 1917: 269; Kant 1978: 176.
61. Kant 1917: 269–70; Kant 1978: 177.
62. Žižek 2009b: 92–3; Johnston 2005c: 368–75.
63. Žižek 2010b: 103–5.
64. Pippin 1989: 6–7, 16–17, 33–5, 79, 120–1, 132, 225, 248; Žižek 1993: 265–6; Žižek 1999a: 290.
65. Lebrun 1972: 145–6; Malabou 2005: 26–7, 37–8, 45, 73–4, 192–3; Pippin 2008: 14–15, 36–64, 112–13.
66. Hegel 1970c: 122; Hegel 1956: 93.
67. Hegel 1970c: 129; Hegel 1956: 98–9.
68. Hegel 1970c: 76; Hegel 1956: 55.
69. Zupančič 2008: 47.
70. Ibid.: 7.
71. Johnston 2007b: 4; Johnston 2008d: 200–1, 240–1; Johnston 2012b: 119–20.
72. Lear 1990: 210–11.
73. Metzinger 2009: 40, 215–16.
74. Johnston 2008b: 172–82; Johnston 2013i.
75. Hegel 1970c: 103; Hegel 1956: 65.
76. Hegel 1990: §292 [196].
77. Hegel 1970c: 121; Hegel 1956: 80.
78. Johnston 2012c: 103–57; Johnston 2014.
79. Žižek 2009d: 117.
80. Žižek 2009b: 71.
81. Žižek 2009b: 71–2; Žižek 2011b: 219–20.
82. Žižek 2012: 186, 188–9, 239, 291, 298, 354, 373, 401, 416, 441, 459–61, 740–1.
83. Dawkins 1976: 207–8, 213, 215.
84. Blackmore 1999: 79–80, 99–100, 235.
85. Dennett 2003: 90–1, 93.
86. Stanovich 2004: xii, 12–13, 15–16, 20–2, 25, 28, 67, 82–4, 142, 247.
87. Johnston 2008d: 174–6, 181, 203–8; Johnston 2011e: 159–79.
88. Žižek 2010b: 104–5.
89. Eldredge and Gould 1972: 82–115.

90. LeDoux 2002: 198.
91. *SIV*: 41–58; Johnston 2011e: 170–5.
92. Žižek 2011b: 217–18.
93. Badiou 2009b: 399–401, 403–35, 437–47, 577, 591; Johnston 2009a: 62–6, 71–5, 80.
94. Johnston 2011e: 159–63.
95. Žižek 2007a: 138–9; Žižek 2008b: 435, 440, 442; Žižek 2009a: 159; Žižek 2009b: 70; Žižek 2009d: 104.
96. Johnston 2010b: 76–100.
97. Johnston 2008d: 16–20, 149–52.
98. Žižek 1993: 129.
99. Johnston 2008d: 18–19, 145–61.
100. Gabriel and Žižek 2009: 13.
101. Žižek 2009c: 277.
102. Žižek 2012: 333–4, 338–9, 344–6, 350, 354, 356, 358, 410.
103. Johnston 2009a: 115–16.
104. Engels 1959: 19–22, 35–9; Engels 1940: 1–34, 279–310; Johnston 2011c: 141–82; Johnston 2014.
105. Mao 2007: 67–102; Johnston 2008b: 170–6.
106. Lukács 1971: 24.
107. Hebb 1949: 63, 70; Johnston 2008c: 41.
108. Colletti 1979: 234, 238–41, 243–6.
109. Agamben 2004: 29–30; Johnston 2008d: 114–16.
110. Žižek 1998: 3–4, 6–7; Johnston 2008d: 11–12, 21–2, 41–3, 55–8, 80, 166–7, 187, 231, 265.
111. Pico della Mirandola 1998: 4–5.
112. Sartre 1948: 27–8, 42–3; Johnston 2008c: 41–2.
113. Badiou 2007: 165–78.

7

Spirit Is a Quark:
Quantum Physics with Žižek

The ongoing debate between Žižek and me, at least as I perceive it, pivots around the question of how to situate materialism, on the one hand, in relation to naturalism and the sciences, on the other hand. Whatever our disagreements, we hold a number of commitments in common, including a fidelity to certain aspects and versions of a robust, ambitious Hegelianism. Thanks to these common commitments, my criticisms of Žižek tend to be immanent (rather than external) ones. This tendency will continue to prevail here too.

Whereas the previous chapter focused largely on the link (or lack thereof) between materialism and naturalism, this chapter addresses the relationship(s) between materialism and the natural sciences. I understand "naturalism" as a term for all those philosophical perspectives according to which "nature," varyingly construed depending on the specific view in question, is a crucial, foundational dimension of philosophy and its assorted explanations of pertinent structures and phenomena. As seen (Chapter 6), Žižek and I have our differences about precisely how naturalism ought to be envisioned. As will be seen below, we also prioritize different natural sciences as the privileged partner of a contemporary (transcendental) materialism: quantum physics for Žižek and biology for me. In what follows, I will both problematize Žižek's philosophical annexations of quantum physics through an immanent critique of them on the basis of Žižekian principles as well as justify my favoring of the life sciences in connection with a materialist theory of subjectivity (with Žižek and I jointly pursuing such a theory).

At the current juncture of our conversation, I find myself facing Žižek's modified redeployment of his previous appropriations of quantum physics elaborated elsewhere (these appropriations are elaborated primarily in the third and final chapter of his 1996 book *The Indivisible Remainder: An Essay on Schelling and Related Matters*, a chapter entitled "Quantum Physics with Lacan"). *Contra* my transcendental materialist concern with tying a carefully qualified quasi-naturalist theory of subjectivity partially to life-scientific foundations, he now argues that the physics of the unimaginably small, instead of the biology of comparatively much larger mid-sized beings and processes, can and should play a singularly special anchoring role in relation to a viable account of the subject as conceived at the intersection of German idealist philosophy, Freudian-Lacanian psychoanalysis, and the natural sciences of today.

According to my immanent critique to be laid out below, Žižek's mode of recourse to quantum physics not only is questionable on general philosophical grounds – it also is awkwardly at odds with the distinctive core tenets of his fundamental ontology. The peak of this self-subverting irony is the fact that the theoretical form of his extensions of quantum physics as a universal economy *qua* ubiquitous, all-encompassing structural nexus (one capable of covering human subjects, among many other bigger-than-sub-atomic things) is in unsustainable tension with the ontological content he claims to find divulged within this same branch of physics (i.e., being itself as detotalized and inconsistent). After replying directly to Žižek's newest addition to our back-and-forth, I will return to his earlier uses (and, arguably, abuses) of quantum physics (especially as contained in "Quantum Physics with Lacan") so as to reassess his materialist deployments of natural science in relation to his contemporary positions taken in the context of our still-unfolding debate.

Before problematizing "Quantum Physics with Žižek" then (1996) and now, I will begin by summarizing and commenting on Žižek's most recent response to me. Therein, he gets well-and-truly underway thus:

> Today, THE scientific discovery which needs philosophical rethinking is quantum physics – how are we to interpret its ontological implications AND avoid the double trap of superficial pragmatic empiricism and obscurantist idealism ('mind creates reality')? Lenin's *Materialism and Empirio-Criticism* has to be thoroughly rewritten – the first thing to do is to abandon the old naïve notion of the existence of fully constituted material reality as the sole true reality outside our minds.

This reality is 'all' and, as such, relying on the overlooked exception of its transcendental constitution. The minimal definition of materialism hinges on the admission of a *gap between what Schelling called Existence and Ground of Existence*: prior to fully existent reality, there is a chaotic non-all proto-reality, a pre-ontological virtual fluctuation of not yet fully-constituted real. This pre-ontological real is what Badiou calls pure multiplicity, in contrast to the level of appearances, which is the level of reality constituted by the transcendental horizon of a world.[1]

I certainly agree that the past century's worth of advances in theoretical physics demand ample additional intellectual labor on the part of philosophers (especially Continentalists typically averse to the mathematical and the scientific). However, I take issue with the "THE" here, namely, with the assertion that a single sub-branch of the natural sciences enjoys a unique privilege for philosophical reflection of a materialist kind. My objection to this is not merely a minor complaint resting on nothing more than the underlining of the simple fact that there are many other scientific disciplines and domains besides quantum physics. A contention central to my reply to Žižek in this particular installment of our extended exchange is that his manner of privileging this one science is incompatible with the fundaments of his ontology and corresponding conception of subjectivity.

The second half of the preceding quotation amounts to a restatement by Žižek of his basic ontological *Weltanschauung*. Mixing Schellingian, Lacanian, and Badiouian terms, he speaks of the Real *Grund* of a *Logos*-eluding zero-level presupposed by onto-*logy*, a ground that is, in itself, a detotalized, un-unified jumble of heterogeneous pluralities and proliferations. Incidentally, Badiou would reject Žižek's equation of the "inconsistent multiplicities" of being *qua* being with quantum-physical structures and dynamics; for the former, his set-theoretic ontology of *l'être en tant qu'être* is put forward as different-in-kind from any and every ontic discipline bearing upon determinate beings, including mathematized physics, with its applied (instead of pure) mathematics. However, I am supportive of Žižek's healthy materialist impulse to root his ontology partially in scientific soil (elsewhere, I cast doubt upon whether Badiou, in light of proclaiming himself to be an ardent materialist, can rely upon a Heideggerian understanding of ontological difference licensing an unqualified, non-dialectical denial of there being any potential ontological implications flowing from the empirical, experimental sciences[2]). But, I believe that Žižek is insufficiently careful in moving between scientific and ontological dimensions on this occasion.

One of the axioms of Žižek's ontology is a philosophical generalization, an appropriation and redeployment, of Lacan's dictum according to which, "The big Other does not exist" (*Le grand Autre n'existe pas*).[3] Within the most minimal of its strata, being is, for Žižek, the barred Real of a non-All not-One (to put it in hybrid Lacanian-Badiouian locution). Or, in other words borrowed from Žižek's German idealist inspirers, the primal *Urgrund* of reality is the groundlessness of an *Ungrund*, an abyssal vortex of out-of-synch entities and forces saturated with antagonisms, conflicts, gaps, negativities, and so on. From a Žižekian standpoint, any portrayal of existence as ultimately governed by a cosmic order, whether above or below, responsible for a harmonious coordination and integration of the entirety of existent objects and occurrences is tantamount to positing the One-All of a big Other (for example, a God-like Nature-with-a-capital-N as a Whole-sustaining homogeneous substance or bundle of eternal universal laws). Although his ontology forbids such a posit, Žižek is at risk of violating this very prohibition through the ways in which he mobilizes quantum physics. This danger of self-contradiction will become increasingly clear and evident shortly.

In his reply to me, Žižek soon proceeds to spell out some of what is required of a scientifically informed materialism. He declares:

> In its effort to grasp reality 'independently of me,' mathematized science erases me out of reality, i.e., it ignores (not the transcendental way I constitute reality, but) the way I am PART OF this reality. The true question is therefore: how do I (as the site where reality appears to itself) emerge in 'objective reality' (or, more pointedly, how can the universe of meaning arise in the meaningless Real). As materialists, we should take into account two criteria that an adequate answer should meet: (1) the answer should be really materialist, with no spiritualist cheating; (2) one should accept that the ordinary mechanistic-materialist notion of 'objective reality' will not do the job.[4]

I endorse almost everything said in these remarks, including the two stipulated criteria. But, looking at this passage in its surrounding context, I want to resist and call into question the move of tethering a materialist philosophical account of the genesis of subjectivity to an interpretation of quantum physics. To state the problem bluntly, Žižek, in flirting with the making of this move, teeters on the brink of falling into either reductive or analogical modes of thinking, both equally incompatible with the true systematic core of his interwoven ontology and theory of the subject.

The twin pitfalls of the reductive and the analogical, to be delineated further momentarily, are both opened up by Žižek's rather un-Žižekian apparent elevation of quantum physics to the status of an ontological master-matrix covering a massive range of being's scales (and not just this specific science's proper disciplinary domain limited to the tiny universes of the extremely small). In his response to me, Žižek makes ground-zero quantum materialization *ex nihilo*, creation arising from the nothingness of a vacuum or void, epitomize everything from the Being of Heidegger's fundamental ontology to drives as per Freudian-Lacanian psychoanalysis (the death drive first and foremost) and the delicate art of fierce socio-political struggle. With reference to the energetics of quantum systems, he asserts, "This is why 'there is something and not nothing': because, energetically, something is cheaper than nothing."[5] Having formulated this abstract ontological principle of economy on the basis of quantum physics, he then leaps into the psychical realm of analytic metapsychology, maintaining apropos the *Todestrieb* that "The paradox of the death drive is thus strictly homologous to that of the Higgs field: from the standpoint of libidinal economy, it is 'cheaper' for the system to repeatedly traverse the circle of drive than to stay at absolute rest."[6] I am of the opinion that Žižek's repeated exercises, here and elsewhere, in employing models taken from theoretical physics so as to elucidate aspects of Lacan's teachings are pedagogically brilliant and amazingly illuminating for anyone interested in grasping key Lacanian concepts.[7] But, however productively suggestive these cross-disciplinary comparisons might be, using "homologies" resting on broad, vague notions of "cheapness" and "energy" to facilitate effortless movement between the "economies" of the ontological, the natural, the libidinal, and the political seems as though it leads right back to the old onto-theological vision of being as an organic Whole of smoothly enmeshed microcosms and macrocosms, a seamless, enchained continuum of recurring patterns embedded within each other in a fractal-like fashion. Succinctly stated, Žižek's sweeping generalization of the "natural economy" of quantum physics courts the peril of a regressive return to the One-All of a big Other supposedly dismantled and banned by Žižekian ontology. Moreover, it brings him into the dubious intellectual company of the Roger Penrose who proposes a quantum-physicalist theory of mind.

The potential for Žižek inadvertently falling into reductivism already should be obvious by now. His selection of quantum physics in particular as the singularly privileged scientific terrain for renewed materialist speculation heightens the chances of stumbling into this theoretical dead-end. Many philosophical materialisms that see themselves as rooted in the "hard" sciences embrace monistic ontologies. Such monisms dictate that, when all is said and done, each and every level and layer of entities and events is expressive of nothing more than whatever the present-best physics of the smallest identified constituents of material reality hypothesizes regarding the purportedly ultimate building blocks of incarnate being. Everything boils down to matter at its most minimal (or, pointing back to Robert Boyle's seventeenth-century corpuscular and mechanical philosophy, one could speak of "Boyling" down). A pre-Kantian, pre-Hegelian, and Spinozistic-style subject-squashing determinism, anathema to a Žižek-inspired proponent of subjects' irreducible autonomy, is only a step or two away, if that. The choice of quantum physics as providing all-purpose cognitive maps for even the biggest and broadest tiers of existence carries with it this sort of unwanted baggage. Additionally, apart from the philosophical fact that reductivism's monism is fundamentally incompatible with Žižekian ontology despite Žižek's evidently unrestricted, free-wheeling extensions of explanatory constructs peculiar to the quantum kingdom of the very small, empirical and experimental constraints (particularly temporal and computational limitations) thwart any efforts whatsoever to carry out an exhaustively thorough reduction of the mid-sized structures and dynamics of human-scale reality to the unimaginably minuscule teeming multitudes of quantum objects and processes. A quantum-based reductivism is in practice impossible to substantiate, condemned to remain a topic of empty speculation straining in the direction of an intangible mirage of a profoundly harmonious universal arrangement of being and beings as a "Great Chain."

As for the status of the analogies Žižek proposes between quantum and other phenomena, these probably are not grounded on anything resembling the monistic reductivism remarked upon immediately above. Although I perceive Žižek's reliance on physics as luring him into the shady neighborhood of these types of scientistic ontologies, I am confident that, self-consciously faced with the looming prospect of this proximity, he would promptly flee from such neighbors by adamantly reaffirming his investment in a One-less ontology of not-Whole being devoid of overarching or undergirding big Others of whatever kind. However, this would be for Žižek to appeal to the same ontology I consider him as compromising his allegiance to through his analogical deployments of bits and pieces borrowed from quantum physics. As I have argued in other texts, the elaboration of a science-shaped materialist ontology of an Other-lacking barred Real is better served by something along the lines of philosopher of science Nancy Cartwright's theoretical landscape of a "dappled world," with Cartwright quite effectively casting a number of weighty doubts, both philosophical and scientific, on the presumed pride-of-place enjoyed in the eyes of many philosophers (Žižek clearly included) and scientists by the quantum-level physics of the microcosmic.[8]

But, if Žižek's quantum analogies are meant to be taken as rather looser homologies – this looseness is entailed by them not resting upon presupposed material continuities licensing, at least in principle, strict explanatory reductions of the larger to the smaller – then several significant questions must be asked and answered: Ontologically speaking, what, if any, hypothesized material forces and factors license comparisons connecting things sub-atomic to realities well above the threshold of the atomic? Epistemologically speaking, how can one know whether discerned resemblances prompting the drawing of analogies are really more than arbitrarily selected or created abstract patterns imaginatively superimposed upon the designated referents thus compared? Methodologically speaking, what principles and restrictions guide constructing certain analogies and not others? Žižek leaves queries of this sort unanswered. Unless and until he furnishes ontological, epistemological, and methodological justifications in support of his philosophical appropriations of quantum physics, they will remain somewhat suspect.

Given Žižek's Hegelianism in all its distinctiveness, a Hegelian problematization of his recourse to physics indeed would count as a far-from-insignificant immanent critique (and, to be mentioned as an aside, Hegel's thinking from his Jena period onward suggests that the only criticisms worth advancing are immanent ones[9]).

A door is opened for a Hegelian reply on my part when Žižek muses:

> what if we transpose ontological difference (the difference between entities and the 'nothingness' of the ontological horizon of their disclosure) into the Thing-in-itself, and (re)conceive it as the ontological incompleteness of reality (as quantum physics implicates)? What if we posit that 'things in themselves' emerge against the background of the Void or Nothingness, the way this Void is conceived in quantum physics, as the Void which is not just a negative void, but the void portent of all possible reality? This is the only truly consequent 'transcendental materialism' which is possible after the Kantian transcendental idealism. For a true dialectician, the ultimate mystery is not 'Why is there something instead of nothing?,' but 'Why is there nothing instead of something?': how is it that, the more we analyze reality, the more we found a void?[10]

Žižek's speculative extrapolation from quantum physics to fundamental ontology might qualify, on a certain construal, as one "truly consequent 'transcendental materialism'" – and, with this phrase, he signals that my own position is in the crosshairs at this moment – but I disagree that it is the "only" version of this materialist stance. In addition to me arguing that Žižek is driven into formulating his specific ontological framework starting first from a particular theory of the subject articulated at the intersection of German idealist philosophy and Lacanian analytic metapsychology,[11] the sub-title of *Žižek's Ontology* is *A Transcendental Materialist Theory of Subjectivity*. What I am getting at is that the genesis of the "something" of material being from the "nothing" of the immaterial void (and the persisting subsistence of the latter within the former) is one thing; the surfacing of subjects out of this thus-generated existent reality is another thing entirely. If Žižek intends for his abstract formal generalizations of quantum-physical phenomena to cover the issue of subjectivity (among a swarm of other issues), then he must supply sound materialist arguments, which I strongly believe cannot be supplied, to the effect that sub-atomic processes can and do resurface directly at scales of materiality (i.e., those at which it is appropriate to speak of minded agents) well above the threshold of the atomic. In other words, he would have to explain how and why quantum-level dynamics are not thoroughly diluted, transmuted, and/or effectively screened-

out at larger-sized levels of material reality. To echo the famous
assessment of phrenology in Hegel's *Phenomenology*,[12] the short
circuit of an infinite judgment along the lines of "Spirit is a quark"
would require supplementation by significant interpretive contortions and counter-intuitive acrobatics so as to amount to more
than the inelegant category mistake of an indefensible reduction or
analogy (an example of such speculative contortions and acrobatics is Hegel's interpretive dance with the phrenological judgment
"Spirit is a bone," a performance greatly appreciated by Žižek and
his close colleague Mladen Dolar[13]). Furthermore, the addition of
such supplements would carry one far beyond the circumscribed
confines of the proper epistemological and ontological jurisdictions of quantum physics itself.

Žižek refers countless times to Hegel's insistence, in the awe-
inspiring preface to the *Phenomenology*, on the (post-Spinoza,
anti-Schelling) necessity of "grasping and expressing the True, not
only as *Substance*, but equally as *Subject*" (*das Wahre nicht als
Substanz, sondern ebensosehr als* Subjekt *aufzufassen und auszudrücken*).[14] Transcendental materialism, at least as I conceive
it, strives to formulate a rigorously materialist and scientifically
responsible delineation of the emergence of, in Hegelese, spiritual
subjectivity from natural substance (incidentally, in the preceding
block quotation, Žižek invokes the idea of emergence, and he, like
me, knows full well of this notion-word's Archimedean position in
the theorizations of various life scientists who exhibit spontaneous
dialectical materialist sensibilities; what is more, the life-scientific
paradigm of strong emergentism consistent with the dialectics of
both Hegelianism and Marxism blocks anything like quantum-
physicalist reductivism and/or the *grand Autre* of an ubiquitous
natural economy of singular universality). At other times, Žižek
refers to biology and its branches in his independent and distinct
efforts, from which I have benefitted enormously and drawn much
inspiration, to outline a narrative recounting those explosive
events in which autonomous subjects spring into being out of
heteronomous matter(s).[15] In sympathy with Malabou's Hegel-
catalyzed and biologically oriented endeavors – her superb book
The Future of Hegel is understandably one of Žižek's favorite
pieces of Hegelian scholarship (along with Béatrice Longuenesse's
Hegel's Critique of Metaphysics and Gérard Lebrun's *La patience
du Concept*)[16] – he sometimes devotes himself to a project dear to
Malabou and me as well: assembling what could be characterized

fairly as a modified, updated reconstruction of the real-philo-sophical transition, within the systematic parameters of Hegel's *Encyclopedia*, from the "Organics" of the *Philosophy of Nature* to the "Anthropology" of the *Philosophy of Mind*.

Given this shared Hegelian project, I feel compelled to propose a twist different from a reversal Žižek proposes when he says, "For a true dialectician, the ultimate mystery is not 'Why is there something instead of nothing?,' but 'Why is there nothing instead of something?'" The twist is this: For a Hegel-indebted transcendental materialist, insofar as a theory of subjectivity is essential to transcendental materialism, the really crucial enigma is "How does the nothing(ness) of the *Cogito*-like subject-as-$ emerge from the something of material substance(s)?" This is my favored question and, from time to time, Žižek's likewise. Moreover, it is the key Hegelian query for any materialist ontology aiming to think the subject as immanently transcending its substantial base as both originary ground and enduring milieu of being.

Before revisiting Žižek's first sustained engagement with quantum physics, I should add a few final clarifications with respect to his most recent reply to me. My manners of responding to him by no means are meant to announce an uncompromising resistance on my part to his appropriations of quantum physics, with their sparkling, promising nuances. Admittedly, I lack the expertise in physics and mathematics to assess with complete confidence the accuracy and validity of select aspects of Žižek's quantum musings. Nonetheless, as hinted earlier, I am wholeheartedly in favor of his inclination partially to ground materialism on natural-scientific bases (this is by contrast with the tendencies either of a caricatured Hegelian hyper-rationalist pan-logism or Badiou's persisting dependence upon the Heideggerian distinction between the ontological and the ontic). From a dizzy-ing high-altitude vantage point surveying such basic, ground-zero categories and concepts as Being and Nothing, Žižek is one-hundred-percent correct that any philosophical materialism genu-inely worthy of the title cannot rightly avoid a sober intellectual reckoning with quantum physics (a genuine materialism also must reckon with whatever further developments unfurl themselves in this scientific realm of the micro and the miniscule – for example, string theory if and when it satisfactorily consolidates its scientific standing). But, if such a materialism is both to be authentically dialectical as well as to include a non-reductive account of a more-than-material subject emergent from nothing more than material substance, then a detailed speculative engagement with biology over-and-above physics alone is absolutely requisite. Furthermore, in fidelity to a Žižekian ontology of an Other-less, barred Real of non-All/not-One material being, I will continue to stick to an emergentist orientation (coupled with a Cartwrightian "nomological pluralism"[17]), an orientation according to which, simply put, the structures and dynamics of biological realities are ontologically as well as epistemologically irreducible to those of physics (especially the physics of the extremely small). A materialist fundamental ontology of the genesis of being by itself might be able to rest content with quantum physics as the sole chosen source of scientific resources for its thinking. But, a viable transcendental materialist theory of subjectivity needs much more than can be extracted and extrapolated from this lone source, particularly if it eschews dependence on the shaky scaffoldings afforded by the big Other of a natural economy.

Keeping all of the above in mind, Žižek's prior reflections on quantum physics in *The Indivisible Remainder* reveal some noteworthy facets, especially with the benefit of present hindsight. Schelling's 1809 *Freiheitschrift* in particular – this text is animated by a desire philosophically to synthesize the apparent opposites of a Spinoza-style system of deterministic natural necessity with a post-Kantian conception of the irreducible spiritual autonomy of free, self-determining subjectivity[18] – is a key source of inspiration for Žižek in his 1996 book and elsewhere.[19] Avowedly inspired by Schelling, Žižek intends to repeat this later-Schellingian synthesizing gesture through a theoretical reinterpretation of quantum-physical experiments and phenomena.

To be more precise, Žižek utilizes quantum physics so as to destabilize and undermine, on a scientific basis, images of nature typically taken for granted and assumed to be valid in various versions of the distinction between, on the one hand, the natural, and, on the other hand (and in the parlance of German idealism), the spiritual (i.e., the more-than-natural as autonomous, cultural, historical, social, etc.). He explains:

> Quantum physics . . . calls into question . . . not the specificity of man, his exceptional position with regard to nature, but, rather, the very notion of nature implied by the standard philosophical formulation of the gap between nature and man, as well as by the New Age assertion

of a deeper harmony between nature and man: the notion of nature as a 'closed,' balanced universe, regulated by some underlying Law or Rule. True 'anthropomorphism' resides in the notion of nature tacitly assumed by those who oppose man to nature: nature as a circular 'return of the same,' as the determinist kingdom of inexorable 'natural laws,' or (more in accordance with 'New Age' sensitivity) nature as a harmonious, balanced Whole of cosmic forces derailed by man's *hubris*, his pathological arrogance. What is to be 'deconstructed' is this very notion of nature: the features we refer to in order to emphasize man's unique status – the constitutive imbalance, the 'out-of-joint,' on account of which man is an 'unnatural' creature, 'nature sick unto death' – must somehow already be at work in nature itself, although – as Schelling would have put it – in another, lower power (in the mathematical sense of the term).[20]

Readers familiar with the full sweep of Žižek's *oeuvre* readily will recognize in this passage a number of thematic threads and trajectories of speculation (not to mention polemical refrains) regularly recurring in texts after *The Indivisible Remainder* up through his most recent publications; considering my precise aims here, I will bypass in what follows many of these motifs and theses so as to retain sharpness of focus. Žižek, short-circuiting the abyss between the very small and the very large (a yawning chasm that has yet to be closed, or even bridged, within physics itself), proceeds in the rest of "Quantum Physics with Lacan" to lay claim to a quantum-physical license for an ontological narrative according to which the existence of the entire universe testifies to a moment of creation sparked by (as he puts it in this quotation) a "constitutive imbalance," namely, "some global 'pathological' disturbed balance, . . . a broken symmetry,"[21] a "fundamental disturbance or lost balance."[22] On this basis, he concludes, "*there is no (balanced, self-enclosed) Nature* to be thrown out of joint by man's *hubris*"[23] (a conclusion with, among other ramifications, obvious ideological-political implications, especially vis-à-vis ecology and "biopower"). Althusser's "aleatory materialism of the encounter" is invoked as a notable precursor of this view.[24]

In addition to insisting on the primacy of imbalance/asymmetry over balance/symmetry, Žižek, via quantum physics, also launches a theoretical line of argumentation resurfacing in his writings of the past few years. This line is adopted in pointed opposition to Lenin's 1908 *Materialism and Empirio-Criticism*. Therein, Lenin rails against allegedly "idealist" (i.e., anti-materialist) philosophical employments of then-cutting-edge physics according to which "matter" (as dense, hefty, solid stuff) "has disappeared."[25] By contrast, Žižek, in both *The Indivisible Remainder*[26] and, for instance, *Organs without Bodies*[27] and *The Parallax View*,[28] maintains that the sole legitimate type of materialism today must be one which joyously affirms the "disappearance of matter," the becoming-immaterial of matter itself as per theoretical physics, in which macro-level sensory-perceptual imaginings of tangible material bodies are rendered null and void and replaced by dematerialized, impossible-to-picture waves/particles, vibrating strings, and the like.

The upshot of the preceding is that, for Žižek, the only nature that exists is dramatically different from the vast majority of standard, traditional envisionings of it by scientists and non-scientists alike (these envisionings usually represent nature as a harmonious, unified, and exhaustively self-coherent Whole of a One-All, the omnipresent lawful order of an inescapable big Other). Whatever there is of "the natural," it is nothing more than a lone expanse of an Otherless barred Real, an "unbearably light" being – in other words, an ontological immanence in which a countless multitude of fragmentary, ephemeral beings come and go with no overarching or underlying governing order centrally controlling this detotalized expanse. Although, in solidarity with Žižek, I too affirm a version of this, so to speak, materialist and science-shaped denaturalization of nature (*à la* a naturalist dismantling of Nature-with-a-capital-N), I am ill-at-ease with his appeals to quantum physics as the scientific cornerstone for a materialist ontology accommodating within itself a non-reductive model of autonomous subjectivity.

My discomfort arises for two reasons. First, as I maintained earlier in responding to Žižek's reply to me in the current round of our debate, his transubstantiation of quantum physics into a catch-all structural web of constellations and patterns applicable across the entire size-spectrum of existence (up to and including not only human subjects, but even the universe as a [non-]whole) amounts to a performative contradiction. How so? He reintroduces the supposedly banished One-All of a big Other in the formal guise of a natural economy generalized precisely from the discipline he holds up as entailing the scientific debunking of any and every version of (material) nature as a totalized, self-integrated Whole

(Žižek's pointing at Schelling's concept of "powers" [*Potenzen*] likewise is symptomatic of this insofar as the Schellingian philosophies of identity and nature, in which this concept features centrally, are what lead Hegel to quip famously and scathingly about the former's "Absolute" as a "night in which all cows are black"[29]).

My second reason for discomfort is that, as I have argued many times elsewhere on combined Hegelian and biological grounds,[30] a reliance upon quantum physics for a thoroughly materialist account of free subjects is neither necessary (this is because of such life-scientific resources as emergentism, neuroplasticity, and epigenetics, all of which break with the deterministic and monistic naturalism of mechanistic/non-dialectical materialisms) nor even remotely feasible (as I observed a while ago here, insurmountable practical limitations having to do with time and number-crunching power thwart in advance attempts at drawing reductive links that would substantiate parallels between quantum worlds and those in which living [and human] beings dwell). Arguably, Žižek's move of going all the way down to the tiny microcosms of quantum realms creates more disturbing difficulties than it resolves and puts to rest. Furthermore, in light of the fact that the scientific disciplines most directly and pressingly relevant to materialist investigations addressing minded subjective agents (i.e., such biological fields as the neurosciences, genetics, and evolutionary theory) have spontaneously on their own come to problematize the same renditions of nature Žižek seeks to dissolve with the help of a theoretical physics at a dauntingly massive distance from human-scale reality, this difficulty-fraught Žižekian move perhaps is better left to the side, if only as the set-aside leftover of an Occam's razor.

Quite interestingly, *The Indivisible Remainder* draws to a close with a set of remarks anticipating a number of my above-voiced objections. At the end of "Quantum Physics with Lacan," Žižek spells out some consequences of his preceding efforts to highlight a series of striking similarities between features of Lacan's conception of the subject as *parlêtre* (i.e., speaking being, socio-symbolic creature of language) and crucial aspects of quantum entities and events,[31] albeit in line with a "realist" reading of physics opposed to well-known anti-realist *cum* subjective idealist and/or sociolinguistic constructivist interpretations of quantum-level science.[32] He observes:

in the strange phenomena of the quantum universe, the human Spirit as it were encounters itself outside itself, in the guise of its uncanny double. Quantum processes are closer to the human universe of language than anything one finds in 'nature' (in the standard meaning of the term), yet this very closeness (i.e., the fact that they seem to 'imitate' those very features which, according to the common understanding of the gap that separates nature from man, define the *differentia specifica* of the human universe) makes them incomparably stranger than anything one encounters in 'nature.'[33]

There can be little doubt that, in this context, Žižek has in mind the specifically Schellingian definition of the uncanny, the one catching Freud's attention and which the latter psychoanalytically paraphrases as "something which ought to have remained hidden but has come to light"[34] and associates with the disturbing, unsettling figure of the *Doppelgänger*.[35] In the senseless mathematized realm of quantum beings and happenings, a weird domain superficially seeming utterly alien from the human standpoint of sense (as both perception and meaning), one is taken by surprise; more precisely, one is startled to find oneself face-to-face with an ensemble of altogether unexpected resemblances (i.e., an "uncanny double"), something "in nature more than nature itself" (to paraphrase the Lacan of the eleventh seminar) as a part of nature eerily mirroring more-than-natural/denaturalized subjectivity (Hegel's absolute idealism, with its objective realism, likely lurks around the edges of these musings as a supporting frame[36]).

Having implicitly waved at psychoanalysis through alluding to the Schellingian-Freudian *Unheimliche*, Žižek immediately proceeds to up the analytic ante. He does so with an eye to a type of reticence apropos his manner of mobilizing quantum physics resonating with some of my reservations articulated earlier:

Is not all we have developed hitherto, however, just a set of metaphors and superficial analogies which are simply not binding? To this criticism, which imposes itself with a self-evident persuasiveness, one can provide a precise answer: the irresistible urge to denounce the homologies between the quantum universe and the symbolic order as external analogies with no firm foundation – or, at least, as mere metaphors – is itself an expression and/or effect of the traditional philosophical attitude which compels us to maintain an insurmountable distance between 'nature' and the symbolic universe, prohibiting any 'incestuous' contact between the two domains.[37]

The final paragraph following immediately on the heels of this penultimate paragraph concludes *The Indivisible Remainder* with a forceful reiteration of the claim that quantum physics vindicates Schelling's 1809 thesis according to which human freedom is an irruptive upsurge, an abrupt resurfacing, of the unruly, always-already-past Real of *Grund* within the tamed and domesticated present reality of *Existenz*; this claim rests on a one-to-one correspondence between the Schellingian "ground" and the quantum universe, on the one hand, and Schellingian "existence" and larger-than-sub-atomic realms, on the other.[38] That said, I want to close this chapter by answering head-on Žižek's diagnosis of critics of his annexations of quantum physics as philosophical neurotics, namely, thinkers hampered by Oedipal incest-issues around "Mother Nature."

To begin with, and without reiterating the multiple criticisms I have already made here that cannot be so easily dismissed in this brusque analytic fashion, Žižek's retort might hit other targets, but it definitely misses me. Why? As should be quite evident, I share with Žižek the desire to overcome the resistances to materialist philosophical engagements with the sciences stubbornly raised again and again by the many species of anti-naturalism, with their suspicions of and hostility to all things scientific – not to mention their underlying nature-spirit ontological dualism, however avowed or disavowed. We concur that a materialist account of the subject requires thinking the Hegelian dialectical-style unity-in-difference/difference-in-unity of natural substance and spiritual subjectivity. We differ in our ways and means of going about this intellectual task.

To operate once again as an immanent critic, I am tempted to hijack Žižek's criterion of uncanniness – for him and on the basis of psychoanalytic (rather than philosophical) standards of evidence, the effect of uncanniness aroused by his quantum considerations is a symptom testifying to the truth of these speculations – and turn it into an additional justification for my insistence that biology, rather than physics, is the key scientific territory for the struggles of today's theoretical materialists. For the sake of clarity and to head off any potential confusions or misunderstandings at this juncture, my privileging of biology over physics rests on two claims. First, in practice, an empirical-scientific substantiation of hypothesized reductions of the biological to the quantum-physical is impossible due to limits of time and computational power (as I have observed here already). Second, in principle – this holds if one affirms, as I do, the sorts of philosophical principles at the core of the ontology and theory of subjectivity Žižek constructs at the intersection of German idealism and Lacanian psychoanalysis – one should not posit a profound continuity between the biological and the quantum-physical. Rather, a science-influenced materialism of an Otherless barred Real and the subjects genetically arising out of this not-One/non-All plane ought to push one into philosophically hypothesizing that the epistemological limit of the gap of irreducibility between biology and physics is, in truth, more than a mere impossibility internal to subjects' practical ability to know. Instead, this impossibility is directly revelatory of a really-existing ontological gap, an actual difference-in-kind, between the physical and the biological. Kant and Hegel insist on this in terms of identifying teleological, self-organizing structures and dynamics as the distinguishing features of organisms over-and-above other material bodies. And, by my lights, a systematic, consistent-with-himself Žižek likewise ultimately would have to abandon his quantum musings so as to stay faithful to his underlying Hegelian-Lacanian fundamental ontology. I also would add that the relevance of biology to reflections on human beings as minded subjects is as solidly established at the empirical-scientific level as reasonably could be demanded, whereas the links (if any there are) between quantum physics and theories of thinking subjectivity, however fascinating and intriguing, have thus far remained a matter of pure (and, as in the case of Penrose, controversial and discredited) speculation and nothing more.

If the uncanny is an effect symptomatic of shocking convergences of phenomena apparently opposed to each other as familiarly near/proximate and foreignly far/distant, then the becoming-unfamiliar of the biological portrait of human beings, à la the radical, subversive transformation of the long-outdated image of nature commonly associated with life-scientific renditions of "human nature," ought to provoke a sense of uncanniness at least as strong and perturbing as the one Žižek alleges arises from an appreciation of select structural isomorphisms between symbolic-subjective and quantum logics. For example, the dysfunctional, conflict-ridden, and kludge-like configuration of the haphazardly evolved human central nervous system, along with the permeating socio-linguistic mediation of body and brain transpiring via epigenetic and neuroplastic conduits, are biological findings presenting a picture of subjects' material substratums (i.e., their "natural" bodies) clashing markedly with a plethora of ideology-laden scientistic caricatures of humanity prevalent and popular in the contemporary societies of biopolitical late-capitalism.

What could be more unnerving than an "incestuous" confrontation with a nature so close to home (i.e., one's own body as *heimlich*, as the skin in which one feels oneself to be at home), hitherto presumably so recognizable as one's own, that nonetheless suddenly has morphed into something dramatically different and unsuspected? What would it be like, as it were, to wake up one day to the realization that who one took all along to be one's mother (Nature) never was, that this figure was, at best, an imposter living on under the cover of the masquerade of a case of mistaken identity? Even worse, what if one couldn't disown and escape from this always-excessively-close *Doppelgänger* "in you more than yourself" – separating oneself from one's own physical body arguably is not really possible – once the mask was off and the ruse was up? Whether viewed psychoanalytically or otherwise, a new materialist incursion into the life sciences in the spirit (if not the letter) of Engels' "dialectics of nature"[39] – political as well as philosophical stakes hang in the balance of this – has a chance to summon forth the powers of *das Unheimliche*, hopefully for the better.

Notes

1. Žižek 2011a.
2. Johnston 2013i.
3. Johnston 2008d: 189, 208; Johnston 2013j.
4. Žižek 2011a.
5. Ibid.
6. Ibid.
7. Žižek 1996b: 189–236; Žižek 2006a: 165–73; Johnston 2008d: 195–203.
8. Johnston 2011d: 71–91; Johnston 2014.
9. Hegel 1977c: 9.
10. Žižek 2011a.
11. Johnston 2013j.

12. Hegel 1977c: 196–210.
13. Johnston 2008d: 211–34.
14. Hegel 1970a: 23; Hegel 1977c: 10; Johnston 2008d: 163–77.
15. Johnston 2008d: 203–9.
16. Žižek 2010c: 68.
17. Johnston 2011d: 71–91.
18. Schelling 1936: 3, 7, 9–11.
19. Johnston 2008d: 19, 69–122.
20. Žižek 1996b: 220.
21. Ibid.: 227.
22. Ibid.: 227.
23. Ibid.: 235.
24. Žižek 1996b: 227; Althusser 2006: 174–5, 188–90.
25. Lenin 1972: 308–18.
26. Žižek 1996b: 229.
27. Žižek 2004b: 24.
28. Žižek 2006a: 165–6, 168.
29. Hegel 1977c: 9.
30. Johnston 2008d: 203–9, 269–87; Johnston 2011d: 71–91; Johnston 2013d: 162–84; Johnston 2013i; Johnston 2014.
31. Žižek 1996b: 220–28.
32. Ibid.: 236.
33. Ibid.: 230.
34. *SE* 17: 241.
35. Ibid.: 234–7.
36. Johnston 2014.
37. Žižek 1996b: 230.
38. Ibid.: 230–1.
39. Johnston 2011c: 141–82; Johnston 2013a: 103–36; Johnston 2013k; Johnston 2014.

Part III

Transcendental
Materialism's
Significant Others:
Psychoanalysis, Science,
and Religion

8

Life Terminable and Interminable: Hägglund and the Afterlife of the Afterlife

From the Religion of Survival to the Survival of Religion – The Difficulties of Atheism

Martin Hägglund is another contemporary thinker who I consider to be a significant other of transcendental materialism. He shares with Žižek and me investments in a number of specific coordinates of reference: German idealism, psychoanalysis, post-war French philosophy, as well as theories of drive, desire, time, religion, and atheism. However, Hägglund's orientation to these matters is significantly inflected by a notable difference (or, I could say, *différance*): He is fundamentally committed to a certain version of Derridean deconstruction. In fact, Jacques Derrida's *oeuvre* arguably provides the foundational building blocks of Hägglund's approaches to the just-mentioned range of issues he addresses that likewise are of concern to the transcendental materialism of Žižek and myself (a materialism strongly preferring, amongst post-war French thinkers, Lacan over Derrida). In this chapter and the one to follow, I will formulate objections of primarily Lacanian inspiration to Hägglundian "radical atheism" and its corresponding "chronolibidinal" alternative to psychoanalytic accounts of the relations between temporal and desiring life.

Lacan's 1974 interview with Italian journalists in Rome, entitled "The Triumph of Religion," implicitly addresses what has come to appear, with the benefit of hindsight, as a failure of vision on Freud's part. In his 1927 text *The Future of an Illusion*, one of the greatest manifestos of atheism in history, the founder of psychoanalysis predicts the inevitable demise of religion, allegedly doomed to wither away in the face of the steadily accelerating advances of the sciences; in accordance with a well-established Enlightenment narrative, Freud has faith that the progress of knowledge is bound to drive an increasing secularization of human societies through its relentless insistence on propagating the desacralizing insights of reason.[1] By the time Lacan gives his interview in Rome – and, this has become ever more evident since then – religion obviously seems to be continuing to enjoy a vibrant afterlife on the world stage in the wake of the Enlightenment emergence of the naturalist and materialist discourses integral to the scientific *Weltanschauung*.[2] Indeed, the potent forces of modernizing techniques and technologies, fuelled by the massive economic energies unleashed by capitalism, have continued to prove themselves to be powerless to liquidate thoroughly the specters of idealisms, spiritualisms, and theisms. Simply put, the problem with the atheism Freud anticipates and celebrates is that it severely underestimates the resilience and persistence of religiosity[3] (borrowing the title from Oskar Pfister's 1928 article responding to *The Future of an Illusion*, one could fault Freud for succumbing to "the illusion of a future"[4]). When asked how he explains the triumph of religion over psychoanalysis, Lacan, speaking with an acute awareness of post-Freudian history's resounding verdict regarding Freud's 1927 prophecy, responds, "If psychoanalysis will not triumph over religion, it is that religion is eternally tireless (*increvable*). Psychoanalysis will not triumph – it will survive or not."[5]

Associating from Lacan's recourse here to notions of eternity and survival to Hägglund's *tour-de-force* manifesto pleading for a "radical atheism" inspired by the philosophy of Derrida, one might be led to ask whether and how religion will survive in the shadow of Derridean-Hägglundian analyses concerning the very concept of survival itself. Without spending too much precious time recapitulating the main lines of argumentation of Hägglund's book in the form of an exegetical summary, suffice it to note a few of its key ideas focused on by the reflections to follow in this response to his work. Hägglund defines radical atheism through contrasting it with familiar varieties of traditional atheism. The latter negates the existence of the divine and everything connected with it (immortality, indestructibility, fullness, flawlessness, etc.) without calling into question whether everything whose existence it denies is desirable. Such pre-Derridean atheism simply takes it for granted that those things vanishing with the renunciation of the transcendent Beyond of an unscathed afterlife obviously are *prima facie* desirable. By contrast, Derridean-Hägglundian radical atheism not only negates what traditional atheism negates – it even contests the assumed desirability of the ostensible "paradise lost" produced by the denials of traditional atheism,[6] thereby refusing perpetually to wallow in the pathetic *pathos* of a position stuck forever pining after disappeared gods and withdrawn heavens. The slogan of radical atheism, apropos the lack jointly posited by both traditional atheism and its religious opponents (specifically, a lack in this material world of a wholly immune eternal life), might be the hopeful declaration that "You have nothing to lose but this loss itself!" In several significant ways, Hägglund offers readers a chance to reject melancholic atheism as a depressing, self-deceiving *doxa* hankering after an Elsewhere modeled on false promises of stagnant, lifeless security and stability.

Hägglund goes so far as to invoke a "law of survival" brooking absolutely no exceptions whatsoever.[7] Viewed from Hägglund's perspective, nobody can or does ever really desire everlasting life as timeless, unchanging being. Rather, the lively kinesis of temporal "survival" (i.e., "living on" in time), and not the deathly stasis of atemporal immortality, is what all desires, without exception, truly desire.[8] One of the justifications for this surprising assertion is the argument that "everlasting life" is a contradiction-in-terms. This is due to the essential temporality of life rendering the insatiable thirst for more life, often (mis)represented as a craving for an eternal life transcending time, a yearning for remaining open to the perpetually renewed alterity of time *à venir* – with the incalculable numbers of dangers and risks this openness to futurity necessarily and unavoidably entails.[9]

Ultimately, Hägglund's case for radical atheism rests on a theory of desire (hence the relevance of bringing psychoanalysis into this discussion). He directly avows this in stating that "Radical atheism proceeds from the argument that everything that can be desired is mortal in its essence."[10] Or, as he reiterates a few pages later, "the radically atheist argument is that *one cannot want* absolute immunity and that it has never been the aim of desire."[11] But, regardless of whether Hägglund is justified in maintaining that what looks to be a desire for immortality is, in truth, a desire for survival in the strict Derridean sense, it is certainly undeniable that neither traditional theists nor their equally traditional atheist adversaries (i.e., the vast bulk of humanity past and present) experience their desire as such. The least one can say along these lines – Hägglund acknowledges this – is that the fiction of the infiniteness of a transcendent immortality, and not the fact of the finitude of an immanent survival, is an enduring mirage which, in its misleading guises, attracts humanity's hopes and aspirations. One does not have to be a practicing psychoanalyst steeped in intricate and subtle metapsychological conceptualizations of unconscious fantasy life to know that illusions are not without an influence on desire. Similarly, time spent between the four walls of the clinical consulting room is not requisite for grasping that desire is far from reasonable, willing and able to be downright unreasonable. Thus, any comprehensive, faithful account of desire cannot be limited to external critical assessments of its object, dismissing the illusions shaping desire itself as mere illusions *qua* ineffective epiphenomena, as unreal by virtue of being irrational when measured by the standards of directed, self-conscious reasoning. One could surmise that this is an aspect of what Lacan is getting at when he warns analysts that "desire must be taken literally,"[12] namely, at its word as well as to its letter.

In this vein, Hägglund notes, "A radical atheism cannot simply denounce messianic hope as an illusion. Rather, it must show that messianic hope does not stem from a hope for immortality (the positive infinity of eternity) but from a hope for survival (the negative infinity of time)."[13] However, at this precise juncture, questions proliferate: Even if "messianic hope" (as an apparent wishing for the saving grace of deliverance from mortal time) can be shown fundamentally somehow to "stem from" the Derridean-Hägglundian "hope for survival," does such a demonstration prove that the passion for salvation is wholly reducible to its finite ground or origin, the "ultra-transcendental"[14] *Ur*-source from which it stems? What does it mean to claim that a desire does not genuinely desire what it takes itself to desire? Are there crucial differences between an atheism, be it traditional or radical, embraced consciously and one internalized unconsciously? Is the unconscious discovered by Freudian psychoanalysis capable of digesting radical atheism? Has this unconscious ever been radically atheist? Will it ever be?

Freud claims that humanity eventually will become atheist. Hägglund claims that humanity always has been atheist. Freud's prediction has failed the test of subsequent history, at least thus far at first glance. Hägglund's thesis has yet to be as thoroughly tested. Its unpredictable, unforeseeable tomorrows await it.

For the sake of contributing to what hopefully will be the long and prosperous future of radical atheism, my response to

Hägglund's theses will put forward a set of three inter-linked proposals (i.e., criticisms/counter-arguments) to be defended below.
To being with, the problem with radical atheism is not that it
is unreasonable, warranting critique due to certain defects or
shortcomings in the reasoning supporting it. On the contrary,
from a psychoanalytic standpoint, it is too reasonable. Ironically
enough, although professional philosophers frequently accuse
Derrida of indulging in anything but philosophy by engaging in
something (whatever it is) that is purportedly beneath the proper
dignity of authentic, respectable philosophy, Hägglund's Derrida
turns out to be too much of a philosopher for psychoanalysis (a
comparable, related irony is that Derridean thought displays the
armchair-philosopher's penchant for challenging psychoanalytic
hypotheses, hypotheses informed by far-from-purely-theoretical
endeavors, with *apriori* assertions without firm anchoring in
any sort of empirical and/or practical discipline apart from the
rarified textual and ideational ethers in which the philosophical
tradition has moved comfortably since its inception in ancient
Greece). Despite deconstruction supposedly eschewing classical,
bivalent logic by questioning the law of non-contradiction as the
fundamental principle on which this logic is based,[15] many of the
manners in which Hägglund argues for a radically atheist vision of
desire exhibit reasoning impeccable by the standards of classical
logic (one imagines that logic professors would be quite pleased
with the argumentative acumen displayed by Hägglund's writing).
If, as Freud adamantly insists, the unconscious thinks in fashions
utterly different than consciousness – the former disregards the
rules of bivalent logic and linear chronology generally adhered to
by the latter – then can Hägglund reason his way to conclusions
about the real nature of unconscious desire (conclusions maintaining that the desire for immortality unknowingly is a desire for
survival) using premises chained together according to the conventions of the logic molding conscious cognition?

Hägglund's reasoning is too reasonable for the unconscious,
his logic too logical. One might remark that he is much too clever
for both the unconscious as well as the bulk of people believing
themselves to desire things Hägglund valiantly tries to prove they
cannot desire and never have desired. He seeks to force rational
constraints upon desire that desire, as generated and sustained in
part by unconscious processes, tends to ignore, for better or worse.
This is not to be denounced and dismissed as a failure of desire

to be true to itself by not experiencing itself as radically atheist. Instead, it is to be diagnosed as a failure of radical atheism to take stock of how and why desire fails to experience itself as radically atheist. There are precise metapsychological reasons for these failures.

A second and related line of counter-argumentation to be formulated is that, judged by the standards of the classical logic on which much of his reasoning rests, Hägglund employs a false dilemma affecting the very core of his radically atheist theory of desire. The mutually exclusive, either/or opposition he thrusts forward between life and death – the former is equated with living on as the time of mortal survival, while the latter is associated with eternity as possible only through the cadaverizing cancellation of life[16] – serves as the basis for his claim that desire always fantasizes about having more (mortal) time, rather than, as with an immortal, no time (and, hence, no life, given the equation of being alive with being-in-time, since "there cannot even in principle be anything that is exempt from temporal finitude"[17]). Departing from Hägglund's related characterization of temporal life as "infinite finitude,"[18] a third possibility in excess of the bivalent binary distinction between mortal life and immortal death is thinkable: the "finite infiniteness" of "undeath" à la the horror-fiction category of the undead as neither alive nor dead in the standard senses of these terms (Žižek, among others, effectively utilizes this fictional category in elucidating the fundamental psychoanalytic concepts of drive [Trieb] and repetition[19]). That which is undead neither heeds the linear, chronological time of survival nor languishes in the frozen immobility of timeless death, these being the only two options allowed for by Hägglund – "If to be alive is to be mortal, it follows that to *not* be mortal – to be immortal – is to be dead. If one cannot die, one is dead."[20] If a satisfactory case can be made for there being a third dimension to the temporality of the libidinal economy, a dimension irreducible to either pole of the dichotomy between the chronological temporality of life and the timeless eternity of death, then some of the load-bearing components of the argumentative architecture supporting the Derridean-Hägglundian radical atheist conception of desire will be weakened and in need of reconstruction.

Not only does Hägglund's deconstructive logic remain, on multiple levels, indebted to classical, non-deconstructive logic – however much the recto of the law of identity (i.e., "A = A") is attacked here,[21] its verso, the law of non-contradiction (i.e., "$A \neq \neg A$"), clearly continues to be operative at select junctures – his, as it were, chrono-logic remains strangely mute with respect to the innovative, non-traditional theorizations of temporality advanced by both psychoanalysis and deconstruction (for example, in his criticisms of my first book, *Time Driven: Metapsychology and the Splitting of the Drive* [2005], he pays too little attention to the role therein of retroactive temporality [as Freud's *Nachträglichkeit* and Lacan's *après-coup*] in the dynamics of the drives, tending instead to think through problems in drive theory via a developmental perspective that privileges linear, chronological time, a perspective closer to phenomenological psychology than Freudian-Lacanian psychoanalysis[22]). The sole form of temporality Hägglund seems to rely upon in pursuing his purposes is a conception that is at least as old as the ancient Greeks, namely, the idea of time as the continuous, ceaseless succession of ever-self-dividing now-points with a past behind them and a future ahead of them. If there is one thing that Freud, Lacan, and Derrida share in common, it is the problematization of thinking time in these terms alone.[23] Additionally, glancing back at the first difficulty I articulated above (i.e., the one proposing that radical atheism is too reasonable for unconscious desire), one can see that the duel staged between classical and deconstructive logics likewise involves the false dilemma of leaving out alternatives over-and-above the two logics thus pitted against each other. At a minimum, what about the logic upon which psychoanalysis bases not only its theory of the psychical apparatus, but also its practice as centered on the "fundamental rule" of free association, that is, the (so to speak) methodical madness of primary-process mentation characteristic of the signifying unconscious? Can this "logic" be reduced to classical logic, deconstructive logic, or some combination of these latter two alone? If not, then further detours lie along the road ahead for Derridean-Hägglundian radical atheism.

The third and final thread of criticism to be unfurled in this response has to do with the familiar-but-crucial difference between description and prescription. Hägglund himself is quite cognizant of the importance of this distinction, deftly employing it to devastating effect in raising a plethora of serious objections to various well-known attempts to interpret Derrida's writings as marshaling ethical and political prescriptions (on Hägglund's highly persuasive reading, Derrida is to be understood as primarily pronouncing a descriptive discourse stating how things are, instead of a prescriptive one proclaiming how things should be). As I will substantiate here later, despite his very effective critical deployment of the description-prescription distinction against depictions of Derrida as the preacher of a theosophical ethics of alterity, Hägglund sometimes sounds as though he succumbs to confusion apropos this difference between "is" and "ought." To be specific, I will make the argument that Hägglund's radical atheism is more prescriptive than descriptive, despite him presenting it as the reverse.

I am extremely sympathetic to the atheism envisioned by Hägglund – albeit sympathetic to it as a vision of what thought hopefully can become in the future, rather than as a picture of what it was in the past and is in the present (like the best of philosophers measured by Nietzschean standards, Hägglund could be characterized as marvelously "untimely"). Succinctly asserted, authentic atheism is a hard-won accomplishment, not an insurmountable, default subjective setting. For Hägglund, the conscientious faithful are nonetheless unwitting atheists. For me, by contrast, even many professed atheists are unconscious believers (a point already made by Lacan through references to both the purportedly atheistic materialists of eighteenth-century France as well as certain features of evolutionary theory[24]). Consciously believing oneself to be rid of religiosity once and for all is one easy thing – another, much harder, matter is the dual-aspect labor of working-through one's atheism past the initial point of its mere intellectual acceptance. This arduous *Durcharbeiten* has two aspects insofar as it entails simultaneously both internalizing atheism at non-conscious levels beyond superficial self-consciousness as well as unmasking hidden, unacknowledged vestiges of beliefs subsisting below the threshold of explicit recognition. Even if, as is sadly unlikely, Hägglund miraculously manages to convince the masses that they are not and never have been faithful to their religions, even this does not amount to succeeding at ridding them of religious revenants, revenants that enjoy defying would-be exorcists and have shown themselves to be devilishly cunning survivalists over the course of recent history, rebelliously lingering on after all atheist eulogies pronounced before. Atheism, including radical atheism, certainly has its work cut out for it. May it triumph against the odds!

The Fantasy of Logic – Thought and Time in the Unconscious

In the spirit of Lacan, a brief return to Freud promises to be productive at this point. Hägglund himself zeros-in on one of Freud's texts of the greatest degree of topicality in this context: the short 1916 piece "On Transience." Therein, Freud succinctly addresses issues and themes at the very heart of Hägglund's undertakings (both in *Radical Atheism* as well as the article "Chronolibidinal Reading: Deconstruction and Psychoanalysis"). Without exhaustively summarizing the various details contained in this three-page Freudian text, suffice it to say for now that the discoverer of the unconscious, himself burdened by a persistent, obsessive concern over his own mortality,[25] here confronts (through two other people as interlocutors) the fleeting, transitory nature of all things, the condemnation of each and every being, without exception, to the cycles of generation and corruption, growth and decay. In response to this undeniable fact, Freud resists falling into a depressive refusal to engage with the world under the shadow of this world's transience. Disputing a contention voiced by one of his walking companions, a poet, that transience, like an inverse Midas touch, lessens the value of everything it envelops, Freud retorts in quasi-economic terms, "On the contrary, an increase! Transience value is scarcity value in time. Limitation in the possibility of an enjoyment raises the value of the enjoyment."[26] Basing himself on this statement by Freud, which he takes to support his radical atheist theory of desire, Hägglund concludes in *Radical Atheism* (in which he calls for a temporalized conception of enjoyment[27]) that *"temporal finitude is the condition for everything that is desirable."*[28]

Already, there are several problems plaguing the conclusions Hägglund draws from this 1916 essay by Freud. To begin with, Freud does not maintain that transience (i.e., temporal finitude) is the ultimate underlying reason or source (in Hägglund's parlance, the ultra-transcendental condition) for the desirability of anything and everything. Rather, he merely observes that scarcity in/of time need not, as is the case for his friend the poet in particular, be bemoaned as a wretched stain indelibly tainting objects and experiences that, in the absence of ubiquitous transience, supposedly would be worthy of committed love and enthralled esteem (or, so this melancholic writer imagines). Freud responds to this poetic pessimism in a very analytic manner, inquiring whether it is obvious and self-explanatory that one necessarily must construe scant time, with its constraining parameters, as poisoning and devaluing all that one might otherwise invest with one's desires. He proposes, to himself, his interlocutors, and his readers, that another attitude toward temporal limits is possible. This is a (self-)analyzed analyst offering those with ears to hear an alternate interpretation, one that opens up the affirmative potential for embracing a superabundant reality full to overflowing with finite things, rather than defensively retreating from this fluctuating existence into a rigid, lifeless pseudo-safety toiling in vain to fend off feeling losses (i.e., neurotically attempting to lose feelings of attachment to temporally finite beings so as to avoid inevitable feelings of loss).[29] Hence, Freud is prescribing another way of positioning oneself vis-à-vis transience, and not describing how transience is an ultra-transcendental condition for each and every instance of desiring something (with this being Hägglund's earlier-mentioned misapplication of the description-versus-prescription distinction). Along these lines, Freud, in "On Transience," does not claim that temporal "scarcity" (i.e., finitude) creates desirable values. Instead, he merely maintains that such scarcity/finitude can become a supplement augmenting or enhancing (i.e., increasing, rather than decreasing) what is already enjoyable in things happening to be transient. All things are temporally finite, including all things desired. This temporal finitude either can decrease or increase the ability to desire one's desire, to enjoy one's enjoyment, of these transient things. But, neither of these two premises leads to and licenses the conclusion that temporality and the fleeting, ephemeral fragility it brings with it are the ultimate causal origins of desirability *tout court*.

To the extent that Hägglund brings Freudian psychoanalysis into the picture of his Derrida-inspired radically atheist theory of desire, additional problems multiply once one turns to the bundle of roughly-contemporaneous texts with which 1916's "On Transience" is inextricably intertwined: "On Narcissism: An Introduction" (1914), the 1915 papers on metapsychology ("Drives and Their Vicissitudes," "Repression," and "The Unconscious"), "Thoughts for the Times on War and Death" (1915), and "Mourning and Melancholia" (1917). To reduce several very long narratives to one very short story – obviously, there can be no attempt here at an exhaustive engagement with this dense cluster of immensely rich slices of the Freudian corpus – these writings, spanning a critical four-year period of Freud's intellectual itinerary, all present ideas cutting against the grain of the Derridean-Hägglundian account of desire. In particular, these essays by Freud contain assertions that, on the one hand, point to deeply engrained patterns of affectively motivated cognition in the psychical apparatus obeying neither classical nor deconstructive logic, and, on the other related hand, cast into doubt whether the unconscious, with its fundamental fantasies, ever was, is, and/or will be radically atheist. Freud's psychoanalytic metapsychology outlines a psyche whose ways and means of thinking, including thinking (or, alternately, the constitutive inability to think) time, must appear to be quite irrational and unreasonable, in a resistant and refractory manner, to a radical atheist equipped with his/her arguments, objections, proofs, and so on (in line with Lacan's warnings against practicing analysis as a knee-jerk hermeneutics of suspicion always on the lookout for intricate, complex hidden meanings of profound significance – he indicates that the truth is sometimes superficially "stupid"[30] – one could say that the unconscious is simultaneously both surprisingly clever as well as unbelievably stupid when measured against the standards of conscious thinking). Will this analytic unconscious listen to these proselytizing efforts at atheistic persuasion? Can conversion take place in this case?

During the conversation in which condemnation to never-enough time is under discussion, neither of Freud's companions are convinced by his rationalizations to the effect that temporal finitude adds to, instead of detracts from, the desire-worthiness of transient beings. Freud notes:

> These considerations appeared to me to be incontestable; but I noticed that I had made no impression either upon the poet or upon my friend. My failure led me to infer that some powerful emotional factor was at work which was disturbing their judgment, and I believed later that I had discovered what it was. What spoilt their enjoyment of beauty must have been a revolt in their minds against mourning. The idea that all this beauty was transient was giving these two sensitive minds a foretaste of mourning over its decease; and, since the mind instinctively recoils from anything that is painful, they felt their enjoyment of beauty interfered with by thoughts of its transience.[31]

He continues:

> Mourning over the loss of something that we have loved or admired seems so natural to the layman that he regards it as self-evident. But to psychologists mourning is a great riddle, one of those phenomena which cannot themselves be explained but to which other obscurities can be traced back. We possess, as it seems, a certain amount of capacity for love – what we call libido – which in the earliest stages of development is directed toward our own ego. Later, though still at a very early time, this libido is diverted from the ego on to objects, which are thus in a sense taken into our ego. If the objects are destroyed or if they are lost to us, our capacity for love (our libido) is once more liberated; and it can then either take other objects instead or can temporarily return to the ego. But why it is that this detachment of libido from its objects should be such a painful process is a mystery to us and we have not hitherto been able to frame any hypothesis to account for it. We only see that libido clings to its objects and will not renounce those that are lost even when a substitute lies ready to hand. Such then is mourning.[32]

If the desires of Freud's companions are grounded upon temporal finitude as an ultra-transcendental condition, they certainly are not willing and able to acknowledge this and make it their own. Additionally, one can see in these passages connections leading back to 1914's "On Narcissism" and forward to 1917's "Mourning and Melancholia." In the former essay, Freud distinguishes between "narcissistic ego-libido" (i.e., libidinal cathexes of one's own ego as a love-object) and "anaclitic object-libido" (i.e., libidinal cathexes of another as a love-object). In certain instances, ego-libido resists being converted into object-libido (in terms of the Freudian economics of psychical-libidinal energy, a zero-sum relation obtains between the narcissistic and the anaclitic).[33] Freud proceeds to speculate that a general resistance to other-oriented sexuality might exist, specifically insofar as sexual reproduction confronts the ego with something injurious to its own sense of itself: its status as a "mortal vehicle of a (possibly) immortal substance"[34] (interestingly for Hägglund's account of desire, it is here not the beloved object's temporal finitude that is the focus, but the lover's own self as mortal). In "On Transience," a preemptive recoiling before loss, an aversion-in-advance to mourning, is said to be operative in Freud's two interlocutors. At least in these two individuals, desire seems to be dampened or turned off by the scarcity of time, by the temporal finitude of all things. Moreover, in both this text and "Mourning and Melancholia," Freud indicates that anaclitic libidinal attachments, once established, are stubbornly sticky; more specifically, in light of mourning, he observes that the psyche is incredibly slow to concede that the loved object is truly gone, that the beloved has departed and is never coming back again.[35] In short, the psyche's desires for others, rather than being aroused by the finite, mortal status of each and every other, persevere in protracted denials of the transient, evanescent quality of whatever can be and is desired, even when faced with the gaping holes of irrevocable loss. Lacan drops similar hints about mourning couched in his own terminology (in the sixth seminar [1958–59], he characterizes mourning as the inverse of his notion of "foreclosure" as per the third seminar [1955–56], that is, as a process in which the void of a Real absence [i.e., the loss of an actual object] is filled in with seemingly indestructible Symbolic signifier-traces of the vanished entity).[36]

Thus, the shadow of death glaringly looms large in the background of "On Narcissism," "On Transience," and "Mourning and Melancholia." It would be neither possible nor productive, in the limited format of this response to Hägglund's project, to dwell at length on the numerous intricacies, inconsistencies, tensions, and contradictions plaguing Freud's conflicted, multifaceted relation to the topic of mortality. However, what Freud has to say about death in two other papers contemporaneous and associated with these three already-mentioned papers (these two being "The Unconscious" and "Thoughts for the Times on War and Death") is highly relevant to the issues at stake in this context. The metapsychological essay "The Unconscious," in seeking to delineate the essential contours of the unconscious as the proper object of psychoanalysis as a discipline, is careful to spell out why the unconscious is not simply a "subconscious" as split-off double of consciousness, a second consciousness hidden from first-person consciousness. The unconscious must not be thought of as akin to consciousness precisely because it itself does not think like conscious thought. The unconscious thinks differently, engaging in mental maneuvers unfamiliar relative to the ideational patterns manifested and recognized by conscious cognition; conscious and unconscious thinking are not the same thing differentiated solely by whether or not there is an accompanying first-person awareness of thinking.[37] In particular, Freud stipulates that the unconscious is not bound by the logical and chronological principles upon which conscious thought generally bases itself. More precisely, the Freudian unconscious disregards both the logical law of non-contradiction (by virtue of the absence of nega-tion in its mental operations) as well as the chronological law of temporal finitude (by virtue of its "timelessness" when measured by the standards of linear time).[38] If psychoanalysis is right that desires fundamentally are informed by the primary-process menta-tion of an unconscious inherently incapable of obeying classical, bivalent logic (as grounded on the function of negation and the corresponding law of non-contradiction) and congenitally blind to the passage of chronological time (with the finitude this inces-sant movement entails), then, without utterly contradicting and discarding psychoanalysis altogether, how can one maintain not only that desire can become radically atheist, but that it always has been? Do Freud's metapsychological axioms pertaining to unconscious psychical life not indicate that indissoluble residues of religiosity (with "religiosity" understood in the broad Derridean-Hägglundian sense as centered on ideas of an immunity unscathed by time and everything time brings with it) cling to subjects' thoughts and desires thanks to the primary-process underpinnings of these subjects' libidinal economies?

In "Thoughts for the Times on War and Death," dating from the same year as "The Unconscious," Freud draws the obvious con-clusion from the metapsychological premises according to which the unconscious lacks cognizance of both logical negation and chronological time: The unconscious is therefore also unaware of its own mortality (at least to the extent that the conscious concept of mortality, one relied upon by Hägglund too, combines the idea-tional components of the negation of the notion of life [i.e., death as "not-life"] and the sense of the limited nature of lived, linear time [i.e., the chronology of life]). The second section of Freud's essay, entitled "Our Attitude Towards Death," repeatedly stresses this imperviousness to the idea of death of those sectors of the psyche lying beyond the circumscribed sphere of consciousness. At the start of this section, Freud remarks:

> To anyone who listened to us we were of course prepared to main-tain that death was natural, undeniable and unavoidable. In reality, however, we were accustomed to behave as if it were otherwise. We

showed an unmistakable tendency to put death on one side, to eliminate it from life. We tried to hush it up; indeed we even have a saying [in German]: 'to think of something as though it were death.' That is, as though it were our own death, of course. It is indeed impossible to imagine our own death; and whenever we attempt to do so we can perceive that we are in fact still present as spectators. Hence the psycho-analytic school could venture on the assertion that at bottom no one believes in his own death, or, to put the same thing in another way, that in the unconscious every one of us is convinced of his own immortality.[39]

Freud is far from the first German-speaking thinker to put forward these proposals apropos death (Kant and Schelling make identical claims[40]). Additionally, twelve years later, Heidegger famously articulates similar propositions in his well-known discussion of "being-towards-death" in *Being and Time*.[41]

But, Freud's arguments regarding mortality and immortality in psychical life do not rest on private phenomenological thought-experiments alone. Rather, his clinical and cultural observations of unconsciously influenced thought processes as well as the metapsychological framework with which these observations maintain a dialectical relationship of reciprocally determining co-evolution lead him to surmise that, at least unconsciously, people cannot shake a "childish," "primitive" belief that they are somehow immortal. Later on in the second section of "Thoughts for the Times on War and Death," he transitions from an analysis of human perspectives on death evidently pervasive in earlier historical periods (i.e., beliefs of "prehistoric men" in "primaeval history")[42] to the contemporary, "civilized" psyche's rapport with mortality (he obviously is relying here on the speculation according to which "ontogeny recapitulates phylogeny," a speculation he entertains in the contemporaneous metapsychological paper on phylogenetic heritage he destroyed unpublished [but a copy of which was found amongst Sándor Ferenczi's possessions][43]). Freud states:

Let us now leave primaeval man, and turn to the unconscious in our own mental life. Here we depend entirely upon the psycho-analytic method of investigation, the only one which reaches to such depths. What, we ask, is the attitude of our unconscious toward the problem of death? The answer must be: almost exactly the same as that of primaeval man. In this respect, as in many others, the man of prehistoric times survives unchanged in our unconscious. Our unconscious, then, does not believe in its own death; it behaves as if it were immortal. What we call our 'unconscious' – the deepest strata of our minds, made up of instinctual impulses – knows nothing that is negative, and no negation; in it contradictories coincide. For that reason it does not know its own death, for to that we can give only a negative content. Thus there is nothing instinctual in us which responds to a belief in death.[44]

A few pages later, he adds, "To sum up: our unconscious is just as inaccessible to the idea of our own death, just as murderously inclined towards strangers, just as divided (that is, ambivalent) towards those we love, as was primaeval man."[45] However, despite the unsubtle allusions to the theory of phylogenetic heritage, Freud's 1915 statements concerning death do not rest on shaky appeals to Haeckel, Lamarck, and/or Darwin. Instead, modern individuals' (unconscious) attitudes to death resemble those of earlier people because, in the view of Freudian (and Lacanian) psychoanalytic metapsychology, there are certain lowest common denominators structuring the psychical apparatuses of human beings living in various historical epochs. The disregard of primary-process cognition for negation and time (and, hence, for death as the negation of life by time) would be something shared by "primaeval" and contemporary psyches alike. And, this trans-historical "logic of the unconscious," freely allowing for the coincidence of contradictories and taking non-chronological liberties with temporal sequences, sounds as though it is a logic closer to a sort of deranged, discombobulated Hegelian dialectics than it is to either classical or deconstructive logical reasoning. Freud subsequently reiterates these assertions, saying of the universal inescapability of death that "no human being really grasps it."[46] Lacan and Žižek echo him[47] (not to mention Otto Rank,[48] Norman O. Brown,[49] and Ernest Becker,[50] among others).

Having reached this point, it appears that Freudian-Lacanian psychoanalysis and Derridean-Hägglundian radical atheism are directly at loggerheads, diametrically opposed to each other. The former denies that individuals' deepest fantasies and desires can and do acknowledge the fact of mortal/temporal finitude; contradicting this, the latter insists that these fantasies and desires cannot help but envision and stage this finitude again and again. In terms of the radical atheist replacement of immortal salvation with mortal survival, Hägglundian Derrideanism relies on a line of argumentation resembling one found in Hobbesian epistemology (this makes for strange bedfellows indeed, given that the British empiricism of which Hobbes is a founding figure is the primary historical ancestor of much of twentieth/twenty-first-century Anglo-American Analytic philosophy, an orientation generally quite hostile to and dismissive of Derrida and other post-war French thinkers). To be precise, Hobbes is critical of philosophers (whether medieval scholastics or Continental rationalists) who participate in endless debates about "absurdities," with an "absurdity" being defined by him as an instance of "senseless speech." Hobbes' empiricist contention is that the sole form of meaningful mental content is that which arises from "sense" (i.e., concrete sensory-perceptual experience). If particular words or phrases seem to refer to things of which no idea (as piece of mental content arising from sense) can be formed in the mind, then they are devoid of a genuine, true referent and, thus, are meaningless (in the parlance of the Saussurian structural linguistics dear to both Lacan and Derrida, Hobbesian absurdities, as instances of senseless speech, are signifiers without signifieds, without corresponding spatio-temporal concepts as ideational materials). One of Hobbes' key examples of an absurdity – the target of his criticism here is not difficult to guess – is the phrase "incorporeal substance" (i.e., metaphysical, and not physical, stuff). In light of an examination of Hägglund's radical atheism, one should not forget that Descartes links his demonstration of the necessary existence of *res cogitans* as incorporeal substance to the theological doctrine of the soul's immortality.[51] All of the above is to be found in the fourth and fifth chapters ("Of Speech" and "Of Reason, and Science") of the first part ("Of Man") of Hobbes' 1651 *Leviathan*.[52] As Hägglund's Derrida has it, immortality basically is a Hobbesian absurdity to the extent that any supposedly "eternal" life one can imagine as an object-referent of desire (i.e., as a desired afterlife, salvation, etc.) must consist of more-time-for-living – and, therefore, this imagined excess of life-beyond-life is anything but timelessly eternal insofar as temporality is an integral ingredient in its imaginary constitution.[53] As Hobbes would put it, when talking about immortality, one thinks either of a mere extension of mortal life (i.e., living on as survival, instead of immortality strictly speaking) or of nothing at all.

204 Adventures in Transcendental Materialism

Hägglund's arguments are as sober-minded as any reasoning spelled out by the hardest-headed modern empiricists or their contemporary offspring this side of the English Channel. But, what in most cases would be a virtue turns out, where a theory of unconsciously shaped desire in relation to mortality is at issue, to be a bit of a vice. In a subtle discussion of Heidegger's treatment of death, Derrida, inspired in part by the writings of Maurice Blanchot,[54] is deliberately unclear about whether any relation to mortal finitude per se is even a thinkable possibility. Simply put, one's "ownmost" death is aporetic, an "x" that cannot be cleanly and decisively categorized along neatly demarcated logical and linguistic lines.[55] Even if Hägglund is absolutely correct that immortality as such, as tied to the timelessness of eternity, is an impossible, unimaginable *telos* for desire's aspirations, Derrida's musings on the aporia of mortality suggest that temporal finitude is at least as elusive and defiant of envisioning as atemporal infiniteness. Or, as Blanchot elegantly encapsulates this conundrum, "To arrive at presence, to die, two equally enchanted expressions."[56] Perhaps desire is stuck stranded between survival and immortality, vainly wanting both, neither, and/or something else. Maybe Sisyphean desire is unreasonable in this futile way, in a way blindly ignoring the cogent, sensible reasons of both classical and deconstructive logics. If indeed there is a third dimension of "something else" in addition to timeless immortality and temporal survival – Hägglund thrusts forward a forced choice between these two alternatives and nothing more – then Hägglund's radical atheist theory of desire must be reconsidered. Exploring whether such a third possibility is at least thinkable is a task to be undertaken below.

The title of Lacan's fourteenth seminar of 1966–67 is "The Logic of Fantasy." As has been and will be maintained here, this logic, as reflective of the unconscious, must be worked with on its own terms, terms that conform to neither of the logics marshaled by Hägglund. A descriptive account of desire that measures desire externally by logical standards not its own ends up being either inaccurate and misrepresentative vis-à-vis its supposed object of description or tipping over into prescription, into informing desire what it should be instead of expressing what it is in and of itself. In telling desire that it does not desire what it takes itself to desire, Hägglund's radical atheist conception of desire suffers from a defect that readily can be conveyed through an inversion of the title of Lacan's fourteenth seminar: the fantasy of logic – that is to say, fantasizing that classical and/or deconstructive logics hold in/ for libidinal mechanisms governed by unconscious primary processes such that what desire appears to desire through its fantasies is epiphenomenal relative to what it really and truly desires despite itself. In this respect, Hägglund is in the best of company. In *The Future of an Illusion*, Freud uncharacteristically indulges himself in a rare bout of utopianism, savoring a tempting intellectualist fantasy (one that flies in the face of much of the rest of his own psychoanalytic insights) in which reason eventually triumphs over religion, establishing an undisputed reign under whose rule unconsciously driven irrationalities are reined in by the patient discipline of the secular sciences.[57] As noted, Hägglund goes further than Freud to the extent that he is not content hopefully to await the future arrival of an atheism *à venir* (insisting instead that atheism always-already has arrived). But, more patience is called for at this moment.

Life, Death, and Undeath in Psychoanalysis – Repetition as Finite Infiniteness

During the course of one of his many musings on the infamous *Todestrieb*, Lacan remarks in passing that "There is nothing so dreadful as dreaming that we are condemned to live repeatedly [*à répétition*]."[58] The nightmare to which he refers is not so much eternal life in the atemporal sense critically scrutinized by Hägglund, but, rather, unending life, survival as a sort of existential insomnia into which one is thrown with no apparent avenue of escape. There can be something awfully horrifying about the prospect of survival-without-end, an existence from which one cannot wake up into the final, resting oblivion of undisturbed nothingness.[59] And yet, at the same time, the alternate prospect of "the End," of the terminal and terminating void of annihilation borne by mortal-making temporality, can seem equally terrible. Could it be said that desire, desiring to have its proverbial cake and eat it too, desires both and neither simultaneously, wanting an unimaginable synthesis combining what is desirable in the ideas of mortality and immortality? Does it want what might be described as a "spectral" (after)life, living on in a mode of being, unknown as such in this world, that would be neither surviving life nor perishing death, neither kinetic time nor static eternity, strictly speaking?

206 Adventures in Transcendental Materialism

Before proceeding to speak of ghosts, specters, the undead, repetition, and infinity – this tangled jumble of terms is quite relevant to a psychoanalytic engagement with Hägglund's Derrideanism – a few clarifications regarding Lacan's theory of desire are in order (keeping in mind that a thorough investigation into Lacanian *désir* alone would require at least a sizable book or two). Hägglund, with ample textual support, claims that Lacan grounds desire on lack.[60] He construes Lacan's account of desire as entailing that an impossible-to-realize filling-up of temporally induced lack is the ever-receding horizon of the Lacanian libidinal economy (in the guise of what Lacan calls "the Thing" [*das Ding*]). Consistent with his radical atheist thesis stating that the undivided fullness of an infinite presence unscathed by the ravages of temporal negativity is not what desire actually desires, Hägglund rejects this psychoanalytic model, claiming that the extinguishing of the desire for immortality in the eternal plenitude of everlasting fulfillment would be tantamount to "absolute death" (as immobility, stasis, etc.), and not the "absolute life" desire desires.[61] Consequently, he concludes, *contra* Lacan, that there simply is no desire for an absent, lacking, impossible fullness. For Hägglundian radical atheism, Lacan's Freudian depiction of desiring remains wedded to a traditional (i.e., non-radical) atheism to the extent that, although Lacan atheistically admits that the "sovereign Good" of "the Real Thing" is intrinsically missing and unattainable,[62] he nonetheless continues to insist that subjects are condemned to long after this always-already departed (non-)being.[63]

Hägglund's reading of Lacan overlooks three crucial, interrelated details: one, the essential, fundamental ambivalence of Lacanian desire; two, the dialectical convergences of opposites incarnated in the figure of *das Ding*; and, three, the positive productivity (i.e., the plus), in addition to the negativity (i.e., the minus), involved with Lacan's "*manque-à-être*" (lack in/of being). First, desire *à la* Lacan is not simply a matter of attraction to the impossible-to-attain, forever-absent, always-already missing Thing; it also consists of a simultaneous repulsion from the Real of *das Ding*. Particularly in the course of analyses of the play of desire in hysterical subjects – for Lacanian psychoanalysis, features of hysteria as a subjective structural position epitomize select facets of subjectivity in general (as the subject of the unconscious)[64] – Lacan is at pains to emphasize the unstable oscillations and erratic vacillations of desire. In fact, when claiming that Lacan mistakenly believes desire to desire its own cancellation through consuming immolation in the fires of the undiluted fullness of the Real *an sich*, Hägglund neglects those instances in which Lacan posits that desire desires its own perpetuation as desire,[65] a perpetuation requiring the avoidance or deferral of any ultimate satisfaction through a direct encounter with the Thing incarnate. Lacanian *désir* is caught between conflicting centrifugal and centripetal movements, splitting subjectivity (as Lacan's "barred S" [$]) because it itself is torn between an inconsistent multitude of uncoordinated pushes and pulls. It is not nearly as univocally coherent and consistent as Hägglund's radical atheism makes it out to be. Although not radically atheist in a strict Derridean-Hägglundian sense, the desire of Lacan is not just traditionally atheist either.

Second, *das Ding*, in Lacanian theory, is a far more paradoxical and multifaceted thing than Hägglund recognizes – and this apart from the questionability of construing Lacan's Thing-with-a-capital-T as a metapsychological equivalent to or synonym for the libidinal *telos* of traditional theisms and atheisms alike (to resort to a flurry of Lacanian jargon, it has much more to do with the desire of/for the absolute alterity of the Real Other as *Nebenmensch* – this Other's desire is what desire desires over and above the answering of signifier-mediated "demands" through the gratification of bodily-driven "needs"[66] – than with full presence, eternal life, and so on [see Chapter 9]). Apropos the Lacanian Real, the register to which *das Ding* belongs, Žižek repeatedly explains how this register exhibits, in a Hegelian manner, paradoxical intersections of seemingly opposed aspects.[67] Specifically, the Real, in the form of the Thing, simultaneously stands for absent presence and present absence,[68] with these two poles each internally split: the former into a presence both alluring and horrifying and the latter into an absence both painful and energizing. Along these lines, the Real Thing both is and is not desired at the same time, functioning as a center of libidinal gravity that the desiring subject as $ neither can live with nor can live without. In one-sidedly emphasizing the Lacanian subject's want relative to *das Ding* as lacking (so as to portray Lacan as complicit with an all-too-traditional atheist theory of desire), Hägglund passes over in problematic silence the plethora of contexts in which Lacan discusses this Thing (as the *jouissance*-laden end of desire, in both senses of the word "end") as a frightening excess, as an overwhelming presence to be kept safely at arm's length (Hägglund here would need to devote sustained attention to select Lacanian reflections, especially those contained in the tenth seminar [1962–63], on anxiety, object *a*, the uncanny, the lack of lack, death drive, and desire's positioning in the face of *jouissance* in particular, intricate motifs/topics into which the present discussion cannot go).[69]

The third flaw in Hägglund's reading of Lacan is closely connected with the second one outlined in the paragraph immediately above. For Hägglund, traditional atheism remains mired wallowing in a bog of mourning for the supposed loss of something never truly loved or possessed in the first place. Such atheism, in negating any exhaustively full presence transcending temporality without correspondingly renouncing its libidinal attachments to what is thereby negated, strands itself in pointless mourning. Lacan is construed as condemning the desiring *parlêtre* to precisely this sad fate. However, Lacanian psychoanalysis does not limit itself to singing traditional atheist hymns which monotonously rehearse the *pathos* of (symbolic) castration. Despite Lacan's frequent employment, in connection with his depictions of desire, of various terms with negative connotations, each Lacanian minus, as it were, is also, at the same time, a plus (the quasi-Hegelian logic behind this thought-theme ought to please the sensibilities of a deconstructive logic founded on the contestation of the bivalent law of identity/non-contradiction). For Lacan, lack is far from being mere lack and nothing else; it is not purely negative. Like Hegel, Lacan celebrates the wonderful productive power of the negative, counter-intuitively viewing the apparent losses of various types introduced into mediated subjective existence as actual gains, as openings through which everything exceeding the stifling, idiotic enclosure of dumb, meaningless being can come to be[70] (in this fashion, Lacanian theory is quite close to Derridean-Hägglundian radical atheism). A cigar sometimes might be simply a cigar. But, absence is never simply absence alone in psychoanalysis.

At the level of the (non-)distinction between presence and absence, it would be worthwhile at this stage to turn to Derrida's "hauntology" in conjunction with certain Lacanian-Žižekian ponderings about ghosts and specters as "the undead." Derrida introduces the neologism "hauntology" in *Specters of Marx*,[71] and Hägglund refers to it several times in *Radical Atheism*.[72] Derrida specifies that he coins this word to designate something that "does not belong to ontology, to the discourse on the Being of beings, or to the essence of life or death."[73] Lacan's hesitations and reservations as regards ontology would not be inappropriate to mention here in connection with Derrida's subsequent deconstructivist take on this domain of philosophy. As is well known, in his famous eleventh seminar of 1964, Lacan answers Jacques-Alain Miller's query regarding a specifically Lacanian ontology by avowing that, in essence, there really is not one – "the unconscious . . . does not lend itself to ontology."[74] And, insofar as Lacan is an analyst theorizing primarily for other analysts about the unconscious as the definitive concern of the practice of psychoanalysis, he does not espouse a psychoanalytic ontology (see also Chapter 4 above). Later on, in both the nineteenth and twentieth seminars, he is critical and dismissive of ontology as a vain philosophical effort at constructing a seamless, totalizing worldview (just as Freud before him cites Heine's derisive depiction of the comical struggles of the philosopher to "patch up the gaps in the structure of the universe" with "the tatters of his dressing-gown"[75]). In the nineteenth seminar (1971–72), he goes so far as to ridicule the discourse of systematic ontology as laughable in light of implications flowing from his "barring" of the Symbolic big Other.[76] In the twentieth seminar (1972–73), while sharply distinguishing between philosophy and psychoanalysis, he treats ontology as a philosophical *Weltanschauung* and, resonating with his remarks about it from the previous academic year, mocks it as "the funniest thing going."[77]

Funnier still, Derrida's term for his in-between, out-of-joint, not-entirely-an-ontology might not be an utterly unprecedented coincidence. Playing with the French word for shame as an actually felt negative affect (i.e., *honte*), Lacan admits to having his own "*hontologie*." He speaks of this sort of shame in the closing session of the seventeenth seminar (1969–70). At the start of that session, with reference to the notion of "dying of shame" and the fact that people often declare "It's a shame" when someone dies, Lacan appeals to a "(h)ontology" as necessary in order to do justice to the non-arriving, always-to-come, deferred (non-) being of death.[78] A couple of years later, he ambiguously remarks that "ontology is a shame."[79] What is one to make of this? Given the issues at stake in this discussion of Hägglund's radical atheist depiction of desire, attention ought to be paid to a common denominator between Lacan and Derrida apropos ontology: When considering mortality and immortality, both thinkers feel compelled to gesture in the direction of a more/other-than-ontology accounting for a spectral netherworld of non-beings, not-quite-beings, not-wholly-existent-beings, and so on. And, for each of them, ghosts turn out to be ideal figures for imaginarily embodying the strange quasi-entities that would be the objects of a Lacanian *hontologie* and/or a Derridean *hantologie*.

Ghosts, as specters condemned to haunt this world, are neither alive nor dead in any conventional sense. They are incompletely dematerialized spirits wandering about between worlds, languishing in a hazy, indeterminate state as misfits bereft of a proper place. These revenants affect the reality of this world here without fully being a part of it. Along these lines, does Lacan, like Derrida, have a hauntology that is not a crying shame? In his commentary on Shakespeare's *Hamlet* contained in the sixth seminar on the topic of desire, Lacan invokes the same ghost Derrida summons in *Specters of Marx* so as to address and further develop Freud's psychoanalytic understanding of mourning (specifically as per "Mourning and Melancholia"). He begins with an observation about mortality – "The one unbearable dimension of possible human experience is not the experience of one's own death, which no one has, but the experience of the death of another."[80] Already, a significant point of contrast with radical atheism surfaces: Whereas Hägglund denies the possibility of one relating to oneself, even in the wildest fantasies, as immortal, Lacan (and, on occasion, Derrida too) denies the possibility of relating to oneself as mortal, save for in a vicarious, displaced manner through the deaths of others. In Lacan's eyes, the void left behind by the absent-because-departed other is the site of mourning. He proceeds to clarify: "Where is the gap, the hole that results from this loss and that calls forth mourning on the part of the subject? It is a hole in the real, by means of which the subject enters into a relationship that is the inverse of what I have set forth in earlier seminars under the name of *Verwerfung* [repudiation, foreclosure].[81] Lacan continues: "Just as what is rejected from the symbolic register reappears in the real, in the same way the hole in the real that results from loss, sets the signifier in motion. This hole provides the place for the projection of the missing signifier..."[82] According to the above, mourning is the precise mirror-image inversion of psychosis within the Real-Symbolic-Imaginary register theory of Lacanian metapsychology. Psychosis, as arising from the mechanism of foreclosure (i.e., the absence/rejection of "the Name-of-the-Father"), entails a dynamic wherein *"what has been rejected from the symbolic reappears in the real"*[83] (i.e., seemingly "real" delusions and hallucinations appear "out there" in place of an intra-subjectively missing constellation of key Oedipalizing signifiers).[84] Mourning, by contrast, amounts to a rift in the fabric of the Real (to be comprehended in this context as an actual, factual material loss of someone) being filled in by the Symbolic return of that which was lost (through, for instance, a proliferation of commemorations, markers, memorials, monuments, rituals, etc. devoted to the vanished one being mourned).[85] Therefore, if psychosis is generated by foreclosure, mourning must be generated by inverse foreclosure. And, in inverse foreclosure, the absences of finite others, absences inevitably and unavoidably brought about by the ravages of temporal negativity, are met with the survivors' stubborn insistences on perpetuating the virtual, spectral presence of those absent through the repetitious incantations of signifier-traces.[86]

From a Lacanian perspective, mourning seems to confirm La Rochefoucauld's maxim according to which "Neither the sun nor death can be looked at steadily."[87] Mixing together Lacan and La Rochefoucauld, it could be maintained that death is a sun that can be stared at only when eclipsed. To be more precise, the work of mourning acknowledges and effaces temporal finitude at one and the same time, bearing witness to mortality through a process that simultaneously struggles to cover over this very same mortality through propping up an ethereal, non-mortal double of the deceased, an enshrined socio-symbolic second body seemingly capable of surviving indefinitely. But, arguably, this work of mourning is not an occasional labor prompted exclusively at those times when another dies and/or disappears.

Surprisingly, the case can be made that the perpetual ontogenetic construction-in-process of a subjectifying ego-level self-identity is spurred, at least in part, by a sort of generally unrecognized mourning. In a passage from the eleventh seminar that Hägglund himself cites,[88] Lacan claims that subjects are haunted by the fantasmatic loss of an immortality never possessed to begin with, perturbed by a living, vital sexuality testifying to individuals' inescapable mortality[89] (he is echoing comments Freud makes about the intimate rapport between sex and death in both biological and psychical life[90]). Incidentally, although Hägglund's radical atheist reading of Lacan as an all-too-traditional atheist emphasizes how Lacan's mortal subjects are left desiring an eternal life radical atheism maintains to be undesirable, Hägglund neglects something very important here: In both the eleventh seminar itself as well as an *écrit* from the same year as this seminar (i.e., 1964's "Position of the Unconscious"), Lacan conjures up a little science-fiction myth of his own making, painting an unsettling portrait of a monstrous entity he christens "the lamella."[91] Without getting into the specifics of its description, this imaginary lamella is the figurative incarnation of the libidinal as excessive vital being, as interminable life idiotically driven to perpetuate itself repetitively. Lacan's myth of the lamella expresses the notion that sexuality is a point at which the opposites of life and death, mortality and immortality, converge (for instance, through sexual reproduction, the mortal individual can live on through transmitting his/her genetic material to subsequent generations of offspring; and yet, sexual reproduction itself is the embodied testimony to the mortality of the individual as the disposable husk carrying this transmissible genetic material). Moreover, the "immortality" embodied by the lamella – this is something Hägglund fails to note – is not, in conformity with traditional atheism, portrayed as desirable. Instead, it inspires revulsion and terror in the face of being smothered by the claustrophobia-inducing immanence of a thriving, parasitical vitality dripping with oozing, obscene *jouissance*. Lacanian desire is profoundly ambivalent about immortality (and this in the same manner as its ambivalence apropos *das Ding*, the Real Thing).

What do mourning and the psychical dynamics of ego formation have to do with these reflections regarding life and death in Lacanian psychoanalysis? In Lacan's account of ego formation through the mirror stage, the complex intertwining of the mortal and the immortal, an intertwining confounding the straightforward dichotomy between life and death relied upon by radical atheism, easily can be discerned. To cut a long story short, the individual's self-alienation through objectification in the form of an *imago-Gestalt* constituting the nucleus of the *moi* introduces this thus-alienated living proto-subject equally to both mortality and immortality through a single process. In becoming an object for itself through the acquisition of an ego, the subject-as-$ is able to imagine its own disappearance, to gaze in fantasies at scenes from which it is absent (such as one's own funeral). Hence, passing through the mirror stage is, according to Lacan, a prerequisite for awareness of one's own mortality since this awareness relies on the use of self-objectification to stage scenarios in which one's self is pictured as non-existent[92] (but, just as Hägglund claims that spatio-temporal visions pretending to envision absolutely infinite immortality are self-refuting,[93] so too could it be claimed that visions attempting to envision life's mortal finitude in itself and as such, visions in which the subject persists as a gaze beyond the outer limits of the very finitude it is struggling [in vain] to glimpse through the windows of fantasies bearing upon matters of birth and death [i.e., fundamental fantasies],[94] are equally self-refuting).

And yet, the mediating images and words into which trajectories of identification are channeled through the mirror stage – this stage facilitates whatever awareness is possible of one's own finitude and mortality – also have the effect of stamping upon subjectivity an impression of its own indelible, permanent duration. The visual and linguistic elements of identity, made of spectral substances consisting of materialities different from the materials composing decomposable bodies, appear to enjoy a capacity for living on different from the survival (as per Derrida-Hägglund) of the terribly perishable lump of flesh-and-blood identifying with them. Indeed, Lacanian considerations lead to the hypothesis that images and words, although making it possible for subjects to be self-conscious of their own mortality, are embraced and held onto in part because they simultaneously make it impossible for subjects genuinely to envision their own non-being. To put it in hybrid Heideggerian-Derridean parlance, the visual and linguistic elements of ego-level subjectification are, at one and the same time, conditions of possibility and impossibility for relating to oneself as a being-toward-death. Subjects cast themselves into what Lacan characterizes as the "cadaverizing," "corpsifying" second bodies of self-images, proper names, personal pronouns, and socio-symbolic statuses so as to accomplish, among other aims, a staving off of temporal negativity and the mortal finitude inherent to it.[95] These alienating identities quietly bear witness to a life-long process of mourning, to a never-finished project of continually recognizing and misrecognizing one's status as a death-bound being.

What makes subjectifying images and words seemingly immortalizing is their iterability, the fact that they appear to possess the potential, in principle, to be repeated without end. Admittedly, both Derrida and Hägglund would be perfectly correct at this juncture to raise the objection that visual and linguistic traces, as traces, are always and essentially exposed to future destruction, erasure, forgetting, and so on. This is indeed true. However, both phenomenologically and structurally, the ghostly, quasi-demate-rialized avatars of its mediated identity lure desiring subjectivity into not being able wholeheartedly to believe in its own mortality, fully to comprehend and digest the radical implications of facing up to the anonymous facelessness of its temporal finitude (and, as I asserted earlier, insofar as illusions of immortality shape desire itself, no defensible theory of desire can dismiss these illusions as merely illusory *qua* epiphenomenal). At the level of its (fundamen-tal) fantasies, the psychoanalytic subject of desire cannot but view itself as surviving without end, as living on interminably. There are two lives, which dialectically interpenetrate each other, cor-responding to the two deaths spoken of by Lacan in his seventh and eighth seminars (1959–60 and 1960–61)[96]: a first, material life (i.e., natural and/or Real being) and a second, more-than-material life (i.e., cultural and/or Imaginary-Symbolic being). The sub-title of Hägglund's *Radical Atheism* refers to "the time of life" without the contents of this thus-sub-titled text going on to distinguish between lives. From a Lacanian vantage point, this presents dif-ficulties. The preceding arguments indicate that, through dispro-portionately stressing a temporal finitude tied primarily to the first, material life, Hägglund neglects temporalities peculiar to the second, more-than-material life. This latter form of living relates to both itself and the former form of living as involving repetition *qua* finite infiniteness (and not, *à la* Hägglund, infinite finitude).

Following Derridean-Hägglundian radical atheism, if infinite finitude refers to life/mortality and infinite infiniteness refers to death/immortality, then finite infiniteness (a third category absent in Hägglund's framework but arguably present in psychoanalytic theory) refers to undeath as neither mortality nor immortality (fol-lowing Žižek, one could propose a tripartite distinction between the mortal, the immortal, and the non/not-mortal[97]). To be undead (i.e., non/not-mortal as different from immortal) would be to go on surviving without foreseeable end, living on indefinitely. This fan-tasmatic prospect splits desire by being simultaneously attractive and repulsive all at once. As I mentioned previously here a while ago, Žižek employs the horror-fiction category of the undead in his efforts to elucidate Freudian and Lacanian concept-terms such as the lamella, *jouissance*, and the death drive. These three things are each related to the fundamental psychoanalytic concept of rep-etition (a concept forming a crucial component of another foundational psychoanalytic concept, namely, that of drive [*Trieb*]). As is the case with the temporality of retroactive "deferred action" uncovered by psychoanalysis (i.e., Freud's *Nachträglichkeit* and Lacan's *après-coup*), the temporality of repetition in its analytic conception does not fit into either of the temporalities operative in radical atheism as per Hägglund (i.e., the time of life and the timelessness of death). One could succinctly encapsulate repetition as an intra-temporal resistance to time itself, a negation of time transpiring within time. As Judith Butler expresses it, "repetition is a vain effort to stay, or indeed, to reverse time; such repetition reveals a rancor against the present which feeds upon itself."[98]

At one point in *Radical Atheism*, Hägglund refers to an aspect of Derrida's interpretation of Hegel. He appeals to the Derridean version of Hegelian "spurious" or "bad" infinity in his efforts to clarify the ultimate underlying mode of temporality posited by radical atheism.[99] Hägglund indicates that extracting this bad/spurious infinity from the relation Hegel places it in with a good/non-spurious infinity – Derridean-Hägglundian radical atheism treats the latter as yet another designation of the impossible, non-existent, self-refuting (idea of the) absolute (as a full, eternal presence-to-itself transcending the negativity of the time of finite life) – permits putting bad/spurious infinity to work for deconstruction as a means of further illuminating temporal finitude as the infinitely finite. Putting aside disputes bearing upon Hegel's genuine, true infinity as the *Aufhebung* negation-of-the-negation of the temporal negativity of bad/spurious infinity (today more than ever, there are various serious philosophical and mathematical reasons for rethinking the infinite), a question must be asked: Is Hegelian bad/spurious infinity, even when deconstructively divorced from its partnership with good/non-spurious infinity, obviously akin or similar (solely) to radical atheist temporal finitude?

One should not forget that Hegel's bad/spurious infinity is still infinite (and not finite), still a mode or variant of infiniteness. With this in mind, a passage from the *Encyclopedia Logic*, in which Hegel discusses bad/spurious infinity, deserves to be quoted:

This *infinity* is *spurious or negative* infinity, since it is nothing but the negation of the finite, but the finite arises again in the same way, so that it is no more sublated than not. In other words, this infinite expresses only the requirement that the finite *ought* to be sublated.

> This progress ad infinitum does not go beyond the expression of the contradiction, which the finite contains, [i.e.,] that it is just as much *something* as its *other*, and [this progress] is the perpetual continuation of the alternation between these determinations, each bringing in the other one.[100]

Particularly considering the deconstructive and psychoanalytic background of this current context in which Hegel is being invoked, a couple of features of these lines from the *Logic* merit close attention. First of all, the descriptive language mobilized by Hegel audibly evokes associations to the undead monsters of horror films cited as fantastic explanatory examples by Žižek in his efforts to elucidate the death-drive-like *jouissance* of the Lacanian Real (not to mention associations to Lacan's 1964 descriptions of the alien lamella-creature itself). In horror films, the undead monster (be it a vampire, mummy, zombie, or, in science-fiction horror, a cyborg, robot, or virus) typically terrifies by being that which nightmarishly "arises again in the same way"; each time the protagonists appear finally to have succeeded at killing off the malevolent beings antagonizing them, these beings reanimate themselves and continue their diabolical pursuits with tireless relentlessness. Perhaps the undead are uncanny in a specifically Freudian fashion (remembering that Freud, citing Hegel's German idealist contemporary Schelling, defines the uncanny [*das Unheimliche*] as "that" which "ought to have remained secret and hidden but has come to light,"[101] and then proceeds to analyze the appearances, in literature, of doppelgangers and entities eerily between life and death). That is to say, they are, in Žižekian parlance, "things from inner space." These figures from myth and fiction both fascinate and disturb people precisely because they represent a return of the repressed, a surfacing, within the out-in-the-open spheres of quotidian popular culture, of elements and aspects of unconscious fantasy life.

Another feature of the above-quoted characterization of bad/spurious infinity from Hegel's *Encyclopedia Logic* enables a bridge to be built between, on the one hand, this Hegelian concept, and, on the other hand, the here-interlinked notions of the undead and unconscious fantasy life. Hegel speaks of an endless iteration generated by a "contradiction." In a very general fashion, one could say, apropos Lacan's register theory (especially as it is configured in the later period of Lacan's teachings in the 1960s and 1970s), that the representational constructs of Imaginary-Symbolic reality circle around unrepresentable antagonisms, conflicts, deadlocks, impasses, etc. in the Real (related to this, and *contra* Hägglund's Hobbesian empiricist insistence that the fantasies of desire are always and necessarily reducible to sensible spatio-temporal inscriptions, one ought to recall Lacan's repeated assertion that parts of *objet petit a*, the center of gravity around which fantasizing desire orbits, are "non-specularizable," that is, impossible to inscribe in spatio-temporal forms[102] – see also Chapter 9). As with the inauthentic infinity of Hegelian repetition, the dynamics of Imaginary-Symbolic reality's always-in-process constructions are driven along by Real "contradictions." In an early period of *le Séminaire* (the third seminar on the psychoses), Lacan observes that "the question of death and the question of birth are as it happens the two ultimate questions that have precisely no solution in the signifier."[103] As defined by Lacan and others (such as Jean Laplanche and Jean-Bertrand Pontalis, André Green, Žižek, and Zupančič), fundamental fantasies are forma-tions of the unconscious straining to stage in fantasy subjectified constellations of images and words answering to the enigmas of birth and death, mysteries lying at the heart of the life of tempo-rally finite beings that nonetheless cannot be answered by images and words in an adequate, satisfactory manner.[104] If, as Hägglund argues, immortality per se (as life-beyond-time) is as unimaginable and self-contradictory as a square circle (and, hence, unable to be a fantasmatic object-referent of desire), so too, might it be argued on psychoanalytic grounds, is mortality as the absolute temporal finitude of a being born to die. In Lacanian locution, the radical negativity of the time of a life-bound-to-death is a Real with "no solution in the signifier," an "x" incapable of proper, appropriate representation by the *Vorstellungen* constituting the contents of the living psyche. Subjects' fundamental fantasies arguably are incapable of envisioning them as either immortal as infinitely infi-nite or mortal as infinitely finite.

Fantasy life is spuriously infinite in two senses: One, its Imaginary-Symbolic formations repeatedly fail to capture the twin Reals of mortality as infinite finitude and immortality as infinite infiniteness. Two, thanks to this failure, unconscious fantasizing repeatedly struggles again and again in perpetual futility to (bor-rowing a turn of phrase from, of all people, Richard Rorty) "eff the ineffable." The result of this is that desiring subjects, with their ego-structures and associated fantasy lives as mediated by images, signifiers, and gazes, relate to themselves as uncanny undead beings, entities unable to leave time in both the Derridean-Hägglundian radical atheist sense (i.e., a true transcendence of time cannot even be imagined) as well as in a psychoanalytic sense (i.e., death, as the only exit from time, also cannot be imagined). If Hägglund is right that people never really have been able to conceive of themselves as immortal strictly speaking, it might additionally be contended that, for analytic reasons, they never really have been able to conceive of themselves as mortal per se either. Making a Kantian gesture, one could stipulate that each and every attempt by the psyche to comprehend mortality and immortality (as finitude and infiniteness *an sich*) lands it in a dialectics of fantasy life (as a correlate of the "transcendental dialectics of pure reason") – more precisely, in the pincers of irreconcilable antinomies (specifically apropos mortal finitude, I have discussed elsewhere a "psychical antinomy" in connection with fundamental fantasies[105]). Appropriating a now-familiar articulation Lacan employs, starting in the twentieth seminar (but foreshadowed beginning in the eighteenth seminar),[106] to characterize the Real of the antagonistic, antinomic deadlock of sexuation (*à la* the infamous non-existent *rapport sexuel*), mortal finitude, as belonging to the Real (and not to Imaginary-Symbolic reality), is an impossibility that "doesn't stop not being written" (*ne cesse pas de s'écrire*).[107] More precisely, impossible-to-subjectify mortal finitude cannot be inscribed at the level of the *Vorstellungen* composing the contents of the psyche. And yet, in spite and because of this, the ideational representations forming the formations of the unconscious repeatedly circulate around this hole-without-a-trace. Mortality, as embodied by the living being's birth and death, is "fundamentally foreclosed" from this being's subjective structure(s).[108]

Jacobi somewhere confesses that he finds the theist idea of ever-lasting-life-without-end and the atheist idea of death-as-the-final-end equally intolerable and unbearable (a sentiment expressible in Leninist-Stalinist style as "both are worse!"). Jacobi's emotional being feels uneasy with both thoughts, with the infinite (as an unending existential insomnia) as well as the finite (as an eventual nocturnal abyss of nothingness). Anything deeper than superficial conscious lip service paid to the intellectual acceptance of the truth that "all men are mortal" is difficult indeed. Saying that one is a radical atheist is much easier than feeling, in the core fibers of one's being, that one is such.

The Desire of Atheist Desire – Radical Atheism's Future(s)

One of the more opaque of Lacan's many cryptic one-liners is a pronouncement about what real atheism would be. In the eleventh seminar, he claims, "the true formula of atheism is not *God is dead* . . . the true formula of atheism is *God is unconscious*."[109] A few years later, in the seventeenth seminar, he explains exactly why, from a Freudian perspective, trumpeting the death of God is not the final act of an accomplished atheism taken to its most extreme, consequent endpoint. This explanation relies upon a reading of Freud's *Totem and Taboo* as a new psychoanalytic twist on the Sophoclean tragedy from which the Oedipus complex takes its name (for Lacan, the tale Freud tells in this exemplary 1913 piece of speculative psychoanalytic anthropology, a story he custom tailors rather than borrows from Sophocles, discloses the true analytic import of the Oedipal[110]). What Lacan highlights is that, in the Freudian myth of the primal horde, the murder of the *Urvater* (i.e., the archaic paternal prototype of the divine, of the gods and God[s] of subsequent religious history[111]) by the band of oppressed, sexually deprived brothers does not open the floodgates releasing a liberated, bacchanalian *jouissance* in which the women formerly monopolized by this alpha male freely circulate in an orgy of unfettered enjoyment. As Freud observes, "The dead father became stronger than the living one had been . . . What had up to then been prevented by his actual existence was thenceforward prohibited by the sons themselves."[112] Lacan resorts to a twist on Dostoyevsky's "If God is dead, then everything is permitted" to encapsulate Freud's insight that the destruction of an incarnation of authority does not automatically and necessarily amount to the liquidation of the rule of this authority's law – "If God is dead, then nothing is permitted."[113] Instead, the living paternal figure murdered returns in the much more potent spectral guise of a guilt-ridden regime of socio-symbolic rules imposing even stricter regulations upon the murderers.

The Lacanian lesson for aspiring atheists is not only that consciously mouthing the words "God is dead" is insufficient for ridding oneself of religiosity once and for all – intoning such a mantra, under the impression that it possesses the power to conjure away the spirits of theism, risks blinding one to the multifarious manners in which ghostly unconscious religious beliefs continue to enjoy a psychical afterlife in the aftermath of a supposed accession to atheism at the level of self-consciousness. In fact, if anything, to be a full-fledged atheist, one must, as Lacan indicates, be warily aware that "God is unconscious" – which, in psychoanalysis, is to be far from dead and gone. In other words, unless and until one is willing and able to accept that theological and quasi-theological residues will subsist in an unconscious that will continue to speak in oneself and despite oneself – this unconscious God does not die if and when consciousness declares the divine to be deceased and departed – one is likely to remain in the thrall of religiosity (even more so the less one believes oneself to believe). How many people, perceiving themselves decisively to have abandoned religion and everything associated with it long ago in their personal histories, discover on an analyst's couch just how persistent and pervasive in their present lives are the lingering spectral traces of a never-really-discarded-faith? Like the ghost of Freud's murdered *Urvater*, God can and does return in even more powerful guises in the wake of having been declared dead. Altering a line from the 1995 film *The Usual Suspects* – radical atheism should take this altered line to heart as a word of warning about the risks ahead of it – maybe the greatest trick God can play is convincing the world he does not exist. The same might be said of (fantasmatic) immortality too.

On several occasions, Lacan indicates that the experience of a psychoanalysis seen through to a proper conclusion (i.e., an analysis that could be said to have been terminated at the right time in the analytic work) must involve an atheistic dimension, namely, in Lacanese, a loss of faith in any and every figuration of an omnipotent and omniscient big Other (whether God, Nature, the analyst, whoever, or whatever).[114] Again in the seventeenth seminar, he forcefully insists that "The pinnacle of psychoanalysis is well and truly atheism"[115] (proceeding to qualify this by saying, "provided one gives this term another sense than that of 'God is dead,' where all indications are that far from calling into question what is in play, namely the law, it is consolidated instead"[116] – the paraphrase of Dostoyevsky immediately follows[117]). A truly completed analysis ends with, among other things, witnessing and accepting the fall of all instantiations of the all-powerful and all-knowing.

In closing, to bring the discussion back to Hägglund's admirable struggle to formulate a rigorous atheism that, in its far-reaching implications, is authentically radical in the most genuine sense of the word, one ought to note that Lacan's construal of atheism shares something with Freud's views on temporal finitude. Recall that, in "On Transience," Freud suggests one can come to experience the limited duration of everything that is as enhancing rather than degrading the worthiness of objects and others to be valued. He offers to his walking companions, who are haunted by a libidinally paralyzing foreknowledge of inevitable decay and disappearance, another way to interpret this ever-changing world of transient beings. But, Freud's succinct account of this walk through the shadow of the valley of death hints that turning the scarcity of time from an inhibitor into a catalyst of desire is an accomplishment that hopefully should be achieved by those laboring to work-through analytic insights. Likewise, Lacan clearly identifies a non-superficial (i.e., radical) atheism worthy of the name as a prescriptive aim of analyses, and not a descriptive default subjective position from which analysands depart in their journeys into the "extimate."[118]

Speaking of desire in the closing minutes of the opening session of his renowned seminar on *The Ethics of Psychoanalysis*, Lacan maintains that "the essential dimension of desire" is that "it is always desire in the second degree, desire of desire."[119] Relating this to the topic of atheism as addressed by psychoanalysis, what the signifier "God" signifies will not drop dead, at least not in the foreseeable future and without a ferocious fight; it will live on under any number of other signifying banners, surviving as an unconscious spirit even in those ignoring it with sealed lips or loudly dancing on its empty grave. This repressed revenant undoubtedly will continue to exert an influence on desiring subjects for quite some time yet. But, radical atheism, whether Lacanian or Derridean, could justifiably be described as the best possible outcome of a good analysis, whether this analysis is "good" judged by clinical-therapeutic standards or by conceptual-theoretical ones. For now, the most that can be hoped for is that Hägglund's superlative conceptual-theoretical analysis, although arguably incapable of killing for good the (unconscious) desire for what the signifier "God" signifies, can arouse in others a "second degree" desire not to have this desire, a redoubled desire for other desires. In this resides the promise of the project of radical atheism.

Notes

1. *SE* 21: 38, 49–50, 53–6.
2. *SE* 22: 34, 160–1, 167–9, 171–4.
3. Johnston 2008a: 67–8.
4. Pfister 1993: 574.
5. Lacan 2005c: 78–9.
6. Hägglund 2008: 1, 111–12.
7. Ibid.: 122.
8. Ibid.: 2, 8, 28, 32–4, 44, 48–9, 130, 132.
9. Ibid.: 121, 129.
10. Ibid.: 111.
11. Ibid.: 119.
12. Lacan 2006l: 518.
13. Hägglund 2008: 136.
14. Ibid.: 27–9, 31–2, 38, 46, 51, 73, 210–11, 220.
15. Ibid.: 24–5.
16. Ibid.: 33–4.
17. Ibid.: 3.
18. Ibid.: 110, 131, 144, 214, 220, 227.
19. Žižek 1989: 4–5; Žižek 1997c: 89; Žižek 1999a: 66, 293–4; Žižek 1999c: 211; Žižek 2001b: 104; Žižek 2002b: 106–7; Žižek 2006a: 182; Žižek 2008b: 54; Johnston 2005c: 368–9; Johnston 2008d: 37, 52.
20. Hägglund 2008: 8.
21. Ibid.: 24–5.
22. Hägglund 2009a: 27–33.
23. Johnston 2005c: 6.
24. *SVII*: 213–14; *SXVII*: 66; Chiesa and Toscano 2005: 10; Johnston 2008b: 166, 168–70.
25. Johnston 2005a: 224–6, 243–5.
26. *SE* 14: 305.
27. Hägglund 2008: 157.
28. Ibid.: 32.
29. *SE* 14: 305–6.
30. *SXV*: 11/22/67; *SXVI*: 41; *SXXIII*: 72.
31. *SE* 14: 306.
32. Ibid.: 306–7.
33. Ibid.: 76.
34. Ibid.: 78.
35. Ibid.: 244–5, 255.

36. *SIII*: 81, 190–1, 321; Lacan 1977: 37–9; Muller 1980: 147, 156; Žižek 2001a: 100; Johnston 2008d: 37–8.
37. Johnston 2010a: 328–30.
38. *SE* 14: 186–7.
39. Ibid.: 289.
40. Kant 1978: 55–6; Schelling 1980: 181–2; Johnston 2008d: 25–6.
41. Heidegger 1962: 280–1.
42. *SE* 14: 292–6.
43. Freud 1987: 11–12, 20.
44. *SE* 14: 296.
45. Ibid.: 299.
46. *SE* 17: 242.
47. *SII*: 211; *SIII*: 179–80; *SV*: 465; *SIX*: 5/23/62; *SXVII*: 122–3; *SXXI*: 12/18/73; *SXXII*: 4/8/75; *SXXIII*: 125; Lacan 2001h: 405; Lacan 2001i: 451; Lacan 2006a: 83; Žižek 1994b: 164; Žižek 2000: 256; Johnston 2008d: 26–9.
48. Rank 1993: 23–5, 60–1, 81; Rank 1958: 55, 116, 119, 124–5, 206–7, 212–13.
49. Brown 1959: 127–8.
50. Becker 1973: 96, 107, 163–4.
51. Descartes 1993: 1–2, 4, 9.
52. Hobbes 1985: 102, 108–9, 112–15.
53. Hägglund 2008: 43.
54. Blanchot 1992: 1, 93–5, 123; Blanchot 1993: 34, 184; Derrida 1993: 87.
55. Derrida 1993: 8, 11–12, 14, 17–18, 21–3, 36–7, 76.
56. Blanchot 1992: 18.
57. Johnston 2008a: 67–8.
58. Lacan 2006a: 83.
59. Žižek 1994a: 29.
60. Hägglund 2008: 192–3; Hägglund 2009a: 25–32.
61. Hägglund 2009a: 25–32.
62. *SVII*: 70, 300; *SXXI*: 3/19/74.
63. Hägglund 2009a: 25–32.
64. Žižek 1997a: 79; Žižek 2002b: 192–3; Žižek 2004a: 144.
65. *SV*: 407; *SVI*: 6/10/59; *SVIII*: 294; *SXI*: 12–13; *SXVIII*: 156; Lacan 2006l: 518, 522–3.
66. *SE* 1: 318, 331; *SIV*: 168–9; *SV*: 381–2, 406, 499; *SVI*: 4/15/59; *SVII*: 39, 51; *SIX*: 2/21/62; *SXVI*: 224–5; Lacan 2006m: 580; Lacan 2006o: 690; Johnston 2005b: 69, 77–81.

67. Žižek 1988: 77; Žižek 1989: 169–70; Žižek 1993: 36; Johnston 2005c: 365–6; Johnston 2008d: 18–19, 109, 146–8, 159–60.
68. Johnston 2001: 414–15.
69. *SX*: 53, 58–61, 67, 98, 102, 360; Johnston 2005c: 280–1.
70. Johnston 2008d: 263.
71. Derrida 1994: 51.
72. Hägglund 2008: 82, 84.
73. Derrida 1994: 51.
74. *SXI*: 29.
75. *SE* 22: 160–1.
76. *SXIX: ...ou pire*: 6/21/72.
77. *SXX*: 30–1.
78. *SXVII* [Fr.]: 209; *SXVII*: 180.
79. *SXIX: ...ou pire*: 3/8/72.
80. Lacan 1977: 37.
81. Ibid.: 37–8.
82. Ibid.: 38.
83. *SIII*: 46.
84. *SIII*: 12–13, 45–6, 149–50; *SV*: 480; Lacan 2006k: 465–6, 479, 481.
85. Johnston 2008d: 37–9.
86. Lacan 1977: 38–9.
87. La Rochefoucauld 1959: 40 [maxim 26].
88. Hägglund 2009a: 30.
89. *SXI*: 204–5.
90. Ibid.: 150.
91. *SXI*: 177, 197–9; Lacan 2006p: 717–20; Johnston 2008d: 22–3, 52.
92. Lacan 2006k: 461; Johnston 2008d: 47–8.
93. Hägglund 2008: 43–4, 93.
94. Žižek 2002a: 197; Žižek 1993: 64; Žižek 1994b: 120; Žižek 1996b: 19, 22; Žižek 1996a: 94; Žižek 2001a: 71; Johnston 2008d: 39–43.
95. *SII*: 169, 238; *SVIII*: 122, 413; Lacan 2006c: 76; Lacan 2006d: 90; Lacan 2001h: 409; Lacan 2005a: 41–3; Dolar 1996: 137; Safouan 1983: 60; Žižek 1997c: 94; Johnston 2008d: 45–51.
96. *SVII*: 320; *SVIII*: 122.
97. Žižek 1994a: 27.
98. Butler 1990: 272.
99. Hägglund 2008: 93, 220.
100. Hegel 1991c: §94 [149].

101. *SE* 17: 225.
102. *SIX*: 5/30/62, 6/6/62, 6/20/62; *SX*: 57, 74, 292–4; *SXIII*: 1/12/66, 3/30/66, 6/1/66; *SXIV*: 5/24/67, 6/7/67; *SXVI*: 300–5; Lacan 2006o: 693, 699; Johnston 2013g.
103. *SIII*: 190.
104. Laplanche and Pontalis 1986: 19, 27; Green 2000: 59; Zupančič 1996: 47–8; Johnston 2008d: 33–6.
105. Johnston 2008d: 30–1, 61, 100.
106. *SXVIII*: 65, 67, 105, 107; *SXIX: Le savoir du psychanalyste*: 11/4/71, 3/3/72; *SXXI*: 2/12/74, 5/21/74; *SXXV*: 11/15/77.
107. *SXX*: 93.
108. Johnston 2008d: 39.
109. *SXI*: 59.
110. *SXVIII*: 68–9.
111. *SE* 13: 147–9, 154.
112. Ibid.: 143.
113. *SXVII*: 119–20.
114. *SX*: 357–8; *SXVI*: 280–1; Johnston 2008b: 170–1.
115. *SXVII*: 119.
116. Ibid.: 119.
117. Ibid.: 119–20.
118. *SVII*: 139; *SXVI*: 224–5, 249.
119. *SVII*: 14.

9

The true Thing is the (w)hole: Freudian-Lacanian Psychoanalysis and Hägglund's Chronolibidinal Reading

The ongoing debate between me and Hägglund is an exchange unlikely to end anytime soon, or so I hope. Our separate bodies of work, especially my 2005 book *Time Driven: Metapsychology and the Splitting of the Drive* and his 2008 book *Radical Atheism: Derrida and the Time of Life*, cover overlapping ground, particularly in their focus on the intertwining of the motivational and the temporal as conceived of at the intersection of philosophy and psychoanalysis. In the background of this present phase of our dialogue (here in Chapter 9) is the first open airing of our points of convergence and conflict in a special issue of the journal *The New Centennial Review* based on the proceedings of an event at Cornell University devoted to Hägglund's *Radical Atheism* (Chapter 8 is a modified version of my contribution to this issue).[1]

Through this dialogue, Hägglund and I have pushed each other to extend, modify, and refine our respective positions on the cluster of topics at the heart of our shared concerns. By virtue of these amiable confrontations, our perspectives have mutually influenced one another to undergo further evolutions. In what follows, my response to Hägglund's newest book *Dying for Time: Proust, Woolf, Nabokov* – given the frame of our prior debates in conjunction with my own specific interests, I will focus my attention on this book's fourth and final chapter entitled "Reading: Freud, Lacan, Derrida" – will reflect certain developments in my own thinking induced by Hägglund's insights. But, at the same time, I also will continue doggedly to hold to many of the core tenets informing both those of my views disputed by Hägglund as well as various of my criticisms of his proposals and arguments (see Chapter 8). As the ensuing will indicate, I remain convinced that a number of objections I already have raised to Hägglund's Derridean alternatives to analyses of time and desire along

Freudian and Lacanian lines either have not been answered or have not been answered in ways I find compelling.

I believe that Hägglund and myself possess in common what could be characterized as an intellectual stubbornness. Put in parlance familiar in this context, the absence of consensus sustained by this commonality of our scholarly temperaments is simultaneously the condition of possibility and impossibility for our fruitful conversations. As regards the impossible side of this dynamic, I strongly suspect that several fundamental differences between us apropos the position of psychoanalysis vis-à-vis philosophy in particular – I anticipate neither of us budging much in relation to certain of these differences – mark fault lines along which we are bound to diverge from each other repeatedly. Definite limits seem to me to be helpfully coming to light, ones perhaps triggering associations to Deleuze's expressed attitude as a philosopher about entering into debates;[2] these limits, as rifts of disagreement, have to do with philosophical methods for interpreting psychoanalytic texts, the relationship between metapsychological theory and clinical practice in analysis itself, and the phenomenology of libidinal life on and off the couch, among other topics. But, at the same time and as regards the complementary possible (as opposed to impossible) side of this dynamic, the back-and-forth we have enjoyed thus far for over five years persuasively indicates that the tensions of these very differences separating our stances are also the galvanizing sources from which spring the most rewarding moments of our thinking with and against each other. Maybe, at least in this instance, Hägglund would be willing to admit that a lack of fullness (in this case, a fiercely maintained absence of complete agreement) can play a central structuring role endowed with ample productive power. Alternately, from the angle of Hägglund's approach, it might be said that, from the start, we perhaps never desired consensus anyway.

These prefatory remarks aside, I want to begin my response to the latest incarnation of Hägglundian chronolibidinalism by making explicit a difficulty I discern afflicting the very foundations of this novel, highly innovative rethinking of the temporal dimensions of desiring life (I hinted at this in my earlier reply to *Radical Atheism* – see Chapter 8). Briefly formulated, Hägglund's reflections on time and desire depend upon an equivocation between that which is ubiquitous, on the one hand, and that which is a cause or reason, on the other hand. This generates several problems for him in my view. First and most obviously, at the level of philosophical argumentation, there is the logical illegitimacy of concluding that temporal finitude is the cause or reason for any particular object being desired merely by virtue of such temporality being an omnipresent feature of all objects of possible desiring. Throughout his work, including in *Dying for Time*, Hägglund regularly makes this move of slippage from underscoring time as a lowest common denominator of libidinal experience to identifying it as the *Ur*-catalyst of the libidinal economy, thereby relying upon a conflation of ubiquity with causality.[3] Even if one concedes to him that the entities and representations invested in by desiring subjects are all finite in his Derridean sense as pervaded by the negativity of ceaseless, unrelenting succession – this itself is a bone of contention in conjunction with the theories of Freud and Lacan – this by no means automatically and necessarily entails that a given desiring subject is invested in a given entity/representation because of temporal finitude.

Furthermore, and directly flowing from the preceding point, I fear that Hägglund's radical atheist chronolibidinalism is vulnerable to the same kind of judgment as passed by Hegel on Schelling (specifically, Schelling's "identity philosophy"). As is common knowledge, in the preface to 1807's *Phenomenology of Spirit*, Hegel precipitates a break with his friend and collaborator when he depicts the Schellingian Absolute as the "night in which all cows are black"[4] (without grandiosely comparing Hägglund and me to these huge figures, I pray that we not suffer the same sad fate, one fueled in their case by mutual misunderstandings, as a consequence of our exchanges). Skipping over the multiple nuances and subtleties both philosophical and historical condensed within Hegel's curt verdict, one of its basic complaints is that explaining everything is as good as explaining nothing (at least if this is done on the basis of a single principle of principles). Hegel sees Schelling, like Spinoza before him, hastily dissolving the kaleidoscopic tapestry of innumerable differences presented by dappled reality into the indifferent abyss of a flat, monochromatic monism (see also Chapters 2 and 3).

Hägglund's ambitious and creative reconstruction of Derridean philosophy on the basis of its central idea of *différance* and related notions elevates and extends temporal finitude into an Absolute as all-pervasive negativity (whether in the guise of a metaphysics weighted toward an ontology or a "logic" weighted toward an epistemology).[5] Especially as regards what is at stake in a psycho-analytic account of desire, the critical upshot of my reference to the Hegel-Schelling split is that Hägglund's chronolibido replaces the illuminations of Freudian-Lacanian drive theory with an undifferentiated darkness in which all actually and potentially desired objects are evenly and comparably blackened by an omnipresent temporality. If, according to Hägglund's Derrideanism, everything is thoroughly permeated by the ubiquitous temporal negativity of *différance*, then, apropos desiring life, what explains why a particular psyche's libidinal economy binds itself to the particular objects it selects and not others? How is his picture of desiring life not tantamount to a libidinal night in which all objects of desire are equally black?

In *Dying for Time*, Hägglund, echoing the early Heidegger of *Being and Time*, connects finitude to caring, claiming that one's care for anything (whether oneself, others, or various beings and states of affairs) is conditioned by the underlying fact of the fragility, vulnerability, mortality, or possible non-being of all things (i.e., their temporal finitude).[6] But, even if this claim is accepted as true – I will raise some doubts about its veracity subsequently – it does not provide Hägglund with the ability to account for the distributions and redistributions of libidinal investments within what, following Derrida, he recasts as the "bindinal economy."[7] He maintains that the intra-psychical economic management of cathexes (*Besetzungen*) as bindings (*Bindungen*) is governed by calculations regarding the threats and dangers circulating within the field of entities and events actually or potentially cathected. In other words, the organizations of libidinal cares are said to alter precisely in response to the psyche's assessments of the risks it and everything else faces under the forever-looming shadow of the grim Absolute Master.

But, at this juncture, Hägglund's theory of chronolibido is confronted by some tough questions: If each and every real and possible object of a binding cathexis is equally affected by temporal finitude, how can appealing to this ostensibly essential feature of all objects contribute to deciphering the shifts of distributions from certain specific objects to other specific objects? That is, if care is solicited always and solely by temporal finitude, how and why would the libidinal economy care about any particular object(s) since they all are temporally finite according to Hägglund's universalization of Derridean *différance*? If, as

Hägglund asserts in dissent from Freud, even the unconscious side of psychical life is acutely aware of death-dealing temporal succession in its purported absolute ubiquity,[8] why do psychical subjects go on desiring along the lines presumed by him, continuing to bother to calculate, distribute, invest, manage, shift, and so on? Asked differently, why would Hägglund's chronolibidinalism not force one into eventually arriving at the implausible conclusion – for obvious reasons, he himself does not draw this consequence from his arguments – that every single desiring subjectivity is always-already libidinally paralyzed as a result of realizing the total impossibility of defending in any effective fashion against the inescapable ravages of time? In still other terms, why would the Derridean-Hägglundian bindinal economy not be stuck in a position analogous to that of the Beast of Buridan, immobilized by its being situated amidst an array of equivalently finite objects from which to select without sufficiently differentiating criteria or incentives?

Incidentally, in the reading of Freud's 1915 essay "Thoughts for the Times on War and Death" laid out in the final chapter of *Dying for Time*, Hägglund justifies his above-mentioned philosophical contradiction of the Freudian thesis positing a fundamental ignorance of death on the part of the unconscious by contentiously claiming that Freud bases it on philosophical rather than clinical grounds (hence bracketing more empirical analytic considerations and thereby aiming to enhance the legitimacy of the non-empirical angle from which he opposes Freud's position). As should be obvious, Hägglund's own stance requires that he contradict Freud on this precise point apropos mortality and the psyche. Hägglund states, "when Freud asserts that the unconscious operates without regard for time and death, or believes that it is immortal, he does not rely on the evidence of psychoanalytic experience but on speculative concepts through which the evidence is interpreted."[9] I think this assertion is inaccurate.

Freud arrives at his thesis in "Thoughts for the Times on War and Death" that mortality is unknown as such to the unconscious thanks to his contemporaneous hypotheses that the unconscious, as a mode of thinking different-in-kind from conscious cognition, is not conversant with negation and (linear) time.[10] Hägglund probably would retort that these hypotheses are contained in his 1915 metapsychological paper on "The Unconscious" and that, as elements of metapsychology, they are "speculative concepts" that do "not rely on the evidence of psychoanalytic experience." However, Freud's metapsychological papers amount to a theoretical consolidation of many years of clinical experience going back to the 1890s.

Although Freud does not operate strictly according to the empiricism of an experimenting natural scientist, he also carefully avoids engaging in *apriori* armchair legislating over his realms of inquiry. Up to the level of the seemingly most speculative tiers of his metapsychology, complex mutual interactions between more empirical and more theoretical dimensions are operative. In this specific instance, the postulated unconscious ignorance of negation and time arises from Freud's observation of primary-process mentation (itself distinct from the secondary-process varieties displayed by conscious thinking[11]) as playing across the surfaces of his analysands' free-associational monologues. In particular, interpretive investigations of countless individual dreams – as is well known, dreams are "the royal road to the unconscious"[12] during Freud's turn-of-the-century creation of psychoanalysis – reveal to Freud formations and styles of mental life foreign to familiar conscious mindedness but profoundly influencing the latter nonetheless. Clinical analytic experience cannot be sidelined even when aspects of Freud's metapsychological apparatus are under discussion.

The fifth section of the metapsychology paper on "The Unconscious," in which this sector of the psyche is said to be unfamiliar with negation and time, is significantly entitled "The Special Characteristics of the System *Ucs.*" Already in my response to *Radical Atheism*, I complain that Hägglund's handling of psychoanalysis rides roughshod over the unique features of unconscious mindedness setting it apart from much of what is taken for granted within the spheres of conscious experience (such as the principle of non-contradiction and the chronological ordering of temporal succession).[13] To cut a long story short, I remain convinced that he fails to take heed of the peculiarities and distinguishing qualities of unconscious thinking as primary-process mentation different-in-kind from conscious thinking as secondary-process mentation. From a location external to analytic experience, Hägglund applies to both conscious and unconscious sides of the psyche without distinction a theoretical framework anchored in a philosophy (i.e., Derrida's) which itself originates with a Saussurian-inspired reinterpretation of Husserl and his phenomenological legacy (with Husserlian phenomenology being focused on consciousness, and extremely wary of the Freudian unconscious[14]). Hägglund discounts discrepancies between separate psychical relationships to time, negation, and death, discrepancies on display in dreams, fantasies, transferences, associations, and other touchstones of analytic work. He also underestimates the illogical tendencies (relative to secondary-process logical standards) and recklessly de-synthesizing powers (through which ideas such as "living on" and "being finite" can be torn asunder and held apart by abstracting ideational violence) of unconscious processes. I must confess that I have difficulty seeing the presence of a genuinely analytic unconscious in Hägglundian radical atheist chronolibidinalism. At most, I detect something closer to Pierre Janet's depth-psychological unconscious as a mere double of consciousness operating according to the same fundamental rules and patterns. I wonder whether Hägglund actually needs or can accommodate a thinking of the unconscious (in both senses of the genitive) so alien to the impressively streamlined and classically logical system he presents.[15]

Returning to the problems generated by the issue of ubiquity for Hägglund, much of the above articulated at the outset of this present chapter suggests that there are descriptive phenomenological shortcomings stemming from Hägglund's sliding between ubiquity and causality in addition to the logical and philosophical difficulties already indicated. Before spelling this out, I ought to mention that one of my reservations in reaction to *Radical Atheism* – this likewise has to do with Hägglund's phenomenology of desire – continues to trouble me up through the present: It seems that Hägglund persists in problematically assuming that desiring subjects can be utterly mistaken about their own desires in manners that would be entirely inconsequential for their desiring subjectivity itself. Although psychoanalysis admittedly is predicated on the possibility and, indeed, inevitability of minded individuals being consciously "mistaken" about what they "really" unconsciously want and wish, neither Freud nor Lacan treats the conscious manifestations of unconscious forces and factors as without significant consequences for the conscious, preconscious, and unconscious strata of the psyche. That is to say, for Freudian-Lacanian analysis, how subjects self-consciously experience and spontaneously self-interpret their emotions and motivations cannot be dismissively written off as inconsequential *qua* purely epiphenomenal, false, fictional, illusory, reducible, and the like.

Conscious and unconscious surfaces of psychical subjectivity thoroughly interpenetrate each other in relations of reciprocally affecting entanglements. But, according to Hägglund's radical atheism, the overwhelming majority of humanity historical and contemporary mistakenly believes itself to desire things other than "survival" as "living on" in Hägglund's Derridean sense. In both *Radical Atheism* and *Dying for Time*, he labors to disabuse theists and insufficiently radical atheists alike of these allegedly erroneous beliefs.[16] Whereas he sees his radical atheist chronolibidinalism as an immanent critique of psychoanalytic descriptions of desiring life,[17] it appears to me to be an external rather than an immanent one.

Related to the distinction between immanent and external critique, since the release of *Radical Atheism* and in response to feedback received from a number of his interlocutors, Hägglund has shifted to describing his Derrida-inspired framework as a conceptual logic that permits raising the contents of other disciplinary domains (such as psychoanalysis) to the dignity of their notions (to phrase this in fitting Hegelian language). Radical atheist chronolibidinalism thereby supposedly allows for the expression of fundamental theoretical truths about space and time (à la the structural dynamics of traces of *différance* as "the becoming-time of space" and "the becoming-space of time") embedded, but perhaps not properly recognized, within whatever regions upon which this conceptual machinery is brought to bear.[18] Hägglund is well aware of the immediately striking resemblance between how Hegel portrays his procedure in, for instance, his three *magnum opera* (*Phenomenology of Spirit*, *Science of Logic*, and *Elements of the Philosophy of Right*) and how he (Hägglund) recently has taken to presenting the "logical" status of his theoretical apparatus with its battery of tightly interlinked concepts. Of course, Hegel tirelessly protests that his "method" is not a method as a formal scaffolding of protocols externally applied with indifference to any and every set of given contents. He adamantly insists that he practices a kind of "hands off" philosophical observation in which he merely witnesses without presuppositions and narrates faithfully how other figures/shapes of consciousness and logical-conceptual worldviews immanently critique themselves if patiently left long enough to their own devices (sooner or later "doing violence to themselves at their own hands"). Recourse to the arbitrary, willfully capricious dogmatism inherent to external philosophical critiques, as awkward, clumsy browbeatings of others' perspectives, is neither requisite nor appropriate from the vantage point of Hegel's systematic philosophy of the genuinely (rather than spuriously) infinite.[19]

As an aside and in conjunction with Hegel on the infinite, I am tempted to ask Hägglund in passing whether the category of the finite, foundational for his entire endeavor, has any ontological and/or epistemological validity apart from the corresponding category of the infinite. If finitude is unthinkable without infinity (or, at a minimum, if it is simply conceded that the idea of infinity is not sheer nothingness), what would this mean for Hägglund's project? What if ideational inscriptions of the infinite, perhaps reflected in mathematical, artistic, religious, and philosophical guises, themselves can be cathected by the bindinal economy? Does temporal finitude hold sway in these instances with the same absoluteness asserted apropos libidinal investments in other sorts of ideational representations (*Vorstellungen*)?

Questions similar to these can be raised from another angle. Hägglund has taken to maintaining that he is modestly claiming temporal finitude to be a necessary (and not also sufficient) condition for the binding cathexes of desire. But, the invocation of the category of necessary condition creates severe problems for Hägglund's larger philosophical stance. In order for something to be identified as a necessary condition, one or more at least hypothetical counter-factuals to this something must be thinkable, if not also knowable. Thus, for Hägglund to be able to pick out temporal finitude as a necessary condition for anything (in his case, desirability as susceptibility to libidinal/bindinal investment), he must concede, at a minimum, the thinkability of temporal finitude not holding, of it not being the case. He would have to allow for the possibility of conceiving of potentially desired entities and events not subject to temporal finitude in order to propose the latter as their necessary condition. Yet, this is precisely what Hägglund's radical atheism deems to be utterly impossible, contending that anything eternal and/or infinite is, despite many claims by many others past and present to the contrary, wholly and completely unthinkable and unknowable. Moreover, his critiques of psychoanalysis rely heavily upon this radical atheist denial of the very conceivability of exceptions to the posited rule of temporal finitude. Of course, for analysis, concerned as it is with "psychical reality" (instead of consensus empirical reality), mere conceivability, the formation of an ideational representation (*Vorstellung*) of some sort (however skeletal), is enough to serve as a point of attachment for desire's cathexes.

Therefore, Hägglund hoists himself onto the horns of a dilemma through his recourse to the logical category of necessary condition. On the one hand, faced with the predicament spelled out in the preceding paragraph, he could relinquish the claim that his purportedly absolute and universal temporal finitude is a necessary condition. However, doing so would deprive him of his response to criticisms flowing from the problem of ubiquity/omnipresence (criticisms articulated both above and below here). On the other hand, for him to stick to his recourse to the logical category of necessary condition would be to persist in contradicting the fundaments of his own position by permitting at least the thinkability of exceptions to the ostensible rule of temporal finitude – and, in permitting himself this, cutting the legs out from under his radical atheist critique of psychoanalysis.

Returning to an earlier point above, regardless of whether or not one grants that Hegel always or even sometimes should be taken at his word apropos his ways of proceeding, I do not think Hägglund should be taken at his similar word when it comes to how he engages with the Freudian field. In other words, I believe his critiques of analysis to be external instead of immanent; put differently, what I am charging is that the chronolibidinal rabbit he pulls out of the analytic hat is the one he put there beforehand. His attempted maneuver of jumping to the purported meta-level of a "logic" – this maneuver feigns Hegelian modesty by pretending to be a discourse in which the desire of psychoanalysis can get clear "for itself" about its supposed "in itself" – definitely does not immunize him against intra-analytic contestations of his arguably loaded descriptions of the phenomenology of desiring existence. Although he denies doing so, Hägglund strikes me as adding from an extra-analytic outside philosophical corrections to how desires are experienced, articulated, and interpreted by analysands and analysts alike (as well as, apart from the restricted circles of analysis, billions and billions of people over the full arc of human history up through today who believe themselves to desire things more and other than Derridean-Hägglundian survival). By my lights, his logic is not a Hegelian-style framework within which the figures and shapes of desire in psychoanalysis are free to express themselves and, in so doing, spontaneously sublate themselves of their own accord into the concepts and categories of radical atheist chronolibidinalism. Instead, Hägglund-the-philosopher artfully ventriloquizes through the non-philosophical (here psychoanalytic) voices of his desiring subjects. Unlike Hegel, Freud, Lacan, and the practitioners of analytic listening, he neither trusts these subjects' self-understandings nor adequately considers that, even if distorted or somehow "incorrect," these self-understandings might function along the lines of the real abstractions theorized varyingly by Hegel, Marx, and Lacan, namely, as concretely efficacious illusions defying dismissal as wholly ineffective and completely epiphenomenal unrealities.

In the remainder of this response to Hägglund, I will substantiate the indictments issued in the immediately preceding paragraphs by concentrating especially on his reading of Lacan's Thing (*das Ding, la Chose*). Before taking up this topic, a few preliminary indications and qualifications are in order. To begin with, Hägglund's pointed, powerful interrogations of *das Ding* and its relation to the place of lack(s) in Lacanian theory, starting in *Radical Atheism* and continuing through *Dying for Time*, have forced me to rethink how I situate myself with respect to these aspects of Lacan's metapsychology. The interpretation of this side of Lacan I advance below in contrast to Hägglund's critical assessment is indebted to Hägglund himself. His pushes against Lacan have pushed me in turn to clarify and refine for myself how I comprehend what I appreciate and appropriate from the latter. This is yet another manner in which Hägglund has proven to be an invaluable interlocutor for me.

Furthermore, as another preliminary remark, I should acknowledge an additional debt to Hägglund. The last two paragraphs of the introduction to *Radical Atheism* provide a lucid synopsis of his interpretive approach as regards Derrida. Within the introduction's penultimate paragraph, he declares, "my main approach is analytical rather than exegetical. I not only seek to explicate what Derrida is saying; I seek to develop his arguments, fortify his logic, and pursue its implications."[20] In the same paragraph, Hägglund adds, "I seek to 'inherit' Derrida in the precise sense he has given to the word. To inherit is not simply to accept what is handed down from the master; it is to reaffirm the legacy in order to make it live on in a different way."[21] The final paragraph immediately following these lines is worth quoting in full:

Such inheritance cannot be accomplished through pious conservation but only through critical discrimination. One question that is bound to arise, then, is whether there are aspects of Derrida's work that do not adhere to the radically atheist logic I develop, especially since it stands in sharp contrast to the readings proposed by many other major interpreters. My response is that even if one is able to find passages in Derrida that cannot be salvaged by the logic of radical atheism, it is far from enough to refute the reading I propose here. Like everyone else, Derrida was certainly liable to be inconsistent. However, in order to turn these inconsistencies into an argument against the logic of radical atheism that I establish, one has to show that they are not in fact inconsistencies but rather testify to the operation in Derrida of a different logic altogether.[22]

At one moment in the fourth chapter of *Dying for Time*, Hägglund seeks to revisit Freud with the same sympathy he unwaveringly bestows upon Derrida.[23] However, most of the time, his interpretations of Freud and Lacan are comparatively less charitable. I wonder, in what is presented as a philosophically systematic edifice, what theoretical axioms and philosophical decisions justify this unevenness of generosity. In what ensues, I will put forward readings of Freud and Lacan arising from a treatment of them modeled on Hägglund's handling of Derrida's texts. Through interpreting Freudianism and Lacanianism as Hägglund interprets Derrideanism, I aim precisely to challenge Hägglund's interpretations of Freud and Lacan through leveling the playing field (and only then seeing where things stand) by doing as much justice to them as he does to Derrida.

One of the goals of my cursory reconstruction here of the Lacanian Thing is to reveal with precision the exact limits of Hägglund's evaluations of Lacan specifically and psychoanalysis generally. But, additionally, another goal of this is to explain why my Freudian-Lacanian version of drive theory (as per *Time Driven*, with which Hägglund engages in *Dying for Time*) is not, as it might appear to be (especially to Hägglund himself), just as guilty as Hägglundian chronolibidinalism of the Schellingian-style absolutism I alleged above in resonance with the Hegel of the *Phenomenology*. This has everything to do with how one understands *das Ding*.

I soon will get well and truly underway with a compressed summary of select aspects of Freud's and Lacan's ideas, after which I will conclude by drawing from this summary a few objections to Hägglund's radical atheist and chronolibidinal critique of analysis. Foreshadowing these concluding objections, I should note here at the beginning the idiosyncrasy of how Hägglund construes Lacan's Thing, especially in *Dying for Time*. He talks about *la Chose* almost exclusively as a fantasmatic avatar of presumably lost immortality; according to his version of Lacanian theory, it amounts to the fictional fullness of an impossibly eternal life purportedly placed by Lacan at the gravitational center of the libidinal economy.[24] I certainly do not intend to repudiate unreservedly Hägglund's rendition of the Lacanian Thing. He indeed discerningly has found some textual hooks in Lacan's corpus on which to hang his portrait of the matter at stake. But, carrying forward a suggestion from my earlier reply to *Radical Atheism*, I do plan to represent this picture as indefensibly selective and partial (or, in Hegelese, "one-sided").

Moreover, I would contend that one of the sources of the undeniable persuasive power of Hägglund's critical analyses of Freud and Lacan is the fact that the preoccupations unbalancing the Hägglundian image of *das Ding* (i.e., fixations on loss and mortality) deeply reverberate with the unresolved issues lying at the foundations of psychoanalysis as partially but significantly laid by Freud's far from fully successful self-analysis. As I have argued elsewhere, what Freud fails to get to grips with thoroughly in his analyses of himself is a debilitating obsessional neurotic *Todesangst*, with this impasse of his self-analysis subsequently resurfacing in the disguised manifestations of displacements onto patients, cultural objects, and metapsychological concepts and problems (including, perhaps most notably, his inconsistent, conflict-plagued pronouncements regarding the death drive [*Todestrieb*]).[25] At one point in his third seminar on *The Psychoses* (1955–56), Lacan observes, "The question of death and the question of birth are as it happens the two ultimate questions that have precisely no solution in the signifier. This is what gives neurotics their existential value."[26] Relying on a figure (i.e., Derrida) who himself draws heavily from existential phenomenology (particularly Heidegger's brand of it), Hägglund offers a philosophical critique of psychoanalysis whose great "existential value" taps into the anxious energies animating obsessional-type symptomatic cathexes of ideas having to do with time and death, energies perturbing both Freud himself as well as the neurotics of whom Lacan speaks in the preceding quotation (not to mention the unnamed poet featuring in Freud's essay "On Transience," a text to which both Hägglund and I refer on other occasions[27]).

Oddly for someone so inclined toward Derrida, Hägglund tends to neglect the profound rapport in Lacan's teachings between *das Ding* and the alterity of Real Otherness (as distinct from Imaginary and Symbolic varieties as the intersubjective alter-ego and the trans-subjective socio-symbolic order respectively[28]). As he notes in *Radical Atheism, la Chose lacanienne* first surfaces in the seventh seminar on *The Ethics of Psychoanalysis* (1959–60).[29] Therein, Lacan explicitly stipulates that his Thing is an extrapolation from the figure of the "neighbor" (*Nebenmensch*) in Freud's 1895 *Project for a Scientific Psychology*.[30] Lacan thereafter persists in associating *la Chose* with Freud's *Nebenmensch als Ding*.[31] Furthermore, Lacan's 1959 introduction of his Freud-inspired Thing already is anticipated in prior musings on an epistemologically inaccessible yet palpably perturbing dimension of unrepresentable Otherness (i.e., Real alterity beyond the little others and big Others of Imaginary-Symbolic realities) at the heart of what is involved with true love.[32] Before, during, and after the seventh seminar, Lacan frequently couples *das Ding* with amorous life (including both courtly and maternal love) and the latter's positioning in relation to the need-demand-desire triad undergirding his vision of the multifaceted libidinal economy.[33]

The full intensities of contradictory swirls of a plethora of libidinal and affective ambivalences – the ambivalences Lacan ties to the interrelated concepts of the Thing, desire, and *jouissance* have come up before between Hägglund and me[34] – are reduced by chronolibidinalism to the see-sawing alternation between "chronophilia" and "chronophobia," a movement hinging on temporal finitude alone.[35] Of course, themes having to do with time and death are overriding fixations for particular incarnations of obsessional neurosis (as embodied by Freud himself and his incomplete self-analysis). Hägglund carefully selects moments in Lacan's texts when the latter associates *das Ding* with these themes, while passing over in silence many others in which this Thing is associated with motifs very different than those directly related to mortality and immortality. I would suggest that when Lacan too zeroes in on such thematic contents, he is doing so in tandem with mapping the libidinal landscape of certain sorts of neuroses and not, as Hägglund portrays it so as to set up his critique of Lacanianism, wholly equating the essence of *la Chose* with the same topics inordinately privileged by chronolibidinal radical atheism.

To make my point here very quickly, I can cite another of Lacan's prefigurations of *das Ding* as properly presented for the first time in *Seminar VII*. *La Chose freudienne*, as depicted in the famous 1955 *écrit* of that title, is identified not with time, death, mortality, immortality, or anything else in this vein, but, more broadly, with the "truth" (*vérité*) of the unconscious (again, in both senses of the genitive).[36] For all subjects, starting out as prematurationally helpless subjects-to-be, the origins of these truths reside in early encounters with ontogenetically primary Real Otherness (as the parental neighbor-as-Thing). However, echoing Freud's admittedly rather enigmatic notion of the primordial "choice of neurosis,"[37] the many varieties of obsessionals, hysterics, perverts, and psychotics are distinguished by how they come to respond differently to *la Chose* as the *Nebenmensch-Ding* (be it Freudian and/or Lacanian). Lacan remarks in the seventh seminar that "It is . . . in relation to the original *Ding* that the first orientation, the first choice, the first seat of subjective orientation takes place, and that I will sometimes call *Neuronenwahl*, the choice of neurosis."[38] Some psyches, but far from all, become preoccupied with trains of thought concerning limits and losses ultimately arising from temporal finitude. Others shift into organizing themselves and their libidinal economies around issues connected with, among many possible things, love, sexuality, pleasure, symbiosis, dependency, control, obedience, law, suffering, and so on in ways not entirely overshadowed and exclusively dominated by oppressive worries about the ticking clock measuring the inexorable unwinding of the mortal coil.

For these reasons, I consider Hägglund's chronolibidinalism to be too narrowly one-sided to encompass the wide range of non-epiphenomenal phenomena to be found in the analytic clinic with its differential diagnoses of idiosyncratic desiring lives. This also dovetails with my prior assertion to the effect that Hägglund thrusts forward what is, in fact, an external instead of immanent critique of psychoanalysis, thereby revealing more about his and Derrida's orientations than about what "truly" lies at the core of each and every analytic experience *an und für sich*. That is to say, the whole truth of *la Chose comme vérité* is not encapsulated in the important but partial truths uncovered by Hägglund's investigations.

Not only are the psychopathologically defining reactions to *das Ding als Nebenmensch* differentiated and particularized – each Thing, as a specific Real Other in an individual's ontogenetic life history, is radically singular despite being separate from the subjectively accessible realities of the distinguishing attributes, characteristics, features, predicates, and qualities displayed by intersubjective alter-egos and/or trans-subjective big Others. Throughout Lacan's teachings, *la Chose* remains invariably subsumed under the heading of the Real.[39] As such, a Real Thing is "no-thing" *qua* entity or object exhibiting Imaginary and Symbolic properties and traits on the basis of which given beings are individuated and differentiated. Nonetheless, unlike the universally self-same anonymity of nothingness epitomized by zero in mathematics, the mysterious facelessness of *la Chose lacanienne* – this Real Otherness is "not without" (*pas sans*) a Borromean-knotted rapport with the Imaginary and Symbolic dimensions of alterity – is anything but universal. This elusive "x" (i.e., *das Ding als Nebenmensch*) is always a unique, irreplaceable, and non-fungible *je ne sais quoi* absolutely peculiar to a singular subject-Other link lying at the base of that particular subject's historical formation.[40]

In this context, it bears remembering that Lacan characterizes his Thing as a sort of black hole around which the drives rotate[41] (in addition to it being a void uniquely outlined by the specific need-demand-desire triangle of a subject related to it). My work on drive theory in *Time Driven*, against which Hägglund raises a number of objections, likewise casts *das Ding* in the role of the, as it were, *Ur*/non-object of all drive-objects, namely, the vanishing attractor point of the unfurling chains of signifier-like *Vorstellungen*, themselves constituting the aim-object configurations of this side of the libidinal economy.[42] Although the drama of the drives as I portray them in my first book centrally involves forms and functions of temporalities, each drive of each subject is inflected and individuated by virtue of its unseverable ties to a singular Neighbor-Thing, an incomparable Real Other inseparable from but irreducible to the images and signifiers of Imaginary-Symbolic realities with their perpetually oscillating dialectics of comparative samenesses and differences. Hence, a Freudian-Lacanian account of the libidinal economy, as centered on a true appreciation of the multidimensional whole of *la Chose à la* Freud as well as Lacan, is not in peril of falling into the darkness of an omnipresent night in which all coordinates of cathexes are rendered *de facto* indistinguishable in being equally blackened (*à la* the monochromatic quality of the night in which all cows are black) by ubiquitous temporal finitude – this being a pitfall I previously suggested Hägglund's theory of chronolibido faces without further future revisions and significant additional supplements.

Moreover, Hägglund, in the recent recentering of his chronolibidinalism around a modified version of the Freudian notion of binding (*Bindung*), repeats a misreading of Freud's drive theory integral to Melanie Klein and her heirs in both the object relations theory and British Middle School analytic traditions. Like these Kleinian and post-Kleinian forerunners, Hägglund accuses Freud of sometimes indefensibly proposing the possibility of an unbound drive, namely, a *Trieb* preceding its subsequent state of being bound to objects through cathexes.[43] This accusation is directed toward the Freud who declares drives to be "objectless."[44] When he makes this declaration, it signifies specifically that drives, unlike instincts, do not have biologically predetermined, innately hard-wired orientations toward pre-programmed *teloi* in the form of given kinds of "objects" as natural types of entities or conditions. However, it does not mean that Freud posits the actual existence of a drive without a drive-object, as, for instance, a quick glance at the metapsychological essay "Drives and Their Vicissitudes" reveals. In this piece, all drives are said by definition to consist of the four components of source, pressure, aim, and object.[45] For Freud, there is no drive without a drive-object, although its objects originate exogenously, rather than, as with instincts, endogenously. This holds for Lacan too.[46]

Yet, there are both Freudian and Lacanian caveats to be attached to the idea of objectlessness in light of Hägglund's construal of the notion of binding. I can begin specifying these by returning to Freud's description of the *Nebenmensch* in his *Project for a Scientific Psychology* (this being, as underlined earlier, the primary source for Lacan's initial presentation of the Thing in *Seminar VII*). Therein, Freud affirms that, given "the initial helplessness of human beings," extraneous individuals are essential in the procurement of "satisfaction" (*Befriedigung*), and that this is the initial impetus behind both communication and morality.[47] He goes on to remark that the other person, as a mental object, can be decomposed into two core components. On the one hand, there is the other as a "thing" (*Ding*), as something with a "constant structure"; on the other hand, there is the other as "understood" on the basis of memory and the acquired knowledge it contains.[48] The two terms italicized by Freud in this distinction are "thing" and "understood," thus suggesting that the Other-as-thing is an enduring enigma that fails to fall easily into the grasp of an understanding grounded upon experientially registered data/information (such as the observable overt behavior of the other as a sensible object within the spatio-temporal perceptual field). Is it any accident that the German word used by Freud is the same one employed by Kant to designate that which forever remains radically unknowable for the thinking subject (i.e., the noumenal *Ding an sich*, the constitutively inaccessible thing-in-itself)? An irreducible margin of alterity, of permanent foreignness, remains a constant (if not always acknowledged) feature of all inter-human relationships. This alterity is, at the everyday level, typically covered over by transferential fantasies and related psychical productions filling in the many gaps and cracks in the fabric of experience resulting from this inherent ignorance – and thus serving as compensations for a constitutional lack of telepathy as an impossible mind-to-mind symbiosis. Reality itself would not be what it is as something seemingly stable and negotiable without these "fictional" elements that mitigate against the Thing-like opacity of the Other.

In one sense, neither Freud nor Lacan would disagree with Klein and Hägglund regarding the always-already bound condition of the drives of the libidinal economy. At this level, I think that Hägglund's radical atheist attack on Freudian-Lacanian metapsychology for allegedly surmising that desiring life orbits around an ontogenetic "paradise lost" of presumably full enjoyment misfires.[49] One manner of putting this is that Heinz Hartmann's ego-psychological "undifferentiated phase" is not a Freudian (or, more obviously, Lacanian) idea. Furthermore, Lacan especially, departing from Freud and in tandem with Klein, vigorously repudiates again and again the myth that infancy is anything close to a blissful repose in the Nirvana of comfortable, contended oneness with the benevolent maternal caretaker. This myth's fictional status nonetheless does not stop analysands from sometimes believing in it, whether consciously or unconsciously.

Additionally, the fundamental fantasies constructed around the ineffabilities of the Real Otherness of *das Ding als Nebenmensch* bear witness to an unconscious disregard for the linear chronology of succession upon which Hägglund so adamantly insists (as per Freud's thesis stating the unconscious is ignorant of [conscious] time, a claim derived from and supported by clinical experience, as I noted a while ago). Of a piece with the neglect of the profound differences between conscious and unconscious mentation I have charged him with before (both here and in Chapter 8), Hägglund's references to the notion of fantasy are indistinguishable from how one would talk about episodic memories or daydreams as consciously familiar quotidian phenomena. In *Dying for Time*, Hägglund understandably expresses frustration with Lacanian waverings and vacillations on the question of whether the fantasmatic centers of cathectic gravity for the libidinal economy are traces of an actual, factual past or illusory retroactive constructions.[50] Considering how Freud himself addresses this distinction in texts such as *Studies on Hysteria* (1894), "Letter 52" to Fliess (1896), "Screen Memories" (1899), and "Creative Writers and Day-Dreaming" (1907), the apparent inconsistency pinpointed by Hägglund is symptomatic, namely, no mere accident to be hastily brushed aside as lamentable intellectual sloppiness.[51] In an analysis, when an analysand asks aloud "Is it A or B?" about a plurality (as two or more) of seemingly incompatible interpretive possibilities surfacing thanks to his/her voiced associations, the analyst's appropriate reply frequently is something along the lines of "Maybe it's a bit of both." That is to say, analytic interpretation often favors inclusive over exclusive disjunction with an ear to the unconscious "logic" of overdetermination, itself unshackled by classical, bivalent logic's laws of non-contradiction and excluded middle. The fitting Freudian and Lacanian response to Hägglund's "Is it past fact or retroactive fiction?" is in this same interpretive spirit.

Primary-process thinking, with its disrespect for chronology, weaves its webs of fantasies through superimposing and condensing slices of psychical life both factual and fictional as well as past and present. Moreover, the drives toward and desires for these unstable, tension-ridden hybrid formations of the unconscious strive after not so much, as Hägglund's criticisms allege, the infinite Absolute of a non-relational and invulnerable afterlife of immortality in the future, but, instead, impossible syntheses combining incompatible elements from disparate bits and pieces of mnemic materials manipulated by an unconscious not bound by conscious concerns over logical consistency or chronological continuity.

However, when it comes to the Neighbor-Thing as the elusive

non-object behind, beneath, and beyond the concatenated series of drive-objects, Freud and Lacan indeed would disagree with Hägglund regarding the latter's employment of the concept-term "binding." In my response to *Radical Atheism*, I observe that Hägglund's Derrideanism, in certain respects, surprisingly resembles the strange bedfellows of Hobbes and his empiricist descendents. I feel this still to be the case in *Dying for Time*. Like the early modern British empiricists and the more critical aspects of Kantian transcendental idealism they help to inspire, the Hägglundian critique of psychoanalysis binds everything to *Vorstellungen* of spatio-temporal objects no different-in-kind from the phenomena of conscious awareness dwelt on at length throughout the modern philosophical tradition (along these lines, Hägglund's occasional talk of retroaction bears little resemblance to Freudian *Nachträglichkeit* or Lacanian *après-coup* but lots to Husserl's quite non-psychoanalytic "phenomenology of internal time-consciousness," with its kinetics involving "retention" and "protention" as inherent specifically to linear chronological time as experienced consciously[52]). In limiting analysis thusly, Hägglund is able to subsume it under his version of the ostensibly universal law of *différance*. But, the price to be paid for this limitation is the outright disavowal of "things" that stubbornly resist or evade altogether capture in and by spatio-temporal representations (i.e., binding in Hägglund's sense). These are some of the very things most integral to the distinctive theory and practice of analysis itself: not only *das Ding als Nebenmensch*, but also, arguably, primal repression, trauma, foreclosure, *objet petit a*, *jouissance*, and the entire register of the Lacanian Real, to name a handful of chronolibidinalism's casualties. To stick with the example of *la Chose à la* Freud and Lacan, the bond to the Real Other is not of the same order as bindings to the inscriptions, marks, traces, etc. of Imaginary-Symbolic reality (i.e., the cathexes of spatio-temporal objects Hägglund speculates about as the lone constituents of the Derridean bindinal economy). Rather, this unforgettable bond to an archaic Thing is, so to speak, a binding to the provocatively and perpetually unbindable.

By my overall estimation, Hägglund, in his radical atheist interest in prohibiting all talk of desiring supposed lost bliss and absent immortality, makes three main moves with which I cannot go along: one, writing off such talk as inconsequentially epiphenomenal in relation to desires themselves; two, collapsing Freudian

246 Adventures in Transcendental Materialism

and Lacanian accounts of libidinal life into a narrative exclusively about the topics of time and death; and, three, applying indifferently a single model of time's linear succession to the multiple heterogeneous dimensions of psychical subjectivity, with its plurality of structures and dynamics. Despite these serious disagreements, I happily and respectfully acknowledge that many of my critical formulations directed against Hägglund owe part of whatever exactitude and clarity they might possess to his own sober, trenchant reflections on the philosophy of psychoanalysis. What is more, I admire the virtuosity with which Hägglund incisively brings to the fore unresolved problems located within the very foundations of analytic metapsychology. Nevertheless, in terms of its solutions to these problems, I judge Hägglund's Derridean chronolibidinalism, in the end, to be too bound by its own theoretical investments to do full justice to the many-sided experiences of psychoanalysis.

Notes

1. Johnston 2009b: 147–89; Hägglund 2009b: 227–52.
2. Žižek 2004b: ix.
3. Hägglund 2008: 27–9, 31–2, 38, 46, 51, 73, 210–11, 220; Hägglund 2009a: 19; Hägglund 2012: 5, 112–13.
4. Hegel 1977c: 9.
5. Hägglund 2011: 122–4.
6. Hägglund 2012: 5, 8–11, 13–14, 111–13, 157–8.
7. Ibid.: 129–30.
8. Ibid.: 114–15.
9. Ibid.: 114.
10. *SE* 14: 186–7; *SE* 14: 289–300.
11. Laplanche and Pontalis 1973: 339–41.
12. *SE* 5: 608.
13. Johnston 2009b: 151–3, 164–5.
14. Fink 1970: 385–7; Johnston 2005c: 13–15.
15. Johnston 2009b: 151–4, 162–5, 181–2.
16. Ibid.: 149–51.
17. Hägglund 2012: 9, 12.
18. Hägglund 2011: 118–19, 122–4.
19. Hegel 1977c: 9, 15–17, 31–3, 35–6, 49, 51–4; Hegel 1969a: 27–8, 31–2, 36–40, 43–4, 53, 55–6; Hegel 1991a: §2 [26], §3 [29–30], §31 [60].
20. Hägglund 2008: 11.

21. Ibid.: 12.
22. Ibid.: 12.
23. Hägglund 2012: 128–31.
24. Hägglund 2008: 192–3; Hägglund 2012: 13–14, 142–5.
25. Johnston 2005a: 222–46.
26. *SIII*: 190.
27. Johnston 2009b: 154–60, 180–1; Hägglund 2009a: 1–4; Hägglund 2012: 110–13, 119–20.
28. Johnston 2013b.
29. Hägglund 2008: 235.
30. *SVII*: 39, 51–2, 76.
31. *SIX*: 3/28/62; *SXVI*: 224–33.
32. *SI*: 180, 276; Johnston 2005b: 67–81.
33. *SIV*: 168–9; *SV*: 499; *SVI*: 4/15/59; *SVII*: 67, 125–6, 161, 214–17; *SVIII*: 141–51, 366; *SIX*: 3/14/62; *SXX*: 39; *SXXIV*: 3/15/77; Lacan 2006o: 690; Johnston 2005b: 67–81.
34. Johnston 2009b: 166–7; Hägglund 2012: 143–4.
35. Hägglund 2012: 9–11, 14, 110–12, 157–9, 167, 186–7.
36. Lacan 2006i: 334–63.
37. *SE* 1: 231, 270–1; *SE* 3: 220, 255.
38. *SVII*: 54.
39. *SXXV*: 1/10/78.
40. Johnston 2005b: 67–81.
41. *SVII*: 111; *SIX*: 6/27/62.
42. Johnston 2005c: xxxiii, 113–14, 184, 186–95, 200–2, 207–9, 211, 213–15, 233–4, 238–40, 242–3, 278, 280–3, 317–25, 327, 346–7.
43. Hägglund 2012: 128–31.
44. *SE* 7: 147–8; *SE* 14: 122–3, 132.
45. *SE* 14: 122–3.
46. *SXI*: 161–86; Johnston 2005c: 184–217.
47. *SE* 1: 318.
48. Ibid.: 331.
49. Hägglund 2012: 138–40, 142.
50. Ibid.: 136–7, 143.
51. Johnston 2005c: 5–22, 218–27.
52. Husserl 1964: 48–79.

Antiphilosophy and Paraphilosophy: Milner, Badiou, and Antiphilosophical Lacanianism

Throughout this book thus far, I repeatedly have invoked Lacan as a key predecessor of transcendental materialism as a specific philosophical system unto itself. Yet, of course, it has become widely known that Lacan appears eventually to denounce the very endeavor of philosophy *tout court*. His later talk of "antiphilosophy" might risk seeming to render him an unsuitable partner for any systematic philosophy. In this chapter, I seek to defuse this potential danger through clarifying, in conversation and debate with many of those who already have explored what Lacan perhaps means by "antiphilosophy," how and why Lacan is far from categorically opposed to philosophy *überhaupt*. In the process, I hope to indicate in what respects Lacan's ideas are, in fact, absolutely invaluable resources for recent and current philosophies unfolding in his wake, transcendental materialism included.

Lacan utters very little about what, late in his life and teachings, he designates as antiphilosophy. This field, labeled as the negation of the oldest of the academic professions, is put forward in 1975 as an area of study for those to be exposed to psychoanalysis in the context of a university education.[1] Five years later, as he is dissolving his École freudienne and winding down *le Séminaire*, Lacan, again speaking of antiphilosophy, declares, "*I rebel*, if I can say, against philosophy."[2]

Despite (or, maybe, because of) the fact that Lacan leaves behind merely two brief mentions of antiphilosophy, a fair amount of ink has been spilled on this topic since Lacan's death by some of his most able readers – in particular, Jean-Claude Milner, Alain Badiou, François Regnault, and Colette Soler. Perhaps they are provoked by understandable perplexity. Of course, Lacan's entire intellectual itinerary involves a sustained, recurrent reliance upon philosophy.[3] As Regnault correctly observes, citations of, among others, Aristotle, Descartes, Kant, Hegel, and Heidegger in his work are nearly as ubiquitous as references to Freud.[4] On Regnault's reading, the philosophy at stake in Lacanian antiphilosophy is not so much philosophy in general as the then-current antipsychoanalytic philosophy of the anti-Oedipal duo of Gilles Deleuze and Félix Guattari.[5] Žižek endorses this reading after asking, "which (singular) philosophy did Lacan have in mind; which philosophy was, for him, a stand-in for philosophy 'as such?'"[6] Žižek proceeds to claim that Lacan has Deleuzian thought in view as a philosophical stance epitomizing a "false subversive radicalization that fits the existing power constellation perfectly" in the climate of post-May '68 Paris.[7] Apropos a generalized concept of antiphilosophy, Badiou advances a claim dovetailing with Regnault's and Žižek's observations – "Each antiphilosopher chooses the philosophers that he intends to make into canonical examples of emptied and vain speech"[8] (i.e., the "anti-" of antiphilosophy is always relative to particular philosophers and/or philosophies, rather than to Philosophy per se, if such a thing even exists at all).

But, as with his technical formalized graphs and "mathemes" (the latter to be discussed below), Lacan's precious few sentences regarding his rebellion against the philosophical, sentences offering no specifications regarding exactly what Lacan takes "philosophy" to be, appear to function as Rorschach ink blots supporting the projections of multiple divergent interpretations. Whereas both Regnault and Žižek detect a disparagement of philosophical tendencies prevailing amongst France's restless student bodies of the late 1960s and 1970s, Soler construes the later Lacanian denigration of philosophy as going with, rather than against, the flow of its contemporaneous socio-cultural *Zeitgeist* in the wake of May '68; she depicts this Lacan as participating in the widespread (quasi/pseudo-)Marxist devaluation of theoretical thought as hopelessly embedded in ideologically compromised superstructural strata of *status quo* society.[9]

Although antiphilosophy *à la* Lacan has given rise to such exegetical discrepancies, those who address this topic nonetheless converge on a specific shared hypothesis apropos its significance: Milner, Badiou, Regnault, and Soler all agree it is no accident or coincidence that Lacan's announced insurgency against philosophy occurs at a time when his institutional circumstances involve issues having to do with the teaching and transmission of psychoanalysis in academic settings.[10] Indeed, Lacan's initial use of the term, in "*Peut-être à Vincennes* ," defines antiphilosophy as an "investigation of what university discourse owes to its supposed 'educational' function."[11] As is well known, the phrase "university discourse" is part of Lacan's theory of the four discourses (the other three being those of the master, hysteric, and analyst), a theory first elaborated at length in the seventeenth seminar of 1969–70, *L'envers de la psychanalyse* (see also Chapter 4).

This chapter will focus on examining Milner's and Badiou's readings of Lacanian antiphilosophy side-by-side with an eye to establishing that Lacan is not so much an antiphilosopher (his isolated 1980 proclamation and associated utterances notwithstanding) as, so to speak, a paraphilosopher whose interweavings of the psychoanalytic and the philosophical pave the way for cutting-edge developments in European/European-inspired philosophy (including transcendental materialism) – developments in connection with which Badiou himself is one of the most prominent figures working today. But, before turning to this focused critical examination, quickly exploring those of Lacan's pronouncements pertaining to university discourse and philosophy roughly contemporaneous with his truncated talk of antiphilosophy is requisite to set the stage for further discussion of this matter.

Lacan tends closely to associate philosophy with university discourse. Since Kant, philosophers usually are professors. In his fifteenth seminar (*L'acte psychanalytique*, 1967–68), Lacan contrasts his analytic discourse with that of these appointed academic "subjects supposed to know," maintaining that the latter likely will resist and be hostile to what he has to say as an analyst.[12] The following year, in a seminar conducted during the immediate aftermath of May '68 (*D'un Autre à l'autre*, 1968–69), Lacan characterizes the reign of (neo-)liberal capitalism as ushering in the dominance of "science" as the authority of university discourse, in which "knowledge" (*savoir* as S_2) is in the "agent" position of this matheme-schema.[13] This claim is reiterated subsequently in the seventeenth seminar,[14] with Lacan pointing out that, according to his formalized theory of the four discourses, the discourse of the university is proximate to that of the master insofar as the former is generated through a mere "quarter turn" of the latter[15] (as Lacan puts it in the eighteenth seminar [*D'un discours qui ne serait pas du semblant*, 1971], "the university discourse can only be articulated if it starts from the discourse of the master"[16]). Similarly, the (apparent) locus of agency in each of the four discourses, knowledge as S_2 in the case of university discourse, is a "semblance" beneath which lies its "truth" (*vérité*), the "master signifier" as S_1 underpinning and governing the *savoir* of academic agents (put crudely, the knowledge of university discourse ultimately rests upon and serves the arbitrary anchors $[S_1s]$ of power).[17] In the academic year 1971–72, the preceding points continue to be stressed: The knowledge produced by the discourse of the university, with which analytic discourse should not be confused, ultimately buttresses and makes more effective the power of capitalism;[18] University discourse, epitomized by the history of philosophy, generates a knowledge that is a dissimulating ideology bolstering whoever happens to be the given *status quo* master.[19] In the twentieth seminar (*Encore*, 1972–73), Lacan flatly identifies "philosophical discourse in its true light" with "a variation on the master's discourse."[20] Soler's reading of Lacanian antiphilosophy as being very much of its time is far from without its justifications. Furthermore, Badiou, with his interest in defending the philosophical tradition from its detractors and eulogizers, insists that philosophy as such is "diagonal" in relation to Lacan's four discourses (i.e., it cannot be reduced to any of these structural schemas).[21]

Curiously, previous discussions of Lacanian antiphilosophy, while citing 1975's "*Peut-être à Vincennes*" and 1980's "*Monsieur A.*," have neglected Lacan's 1974 interview with journalists in Rome entitled "*Le triomphe de la religion*." The section of this interview entitled by Jacques-Alain Miller "*Ne pas philosophe*" begins with an interviewer prefacing a question with "In your philosophy..." Lacan interrupts, snapping back, "I am not at all a philosopher."[22] When the questioner specifies that he/she means by "philosophy" an "ontological concept" (*nozione ontologica*) such as Lacan's "metaphysics of the real," he/she is met by another, similarly blunt negation – "It is not at all ontological."[23] Evidence from this period of Lacan's theorizing strongly suggests he entirely equates philosophy with ontology, unsympathetically viewing the latter as a systematic *Weltanschauung*, an intellectually bankrupt and laughable "theory of everything" grounded on the supposition that being is an ultimately coherent and unified substantial whole, a seamless One[24] (see also Chapter 4). Regnault reasonably proposes that the undermining of the ontological worldviews of academic/university philosophy is a key mission of Lacanian antiphilosophy, which does not strive to pose itself in turn as an alternate worldview.[25] When the interviewer then speaks of the Lacanian Real as Kantian, Lacan, evidently interpreting Kant (in line with Hegel) as assuming that the noumenal realm of thing-in-themselves beyond the limits of possible experience forms a consistent totality, retorts: "But this is not at all Kantian. It is even on this that I insist. If there is a notion of the real, it is extremely complex, and on this account it is not perceivable in a manner that would make a totality. It would be an unbelievably presumptuous notion to think that there would be an all of the real."[26] A short while later in the conversation, Lacan exclaims, "I do not make any philosophy; on the contrary, I am wary of it like the plague."[27] He immediately proceeds to mention his topological Borromean knotting of the registers of the Real, the Symbolic, and the Imaginary as central to a non-philosophical, non-Kantian handling of the Real in analysis[28] (similarly, Soler and Badiou both note Lacan's opposition to a Kantian-style critical cordoning off of the Real as an absolutely inaccessible noumenal "x"[29]). At this juncture, things get particularly puzzling.

Clearly, the Lacan of "*Le triomphe de la religion*" thrusts to the fore his topologized analytic register theory as antithetical to the all-encompassing fictions of philosophical ontology (with even Kant's critical-transcendental framework implicitly being accused of dogmatically harboring unanalyzed vestiges of traditional substance metaphysics). By contrast, the temporally proximate Lacan of the twenty-third and twenty-fifth seminars (*Le sinthome*, 1975–76 and *Le moment de conclure*, 1977–78) sings what sounds like a quite different tune. The Lacan of *Le sinthome* wants to forge a "*foliesophie*"[30] (i.e., a neologism involving an acoustic resonance between "philo-" and "*folie*" [madness]); he speaks of "supplementing" a "certain lack" in philosophy with his Borromean knot, thereby creating "the first philosophy that it appears to me supports itself"[31] (see also Chapter 4). Stranger still, in 1977, Lacan, addressing his lifelong engagement with the theory and practice of analysis, confesses: "That which I do there . . . is of philosophy . . . My Borromean knots are philosophy too. It is philosophy that I have handled as I have been able to in following the current, if I can say, the current that results from the philosophy of Freud."[32] All of these vacillations on Lacan's part are sandwiched in time between his two explicit uses of the word "antiphilosophy." Two reactions to the above are to be avoided, at least at the present stage: one, leaping to the conclusion that Lacan is being merely inconsistent, carelessly contradicting himself in rapid succession as regards his fraught rapport with philosophy; two, rushing to smooth over these inconsistencies with various possible interpretations of an extremely (perhaps excessively) charitable nature. Instead, the approach to be adopted in what follows will be to pass through an exploration of Milner's and Badiou's overlapping treatments of Lacanian antiphilosophy (with additional references to Regnault, Soler, and Žižek) so as to arrive at a better perspective on Lacan's final positioning of himself and psychoanalysis vis-à-vis philosophy.

In 1990, Milner and Badiou each present a paper at a conference organized by the Collège international de philosophie on *Lacan avec les philosophes*. Moreover, they both make references to Lacan's antiphilosophy on this occasion.[33] As will become increasingly evident here, Milner's and Badiou's interpretations of Lacan's ambivalent relationship with philosophy overlap considerably. Beginning with Milner, toward the end of his 1995 book *L'Œuvre claire: Lacan, la science, la philosophie*, the fifth and final section of the penultimate fourth chapter (*"Le second classicisme lacanien"*) is devoted to *"L'antiphilosophie."* Therein, one of Milner's arguments is that Lacan's late turn against the philosophical tradition to which he refers constantly must be understood as intimately bound up with what Milner characterizes as the "hyperstructuralism" of Lacan's "second classicism,"[34] namely, the paradigm holding sway in the later period of his teachings (especially during the 1970s) centered on the doctrine of the matheme.[35] Milner equates Lacanian antiphilosophy with this doctrine, thus positing an antinomy between, on the one side, a transmissible, mathematical-style formalization of psychoanalysis, and, on the other side, what Lacan understands by "philosophy" in the final phase of his theorizing.[36]

Lacan's mathemes, consisting of a plethora of letters, numbers, formulas, and diagrams, constitute his attempts to formalize his analytic insights. Why does he engage in this struggle to distill his reflections on psychoanalysis into the skeletal configurations of scientific-style symbolizations? Arguably, Lacan reaches for such representations motivated by his suspicion that part of what delivers Freud into the hands of his bastardizers and betrayers (i.e., non-Lacanian post-Freudians) is the latter's speciously accessible and deceptively clear prose, a writing style that lulls readers into complacent misreadings because its apparently ordinary language too easily seems evidently to "make sense" (an illustration of Lacan's dictum according to which understanding entails misunderstanding[37]). Of course, this goes some way toward explaining Lacan's notoriously cryptic fashions of expressing himself in light of his "return to Freud." But, what is more, it also clarifies the link between the doctrine of the matheme and the recurrent theme of transmission. Contemporaneous with his declaration of insurgency against philosophy during a period when the place of psychoanalysis in the university is at stake, Lacan, speaking of the matheme in the ancient Greek sense of *ta mathēmata* (i.e., that which can be taught and passed on without loss),[38] repeatedly emphasizes that his formalizations function in the service of rendering his analytic concepts integrally transmissible.[39] The implicit contrasting case looming in the background is Freud, whose concepts, couched in non-formalized writing, proved themselves vulnerable to corrupting, perverted mistransmissions. And yet, an irony not to be missed is that, as indicated above, Lacan's mathemes can be seen as pillars of a new Tower of Babel inasmuch as, to the extent that they do not just interpret themselves as self-evident, they have given rise to thriving pluralities of incommensurable interpretations (although, admittedly, Lacan evinces an awareness of this danger – for instance, with respect to these mathemes, he remarks, "they are not transmitted without the help of language, and that's what makes the whole thing shaky"[40]).

However, the significance of Lacan's steadily increasing mobilization of mathemes in the '60s and '70s also has to do with issues of communication and understanding (as miscommunication and misunderstanding) apropos not only the practice of analytic pedagogy (i.e., the educational teaching and transmission of analysis), but also the very objects of metapsychological theory (i.e., the *parlêtre* as subject of the unconscious). In his discussion of Lacanian antiphilosophy, Milner asserts that philosophy (at least in this context) remains completely wedded to its archaic roots in a pre-modern ethos concerned with the enrichment of the soul (*psuchê, âme*) through the acquisition of meaningful wisdom. Milner's contention is that the advent of modern science – following Koyré, as does Lacan, he privileges Galileo's mathematization of the study of nature as the founding gesture of scientific modernity[41] – shatters the pre-modern fantasized wholeness of the closed cosmos with which the wisdom-loving soul of the philosopher is entangled.[42] By contrast, according to Milner, psychoanalysis, unlike the philosophical tradition which (still) allegedly lags behind the early-seventeenth-century revolutionary rupture signified by the proper name "Galileo," is entirely in synch with modern science[43] (of course, as is common knowledge, Lacan considers this new scientificity to be a historical condition of possibility for the subsequent emergence of Freudian psychoanalysis almost three centuries later[44]). Hence, among other of its agendas, Lacan's antiphilosophy perhaps aims to draw attention to the fact that the philosophical (and quotidian) conception of psychoanalysis as a depth hermeneutics in search of the profound meaning of psychical suffering is a hopelessly wrong-headed misreading of Freud and his place in the history of ideas.

Soler rightly reminds readers that Freud's discovery of the unconscious poses a series of fundamental challenges to traditional philosophy.[45] Buttressing Milner's perspective, she maintains that the later Lacan comes to place his faith in mathemes modeled on scientific formulas because anti-ancient, mathematized modern science does not "think,"[46] with thinking here being associated with modes of cognition prone to endow things with sense and significance (indeed, traditional philosophy certainly thinks in this manner). In the post-Galilean universe, the Real of mathematically parsed material being, although anything but ineffable and unknowable, is meaningless, decoupled from the ordered, organizing plans of final causes as guarantees of rhyme and reason.

A couple of months prior to his second and last self-identification as an antiphilosopher, Lacan, in his "Letter of Dissolution" announcing the end of his École freudienne, presents his "obstinacy on the path of mathemes" as a struggle against "meaning" as "always religious."[47] In other words, atheistic psychoanalysis is opposed to the essence of religiosity, the latter being rendered as the infusion of purposiveness, sense, or significance into being, existence, reality, the world, etc. (in his seminar on Lacan's antiphilosophy, Badiou indisputably has this 1980 statement in mind when he describes the doctrine of the matheme as a countermeasure against the fact that psychoanalysis is "constantly threatened with being a hermeneutic of sense," with "Lacan imputing to philosophy a religious recovery of sense"[48]). Combining this with the observations of Milner and Soler mentioned previously, a stark opposition between two chains of equivalences becomes visible during the final stretch of Lacan's teachings: religion-philosophy-meaning (grounded and totalized in the ancient finite cosmos) versus psychoanalysis-antiphilosophy-meaninglessness ([un-]grounded and detotalized in the modern infinite universe).

In her exegesis of Lacan's revolt *contra* philosophy, Soler refers to the Lacanian "anticognitivist thesis" according to which "Thought is *jouissance*,"[49] a thesis she dwells on at some length.[50] Both Badiou and François Balmès similarly identify *jouissance* as that which is granted no proper place in classical philosophy/ontology.[51] As with so many instances of things that initially appear enigmatic and mysterious in Lacan's musings, returning to Freud is both helpful and crucial for illuminating the reasoning behind the preceding assertions. At root, what connects all of the above is Freud's conception of primary-process-style mentation as characteristic of unconscious thinking.[52] Devoid of innate ideas, Jungian archetypes, and the like as a hard-wired foundational basis of necessary deep meanings, the Freudian psyche acquires its contingent contents over the course of temporally elongated ontogenetic subject formation. These thus-furnished contents, registered in the form of ideational representations (Freud's *Vorstellungen* and Lacan's signifiers), come under the driving influence of primary processes as libidinally charged (i.e., *jouissance*-saturated) psychical dynamics chaining together concatenations of mental materials with no regard whatsoever for considerations of sense, significance, communicability, or comprehensibility, these being the concerns of secondary-process-style mentation as typically governing conscious cognition (gesturing back at one of Soler's earlier remarks, philosophy "thinks" in a secondary-process mode, a mode circumvented by Lacan's analytic mathemes – the thinking she equates with *jouissance*, on the other hand, is quite distinct and different, being of a primary process sort).

An ensemble of Lacan's later concepts contemporaneous with his announced move onto the terrain of antiphilosophy (for example, the letter, *lalangue*, and *jouis-sens* [enjoy-meant]) can be examined as extensions of the Freudian insight into the primary processes. According to this insight situated at the origins of psychoanalysis, networks and webs of associations meaningless from the standpoint of the awareness of self-consciousness (associations hinging on the acoustic and graphic resemblances between *Vorstellungen*/signifiers as material rather than meaningful) constitute the unconscious grounds of psychical life itself. If philosophy introspectively peers into the presumed depths of the soul (*âme*) so as to discover profound *apriori* meanings anchoring the unified self in its relations with the world as a coherent global whole, Freudian psychoanalysis as developed by Lacan is antiphilosophical insofar as it scans the surfaces of the $-*qua-parlêtre* so as to detect traces of the Real of a strange thoughtless thinking out-of-joint with sensible worldly reality, a thinking in which currents of *jouissance* (as *jouis-sens*) concatenate *aposteriori* fragments of phonemes, words, images, and memories in movements whose susceptibility to formal delineation and analytic interpretation makes them no less senseless relative to common, conscious sense. And, this can be connected back to the sub-title of Milner's *L'Œuvre claire*, in which Lacan's name is linked to science as well as philosophy ("*Lacan, la science, la philosophie*"): Just as scientific equations such as "$E = mc^2$" ultimately do nothing more than descriptively encircle facets of a universe with no transcendent, metaphysical Other or Elsewhere – the sheer, brute givenness of immanent materiality in its inexplicable contingency is science's one-and-only ground-zero, that which it represents without adding any supplementary meaning or guarantee of necessary significance – so too do Lacan's mathemes, equally as meaningless as the mathematical formulas of physics, reflect the baseless base of subjectivity's structures as beneath or beyond the spheres of sense.

Milner concludes his remarks on antiphilosophy in Lacanian psychoanalysis by comparing and contrasting psychoanalysis and philosophy in relation to a dialectic between contingency and necessity foreshadowed in the prior paragraphs here. Focusing on the subject, the notion constituting the core hub of intersection between Lacanian theory and the philosophical tradition, he states:

> The point of intervention of psychoanalysis is very nicely summarized thus: the passage from the anterior instant where the speaking being would have been able to be infinitely other than it is – in its body and thought – to the ulterior instant where the speaking being, due to its very contingency, has become entirely the same as an eternal necessity. For in the end psychoanalysis speaks of only one thing: the conversion of each subjective singularity into a law as necessary as the laws of nature, also as contingent as them and as absolute.[53]

Milner continues:

Yet, it is true that philosophy has not ceased to treat this instant. In a sense, one would be able to maintain that it has properly invented it. But, to describe it, it has generally taken the paths of the outside-the-universe (*hors-univers*). Yet, psychoanalysis is nothing if it does not maintain, as the pivot of its doctrine, that there is no outside-the-universe. There and only there resides that which is structural and non-chronological in its relation to modern science.[54]

In a way, the claims in these quoted passages tap into a line of thought present in Lacan's theorizations at least as early as his mid-1950s utilizations of Poe's "The Purloined Letter"[55] (i.e., well before the dominance of the antiphilosophical mathemes in the 1970s and start of the 1980s). Simply put, Lacan consistently remains committed to models of subject formation in which a scaffolding of firm, law-like structural constraints shaping subjectivity (i.e., apparent necessities regulating the vicissitudes of psychical life) emerge via a bottom-up genesis out of the interplay between primary-process-level dynamics (including the libidinal economy, *jouissance*, drives, and desires) and arbitrary sets of signifiers as *Vorstellungen* (i.e., imposed contingencies stamped upon the psyche by chance experiences, encounters, relationships, etc.). On Milner's reading, philosophy errs in that it seeks to stabilize this groundless ground of contingency by slipping under it the imagined depth of a supposedly solid bedrock of final, irreducible meaning/sense (i.e., an "outside-the-universe," with "universe" designating the post-Galilean plane of mathematized materialities, as a metaphysical and/or theological "other scene" giving reason to existence by rationally orchestrating the order of things). As Badiou puts it, "Philosophy operates, in Lacan's eyes, by affirming that there is such a thing as a meaning or sense of truth (*sens de la vérité*)."[56]

Milner, Regnault, and Badiou all agree that, for Lacan, philosophy and antiphilosophy are not simply and diametrically opposed to one another as mutually exclusive. For Milner, "psychoanalysis has not only the right, but the obligation to speak of that which philosophy speaks, because it has exactly the same objects."[57] For Regnault, the "anti-" of "antiphilosophy "is to be understood, no longer in the sense of contradiction."[58] For Badiou, the issue is particularly complicated. On the one hand, just as Regnault describes psychoanalysis as being on "the opposite shore"[59] bordering the same river bordered by philosophy – this is another way of articulating Milner's assertion that philosophy and psychoanalysis share common points of reference – Badiou too grants that Lacanian theory especially is quite proximate to philosophy in that it applies itself to an identical ensemble of topics[60] (in a related vein, he recognizes Plato's Socrates as the first analyst[61]). Nonetheless, he repeatedly and emphatically insists that Lacan is unambiguously the partisan of an antiphilosophy to be rigorously and sharply distinguished from philosophy proper.[62]

In fact, Badiou devotes his seminar of the academic year 1994–95 to "The Antiphilosophy of Lacan," itself preceded by annual seminars on the two other figures he singles out, along with Lacan, as the great antiphilosophers of the current age: Nietzsche ("The Antiphilosophy of Nietzsche," 1992–93) and Wittgenstein ("The Antiphilosophy of Wittgenstein," 1993–94). In addition to the seminar on Lacanian antiphilosophy, three other texts by Badiou focus on Lacan's tricky placement of himself with respect to philosophy (apart from, in addition, the numerous lines of influence stemming from and references to Lacan scattered throughout Badiou's corpus from its earliest years up through the present): "La psychanalyse a-t-elle des fondements philosophiques? (1989), "Lacan et Platon: Le mathème est-il une idée?" (1990/91), and "The Formulas of l'Étourdit" (2006). In this context, exhaustively surveying and unpacking Badiou's relationship to Lacan, or even his multifaceted glosses on Lacanian antiphilosophy, is out of the question – let alone encompassing Badiou's extremely wide-ranging elaborations regarding antiphilosophy as a broad, fundamental category (Bruno Bosteels' article "Radical Antiphilosophy," which will serve as his translator's introduction to a forthcoming collection of Badiou's texts on Nietzsche, Wittgenstein, and Lacan entitled What Is Antiphilosophy?, provides a superlative overview of the antiphilosophical as it functions in the philosophy of Badiou[63]). Instead, the ensuing engagement with Badiou's meditations on Lacanian antiphilosophy will be guided primarily by Milner's remarks as spelled out above and generally will restrict itself to citing only those pieces by Badiou mentioned explicitly by title in this paragraph.

Not only does Badiou, as he openly acknowledges, borrow the very word "antiphilosophy" from Lacan for his own philosophical purposes[64] – his philosophy relies heavily upon a distinction between "knowledge" (savoir) and "truth" (vérité) echoing Lacan's fashion of distinguishing between these two terms. In the first session of his 1994–95 seminar, Badiou notes that Lacan, unlike Nietzsche-the-antiphilosopher, retains a notion of truth[65] (although, in his lecture on the question of the philosophical foundations [or lack thereof] of psychoanalysis, Badiou contrasts the analytic concept of truth-as-cause, situated as the originary catalyst of the subject's trajectory in analysis, with the philosophical idea of truth-as-end, situated as the ultimate *telos* of the inquirer's quest[66]). However, whereas one might be tempted to think of unconscious truths exceeding the scope of (conscious, thematized, self-reflexive) knowledge as elusive and imponderable eternal mysteries (i.e., as belonging to a Kantian-style noumenal Real), Badiou correctly draws attention to the fact that Lacan, as it were, wants to eff the ineffable, to produce analytic knowledge (*savoir*) regarding those truths (*vérités*) anchoring the being(s) of speaking subjects. He insightfully explains later, in the penultimate session of this seminar, that Lacan seeks "to subtract the real from knowing (*connaître*) without falling into a doctrine of the ineffable or the unknowable."[67] It is crucial to appreciate here the difference between knowing/knowledge as involving conscious acquaintance or familiarity (*connaître/connaissance*) versus knowing/knowledge (*savoir*) as entailing conceptual, intellectual comprehension. As Badiou is well aware, the Real truths constituting the arbitrary, senseless kernels of the unconscious of the *parlêtre*, according to Lacan, are not known *qua* consciously recognized as customary or familiar, although they can be known *qua* theoretically grasped or symbolically interpreted (through the discourse of psychoanalysis). Along these same lines, in "The Formulas of *l'Étourdit*," he stipulates that Lacan's "twist is not at all to put forward that the Real is unknowable, nor that it is knowable either. Lacan's thesis is that the Real has an exteriority to the antinomy between knowing and being unaware."[68] The truths of the unconscious, situated in the register of the Real, defy *connaissance* but not (analytic) *savoir*. This *savoir* is what Lacan situates "between knowing" (*connaître*) – *connaître* inevitably brings with it the quotidian and philosophical temptations to render things recognizable through infusions of communicable meaning and significance, thus guaranteeing misrecognition (*méconnaissance*) of the meaningless contingencies (i.e., Real truths) brought to light by analysis – "and being unaware."

As does Milner, Badiou assigns the doctrine of the matheme a great deal of importance in the later period of Lacan's teachings.

From Badiou's perspective, registering Real *vérité* by tracing its edges within the Symbolic field of transmissible *savoir* is the crucial task assigned to the mathemes by Lacan.[69] More specifically, the act (in the precise Lacanian sense of "act"[70]) of each unique, unrepeatable analysis can and should be captured as replicable, iterable knowledge, as *ta mathēmata*; Lacanian analysis thus attempts to be a paradoxical "science of the singular"[71] (i.e., a Symbolic *savoir* of Real *vérité*, the latter being idiosyncratic and peculiar to the experience or event of an analysis). Several times, Badiou connects this matheme-mediated knowledge, a knowledge of those truths causally influencing the subjects at stake in analytic acts which target the unconscious, to a Lacanian neologism featuring prominently in Lacan's 1972/73 paper "*L'étourdit*": *ab-sens* (ab-sense).[72] In Badiou's reconstruction of the Lacan of this period, the *savoir* that is neither *connaissance* nor directly *vérité* (although it sustains a relationship to the latter) is that which "touches ab-sense."[73]

Before saying more with respect to the manner in which Badiou reads "*L'étourdit*," a succinct definition of *ab-sens* is requisite. Stated with relative brevity, this neologism refers to the absence of a "sexual relationship" (*à la* Lacan's infamous contemporaneous *dictum* asserting that "*il n'y a pas de rapport sexuel*") as a Real around which takes shape the Imaginary-Symbolic realities of the sexuated subjects with sexual and gender identities, the *parlêtres* spoken about in psychoanalysis from Freud onward. Additionally, Lacan makes clear that ab-sense involves the formal delineation-without-meaningful-signification (via mathemes, topology, and the like) of the consequences of this lacking *rapport*[74] (as Badiou observes along these lines, "the lone form of transmissibility for ab-sex sense that is possible is found in the figure of the matheme. There is no language of the Real, there are only its formulas"[75]).

In the closing pages of the second chapter of *L'Œuvre claire*, Milner, although not explicitly referring to "*L'étourdit*," helps to illustrate what Lacan has in mind when resorting to *ab-sens* as a neologism. Considering the central grounding role sexuality is assigned in psychical-subjective life by Freudian-Lacanian analysis, he declares:

> I will advance that sexuality, inasmuch as psychoanalysis speaks of it, is nothing other than this: the place of infinite contingency in the body. That there is sexuation, rather than not, is contingent. That there are two

sexes rather than one or many is contingent. That one is on one side or the other is contingent. That such somatic characteristics are attached to a sexuation is contingent. That such cultural characteristics are attached to it is contingent. Because it is contingent, it touches infinity.[76]

This "touches infinity" can be interpreted as synonymous with Badiou's above-quoted "touches ab-sense." Milner proceeds to state, "The Freudian unconscious, inasmuch as it is sexual, is the unconscious inasmuch as it would be able to be other than it is . . . In its place, as it admits, the infinite and the contingent therefore pass into each other."[77] Of course, human beings, as organisms produced through sexual reproduction, each owe their very existences to sexuality. But, humans as speaking beings, unlike other animals, somehow have to subjectify, whether consciously and/or unconsciously, overwhelming knowledge of the infinite contingencies this condition brings with it (one need only consider the sheer improbability of the existence of any given person – if this one sperm of this one man had not inseminated this one egg of this one woman . . . extrapolating chains of circumstances and happenings outward from this incredibly chancy point, one eventually arrives at a confrontation with the inexplicable facticities of the very existences of humanity and even the universe, right up to the question, "Why is there something rather than nothing?").[78] With ample justification, Milner suggests that the formations of the unconscious (in particular, various sorts of fantasies) orbit around and reflect the impressions made on subjectivity by the limitless versions of "it could have been otherwise" which come to be inseparably bound up with sexuality as theorized analytically. Ab-sense is this Real of infinite contingency, an absence of meaning that subsists within the heart of those beings condemned to make meaning out of it nonetheless. Ab-sense entails condemnation to the making of sense out of senselessness.

Badiou's "The Formulas of L'Étourdit" devotes a lot of attention to ab-sens. Badiou introduces this Lacanian concept-term as follows: "the Real may be defined as a sense which is ab-sense. The Real is ab-sense, and therefore an absence of sense, but which absence of course implies that sense does exist."[79] He immediately adds:

The point that needs to be understood, as concerns the complex decision Lacan is formulating here, is that ab-sense must be held absolutely distinct from nonsense. Lacan's argument is not absurdist or in a general sense existentialist. He is not asserting that the Real is nonsense. He is asserting that an opening onto the Real cannot be breached save through the presupposition that it is an absence in sense, an ab-sense, or a subtracting of something from, or out of, sense. Everything depends on this distinction between ab-sense and non-sense.[80]

Rejoining the theme of antiphilosophy, Badiou subsequently emphasizes in this same essay that philosophy is both unwilling and unable to acknowledge and incorporate ab-sense.[81] Badiou's accurate remarks touch upon two crucial details. First, the Real as ab-sense (which is bound up with *jouis-sens*, *lalangue*, and related concept-terms) is posited and parsed from within the fields of socio-symbolic realities, remaining inaccessible to any sort of (non-existent) intellectual intuition of or mystical union with *le réel du ab-sens*. Put differently, the, so to speak, ab-meant Real is not a sublime and utterly withdrawn transcendence, but, instead, that which subsists immanently with respect to the accessible planes of articulable knowledge (specifically, the *savoir* of formulas consisting of mathemes[82]). In his seminar on Lacanian antiphilosophy, Badiou emphasizes that *"le savoir qui touche à l'ab-sens"* can be testified to and conveyed, which leads him to concede that Lacan, unlike most of those he identifies as antiphilosophers, refuses to succumb to the allure of a transcendent *je ne sais quoi* beyond all possible as well as actual knowledge, an unspeakable and ineffable *"x"*[83] (implicitly supported in the historical background by Hegel's critique of Kant's antirealist-as-subjective transcendental idealism [see Chapter 2] and explicitly supported by Koyré's Galilean-Cartesian rationalism [see Chapter 4], such French thinkers as Lacan, Badiou, and Meillassoux, among many others, are realists specifically as regards a Real knowable with exact precision through mathematical or quasi-mathematical formalizations [see also Chapter 4 once more]). Second, ab-sense is, as it were, the method in the madness, namely, the primary-process dynamics and non-classical logics of a thinking other than the secondary-process mentation familiar to everyday and philosophical consciousness alike, a thinking unfolding itself as the free-associative *lalangue* of *jouis-sens* constructing the rudiments of the formations of the unconscious. Such *ab-sens* is an integral part of Lacan's psychoanalytic antiphilosophy insofar as classical/

traditional philosophy tends to deploy a black-and-white, either/ or distinction between sense (associated with secondary-process conscious thinking as reasoning in obedience with the constraints of bivalent logic and the syntaxes and semantics of recognized natural languages as systems for the production of communicable meanings) and nonsense (i.e., that which is not sense as per the preceding definition, envisioned as totally random and anarchic).[84] Clearly, as Badiou aptly discerns, Freudian-Lacanian analysis is centered on, among other things, the hypothesis that something in-between strictly structured sense and completely unstructured nonsense not only exists, but even underpins sense itself (hence, Badiou's reflections on ab-sense intersect with Soler's above-cited insistence on equating unconscious thinking and *jouissance*).

In this contextual vein, Badiou highlights Lacan's theory of the material signifier. Without the time to explain this theory, which runs uninterrupted as a red thread through the full span of *le Séminaire*, suffice it to say that *ab-sens* is a neologism referring to the sonorous and/or visual materialities of ideational-psychical *Vorstellungen* that, although not meaningful, are nonetheless not sheer nonsense as transcendent and chaotic meaninglessness lurking silently beyond the confines, circumscribed by accepted logic and grammar, of consciously recognized and reassuring significance.[85] Badiou speaks of a Lacanian "meta-physics" of material signifiers as incorporeal bodies.[86] For him, the "meta-" indicates that the intra-signifying motions of psychical causality, bound up with material signifiers, are irreducible to physical causality. As such, any sort of psychoanalytic scientism, in which a reduction of the psychical to the physical would be at stake, is out of the question.

Badiou praises Lacan as opening up vectors of speculation promising to maneuver around twin dangers emanating from theology- and science-inspired ideologies. In *Logics of Worlds*, he comments, "traversing Lacan's anti-philosophy remains an obligatory exercise today for those who wish to wrest themselves away from the reactive convergences of religion and scientism."[87] This comment should be connected up with some remarks Badiou makes regarding "all hermeneutic conceptions of philosophy" in a eulogy for Althusser:

> The idea of philosophy as questioning and openness always paves the way, as we know, for the return of the religious. I use 'religion' here

to describe the axiom according to which a truth is always a prisoner of the arcana of meaning and a matter for interpretation and exegesis. There is an Althusserian brutality to the concept of philosophy that recalls, in that respect, Nietzsche. Philosophy is affirmative and combative, and it is not a captive of the somewhat vicious delights of deferred interpretation. In terms of philosophy, Althusser maintains the presupposition of atheism, just as others, such as Lacan, maintain it in antiphilosophy. That presupposition can be expressed in just one sentence: truths have no meaning.[88]

Insofar as Lacanian psychoanalysis concerns itself with a distinctive meta-physics of the incorporeal-yet-material signifier, it avoids a scientism submitting to and imitating the physical sciences. But, it does so without lapsing back into religiosity, as happens all too often to those who pit themselves against scientistic reductivism. The Symbolic of an analytic *savoir* outlining and capturing, through the formal "literalization" (as Milner has it[89]) of mathemes, the play of Real *vérité*, itself without meaning or sense, bypasses the Imaginary lures of a *connaissance* fixated upon visions of a corporeal wholeness (biologistic scientism) and/ or enveloping world of significance (onto-theological religion and, as observed previously here, the majority of traditional philosophies as Lacan and Badiou see them). For anyone acquainted with both Lacan and Badiou, it is impossible not to hear profound cross-resonances between the antiphilosophy of the former and the philosophy of the latter.

In response to these cross-resonances, one could go so far as to maintain that Badiou's opposition between philosophy and antiphilosophy comes undone in confronting Lacan-the-supposed-antiphilosopher (Milner's endorsement of Lacan's few self-identifications as an antiphilosopher likewise becomes problematic at this juncture too). Arguably, some of Badiou's own statements indicate this. His 1990 Collège international de philosophie presentation contains an admission that Lacan's thought is uncannily proximate to his own philosophy[90] (Regnault, in his discussion of Lacanian antiphilosophy, also highlights the relevance of Badiou's thought to analysts interested in Lacan's later teachings[91]). Near the end of this same presentation, Badiou, avowing that Plato and Lacan, side-by-side, both are crucial inspirations for his own thinking, describes a "Cross-fertilization in torsion, without unity of plan, between antiphilosophy and philosophy."[92] Quite recently, he invokes "Lacan the philosopher, as much as antiphilosopher. Or, philosopher of that which in psychoanalysis is antiphilosophical," proceeding to propose that Lacan offers "no reason to conclude as to the triumph of antiphilosophy."[93] Similarly, in "*La psychanalyse a-t-elle des fondements philosophiques?*," he states that "Inasmuch as there is a philosophy of Lacanianism, it's the philosophy of antiphilosophy."[94] The precise formulation of this statement signals that Lacan's thought represents, for Badiou, a paradoxical node of convergence at which the apparent opposites of philosophy and antiphilosophy pass into each other, a short circuit in which these seemingly antinomic poles are rendered fluid, unstable, and, perhaps, even indiscernible at times. Such an interpretation is further supported through reference to the 1994–95 seminar on Lacan's antiphilosophy, in which Badiou posits that "Lacan elaborates the first immanent antiphilosophy and, as such, it's the last antiphilosophy."[95] By "immanent," he means here that Lacan, by treating ab-meant Real truths as attested to in and through transmissible knowledge, eschews the standard antiphilosophical gesture of pointing at unsayable mysteries transcending any and every possible *savoir* (i.e., truths absolutely refractory to all efforts at knowing). According to this characterization, Lacan's name designates a historical switch point at which, to resort to Hegelian language, antiphilosophy becomes self-sundering, surpassing itself at the very moment it reaches an apex of culmination. As I noted earlier, Lacan himself, during the years 1975 to 1980, oscillates back-and-forth between embracing and repudiating philosophy as his key intellectual partner in thinking through everything at stake in Freudian psychoanalysis. Hence, Badiou's ambivalences, hesitations, and qualifications surrounding the identification of Lacan as an antiphilosopher echo Lacan's own vacillations apropos this issue. Can anything more satisfactory be said about this matter?

Interestingly, Žižek's very first reference to Badiou in print – this occurs in the introduction to his 1993 book *Tarrying with the Negative: Kant, Hegel, and the Critique of Ideology*, a text essential for an understanding of the philosophical foundations of Žižekian theory in its various guises and manifestations – hinges on the question of whether or not Lacan is an antiphilosopher in the Badiouian sense. Žižek argues at length:

According to Alain Badiou, we live today in the age of the 'new sophists.' The two crucial breaks in the history of philosophy, Plato's and Kant's, occurred as a reaction to new relativistic attitudes which threatened to demolish the traditional corpus of knowledge: in Plato's case, the logical argumentation of the sophists undermined the mythical foundations of the traditional mores; in Kant's case, empiricists (such as Hume) undermined the foundations of the Leibnizean-Wolfian rationalist metaphysics. In both cases, the solution offered is not a return to the traditional attitude but a new founding gesture which 'beats the sophists at their own game,' i.e., which surmounts the relativism of the sophists by way of its own radicalization (Plato *accepts* the argumentative procedure of the sophists; Kant *accepts* Hume's burial of the traditional metaphysics). And it is our hypothesis that Lacan opens up the possibility of another repetition of the same gesture. That is to say, the 'postmodern theory' which predominates today is a mixture of neopragmatism and deconstruction best epitomized by names such as Rorty or Lyotard; their works emphasize the 'anti-essentialist' refusal of universal Foundation, the dissolving of 'truth' into an effect of plural language-games, the relativization of its scope to historically specified intersubjective community, etc. etc. Isolated desperate endeavors of a 'postmodern' return to the Sacred are quickly reduced to just another language game, to another way we 'tell stories about ourselves.'[96]

He continues:

Lacan, however, is not part of this 'postmodern theory': in this respect, his position is homologous to that of Plato or Kant. The perception of Lacan as an 'anti-essentialist' or 'deconstructionist' falls prey to the same illusion as that of perceiving Plato as just one among the sophists. Plato accepts from the sophists their logic of discursive argumentation, but uses it to affirm his commitment to Truth; Kant accepts the breakdown of the traditional metaphysics, but uses it to perform his transcendental turn; along the same lines, Lacan accepts the 'deconstructionist' motif of radical contingency, but turns this motif against itself, using it to assert his commitment to Truth *as contingent*. For that very reason, deconstructionists and neopragmatists, in dealing with Lacan, are always bothered by what they perceive as some remainder of 'essentialism' (in the guise of 'phallogocentrism,' etc.) – as if Lacan were uncannily close to them, but somehow not 'one of them.'[97]

Of course, this inaugural invocation of Badiou, one that inaugurates a subsequent sustained engagement with Badiou's ideas, implicitly contests the Badiouian depiction of Lacan as an antiphilosopher. As I mentioned at the beginning of this chapter, Žižek (like Regnault) insists that Lacan's antiphilosophy is not an antagonistic dismissal of Philosophy *tout court*, but, instead, a rejection of particular philosophies (such as Deleuze and Guattari's anti-Oedipal philosophy of nomadic desiring machines *en vogue* during the period when Lacan declares himself to be an antiphilosopher – or also many metaphysical and/or ontological systems of the philosophical past). And, as the above quotations reveal, he goes so far as to situate Lacan in a classical Western philosophical lineage tracing all the way back to Badiou's dear Plato, contending that the Lacanian "anti-" signifies hostility specifically to the new postmodern sophists, namely, many of his intellectual contemporaries in post-war France. Given that Badiou subsumes what Žižek refers to as "postmodernism" under the heading of antiphilosophy, Žižek's assertions in these quoted passages regarding Lacan, if they were to secure Badiou's agreement (which it is not evident they would fail to do), would mean that Lacan's antiphilosophy actually is an anti-antiphilosophy (to be interpreted here according to a dialectical, rather than a classical, construal of double negation, meaning that the Lacanian "philosophy" resulting from the negation of the negation is different from the [traditional] philosophy initially/originally negated by the first "anti-"). Moreover, apropos the Žižekian rendition of Lacanian *vérité* "*as contingent*," Badiou's (conception of) philosophy, based as it is on truths generated by aleatory events in the four "generic procedures" of truth-production (i.e., art, love, politics, and science) as "conditions" for philosophy, now looks to be itself an heir inheriting from Lacan some of its decisive defining features (the fact that the thirty-seventh and final meditation of *Being and Event*, his 1988 *magnum opus*, is entitled "Descartes/Lacan" is telling in this regard as well).

Lacan's influence on Badiou is no secret. The latter is quite forthright about his profound indebtedness to the former ("my master Jacques Lacan"[98]). For instance, 1989's *Manifesto for Philosophy* speaks of Lacan-the-antiphilosopher as "the greatest of our dead."[99] It goes on to identify the names of Freud and (especially) Lacan as marking a proper event at the level of thinking the generic procedure of love, itself one of philosophy's four conditions.[100] This leads Badiou to declare that "the anti-philosopher Lacan is a condition of the renaissance of philosophy. A philosophy is possible today, only if it is compossible with Lacan."[101] In the immediate wake of *Being and Event*, Badiou's confining of Lacan's importance to a radical transformation of the amorous risks striking the eye as an exercise in shoehorning Lacan into a pre-arranged picture in which love is the category of truth-production left over once Badiou has identified the artistic, political, and scientific events conditioning his philosophy; anyone possessing even a passing acquaintance with Lacan's texts is aware that he has a great deal to say about art, politics, science, truth, subjectivity, and so on (i.e., love is hardly the only thing with respect to which Lacan makes crucial theoretical contributions pertinent to Badiouian philosophy). Additionally, anyone possessing even a passing acquaintance with Badiou's texts is aware that Lacan is deeply significant for Badiou beyond the topic of amorous matters alone. Prior to *Being and Event*, this is frankly admitted. For the relatively younger Badiou, faithful to a Maoist version of Marxism and a certain materialist deployment of dialectics, "Lacan . . . is our Hegel,"[102] "Like Hegel for Marx, Lacan for us is essential,"[103] and "For today's French Marxists, the function of Lacan is the function that Hegel served for the German revolutionaries of the 1840s."[104] In hybrid Hegelian-Žižekian parlance, Lacan could be construed, in this light, as a vanishing mediator between philosophy and antiphilosophy, with his determinate negations of given philosophies rendering possible the birth of novel philosophical trajectories.

In the opening session of his seminar on Lacanian antiphilosophy, Badiou proposes that Lacan's specific brand of antiphilosophy requires passing through philosophy, hence the frequent, extended forays into the philosophical canon by Lacan.[105] Combined with the portions of the *Manifesto for Philosophy* I cited in the preceding paragraph, Badiou's position mandates two inverse-yet-complementary movements: a philosophical traversal of antiphilosophy (as Lacanian psychoanalysis) and an antiphilosophical traversal of philosophy. Badiouian thought arises, in part, out of what forms at the center of these crosscurrents. Already in 1972, during a session of his nineteenth seminar (*...ou pire*, 1971–72), Lacan retroactively can be viewed, with the benefit of hindsight informed by the advent of Badiou's work, as heralding the eventual arrival of a new mode of philosophy, a post-Lacanian philosophical orientation. After speaking of Plato's *Parmenides* and the theme of "the One" (key references precious to Badiou), Lacan predicts that "one surely will be found one day to make an ontology with what I am telling you."[106] The temptation to crown Badiou an at-least-one-philosopher who fulfills this prophecy is well nigh irresistible. What is more, doing so demonstrates that Lacanian theory is neither opposed to Philosophy as such nor incapable of serving as a foundation for the construction of new philosophical edifices freed from the burdens imposed by a range of intellectual-historical constraints. The contemporary flourishing of philosophies without Ones or necessities, such as those articulated by Badiou, Žižek, Meillassoux, and others, bears witness to the philosophical fecundity of Lacan's reflections.[107]

A prolific neologizer, Lacan employs the prefix "para-" for a number of his neologisms. Of particular relevance in this context are his utterances concerning the *"paraître"* of *"parêtre"* (roughly translated, the appearing-being of parabeing).[108] Although he portrays himself as scrupulously skirting around philosophical ontology[109] – nobody who splits with bars both symbolic orders as big Others and the Real itself could buy into what presents itself as a consistent discursive system mirroring a consistent field of Being – he nonetheless is "not without" (*pas sans*)[110] many things to say about matters ontological,[111] things maybe better said (or half-said [*mi-dire*]) through an indirect, circumspect style unfamiliar by comparison with accepted philosophical conventions of speech and writing (see also Chapter 4). In the end, as regards the topological placement of the philosophical vis-à-vis the antiphilosophical, perhaps Lacan is best thought of as, so to speak, a sort of slant philosopher developing a paraphilosophy twisting and subverting the surfaces supposedly dividing philosophy from its others.

Notes

1. Lacan 2001e: 314–15.
2. Lacan 1980: 17.
3. Milner 1995: 146.
4. Regnault 1997: 61.
5. Ibid.: 61–2, 73.
6. Žižek 1999a: 250.
7. Ibid.: 250–1.
8. Badiou 2009a: 9.

9. Soler 2006: 122.

10. Milner 1995: 146–8; Badiou 1994–95: first course; Badiou 2006a: 81; Regnault 1997: 62–3; Soler 2006: 122.

11. Lacan 2001e: 314.

12. *SXV*: 2/28/68.

13. *SXVI*: 239–40.

14. *SXVII*: 31.

15. Ibid.: 168.

16. *SXVIII*: 43.

17. *SXVII*: 169; Johnston 2008d: 251–2.

18. *SXIX: Le savoir du psychanalyste*: 12/2/71.

19. *SXIX: Le savoir du psychanalyste*: 5/4/72; *SXIX: ...ou pire*: 6/21/72.

20. *SXX*: 39.

21. Badiou 1991: 148.

22. Lacan 2005c: 96.

23. Ibid.: 96.

24. *SXIX: ...ou pire*: 6/21/72; *SXX*: 30–1; Johnston 2008b: 184–5; Johnston 2009b: 168–9.

25. Regnault 1997: 64, 66, 73.

26. Lacan 2005c: 96–7.

27. Ibid.: 101.

28. Ibid.: 101.

29. Soler 2006: 123–4; Badiou 1994–95: seventh course; Badiou 2006a: 91–2.

30. *SXXIII*: 128.

31. Ibid.: 144–5.

32. *SXXV*: 12/20/77.

33. Badiou 1991: 135; Milner 1991: 348.

34. Milner 1995: 117–58; Milner 2002: 153–68; Milner 2012: 229–44.

35. Milner 1995: 147–8.

36. Ibid.: 148, 150–1, 154.

37. *SIII*: 163–4.

38. Heidegger 1993: 273–8.

39. *SXIX: ...ou pire*: 12/15/71, 4/19/72; *SXIX: Le savoir du psychanalyste*: 5/4/72; *SXX*: 110, 119; Lacan 2001i: 472, 482–3; Milner 1995: 122–3.

40. *SXX*: 110.

41. Koyré 1958: 99, 278; Lacan 2006g: 235–9; Lacan 2006h: 299–300; Lacan 2006n: 608; Lacan 2006q: 726–7; *SII*: 298–9; *SIII*: 238;

SXIII: 12/8/65; *SXX*: 81–2; Milner 1995: 9, 37–53; Milner 2000: 8; Johnston 2012b: 105–21.

42. Milner 1995: 148–9.
43. Ibid.: 149.
44. Lacan 2006p: 712; *SXI*: 47, 231; Johnston 2005c: 61–71; Johnston 2012b: 105–21.
45. Soler 2006: 124–5.
46. Ibid.: 142–3.
47. Lacan 1990d: 130.
48. Badiou 1994–95: third, fourth, sixth, and seventh courses.
49. Soler 2006: 127.
50. Ibid.: 128–9, 131–2, 134.
51. Badiou 1994–95: sixth course; Balmès 1999: 206.
52. Johnston 2010a: 328–30.
53. Milner 1995: 153.
54. Ibid.: 153.
55. Lacan 2006b: 30–48; *SII*: 181–6, 192–4.
56. Badiou 2006a: 82.
57. Milner 1995: 153.
58. Regnault 1997: 73.
59. Ibid.: 73.
60. Badiou 1991: 153–4.
61. Ibid.: 147.
62. Badiou 1991: 135; Badiou 2006b: 7.
63. Bosteels 2008: 155–87.
64. Badiou 2009a: 7.
65. Badiou 1994–95: first course.
66. Badiou 1989.
67. Badiou 1994–95: sixth course.
68. Badiou 2006a: 92.
69. Badiou 1994–95: first course; Badiou 2006a: 92–3.
70. Johnston 2009a: 144–56.
71. Johnston 2012b: 105–21.
72. Badiou 2006a: 91–2.
73. Badiou 1994–95: third course.
74. Lacan 2001i: 452, 458–9, 477, 490.
75. Badiou 2006a: 92.
76. Milner 1995: 68–9.
77. Ibid.: 69.
78. Johnston 2008d: 35–6.
79. Badiou 2006a: 82–3.

80. Ibid.: 83.
81. Ibid.: 85, 88.
82. Ibid.: 93.
83. Badiou 1994–95: fourth course.
84. Badiou 2006a: 85.
85. Johnston 2008d: 85–90; Johnston 2009a: 118–24.
86. Badiou 1994–95: second course.
87. Badiou 2009b: 523.
88. Badiou 2009d: 67.
89. Milner 1995: 141–6; Milner 2002: 149–50; Milner 2000: 8; Milner 2012: 229–44.
90. Badiou 1991: 138.
91. Regnault 1997: 76.
92. Badiou 1991: 154.
93. Badiou 2010: 107–8.
94. Badiou 1989.
95. Badiou 1994–95: fourth course.
96. Žižek 1993: 4.
97. Ibid.: 4.
98. Badiou 2008: 27.
99. Badiou 1999: 28.
100. Ibid.: 81–4.
101. Ibid.: 84.
102. Badiou 2009e: 132.
103. Ibid.: 133.
104. Badiou 2009c: 4.
105. Badiou 1994–95: first course.
106. *SXIX: ...ou pire*: 5/17/72.
107. Johnston 2013i.
108. *SV*: 350, 453–4; Lacan 2006m: 582; *SXX*: 44–5; Lacan 2001i: 488; *SXXIV*: 2/15/77, 3/8/77.
109. *SXI*: 29.
110. *SVI*: 2/11/59; *SIX*: 4/4/62; *SX*: 105.
111. Johnston 2009b: 168–9.

II

The Real Unconscious:
Malabou, Soler, and Psychical Life
After Lacan

Having just attempted to redeem Lacan as important for and com-patible with contemporary philosophy in the preceding chapter immediately above, I feel that, for a plethora of reasons, it is now fitting to turn attention to the work of Catherine Malabou in this chapter. Malabou is another contemporary thinker who is an utterly irreplaceable interlocutor for me. Between us, she and I enjoy a wonderful equilibrium productively blending agreement and disagreement.

In particular, Malabou and I both are devoted to reassessing philosophy and psychoanalysis in light of the life sciences (as seen in Part II, Žižek also is engaged in this project). Moreover, we both are committed to resuscitating the tradition of dialectical materialism (as, again, is Žižek too). However, when it comes to the place of psychoanalysis in relation to philosophy and biology, she and I part company. To paint in broad brushstrokes at this preliminary stage here, Malabou tends to interpret neurobiology as seriously undermining Freudian-Lacanian analysis, whereas I tend to interpret it in an opposite manner, namely, as largely cor-roborating and/or enriching the theory and practice of analysis. In what follows below, I strive to extend and deepen the debate between Malabou and me as it already has taken shape along these lines.

To be even more precise, my agenda in this chapter is simple and straightforward: to problematize select dimensions of Malabou's critique of psychoanalysis and, in so doing, to clarify and nuance the analytic concepts in the crosshairs of some of her criticisms. Although I am much more sympathetic to analysis than Malabou, I readily admit that the multiple challenges which she poses to both Freudian and Lacanian schools are serious ones; they demand a substantial, detailed response from anyone who maintains, as I do, that analysis theoretical and clinical has a viable, vibrant future in the twenty-first century. Her neuroscientifically grounded objections to analysis, unlike many neuroscientific (and, all too often, pseudoscientific) dismissals of it, are informed by a profound knowledge of the discipline of the unconscious manifestly evident in her subtle, thought-provoking readings of key texts by Freud and Lacan.

As a highly informed and talented critic of analysis, Malabou clearly has the power to help push forward the analytic field precisely through how she pushes back against some of its most cherished and established doctrines. Partisans of Freud and Lacan stand to gain a great deal from engaging with her ideas. I hope my reply to Malabou in what follows both does justice to her significant contributions to contemporary thought as well as assists, if only to a very small extent, in the ongoing work-in-progress of refining and enriching the living psychoanalytic tradition.

Of what Malabou has released in print thus far, her 2007 book *Les nouveaux blessés: De Freud à la neurologie, penser les traumatismes contemporains* and 2009 book *Ontologie de l'accident: Essai sur la plasticité destructrice* contain the material most relevant to me in this context. However, in addition to these two published books, she and I recently published a co-authored book with Columbia University Press entitled *Self and Emotional Life: Philosophy, Psychoanalysis, and Neuroscience*. At certain points below, I will draw on content from this text. In fact, this response to Malabou constitutes an additional installment in the dialogues and debates we initiated with each other in our co-authored book.

To put my cards on the table right up front, I believe that Malabou's criticisms of psychoanalysis sometimes hinge on tacitly construing it as essentially a type of hermeneutics lop-sidedly favoring continuity over discontinuity. Such a construal is far from unusual or unprecedented, in the past as well as the present, amongst its proponents and critics alike. Nonetheless, despite intuitive appeal and wide acceptance within and beyond analytic circles, this portrayal of analysis as an activity of uncovering and/or constructing threads of signification running seamlessly through all the moments and periods of entire life histories distorts Freud's foundational framework – with Lacan going furthest amongst the inheritors of the Freudian legacy toward correcting this misrepresentation of what is at stake in analysis. Through turning to Lacanian analyst Colette Soler's presentation of Lacan's "real unconscious" in her two latest books, *Lacan, l'inconscient réinventé* (2009) and *Les affects lacaniens* (2011), I will assemble, *contra* Malabou, a counter-image of Freudian-Lacanian psychoanalysis as a non-hermeneutical orientation open to the possibility of radical discontinuities. More than any other expert on Lacanianism, Soler, in her recent publications, spells out with exquisite precision just how far the unconscious arising out of Lacan's "return to Freud" is from being the continuous expanse of a deep, dark reservoir of hidden meanings.

Before turning to Freud, Lacan, and Soler, I must take the time to furnish a faithful sketch of those aspects of Malabou's critical position which I wish to address (and periodically I will punctuate this synopsis with rejoinders to certain points made by Malabou, particularly apropos matters having to do with Freud's ideas). Her general strategy relies upon confronting psychoanalysis with examples and cases taken from contemporary neuroscience, instances in which "it is not possible to separate the organic wound from its psychical repercussions."[1] To be more specific, she sees "the new wounded" (*les nouveaux blessés*) of neuropathology – the ranks of this corps include Alzheimer's patients, sufferers of senile dementia, and all those with various kinds of brain damage or neurophysiological alterations resulting from disease, injury, malnutrition, poverty, war, and/or substance abuse – as disturbing figures facing analysis with what, allegedly up until now, it has failed to recognize as incarnations of its conceptual and curative limits.[2] Those unfortunates whose socio-symbolic selfhood is severely diminished or utterly destroyed by neurophysiological traumas embody, according to Malabou, something analysis has yet really to think through: meaningless material events of destruction, brutal and total breaks, in which the human organism survives the ordeal of a senselessly imposed erasure of its prior accompanying form of subjectivity.[3]

Motivated by her particular argumentative agenda, Malabou is especially preoccupied with rather extreme instances of neuropathology in which personality and the capacity to feel emotions are obliterated as a consequence of lesions compromising the central nervous system (i.e., neuro-traumas resulting from any number of causes). In relation to his/her significance-saturated ontogenetic life history as a proper psychical subject, such a victim of major neuro-trauma undergoes a radical, irreversible change without analytically interpretable rhyme or reason. Malabou insists that

trying to make sense of such senseless shocks of contingent ruptures[4] in terms of regression,[5] repression,[6] and/or (de)negation[7] is
an invalid and impossible endeavor.

Additionally, even if the sufferer's trauma could be inscribed
into the narrative of analytic interpretation, the biological body
living on after the infliction of its wounds, now bereft of its former
subjective identity, would be incapable of benefitting from such
interpretive (re)inscriptions. With such a body on his/her couch,
the analyst would have no one to address, given the absence in this
semblance of an analysand of a psychical life sufficiently rich for
productive participation in the analytic process as driven by interactions between analyst and analysand. As Malabou voices this in
Ontologie de l'accident, "The body can die without being dead"[8]
(one cannot help but hear echoes of Lacan's interrelated notions
of the "second death" and the state "between-two-deaths" [*entre-
deux-morts*] here[9]). Deprived of both a robust sense of personhood as well as an ability affectively to register and digest his/her
post-traumatic circumstances, the representative of Malabou's
new wounded (for instance, someone at the stage of very advanced
Alzheimer's or an individual with anosognosia) has no hope of
finding healing anamnesis and liberatory working-through within
the four walls of the analyst's consulting room. And, no matter
what the analyst says, he/she has no real analytic explanation
regarding the absence of positive therapeutic prognoses for these
neuropathological patients.

Malabou frequently emphasizes the "indifference" and "coldness" of the post-traumatic survivors that preoccupy her most.[10]
In this vein, she contrasts the Freudian death drive (*Todestrieb*)
with the neurobiological death of (all) drive.[11] Given the entangle-
ment of emotion and motivation in the functional living brain (as
per the neuroscientific triad of the emotional, the motivational,
and the cognitive as the three basic dimensions of brain-based
mental life), the second term of this contrast (i.e., the neurobiological death of [all] drive) suggests the dissipation of affective life,
the demise of the "emotional brain." The detached, disinterested
being who lives on after the "event" of his/her neuro-trauma
– Malabou speaks of both "cerebral events"[12] and "material
events"[13] in connection with sufficiently drastic transformations of
the central nervous system – has neither the means nor the motives
to attempt a cathartic reckoning with what happened to him/her
(such as the type of catharsis-through-*Durcharbeiten* aimed at by

analysis). In the wider context of contemporary French philosophy, the Malabouian event could be seen as the dark underside
of the Badiouian event, the latter being frequently celebrated
nowadays as the brilliantly bright source of novelty, invention,
creativity, etc. Conceptions of contingent disruptions bring with
them a negative backside in addition to a positive front side.

In *Les nouveaux blessés*, Malabou claims that "*Every brain
disease or cerebral lesion affects the brain's auto-affection.*"[14]
The concept-term "auto-affection" has become, over the past
several years, a cornerstone of Malabou's philosophical reflections on the neurosciences. Consequently, it has taken on a range
of distinguishable senses in her recent writings. However, for the
moment and in line with the immediately preceding, the sense of
most relevance here has to do with affect as emotion. After the
exogenous hetero-affection of certain neuro-traumas (i.e., "brain
disease or cerebral lesion" as a non-emotional affecting of a person's central nervous system), the auto-affection characteristic
of the human brain (i.e., its largely non-conscious, endogenous
self-regulation[15]) is interrupted and altered. In the more extreme
examples foregrounded by Malabou, this interruption/alteration
can be so severe as to obliterate the possibility of the traumatized
individual being affected emotionally thereafter in relation to him/
her-self (i.e., to be auto-affected emotionally, such as being sad-
dened or dismayed at one's impaired condition) or other persons
and things (i.e., to be hetero-affected emotionally, feeling various
feelings in response to one's material and social surroundings). At
the outer limits of neuropathology, one encounters, so to speak,
the living dead of human organisms traumatically hetero-affected
so brutally that, in the realms of affective-as-emotional life, they
can no longer be further auto- or hetero-affected.

With respect to the dire cerebro-lesions on which she zooms
in, Malabou contends that psychoanalytic conceptions of trauma
are quite inadequate for truly thinking the severity of the traumas
producing her new wounded.[16] Post-traumatically, Malabou's
zombie-like survivors, stripped of a subjectivity emotionally and
motivationally inclined toward the kind of laborious process
epitomized by analysis, are uninterested and unable to undergo the
sorts of experiences crucial to a therapeutically beneficial analysis
(unlike those differently traumatized analysands committed to
remembering, repeating, and working-through their painful pasts
on the analyst's couch). Pre-traumatically, the impossible-to-

imagine ordeal of living death as the physically inflicted erasure of one's very selfhood and personal identity – this defies depiction via representations and expectations in the non/not-yet-traumatized subject's psyche – cannot, by virtue of this very impossibility, be foreshadowed by prior fantasies and similar formations of psychical subjectivity[17] (however, at least as regards literal death per se, Freud likewise maintains that this unavoidable eventuality cannot be grasped as such by the psychical apparatus[18]; more generally, Lacan frequently depicts the fantasmatic and desiring life of psychical subjectivity as orbiting around the Real *qua* unrepresentable, non-specular centers of libidinal gravity). Hence, for Malabou, considering the total absence in the non/not-yet-traumatized subject's psyche of any trace of accurate anticipatory imagining of dramatic neuro-trauma, if and when such a trauma occurs, it cannot plausibly be fastened back onto an unbroken thread of an uninterrupted ontogenetic life history of a particular subject. The lack of preceding pre-traumatic *Vorstellungen*, as intra-psychical coordinates anchoring desires, fantasies, and the like, blocks the standard analytic gesture of establishing links between the endogenous libidinal economy and various arrays of exogenous forces and factors. Related to this, Malabou criticizes Freud for invariably privileging the endogenous over the exogenous to such an extent that he purportedly denies the reality of purely exogenous traumas,[19] such as the meaningless material events profoundly impacting the brain upon which she ruminates (but, Freud's later revisions of his account of trauma in light of those suffering from a single, adult, and non-sexual violent event breaking the history of their lives in two through a sudden horrible glimpse of death arguably present evidence conflicting with Malabou's interpretive assessments[20]).

To Malabou's ears, neuropathology's new wounded testify against the analytic assumption of there being an underlying, indestructible continuity of significances and temporalities at the foundational base of psychical life, an unbreakable continuity licensing the art of analytic interpretation.[21] They do so by bearing witness to the ineliminable and omnipresent possibility, one haunting everyone for whom this threat has not (or not yet) become a materialized actuality, of undergoing and surviving a senseless, random, unforeseeable neuro-trauma eventuating in an ontogenetically unprecedented post-traumatic subjectivity (or even in the non-existence of any fleshed out socio-symbolic and/or affective subjectivity altogether). Already in *Les nouveaux blessés*, but especially in *Ontologie de l'accident*, Malabou strives philosophically to generalize into a fundamental ontology aspects of what is involved here in her neuroscience-informed critique of psychoanalysis. The roots of this larger philosophical pursuit lie in Malabou's first major work, *The Future of Hegel: Plasticity, Temporality and Dialectic* (originally her doctoral dissertation). Therein, she extracts from a close reading of Hegel (particularly his "anthropology" as laid out in the third volume of the *Encyclopedia of the Philosophical Sciences*, the *Philosophy of Mind*) what arguably has become since then the master-concept of her whole *oeuvre*: "plasticity."[22]

The cardinal feature of plasticity *à la* Malabou is its two-sidedness, its peculiar ambiguity (this is quite fitting for a notion initially taken from Hegel's dialectical-speculative philosophy). Throughout each and every one of her works, she regularly insists that the plastic simultaneously involves, on the one hand, flexibility, fluidity, and malleability, and, on the other hand, inflexibility, rigidity, and fixedness. The balance (or lack thereof) between these negative and positive poles of plasticity, as the recto and verso of what also could be called "forming," can and does shift into unevenness in any number of ways. What is more, anything properly plastic has a form it can lose and, if and when it loses one form, it usually has the potential to take on another. Her 2004 *tour de force*, *What Should We Do with Our Brain?* (a project hinted at in the concluding pages of *The Future of Hegel*[23]), convincingly combines her notion of plasticity with the scientific conception of neuroplasticity. This combination sets the stage for much of what she does in *Les nouveaux blessés* and *Ontologie de l'accident*.

In *Les nouveaux blessés*, Malabou describes the neuro-traumatic termination of a pre-traumatic subjectivity as a *"creation by destruction of form,"* namely, as a "destructive plasticity."[24] Put differently, cerebro-lesions cancel/negate a prior subjective form and, at one and the same time, create a new one discontinuous with the old, with this creation sometimes producing instances of an absence of subjective form *tout court* as a paradoxical type of subjectless subject (i.e., the zombie-like living dead surviving in cold, indifferent anonymity). In *Ontologie de l'accident*, a book whose sub-title includes the phrase "destructive plasticity," she carries these speculations further. With the more extreme examples of post-traumatic subjects-without-subjectivity evidently in mind, she maintains that all established disciplines, and not just psychoanalysis, have failed to contemplate the idea of destructive plasticity in its most striking manifestations.[25] Even the neurosciences themselves are judged guilty of this shortcoming. Defensively averting their gaze from the upsetting sight of irreparably shattered lives, the neuroscientists prefer to restrict their attention to the regenerative side of neuroplasticity and their curative role in helping along the recuperative process. Through keeping themselves preoccupied with the contingent, circumstantial causes of the individual cases of trauma which they treat, they avoid acknowledging the necessary universality of each and every person's inherent vulnerability to such wounding accidents and misfortunes[26] (Freud offers a similar analysis of defensive mental maneuvers vis-à-vis the fact of death's inevitability[27]). Addressing both the psychoanalytic doctors of the soul and the neuroscientific doctors of the brain, Malabou asks about "How to think, without contradicting oneself, a plasticity without cure (remède)?"[28]

Ontologie de l'accident, as its very title already indicates, is devoted to laying the groundwork for an ontology finally taking into account, as previous orientations have not yet done, explosive events of indigestible, meaningless traumas in which destructive plasticity goes so far as to destroy plasticity itself, in which plasticity is exposed, thanks to itself, to its own disruption.[29] That is to say, in a Hegelian/dialectical-style self-subversion, destructive plasticity, on Malabou's account in *Ontologie de l'accident*, can (and does) make possible a cutting off of the openness to the possibility of taking on subsequent forms *à venir*, a possibility characteristic of plasticity per se. She speaks of this possibility of no more possibilities as the "negative possible."[30] The massive cerebro-lesions of catastrophic neuro-traumas produce the bodies of human organisms living on but not, as it were, living for, that is, not inclining toward future plans, projects, and prospects in the manners in which full-fledged human subjects proper continually do. As the ontologically essential dynamics of acquiring and losing form (i.e., "forming"), plasticity (including neuroplasticity) stands permanently under the shadow of the virtual danger of its liquidation, an elimination with which it cannot help but be complicit (specifically in terms of its propensity for loss of form) when this elimination eventually comes to pass. Old age, if nothing else, will bring this about sooner or later.

According to Malabou, both psychoanalytic and neuroscientific theories are forced to balance delicately between "system" (as the continuity of self-regulating structures and dynamics) and "event" (as the discontinuity of disturbances and breaches disrupting systems).[31] In her view, whereas neurobiology allows for conceiving of the primacy of event over system (in terms of the utterly system-destroying events of neuro-traumatic destructive plasticity), analysis, by contrast, unwaveringly insists on the supremacy of system over event (in terms of a psychical apparatus sustaining indestructible threads of connection across vast temporal swathes of an ontogenetic life history). Analytic metapsychology à la Freud and Lacan allegedly clings to continuity at all costs.[32] But, how so, exactly?

Malabou begins setting up the argumentative details buttressing this objection to analysis' ostensible privileging of continuity over discontinuity by observing that, in the Freudian corpus, death is an ubiquitous (albeit sometimes shadowy) presence throughout Freud's elaborations of the different versions of his drive theory well before 1920's *Beyond the Pleasure Principle*.[33] In other words, it is not as though Freud abruptly introduces mortality into sexuality – some readers of Freud's *oeuvre* might be tempted to believe that his pre-1920 drive theory is, as it were, all sex and no death – only starting with the initial formulations of the notion of the *Todestrieb* in 1920. On this point, Malabou is absolutely correct. Any minimally attentive reading of the *Standard Edition* reveals the omnipresence of reflections related to death across the entire arc of Freud's long intellectual itinerary from the 1890s onward.[34] And yet, anticipating the subsequent moves Malabou makes on the basis of this, one reasonably might ask: Even though Freud often, both before and after 1920, muses about mortality in relation to sexuality, does this mean that death is always and invariably sexualized for him? I am convinced that the answer to this question is negative, with this "no" complicating Malabou's line of argumentation.

Anyhow, for Malabou's purposes, the crucial upshot of her preceding observation about mortality in Freud's corpus is that mortal finitude is a tangible reality for the analytic psyche exclusively in a derivative, indirect fashion. That is to say, according to Freudian analysis, the psychical subject, both consciously and unconsciously, relates to death (its own in particular) solely as refracted through the prism of sexuality: for instance, death fantasmatically represented as a variant of castration and/or as related to the hateful, id-level sadism of the death drive as a dimension of the psyche's affective and libidinal economies[35] (I must note that I consider this depiction to oversimplify, through excessively generalizing from a handful of select remarks by Freud, his complex, shifting positions with respect to mortality). Malabou is overridingly concerned with theorizing death as both the destruction of prior forms of subjectivity in addition to the random, unpredictable annihilation of the supporting body of any and every form of subjectivity (a body also capable of supporting the desubjectified lives, the living deaths, of the new wounded). As I noted earlier, she contends that these sorts of cuttingly abrupt ends cannot be foreseen and rehearsed in advance by psychical subjects prior to the event of a (neuro-)trauma; no ideational, representational imaginings or symbolizations can or do capture and bind these spectral terminators from a black future refractory to anticipations, forecasts, and predictions. Therefore, Freud's treatment of mortality, insofar as this finitude features in his models of the psyche as an ontogenetically continuous permutation of sexuality past and present, in no way grasps or addresses the sorts of deaths Malabou dredges up from biological fields. Not only are the kinds of new wounded spoken of by Malabou post-traumatically indifferent to sexuality (as per a libidinal coldness in line with their affective coldness)[36] – pre-traumatically, the psychical subjectivity of Freudian psychoanalysis is constitutively incapable of envisioning a death that would erase it (i.e., this very subjectivity itself) and its accompanying matrices of desires, drives, fantasies, and feelings. Malabou challenges analysis to try to think a death of the psyche carrying it beyond the sexual-libidinal coordinates of pleasure and pain, love and hate.[37] She thereby pits the discontinuity of neuroscientific "cerebrality" against the continuity of psychoanalytic "sexuality"[38] (with the cerebral brain, unlike the sexual unconscious of Freud as constitutively ignorant of its own mortality, being extremely sensitive to its frail finitude, a sensitivity intrinsic to its auto-affective self-regulation[39]).

Malabou considers Lacan to be as guilty as Freud of holding fast to a fatally flawed sexual etiology of even the most shattering of traumas.[40] And, in the context of her provocative reading of pivotal sessions of Lacan's renowned eleventh seminar, she claims that "*automaton*" (i.e., "system" in her sense as highlighted above) always triumphs over "*tuché*" (i.e., "event" in her sense) in the Lacanian envisioning of trauma.[41] In general, she accuses Lacan of completely disregarding the central nervous system.[12] Elsewhere, I have defended Lacan against this charge of utterly neglecting the brain and all things biological[43] (as has Soler too in her own fashion[44]). Moreover, on another occasion, I have responded directly to a number of Malabou's criticisms of Freudian-Lacanian analysis as summarized here thus far.[45] I also cannot resist mentioning as an aside that the theory of drive proposed in my first book, *Time Driven: Metapsychology and the Splitting of the Drive*, redeems Freud in the face of Malabou's charges to the effect that he fails to incorporate plasticity (in her precise meaning) into his metapsychological theories[46] – and this to the extent that my Freud-inspired temporal model of drives as a combination-in-tension of a repetitive "axis of iteration" (parallel to plasticity-as-fixity) and a differentiating "axis of alteration" (parallel to plasticity-as-fluidity) reveals the Freudian *Trieb* to be plastic according to the exact Malabouian definition of plasticity. But, instead of repeating these pro-analytic defenses and responses already elaborated, I will, in what follows, try to articulate a new set of additional replies to Malabou's indictments of Freud and Lacan – and this, as signaled at the start of the present chapter, through drawing on the recent work of Soler.

As the title of Soler's 2009 book promises (*Lacan, l'inconscient réinventé*), she pursues the elucidation of Lacan's "reinvention" of the unconscious. The word "reinvention" is well chosen, conveying the dialectical double-sidedness of the famous Lacanian "return to Freud" as simultaneously both an orthodox recovery of the core of Freud's thought (i.e., "re-") as well as a heterodox modification of this same core (i.e., "invention"). Specifically apropos Lacan and his unconscious, Malabou makes several related assertions. To begin with, she claims, "Psychical energy is, in a certain way, the rhetorical detour of nervous energy"[47] (this claim is reiterated by her in our co-authored book[48]). The choice of the adjective "rhetorical" (*rhétorique*) undoubtedly hints that Lacan's metapsychology of psychical subjectivity is being targeted here. Then, making this glaringly explicit on the following page, she posits that "*The unconscious is structured like a language only to the extent that the brain does not speak.*"[49] In both *Les nouveaux blessés* and *Self and Emotional Life*, she contests the assumption that the brain is organically closed in upon itself in the mute, sealed-off dumbness of inert material silence.[50]

On my reading, Malabou seeks to attribute directly to the auto-affective central nervous system various aspects of Lacan's (subject of the) unconscious. Cerebral auto-affection is neither conscious nor self-reflective/reflexive[51] (as is the Freudian-Lacanian unconscious that knows without knowing that it knows and thinks without thinking that it thinks). Along the same lines, there is no "mirroring" in the brain[52] (just as the Lacanian *sujet*, as different-in-kind from the specular ego [*moi*] born within the frames of the reflective surfaces of mirrors both literal and figurative, eludes being captured in the visible worlds of Imaginary-Symbolic reality). Finally, the physical brain is a Real material Thing similar to, but nonetheless different from, Lacan's Real Thing (*la Chose du Réel*)[53] (to remark in passing, Lacan often links his register of the Real to materialities along the lines of what Malabou is after too). With Lacan's apparent anti-naturalist distaste for things biological in mind, Malabou contends that the brain he seems disdainfully to ignore embodies key features of his subject of the unconscious while, all the same and at the same time, complicating and/or contesting other facets of his analytic discursive apparatus. Assuming that Soler and I, each in our own ways, already have managed to call into question whether Lacan is as hostile to the life sciences and as neglectful of the brain as Malabou and most others assume,[54] what might Soler have to say in response to the preceding?

In both *Lacan, l'inconscient réinventé* and *Les affects lacaniens*, Soler seeks to illuminate what she christens "the real unconscious" (*l'inconscient réel* [ICSR]), namely, the unconscious as related mainly to the Lacanian register of the Real. Although, in these efforts, she relies heavily on the later Lacan of the 1970s, Soler justifiably rejects the standard periodization of Lacan's intellectual itinerary dividing it, as per his register theory, into the early primacy of the Imaginary (the 1930s and 1940s), the middle primacy of the Symbolic (the 1950s), and the late primacy of the Real (the 1960s through 1981). Along these lines, she states that the Lacan of the 1950s never really was a classical structuralist properly speaking; even then, his subject is, according to her, "the living being marked by language" (*le vivant marqué par le langage*).[55] In fact, Soler tirelessly stresses again and again that Lacan unwaveringly, throughout the vast span of his teachings, grounds unconscious subjectivity in the living being as a material incarnation of the Real[56]; in this vein, she speaks of "living *jouissance*,"[57] "the Real of the living being,"[58] "the organism affected by discourse,"[59] and "the affected living being."[60] Her Lacan, over the time of his thinking, moves seamlessly from talking about "the Freudian Thing" to dwelling on a *parlêtre* (speaking-being) that itself morphs into the subject of the real unconscious.[61]

The Solerian ICSR and the subjects associated with it have everything to do, on Soler's reconstruction of Lacanianism, with what the Lacan of the 1970s baptizes "*lalangue*."[62] It can be defined thusly:

> This neologism is formed through collapsing the space between the definite article and the noun in the French '*la langue*' (which could be translated as 'the tongue' or 'the natural language'). One could say that a nonsense word is created through skipping over the spacing so crucial to the syntactical and grammatical structures of recognizably meaningful (uses of) natural languages. Moreover, the sound of the word *lalangue* recalls, through its first two repeating sounds (*lala*), the murmurings of infants before mastering their 'mother tongue' (*la langue maternelle*) as a transparent medium of socially comprehensible communication. An infant's babbling, prior to his/her acquisition of and accession to *la langue* as a system of signifying signs employed in exchanges of ideas, frequently involves playing with phonemic elements of his/her auditory milieu as meaningless materials to be enjoyed for the sensations they produce in the libidinally charged orifices of the mouth (when vocalized) or the ears (when heard). The nonsense neologism *lalangue* is coined by Lacan to designate, among other things, the nonsense uttered by babbling infants joyfully and idiotically reveling in the bodily pleasures of pure, senseless sounds.[63]

Soler offers identical specifications of what Lacan intends to covey with this notion.[64] Additionally, she shows that Lacan's privileging of signifiers as material rather than meaningful long pre-dates such interrelated 1970s-era concept-terms as *lalangue*, "letter," and "*jouis-sens*" (enjoy-meant). I too have insisted repeatedly, like Soler, that the signifier as meaningless materiality, instead of as significance-laden unit of communicative natural language, is a red thread running through the Lacanian corpus from the 1950s until his death.[65]

What is more, Soler correctly traces back all of this (i.e., the *jouis-sens* of *lalangue* as the associative play within the unconscious of meaningless signifier-letters in their acoustic and/or graphic materiality as tied up with the orifices of the living organic

body) to the pioneering Freud of the 1890s and first years of the
1900s (especially the author of *The Interpretation of Dreams*,
The Psychopathology of Everyday Life, and *Jokes and Their
Relation to the Unconscious*).[66] Hence, from the early Freud to
the late Lacan, a fundamental dimension of the psychoanalytic
unconscious, whether this be dubbed Freudian "primary process"
or Lacanian *lalangue*, reveals itself to be independent of and
unconcerned with constraining strictures of meaning/significance.
Already apart from various sorts of traumas (including those of
interest to Malabou), many of the fundamental underpinnings
of the Freudian-Lacanian unconscious precipitate out of the
senseless accidents of events of contingent collisions between, on
the one hand, the "living substance" of the Real corporeal body
laden with its libidinal and affective *jouissance* (as Soler renders
this[67]), and, on the other hand, the universe of material signifiers
into which the prematurationally helpless and uncomprehending
young human being is randomly thrown through the accidental
circumstances of conception and birth (tangentially related to
this, it would be very interesting to see Malabou engage with
Otto Rank's unjustifiably marginalized 1924 analytic classic *The
Trauma of Birth*).

   Soler's ICSR becomes, over the course of her theorizations, synonymous with what she refers to as the "*lalangue*-unconscious."
The Real unconscious of *lalangue* has several features by her
account. First, this ICSR consists of a *savoir* (as well as a *savoir
faire* with meaningless material signifiers) as a set of "unknown
knowns" (to resort to Donald Rumsfeld's irresistible phrasing).
This peculiar type of unconscious knowledge continually over-
flows and escapes from the grasp of (self-)conscious cognition,
including from that of the analyzing analyst (who nonetheless,
with his/her analytic *savoir* [*faire*], knows how to attempt going
with the flow of this free-associative slipperiness).[68] Second, the
ICSR as *lalangue*-unconscious remains immanent to the signifying planes of Imaginary-Symbolic reality, albeit as inevitably mis/
un-recognized by the ego-endowed inhabitants of these planes; it
subsists "extimately" (as per Lacan's neologism "*extimité*") as
singular "a-structural" idiosyncrasy within-but-beyond reality's
socio-linguistic configurations and constellations.[69] Third, Soler
stipulates that "The *lalangue*-unconscious has effects at the level of
jouissance, but remains, in essence, unknown."[70] In other words,
the primary-process-style *jouis-sens* interwoven with acoustic

and/or graphic letters produces libidinal and affective effects likely to appear mysterious and opaque to the speaking being thus affected.[71] Fourth, this Real unconscious is grounded on senseless neologistic signifiers. It consists of peculiar material elements of a *lalangue* that is always private as meaningless relative to the codes and conventions of socio-symbolic big Others.[72]

This fourth and final feature explains the previous three in that the conscious selves of personal identities, with their secondary-process mentation and fixation on what is recognizably significant as per the established standards and norms of given Imaginary-Symbolic realities, are bound to be perplexed and puzzled by symptomatic manifestations of the (il)logics of the ICSR – and this insofar as these primary processes (as *jouis-sens*) by no means obey the shared principles and rules of inter- and trans-subjective structures psychically introjected to become egoistic and super-egoistic assemblages. Thus, ego-level self-consciousness tends to experience the Real of the *lalangue*-unconscious in the guise of strange, incomprehensible phenomena (such as enigmatic affects and inexplicable impulses). The Lacanian-Solerian unconscious of the Real is both too clever (in its unchained playfulness) and too stupid (in its uncommunicating idiocy) to be reliably known (in the sense of both *savoir* and *connaissance*) by mindsets embedded in Imaginary-Symbolic realities (see also Chapter 8).

Before I conclude by enumerating the implications of Soler's illuminating reflections on Lacan's conception of the unconscious for Malabou's critique of Freudian-Lacanian psychoanalysis, I want briefly to refer to a single text by Lacan quite relevant to some of what is up for grabs above. As shown, Malabou, in *Les nouveaux blessés*, latches onto Lacan's 1964 distinction between *automaton* and *tuché* so as further to substantiate her contention that, supposedly like Freud, he too subordinates the discontinuities of the accidental and contingent (i.e., *tuché*) to the continuities of a randomness-squelching *automaton*, namely, the signifying unconscious sustaining an indissoluble temporal-ontogenetic unity across the whole span of psychical life. Consistent with the sustained underlying systematicity Soler and I claim runs through Lacan's teachings from at least as early as the 1950s all the way through the 1970s, the *tuché-automaton* pair of the eleventh seminar expresses a trajectory of thought already articulated in the postface to the "Seminar on 'The Purloined Letter'"[73] (Bruce Fink rightly comments that this postface has not received the

exegetical attention it deserves, an injustice he helps to rectify[74]).
To cut a long story short, one of the basic lessons of this supplement to the opening chapter of the *Écrits* is that the *automaton*
of the Symbolic unconscious (represented, in this postface, as the
combinatory laws for consecutive-but-overlapping sets of two or
more binary units [os and 1s, plusses and minuses, heads and tails,
and so on] marking random events) emergently arises from and
parasitically rests atop unfurling sequences of utterly accidental
and contingent happenings (i.e., the *tuché* of chance occurrences
represented as the non-necessary, unpredictable impacts of real
material events as random and disconnected as coin tosses).

How is this lesson from the "Seminar on 'The Purloined
Letter'" relevant to certain of Malabou's interpretations of Lacan?
Expressed in her own philosophical terminology, the groundless
ground of the Freudian-Lacanian unconscious is composed of
nothing other than a tissue of instances of exogenous hetero-
affections without ultimate meaning; the zero-level of auto-
affective psychical life is a baseless base of externally imposed
random accidents and contingencies *sans* sense. The subjects at
stake in analysis take shape through their endogenous subjec-
tifications (or lack/failure thereof) compelled by the Outside of
these chances beneath all rhyme and reason, these episodes and
encounters always-already exceeding any and every rational con-
catenation of "Whys?" This goes some way toward turning what
Malabou puts forward as a strict difference-in-kind between the
analysands of psychoanalysis and the patients of neuropathology
into a mere difference-of-degree, however great (a point to which
I will return in my closing observations momentarily).

Furthermore, as Lacan's 1956 postface openly acknowledges, the
law-like continuities created and sustained in/by the *automaton*-
like unconscious are fictitious pseudo-laws superimposed upon the
discontinuities of lawless successions of isolated *tuché*-like events
with no real connections between them. In response to Malabou's
charge that he (and Freudian analytic theory as a whole) is the one
who projects this continuity onto actually discontinuous material happenings, Lacan might reply that, as an analyst devoted to
describing what he deals with in the practice of analysis, he is just
theoretically mirroring what hetero-affected-but-auto-affecting
psychical subjectivity perpetually does on its own to itself and
its lived real(ity). If and when an analyst comes across a human
being who is no longer capable of and invested in continuing such

superimpositions and projections – faced with the postface to the "Seminar on 'The Purloined Letter,'" Malabou probably would use the model of the coin toss to suggest that Lacan falls short of speculating about a toss resulting in the disappearance through loss or destruction of the heads-and-tails-generating coin itself (or at least of the function of retaining and extrapolating from past tosses) – an analyst might curtly concede that this person has suffered a misfortune placing him/her on the nether side of the outer boundaries of analyzability even for those analysts with the widest of wide scopes. Such an individual simply does not have enough coin for analysis, as it were. But, this concession does not mean that those impoverished by severe neuro-traumas bring about the complete bankruptcy of analysis as both theory and therapy (something I defend in *Self and Emotional Life*[75]).

What about Soler's contributions to a more refined appreciation of the Lacanian unconscious? As is perhaps obvious by now, my succinct gloss on Lacan's postface to the "Seminar on 'The Purloined Letter'" dovetails for the most part with what Soler stipulates regarding the ICSR of *lalangue*. Her rendition of the real unconscious sets up with special lucidity a twist on Malabou's critique of psychoanalysis with which I will conclude. If *l'inconscient du Réel* is the rock-bottom basis sought after over the course of analyses, then the appropriate termination of an analysis must involve bringing to light previously eclipsed extimate dimensions of psychical life eerily resembling the new wounded of the brain sciences: the ghosts of an acephalous subjectivity of the unconscious produced out of meaningless material events; the specters of an impersonal subjectless subject often cold and indifferent in relation to the emotions and motivations moving the ego of conscious selfhood; unknown and unknowable vicissitudes of aimless drifting and dissolving cut loose from the plans and purposes of the reasonable self. Malabou's *nouveaux blessés* would thereby be "uncanny" exactly *à la* the Freudian *Unheimliche* as embodying something repressed that, although it was not supposed to, comes to light unexpectedly nevertheless.[76] For those who are analytically minded, close, unflinching scrutiny of many characteristics of the traumatic cases put on display by Malabou would lead them to view these living dead as embodiments of something "in you more than yourself" (as the Lacan of *Seminar XI* would phrase it). Maybe one of the most unsettling qualities of Malabou's trauma victims has to do with their disavowed familiarity rather than different-in-kind foreignness. Not only, as per Malabou's accidental ontology of destructive plasticity, do they incarnate destructions and deaths unavoidable in the future for everyone when all is said and done – from a Lacanian-Solerian perspective, these shocking sufferers represent, with the potent effectiveness of exaggerated degree, the past and present of those subjects not impacted by neuro-traumas who nonetheless unknowingly suffer daily from the senselessness of material signifiers.

The end of a properly terminated Lacanian analysis is varyingly described as entailing the dissolution of the transference onto "the subject supposed to know," "subjective destitution," the confrontation with the non-existence of the big Other, "traversing the fantasy," and similar things. To risk an oversimplification, one lowest common denominator of what these various phrases designate is the ordeal, at the conclusion of an analytic process, of facing up without illusions to several hard, connected truths. The one-and-only universe of material beings is not a cosmos as a meaningful order created and administered by the highest author-ity of a big Other such as God or Nature. There is no profound and significant teleological undercurrent responsible for the shape of one's life history as a presumably meaningful narrative. Neither the analyst nor anyone else can provide a cure for the vulnerable, mortal human condition, for a death one must at some point meet up with in final, absolute aloneness. What Malabou, via the neurosciences, advances as a limit *qua* external check on analysis both conceptual and clinical arguably could be recast as a limit *qua* internal culmination of the analytic experience, namely, as the limit-experience of the true end of a real analysis. Registering the uncanniness of one's otherness to oneself, glimpsing an extimate unconscious subject alien to one's sense of self in fashions akin to Malabou's new wounded, is an essential component of any analy-sis worthy of the name.

Although defending Freudian-Lacanian analysis against Malabou's neuroscience-inspired criticisms of it, I do not in the least want to run the risk of conveying the impression that her philosophical engagements with neurobiology are not to be taken with the utmost seriousness. As I hope is already crystal clear, I am profoundly solidary with her insistence on the ultimate unavoid-ability for the various traditions and orientations of Continental philosophy (the majority of them still remaining vehemently anti-naturalistic and, accordingly, averse or antagonistic toward the natural sciences) of a sustained reckoning with empirical, experimental investigations into the brain (as well as the biological body and its place in evolutionary natural history overall). Malabou and I fundamentally concur that, especially for materialist and/or embodied theories of subjectivity, neglect of things biological sooner or later consigns such thus-neglectful philosophies to obscurantist idealism and intellectual irrelevance.

Notes

1. Malabou 2007: 47.
2. Ibid.: 309–10.
3. Malabou 2007: 37–8, 45, 94, 253–4, 258–60, 272–3, 293; Malabou 2009d: 9–10, 18–19, 23–4.
4. Malabou 2007: 34–5.
5. Ibid.: 94.
6. Malabou 2009d: 75–7.
7. Ibid.: 83.
8. Ibid.: 36, 66–7.
9. *SVII*: 260, 294–5, 320; *SVIII*: 122.
10. Malabou 2009d: 21, 24, 27–31, 39–40; Malabou 2013a: 7–8, 10–11, 33–4, 58–60, 64, 71.
11. Malabou 2007: 53.
12. Ibid.: 62.
13. Ibid.: 343.
14. Ibid.: 92.
15. Malabou 2007: 83, 85, 88; Malabou 2013a: 5–6, 20–1, 26, 31, 33–4, 42, 51, 55, 64, 221–3.
16. Malabou 2007: 223–4.
17. Ibid.: 34–5.
18. *SE* 14: 186–7, 296.
19. Malabou 2007: 32, 34–5, 241–2, 251–2.
20. *SE* 18: 12–14, 29–33.
21. Malabou 2007: 51–2; Malabou 2009d: 20–1.
22. Malabou 2005: 6, 8–9, 26, 71, 73–4, 192–3.
23. Ibid.: 192–3.
24. Malabou 2007: 49.
25. Malabou 2009d: 12–13, 15.
26. Malabou 2007: 52–3, 274; Malabou 2009d: 10–13, 33–4.
27. *SE* 14: 290.
28. Malabou 2007: 307.

29. Malabou 2009d: 33–4.
30. Ibid.: 72–3, 82–4.
31. Malabou 2007: 59–60; Malabou 2009d: 12.
32. Malabou 2007: 233–4.
33. Ibid.: 179, 217.
34. Johnston 2010c: 35–59.
35. Malabou 2007: 219.
36. Ibid.: 314–15.
37. Ibid.: 314–15, 322–3, 344–5.
38. Ibid.: 234, 256.
39. Ibid.: 89–90.
40. Ibid.: 233.
41. Ibid.: 231–2.
42. Ibid.: 341–2.
43. Johnston 2011e: 159–79; Johnston 2012a: 23–52; Johnston 2013e; Johnston 2013i.
44. Soler 2009: 138–9, 204.
45. Johnston 2013c: xi-xv.
46. Malabou 2007: 280, 288–9, 290–1.
47. Ibid.: 74.
48. Malabou 2013b: 213–20.
49. Malabou 2007: 74.
50. Malabou 2007: 76–7, 80; Malabou 2013b: 213–14, 216–23.
51. Malabou 2007: 85, 234–5.
52. Ibid.: 234–5.
53. Ibid.: 234–5.
54. Johnston 2011e: 159–79; Johnston 2013i; Soler 2009: 138–9, 204.
55. Soler 2009: 5–7.
56. Ibid.: 12, 69–70.
57. Ibid.: 29.
58. Ibid.: 61.
59. Ibid.: 120.
60. Soler 2011: 49–51.
61. Soler 2009: 15–16.
62. Ibid.: 21.
63. Johnston 2013d: 141–2.
64. Soler 2009: 25; Soler 2011: 41, 54–5, 109–10.
65. Johnston 2008d: 87–90; Johnston 2009a: 122–4.
66. Soler 2009: 32.
67. Soler 2009: 37–9, 61, 119, 141; Soler 2011: 112.
68. Soler 2009: 24, 31, 60, 121–3; Soler 2011: 102, 108–9, 166–7.

69. Soler 2009: 26–7, 40, 59.
70. Ibid.: 27.
71. Soler 2009: 29–31; Soler 2011: 84, 103, 105–7.
72. Soler 2009: 41, 48, 88.
73. Lacan 2006b: 30–46.
74. Fink 1996: 173–91.
75. Johnston 2013c: xi–xv.
76. *SE* 17: 217–56.

Toward a Grand Neuropolitics:
Why I am Not an Immanent Naturalist
or Vital Materialist

I have indicated periodically throughout this book that transcendental materialism involves practical-political, in addition to theoretical-philosophical, dimensions. Here, I would like to bring *Adventures in Transcendental Materialism* to a close in this twelfth chapter by providing a few preliminary specifications and concretizations of exactly what a politics informed by this brand of materialism might look like in relation to certain current socio-economic challenges. I will do so by addressing two more contemporary thinkers: William Connolly and Jane Bennett, colleagues in the Department of Political Science at Johns Hopkins University. Harking back to Part I above, Connolly and Bennett, on my reading, represent neo-Spinozist stances, whereas transcendental materialism is definitely and avowedly neo-Hegelian in manners fundamentally incompatible with Spinozism of any sort (see especially Chapters 2 and 3). The present chapter reveals some of the very tangible differences this divide separating neo-Spinozism from neo-Hegelianism (a divide marking fault lines of tension quite alive and charged today) makes to both the theory and practice of politics.

But, before engaging with Connolly and Bennett, I should say a little more at a general level about the practical-political dimensions of transcendental materialism. To begin with, this materialism, as I already have noted several times, stands on the shoulders of its historical and dialectical precursors *à la* Marx, Engels, and various of their offspring. But, Marxism provides not only theoretical-philosophical resources for transcendental materialism – to put my cards squarely on the table, I also am axiomatically committed to the spirit (as well as many of the letters) of Marxist politics as anchored by its historical materialist critique of political economy. Put differently, I am a Marxist not only of the first, but also of the eleventh, thesis on Feuerbach. As I specify elsewhere apropos transcendental materialism as an "approach":

> Broadly and summarily speaking, I see four primary ways in which this approach is constructive and useful for Marxism. One, my repetition of a gesture first boldly performed by Engels and Lenin (i.e. recruiting the natural sciences to the side of Marxist materialism) turns the life sciences, themselves in a pre-eminent cultural and institutional position in the Western world today, from supporting to contesting the Hobbesian-Smithian portrait of 'human nature' – and along with this lending further support to Marx and Engels's load-bearing materialist hypotheses regarding the species-being of humanity. Two, transcendental materialism's meta-dialectics of nature helps to debunk, both philosophically and scientifically, contemporary scientistic ideologies . . . that falsely naturalize status-quo social relations and forms of subjection, as ideology in various socio-historical guises typically tries to do; on the active front of a live intellectual war of position, this updated materialism strives to unmask bio-scientism's specious rationalizations for a mind-boggling array of infrastructural and superstructural features of late capitalism. Three, it pursues what I see as the valuable goal of thoroughly immunizing Marxist materialism from the threats of three intellectual and ideological dangers: covert idealisms (à la post-Lukácsian antipathy to the natural sciences in Western Marxism), overt idealisms (if only by association with the dubious company of conscious or unconscious neo-Kantians or the theologically inclined), and non-dialectical materialisms (to take a handful of examples, what Badiou dubs democratic materialism, what I describe as capitalist biologism, Rose's neurogenetic determinism, and similar manifestations that are now ubiquitous). Four, despite carrying out this immunization, my position allows for the outlining of a contemporary materialism that is both fully compatible with the core of Marx and Engels's shared *Weltanschauung*, as well as for striking a delicate balance between affirming freedom and admitting determinism, in such a way that optimism about revolutionary subjective agency and realism about objective material conditions and constraints can be varyingly combined in ways appropriate and sensitive to shifting concrete conjunctures (thereby allowing for a tactically and strategically wise, sober conviction that avoids deviating in the direction of either wild-eyed Panglossianism or dull-eyed resignation).[1]

I feel that this quotation provides the best single, succinct synopsis of transcendental materialism's relationships to foundational political matters. With this overview in place, I can now turn productively to Connolly and Bennett themselves.

Connolly's 2002 book *Neuropolitics: Thinking, Culture, Speed* is one of the more interesting attempts in recent years to reflect on the socio-political implications of cutting-edge developments in the neurosciences. Therein, Connolly constructs a position he labels "immanent naturalism," a position inspired, at its root in the history of philosophy, by the ontology of Spinoza's dual-aspect monism[2] (Bennett likewise appeals to Spinoza in pleading for her materialism of "vibrant matter"[3] – certain clearly visible overlaps between immanent naturalism and vital materialism will be addressed by me below). On the basis of his immanent natural-ist appreciation of current research in biology and its branches (neurobiology first and foremost), Connolly argues that a non-reductive interfacing of the life sciences and those varied fields sur-veying the domains of human culture(s) points political thought in the direction of focusing on (to use the Foucauldian language he uses) "micropolitical techniques of the self" (i.e., the fine-grained dimensions of persons' quotidian, embodied existences as their daily ways of being, doing, feeling, and thinking, existences shot through with a plethora of multiple-speed layers of emotions, awarenesses, stimuli, sensations, and so on).[4]

Through a tacit but evident contrast between a micropolitics of bottom-up reform (tied to a pluralist democratic framework) and a grand-scale macropolitics of top-down regulation (if not revolution) – Michel Foucault's reflections on "biopolitics" and "biopower," reflections crucial for Connolly's project in a number of ways, are peppered with sweeping, provocative dismissals of revolutionary Marxism[5] – Connolly flirts with hinting that the surest road to desirable political progress involves small-scale tink-ering by subjects with their own complex, interconnected webs of cognitions, affects, and motivations. He likewise indicates that, in his view, contemporary neurobiology supports shifting attention increasingly in the direction of the micropolitical. For instance, at one three-page juncture in his fourth chapter (entitled "Techniques of Thought and Micropolitics"), he provides a long, detailed list of concrete examples of neuropolitical techniques of the self, namely, strategies of individual self-modification purportedly apt to bring about changes and reinforcements conducive to the greater collec-tive realization of more open forms of democracy, of new, creative manners of being together[6] (a shorter version of this list reappears in his 2011 book *A World of Becoming*[7]). Immediately after running through this list, Connolly acknowledges, "Such examples could be modified along several dimensions and proliferated indefinitely, for technique, in film, institutional life, and everyday life, is ubiquitous."[8]

However, this indefiniteness and ubiquity arguably are at least as much weaknesses as strengths of Connolly's position, particularly in the register of political thinking. Succinctly stated, if, under the influence of a carefully qualified quasi-naturalism, one so broadly (and, perhaps, carelessly) construes "politics" as to see it everywhere within the tiniest features and facets of mundane, day-to-day affairs, then the pursuit of political projects is in danger of losing focus by being distractedly scattered into a diffuse array of trifling entities and events. What is worse, if even the slightest banal experiences introduce modifications into the delicate calibrations of shifting brain-body-milieu systems – the plasticity of the central nervous system indeed means that quite fleeting phenomena leave traces behind in the neural connections of the brain – then rationalizations can be provided for, for instance, believing that simply going to a movie theater to watch the latest Hollywood blockbuster is a politically transformative gesture. Along these exact lines, Connolly's micro-dimension neuropolitics is at risk of running into the same impasses as his French predecessors' sixties-era philosophies of desire-in-revolt (*à la* Deleuze and Guattari as well as Foucault) – not to mention the comparable dead ends of the American hippie sex-drugs-and-rock-and-roll rebellion (as is now well known, orgasms, intoxicants, and music all have mind-altering neurological effects).[9] Additionally, although Connolly's immanent naturalism and its sophisticated, nuanced engagement with the natural sciences has much to recommend it on both philosophical and scientific grounds, its implications at the levels of political theory and the practice of politics are significantly more ambiguous than Connolly's glosses and illustrations present it as being. The vaguely Heraclitian flux doctrines palpably lurking in the background – Connolly relies on philosophers recent and not-so-recent who share such ontological tastes in common – hardly are conducive to a targeted and disciplined set of coordinated political practices. Considering the disheartening record of leftist political movements in disarray from the post-'68 era through today, it is quite questionable whether more of the same rhizomatic micropolitics should be prescribed.

Bennett, in her beautifully written 2010 book *Vibrant Matter*, makes an important observation: She admits that there is no direct, one-to-one link between ontology and politics, namely, that philosophical perspectives on the nature of being(s) do not automatically recommend a given corresponding set of political perspectives.[10] Connolly displays an appreciation of this same non-correspondence. But, both Connolly (on the basis of his immanent naturalism) and Bennett (on the basis of her vital materialism) nonetheless evince a shared conviction that their ontologies strongly push thinking to leap in certain directions rather than others, to jump the gap from philosophy to politics toward specific forms of the latter. At a minimum, this chapter seeks to show that leaping this gap in a dramatically different way, one aiming toward a revolutionary macropolitics rather than a reformist micropolitics, is at least as justified, starting from a cluster of philosophical and scientific claims shared with Connolly and Bennett, as the directed fashion in which both of them choose to leap.

So, before further elaborating the critique of Connolly's brand of neuropolitics outlined in the preceding two paragraphs, a sympathetic summary of his theoretical framework is requisite. To begin with, Connolly defines "neuropolitics" in his sense thusly – "By *neuropolitics* . . . I mean the politics through which cultural life mixes into the composition of body/brain processes. And vice versa."[11] Especially considering that he comes from the background of a discipline (i.e., political science) that tends, like much of the humanities and social sciences overall, to ignore ontologies integrating the sciences of nature, his open-minded, insightful recognition that up-to-date neurobiological investigations of human beings are pregnant with implications for a wide range of disciplines is laudable. Connolly realizes that political science ought to be concerned with things biological not only at the levels of such practical, applied issues/problems as stem-cell legislation, the ethics of cloning, the socio-economic ramifications of genetic engineering, and so on – he understands that the recasting of human nature and subjectivity underway in the life sciences entails major consequences for assumptions lying at the very foundations of the metaphysics, however implicit or explicit, of any and every general theory of politics.

Connolly's above-quoted definition of neuropolitics unambiguously signals from the get-go that his program is not a naturalist one if naturalism is conceived of, as it still too often is, as exclusively wedded to the old ontology of a mechanistic materialism – that is to say, a materialism calling for the elimination of the domains of the cultural and the subjective through the reduction of these phenomena to the sum of their supposed physical parts as material units bumping and grinding against each other according to nothing more than the efficient causality of mechanical laws. Connolly has no sympathy whatsoever for mechanistic materialism.[12] Likewise, Bennett correctly notes that "The machine model of nature, with its figure of inert matter, is no longer even scientific."[13] Connolly too rightly maintains that anti-reductivism can and should be defended intra-scientifically (i.e., through immanent, rather than external, critiques of scientisms). In other words, a viable theoretical option nowadays is to point out how advances internal to the natural sciences (for example, research bearing upon epigenetics, neuroplasticity, mirror neurons, and emergence) testify against the plausibility of now-dated reductivist agendas (in the neurosciences, such agendas appear to be grounded and modeled upon earlier states of those sciences many decades ago).[14] Catherine Malabou nicely makes this point when she remarks, "it is within the very interior of the conceptual apparatus of the neurosciences, and not from the exterior, that it has appeared to me opportune to seek to contest strict reductivism."[15] As Connolly claims in this same vein, "different levels of biological complexity are mixed into culture to varying degrees, and ... you can include genetics in cultural theory without succumbing to genetic determinism."[16]

Anti-reductivism no longer demands of its partisans that they advocate their stance through trying to exercise an interdisciplinary check on the explanatory ambitions of the natural sciences, through struggling externally to impose limits on these sciences based on non-scientific (for instance, philosophical) considerations and claims (as the critical analyses of biopolitics offered first by Foucault and then by Agamben continue to do). Veterans of past wars against mechanistic and eliminative scientisms in the humanities and social sciences can be forgiven for their lingering hostility to and wariness of the natural sciences. But, as Connolly demonstrates, it is high time for this persisting animus to dissipate. Moreover, insofar as "neuropolitics" is a hybrid term blending together the two sides of the "natural" (i.e., the "neuro-" of neuroscience) and the "cultural" (i.e., the "-politics" of political theory), it must be specified that this hybridity redoubles itself as internal to both sides. What is meant by this? The non-reductive neurosciences intra-scientifically delimit the boundaries of their explanatory jurisdictions in pinpointing biological evidence for more-than-biological (i.e., cultural/political) forces and factors operative within the bio-materiality of the body itself;[17] in this, the neurosciences already are neuropolitical sciences. In a parallel, mirroring fashion, political theory *à la* Connolly also becomes neuropolitical science in acknowledging the pervasiveness of biological influences at work in the flows and strata composing the kaleidoscopic arrays of socio-cultural realities.

As already mentioned, Connolly (and Bennett too) displays a sensible cognizance of the fact that reading off a singular, specific political program from a fundamental ontology is difficult if not impossible. This cognizance is on display when he states that "every image of nature does set conditions and restraints that must be negotiated somehow to support a specific conception of culture."[18] He re-emphasizes this same line of thought several times later.[19] Carefully parsing the sentence just quoted, the "conditions and restraints" are not dictates compelling one and only one "conception of culture." Instead, they establish a bandwidth of parameters and permutations for a range of possible representations of the more-than-natural, a bandwidth that constrains (by ruling out some representations, such as absolutely anti-naturalist ontological dualisms) but does not compel. Moreover, Connolly leaves himself and his readers plenty of wiggle room with the words "negotiated somehow."

Nonetheless, such caveats notwithstanding, Connolly maintains that "each speculative theory . . . helps to set a specific agenda for cultural and political thought."[20] He then proceeds to advance a wholistic, quasi-Spinozistic *Weltanschauung* of a single, non-stratified ontological field of complexity in which the bio-natural and the socio-cultural swirl together in various hybrid formations and mixtures, a worldview allegedly more conducive to, among other things, a politically beneficial ecological sensitivity (at this point, Connolly is foreshadowing what he later explicitly names his "immanent naturalism").[21] Along these lines, he asserts: "If thinking is part of nature, as the largest whole in which we are encompassed, then the experience of creativity in thinking provides a piece of testimony in support of the idea that *other* aspects of nature may have variable capacities for creative production as well."[22] Bennett's vital materialism readily can be construed as an extended development of this intuition regarding "*other* aspects of nature"[23] (with Connolly's addition of the adjective "realist" to his rearticulation of immanent naturalism in 2011's *A World of Becoming*, itself presented "as a companion to her [Bennett's] recent book on the vibrancy of material assemblages,"[24] signaling his endorsement of the anti-anthropocentric opposition to subject-centered philosophies expressed in *Vibrant Matter*[25]). I will touch again upon this anti-anthropocentrism thematic note common to Connolly and Bennett subsequently. For the time being, suffice it to observe that Connolly's Spinoza-style wholism entails emphasizing continuity over discontinuity, leading to a perspective that prefers to eliminate both a vertical hierarchy between thinking subject and natural substance as well as any hard-and-fast horizontal distinctions amongst inhabitants of a sole plane of immanence exhibiting multiple powers of creativity. As will be seen, this motif comes into subtle tension, if not overt conflict, with other dimensions of his immanent naturalism.

So, what about this immanent naturalism? Connolly introduces it through a basic materialist proposal:

> The key move is to translate the Kantian transcendental field into a layered, immanent field . . . the unconscious dimension of thought is at once *immanent* in subsisting below the direct reach of consciousness, *effective* in influencing conduct on its own and also affecting conscious judgment, *material* in being embodied in neurological processes, and *cultural* in being given part of its shape by previous inscriptions of experience and new experimental interventions . . .[26]

As he adds a few pages after this, "The transcendental – which for Kant lies beyond human knowledge even as it regulates thinking – is translated by immanent naturalists into an infrasensible field that transcends consciousness and exceeds mechanistic models of scientific explanation."[27] Philosophically speaking, there is a momentary misunderstanding at work here (one that Connolly, as will be seen in the block quotation contained in the paragraph immediately below, rectifies himself): In opposing his "immanence" to the Kantian "transcendental," Connolly betrays a commonplace conflation of the latter with "transcendence." The transcendental and the transcendent are not synonymous. Within Kant's transcendental idealism, although transcendent things-in-themselves are unknowable (i.e., lying "beyond human knowledge," as Connolly puts it), the transcendental conditions of possibility enabling and structuring the subject's experiences are knowable (in fact, the *Critique of Pure Reason* purports precisely to elaborate a detailed knowledge of the possibility conditions of knowledge itself). In this sense, there is not a real difference between what Kant means by "transcendental" and what Connolly means by "immanent," insofar as Connolly's immanence likewise designates a field making possible the experience of subjectivity. The real difference consists in the fact that Kant espouses an idealism ruling out any idea according to which the realm of the transcendental (consisting of conditions of possibility) could be conceived of in a naturalist and/or materialist fashion.

This aside, Connolly's thorough, substantial characterization of his immanent naturalist position is worth quoting at length. He explains:

> By *naturalism*, I mean the idea that all human activities function without the aid of a divine or supernatural force. The specific form of naturalism I embrace questions the sufficiency of the lawlike model of nature endorsed by classical natural science. And it emphasizes how culture gets differentially mixed into natural processes, depending upon the capacity for complexity of the mode of being in question. Let us construe *eliminative naturalism* to be a philosophy that reduces the experience of consciousness to nonconscious processes. Let us construe *mechanical naturalism* to be one that denies any role to a supersensible field while finding both the world of non-human nature and the structure of the human brain to be amenable 'in principle' to precise representation and complete explanation. I am not sure how many eliminative or mechanical naturalists there are today, although many philosophers and cognitive scientists are represented as such by those critics who endorse transcendentalism. An *immanent naturalist*, by comparison, does not repudiate the transcendental. Rather, it is translated into an immanent field that mixes nature and culture. To immanent naturalism, consciousness emerges as a layer of thinking, feeling, and judgment bound to complex crunching operations that enable and exceed it. The immanent field is efficacious and inscrutable (to an uncertain degree), but not immaterial. It is, you might say, infrasensible rather than supersensible. Moreover, the immanent field, while currently unsusceptible to full explanation and unsusceptible in principle to precise representation, may retain some amenability

to both cultural inscription and experimental tactics of intervention. That is, as the practices of Buddhists, Epicureans, and several monotheistic religions have presumed for centuries, human powers of cultural inscription and experimental intervention into the inscrutable domain, while limited, nonetheless *exceed* those of direct conscious control and scientific explanation.[28]

The last two sentences of this quotation gesture not simply at micropolitics in general, but at a version of it in which a materialist approach to subjectivity leads to endorsing non-Western and/or pre-modern practices of caring for small-scale selfhood. A little further on, Connolly underscores the intimate rapport between immanent naturalism and a micropolitical attentiveness to Foucauldian "techniques of the self."[29] However, not only, as I have already remarked, is there no overwhelmingly compelling connection between, first, an ontological theory registering problematizations of the old nature-nurture dichotomy arising within the natural sciences themselves, and, second, ethico-political practices allied to Eastern and/or ancient worldviews and focused on the fine-grained texture of individuals' quotidian existences – features of Connolly's own articulations of immanent naturalism point to an alternate theory-practice ensemble simultaneously proximate to and distant from his guiding intuitions and visions in both *Neuropolitics* and *A World of Becoming*.

In the lengthy block quotation above, Connolly invokes the notion of emergence ("To immanent naturalism, consciousness emerges as a layer of thinking, feeling, and judgment bound to complex crunching operations that enable and exceed it."). A few pages after this invocation, it becomes evident that he intends this in the sense of emergentism as a general theoretical model in the natural sciences – "Thinking is irreducible to any of the preliminary ingredients that enable it, but it is affected profoundly by the material medium of its occurrence."[30] A tension subsists within this single sentence: On the one hand, Connolly affirms a certain autonomy or independence of emergently generated cognitive activity as "irreducible" to its bio-material bases; on the other hand, he appears to retract/revoke this very freedom though simultaneously insisting on thinking's impinged-upon position relative to its physical ground (with the former stuck being perpetually "affected" by the latter). As small as it might seem at first glance, this tension testifying to Connolly favoring a weak over a strong strain of emergentism – strong emergentism would contend that certain emergent entities and events can and do achieve a complete and full separation from their originary sources of emergence, rather than remaining subservient to these origins as effect to cause – has huge political implications.

Putting to one side the gargantuan fundamental ontological question of if, following Spinoza, one ought to conceive of being itself (whether called "nature" and/or "God") as a substantial whole (i.e., a One, All, totality, unity, etc.),[31] the issue of Connolly's Spinozistic wholism, as per his broad definition of the natural, is open to critical examination within the comparatively narrower scope of neurobiology and the theoretical topic of subjectivity. To begin this critical examination, it is worth noticing that both Connolly and Bennett refer to mid-twentieth-century French phenomenologist Maurice Merleau-Ponty, whose monistic inclinations and attention to "embodiment" make him an obvious predecessor of and inspiration for orientations such as immanent naturalism and vital materialism.[32] Likewise, in their 1991 book *The Embodied Mind: Cognitive Science and Human Experience*, Francisco J. Varela, Evan Thompson, and Eleanor Rosch appeal to Merleau-Ponty's philosophy throughout their efforts to weave together, in a non-reductive manner, (existential) phenomenology and science-inspired cognitivist approaches to human mental life (plus ingredients from Buddhist psychology – one should recall that Connolly too is interested in supporting Eastern outlooks using Western science).[33] Not only does Connolly cite Varela and his collaborators several times[34] – Varela promotes, among other things, emergentism as a non-reductive paradigm in the life sciences – he employs a quotation from *The Embodied Mind* as one of the epigraphs for *Neuropolitics*.

In fact, close scrutiny of the passage in *The Embodied Mind* from which Connolly extracts his epigraph reveals the possibility for a different neuropolitical interpretation of the work of Varela et al. than that offered by immanent naturalism. Here is the passage in question:

> an important and pervasive shift is beginning to take place in cognitive science under the very influence of its own research. This shift requires that we move away from the idea of the world as independent and extrinsic to the idea of the world as inseparable from the structure of these processes of self-modification. This change in stance does not

express a mere philosophical preference; it reflects the necessity of understanding cognitive systems not on the basis of their input and output relationships but by their *operational closure*. A system that has operational closure is one in which the results of its processes are those processes themselves. The notion of operational closure is thus a way of specifying classes of processes that, in their very operation, turn back upon themselves to form autonomous networks. Such networks do not fall into the class of systems defined by external mechanisms of control (heteronomy) but rather into the class of systems defined by internal mechanisms of self-organization (autonomy).[35]

Connolly's epigraph quotes only the first two sentences of this stretch of text. The first quoted sentence dovetails with the earlier-made observation that intra-scientific immanent (self-)critiques are bringing about shifts within the sciences usually advocated by external critiques coming from non-scientific quarters (such as philosophy and the humanities in general). The real bones of contention in the present context have to do with both the second sentence as well as the rest of the content of this quotation.

As for the second sentence, one could argue that Connollian immanent naturalism reads the inseparability spoken of by Varela, Thompson, and Rosch between "the world" and "these processes of self-modification" in a lop-sided, one-way fashion. That is to say, Connolly overemphasizes the fusion of the reflexive mind with the stuff of wider nature to such an extent that mental life threatens to be deprived of its freedom as self-relating, auto-transformative dynamics (given that his philosophical heroes are Spinoza, Nietzsche, Merleau-Ponty, Foucault, and Deleuze,[36] it is no surprise that Connolly runs the risk of squelching the subject altogether – see also Chapter 3). Correspondingly, under the influence of monist ontologies hostile to robust theories of radically autonomous subjectivity, he downplays the other side of Varela and company's assertion regarding this inseparability: To the extent that "the world" is inseparable from the gaze it casts upon itself through sentient and sapient subjects as twisting folds of a universe staring back at itself thusly, this world (as nature) must be reconceived so as account for how it produces such reflexive ruptures out of itself in the form of self-determining subjects, designated here by Varela and his colleagues with the phrase "operational closure" (elsewhere, Varela and Humberto R. Maturana famously explain subjective autonomy in terms of a life-scientific theory of "autopoietic organization,"[37] a theory echoing, however wittingly or unwittingly, Kant's discussions of the idea of organic life in his *Critique of the Power of Judgment*[38] and Hegel's Kant-inspired treatments of the same topic[39] in both the *Phenomenology of Spirit* [as per the section on "Observing Reason"][40] and the *Philosophy of Nature*[41] – in *A World of Becoming*, Connolly repeatedly refers to emergentism and autopoiesis together[42] while, in the same book, falsely accusing Hegel of ignoring the natural altogether in favor of an exclusive focus on the socio-historical[43]).

Having reached this juncture, the core differences between Connolly's immanent naturalism and my transcendental materialism can begin to be spelled out by playing off transcendental materialism's Hegel (as a sort of strong emergentist *avant la lettre*) against immanent naturalism's Spinoza (as a sort of weak emergentist *avant la lettre*). The strong emergentism of Varela and company arguably is misread by Connolly in light of his weaker version of this paradigm, a diluted strain of emergentism according to which the monistic, unified wholeness of natural substance is not fundamentally torn or shattered to pieces by creating within itself the weird cognitive-emotional-motivational beings that can and do turn back upon it (with these beings achieving an auto-reflexive self-determination thanks to natural materiality sundering itself in giving rise to them). But, in what way(s) is Hegel's nineteenth-century philosophy relevant in this contemporary context? Both Hegel and Schelling, although beginning their intellectual adventures as supporters of Spinozism while students in theological seminary at Tübingen during the end of the eighteenth century, quickly come to find Spinoza's dual-aspect monism to be unsatisfactory specifically insofar as it is a system depicting, as it were, substance *sans* subject (however, starting in 1807, Hegel initiates his thereafter regularly reiterated assertion that Schelling, somewhat unfairly in that he considers only the juvenilia of the latter's relatively early philosophies of nature and identity, is just as guilty as Spinoza of dissolving "the Absolute" into a static, undifferentiated "night in which all cows are black" – see Chapter 2). That is to say, the ontology of the *Ethics* not only promotes a thoroughgoing determinism in which the strength of one's sense of being free in thinking and acting is precisely correlative and proportional to the degree of one's ignorance of the sum total of causes converging upon one's thoughts and actions as mere effects[44] – this is something that obviously would be anathema to two young men from Protestant backgrounds who are enthusiasts of the French Revolution, with its explosive political affirmation of human freedom – this ontology cannot and does not explain exactly how and why the One of the natural substance named "God" reflects/refracts itself into the domain of appearances in which it is split into two attributes (i.e., the incommensurable aspects of thinking and extension) and multiple modes. For instance, the later Schelling's draft manuscripts of his unfinished *Weltalter* project (1811–15), centered on a cosmo-theological narrative of God's creation of the world, can be viewed as struggling to tell a story Spinoza utterly failed to tell, but, by German idealist lights, was obliged to articulate nevertheless.

Of course, Hegel's most renowned (and succinct) expression of his dissatisfaction with Spinoza's dual-aspect monism, as an ontology of substance *sans* subject, is to be found in the magisterial preface to his 1807 *Phenomenology of Spirit*. Therein, he declares, "everything turns on grasping and expressing the True, not only as *Substance*, but equally as *Subject*."[45] Returning to a comparatively neglected textual fragment from Hegel's time as a *Hofmeister* in Bern, a piece entitled "The Earliest System-Program of German Idealism," both will help illuminate this well-known line from the later *Phenomenology* as well as allow for reconnecting with the intertwined topics of today's natural sciences and politics. In fact, the opening two paragraphs consist of Hegel (or Hölderlin or Schelling, depending on who one credits with authorship of this fragment) discussing science and ontology with an eye to the philosophical consequences of France's then-recent momentous political upheaval and its cultural reverberations in German-speaking circles next door:

> Since the whole of metaphysics falls for the future within *moral theory* ... this ethics will be nothing less than a complete system of all ideas or of all practical postulates (which is the same thing). The first idea is, of course, the presentation of *my*self as an absolutely free entity. Along with the free, self-conscious essence, there stands forth – out of nothing – an entire world, the one true and thinkable creation out of nothing. – Here I shall descend into the realms of physics; the question is this: how must a world be constituted for a moral entity? I would like to give wings once more to our backward physics, that advances laboriously by experiments.[46]

Hegel (or Hölderlin or Schelling) adds immediately on the heels of this: "Thus, if philosophy supplies the ideas, and experience the data, we may at last come to have in essentials the physics that I look forward to for later times. It does not appear that our present-day physics can satisfy a creative spirit such as ours is or ought to be."[47] From the perspective of Hegel and certain of his contemporaries, the philosophies of freedom propounded by Kant (as per his deontological "metaphysics of morals") and Fichte (starting with the first version [1794] of his *Wissenschaftslehre*) in the 1780s and 1790s represent the, loosely speaking, "spiritual" (as cultural-intellectual) furtherance of the progressive, albeit violent, historical leap forward achieved in France at the level of the practical-political. In Hegel's view of world history, what began within the *Sittlichkeit* of the Germans with Martin Luther's Reformation in the sixteenth century comes full circle and returns to its homeland thanks to the surfacing of Kantian and post-Kantian philosophical idealisms, after passing through its intervening worldly development as concentrated in Enlightenment-era Paris. Basically, a sixteenth-century German religious reformation becomes an eighteenth-century French political revolution, which then in turn becomes a nineteenth-century German philosophical reformation.[48] According to the *Philosophie der Geschichte*, Hegel and his fellow idealists of the period theoretically consolidate and help bring to completion the post-1789 sequence in that "it is a false principle that the fetters which bind Right and Freedom can be broken without the emancipation of conscience – that there can be a Revolution without a Reformation."[49]

In this early set of notes quoted from above, the young, post-Fichtean idealists announce that, following upon their construal of Kantian and Fichtean subjective idealisms as fundamentally centered upon and concerned with a radical (re)thinking of freedom,[50] they too intend to base their philosophy *à venir* on the autonomy embodied by self-reflective/reflexive subjectivity. What is more, already before his Jena period, Hegel (in whose handwriting this surviving fragment, "The Earliest System-Program of German Idealism," is written) signals his commitment to the objective and absolute forms of idealism (as distinct from subjective forms) he soon comes to espouse ever more forcefully and systematically – a commitment held to in common with Schelling and partially rooted in their shared Spinozist sympathies. Implicitly mixing together Spinoza, Kant, and Fichte, the start of "The Earliest

System-Program of German Idealism" indicates an intention not only, as later announced by Hegel in the *Phenomenology*'s preface, to think substance as subject, but also, in an inversion necessitated by dialectics, to think subject as substance.

To be more exact, when the author of "The Earliest System-Program of German Idealism" asks, "how must a world be constituted for a moral entity?," he is raising the question of how to reconceptualize ontological substantiality so as to incorporate, as (still) fully immanent to such substantiality, the more-than-substantial free subjects (as sentient and sapient auto-relating self-determinants not directly determined by iron-clad mechanical laws of externally dictated efficient causality, whether physical and/or biological) back within this ground of being which gave rise to such subjects to begin with.[51] It appears that this author's use of the term "physics" (*Physik*)[52] in this same context refers, in line with a standard usage at the time, to the modern natural sciences in their entirety as modeled on the organon of Francis Bacon's "new method" as deployed by Newtonian mechanics. During this stage in his career (i.e., in Bern in 1796), Hegel is engaged in a post-Kantian recovery of Spinoza's key insight into the impossibility of consistently affirming both the infinitude and transcendence of being as God/Nature. According to this insight, given what is entailed by the very concept of infinity, an infinite being cannot stand separately over-and-above (i.e., be transcendent) in relation to the finite, since the finite would thereby be purely external to the infinite, thus de-infinitizing the infinite, namely, rendering it less than infinite insofar as it is not all-encompassing by being bounded/limited in its rigid, *Verstand*-type binary opposition to the finite as erroneously situated on an other side supposedly beyond the infinite[53] (see also Chapter 2).

In a related vein, one of the lessons of Hegel's lifelong argumentative assault on Kant's critical-transcendental epistemology of the finite subject's "limits of possible experience," with this epistemology's problematic noumena and things-in-themselves, is that the actual notions of finitude and limitation upon which Kant relies are self-subverting in such a way as to demonstrate the ultimate unavoidability of eventually coming to know the absoluteness of infinite being *an sich* (or, in stricter Hegelese, "in and for itself" [*an und für sich*], rather than just "in itself" [*an sich*]).[54] For a post-Spinoza objective/absolute idealism, unlike subjective idealism (first and foremost, Kant's transcendental variety), the being of the infinite Absolute (i.e., the real, non-spurious infinite), as what it is in truth, cannot be something noumenally transcendent standing apart from a self-enclosed realm of finite subjectivity with its circumscribed field of phenomenal experience. If the latter is external to the former – again, unlike Hegelian speculative reason (*Vernunft*), non-speculative understanding (*Verstand*) invariably tends to treat the finite as the bivalent, mutually exclusive negation of the infinite and vice versa, thereby partitioning these two dimensions as utterly separate and distinct from each other – then what is called and conceived of as the infinite Absolute is neither infinite nor absolute properly speaking. Once more, if the finite stands outside of the infinite, then the infinite is not truly infinite; if the less-than-Absolute stands outside of the Absolute, then the Absolute is not truly absolute. In his Jena-period 1804–05 *Logic and Metaphysics*, Hegel explains:

> Genuine infinity . . . is not a series that always has its completion in some other yet always has this other outside itself. Rather, the other is in the determinate itself; it is a contradiction, absolute on its own account: and this is the true essence of the determinacy. In other words, [it is] not [the case] that a term of the antithesis is on its own account, but that it only is within its opposite or that only the absolute antithesis is, while the opposite, since it only is within its opposite, annihilates itself therein, and annihilates this other as much as itself. The absolute antithesis, infinity, is this absolute reflection into itself of the determinate that is an other than itself (that is, not an other in general against which it would be indifferent on its own account, but its immediate contrary), and as that, it is itself. This alone is the true nature of the finite: that it is infinite, that it sublates itself in its being. The determinate has as such no other essence than this absolute unrest: not to be what it is.[55]

To tie the above back into the contemporaneous substance-as-subject thread, if, following in Spinoza's footsteps, substance is identified as absolute infinity, then, according to Hegel, the subject philosophically reflecting upon this substance cannot merely be a less-than-absolute finitude entirely external to substance in the non-dialectical manners envisioned by the sub-rational understanding. When the Hegel in whose hand is penned "The Earliest System-Program of German Idealism" anticipates, as quoted above, a new (meta)physics capable of satisfying "creative spirit" (*schöpferischen Geist*)[56] – arguably, this phrase could count as a pleonasm in the language of Hegelianism – the *Geist* he has in mind is the "unrest" of subjective negativity as immanent to substantial material being (i.e., the world of *Physik*). Ambivalently indebted to Spinoza and, like his fellow post-Kantian idealists, deeply dissatisfied with what he takes to be the two-worlds metaphysics of Kant's critical-transcendental idealist philosophy distinguishing sharply between noumenal and phenomenal realms, Hegel announces the genesis of a new ontology of freedom in which not only is subjectivity re-envisioned as part of substantiality (a one-sided re-envisioning already carried out by Spinoza and which [mis]leads him into thoroughgoing, fatalistic determinism), but, in an inverse complementary movement, substantiality is correspondingly re-envisioned as containing within itself autonomous subjectivity. Acknowledging the importance of the latter move obligates any materialist theory of the subject after Hegel to carry out a transformation of still-standard images and ideas of nature in tandem with rendering the subject immanent to the natural realm of given materialities (see Chapters 2 and 3).

Both Hegel and Connolly at least would agree, as the former puts it in his Berlin *Lectures on the History of Philosophy*, that "thought must begin by placing itself at the standpoint of Spinozism; to be a follower of Spinoza is the essential commencement of all Philosophy."[57] Moreover, both these thinkers seek to conceive of a politics unshackled from the imaginings of the spontaneous metaphysics of the understanding, a *Weltanschauung* that pervades much of philosophy itself and virtually all of non-philosophical "common sense" (and, in political terms, leans in the direction of underpinning political economies of a traditional liberal/social-contractual sort as per the atomized collective universes of Thomas Hobbes and Adam Smith). But, the mature Hegel, in his later history-of-philosophy lecture on Kant, makes an observation flowing from his modified Spinozism (as an absolute idealism of a rationally apprehended infinite substance-as-subject), an observation that signals some crucial differences between anything properly Hegelian and Connolly's immanent naturalism:

> People of this kind say: We are good for nothing, and because we are good for nothing, we are good for nothing, and wish to be good for nothing. But it is a very false idea of Christian humility and modesty to desire through one's abjectness to attain to excellence; this confession

of one's own nothingness is really inward pride and great self-conceit. But for the honour of true humility we must not remain in our misery, but raise ourselves above it by laying hold of the Divine.[58]

Hegel undoubtedly would detect in both Connolly's and Bennett's writings – Connolly and Bennett belong to a broader current trend of de-anthropomorphizing theory continuing certain trajectories internal to prior strains of anti-humanism in post-war French thought – notes of "humility and modesty" qualifying them as "people of this kind" unwilling or unable to follow through to the ultimate end their avowed allegiances to the Spinoza who intellectually reaches the intuition of genuine, non-spurious infinity (incidentally, although Hegel utters these remarks in a lecture on Kant, Pascal is clearly in mind too ["Man's greatness comes from knowing he is wretched: a tree does not know it is wretched"[59]]). *Contra* this miserable self-effacing masochism of those who are ashamed to be human beings while suffering from theological hangovers worsened in an era of looming ecological crisis, a Hegelian is not limited to affirming that one must be confident enough to run the risk of the grand gesture of "laying hold of the Divine." A Hegelian, in accepting the joint insight of both Spinozism and Hegelianism that there is no God-like Absolute as transcendent (in Lacanian parlance, a "big Other"), likewise accepts that his/her deeds cannot but sometimes "lay hold of the Divine" – and this insofar as he/she and his/her reality amount to the only divinities left as beings immanent to the lone, one-and-only ontological plane of substantiality, a plane bereft of redoubled foundational/meta-level layers. Relatively recently, Žižek echoes this Hegelian condemnation of Pascalian-Kantian false humility – "the true source of Evil is not a finite mortal man who acts like God, but a man who . . . reduces himself to just another finite mortal being."[60] But, what does all of this have to do with politics and/or neuroscience?

Connolly, as quoted a while ago, rightly remarks that "each speculative theory . . . helps to set a specific agenda for cultural and political thought." His non-Hegelianized Spinozism (as channeled through Merleau-Ponty, Foucault, and Deleuze, among others) steers his political theorizing, as I highlighted previously, in the direction of a modest micropolitics of nudging and tinkering with one's selfhood; this is a self-restrained, small-scale neuropolitics of subtle shifts and fine-tuned recalibrations of neural networks enmeshed in local phenomenal environments. Additionally, Connolly's book indicates that his immanent naturalism is more conducive than its alternatives to ecologically conscious thinking.[61] Of course, the sub-title of Bennett's later book is *A Political Ecology of Things*. And, this "political ecology"[62] of hers, framed by her paradigm of vital materialism, shares with Connolly's neuropolitical immanent naturalism an avowed reliance on Spinoza's ontology and a select cross-section of its heirs.[63] What is more, the topic of ecology provides a perfect example allowing for drawing out the key contrasts between, on the one hand, an organic-wholistic Connollian-Bennettian Spinoza-inspired immanent naturalist vital materialism of a flat, even, and democratic first nature of weakly emerging not-quite-subjects, and, on the other hand, a Hegel-inspired (but not organic-wholistic) transcendental materialism of transcendent-while-immanent subjects internal to an uneven, unequal, and stratified self-sundering nature disruptive of itself thanks to the second natures strongly emerging from it as its own products.

In the opening paragraphs of the preface to *Vibrant Matter*, Bennett associates the "vital materiality" of "vibrant matter" to childhood animism.[64] She maintains that the child's tendency to anthropomorphize willy-nilly anything and everything in his/her surrounding contexts harbors the germinal seed of an insight animating her own project, namely, the notion that the world of non-human entities and events is a lively kingdom of agent-like actants (instead of a mechanical expanse of inert stuff).[65] Given her previously mentioned anti-anthropocentric agenda, this initially might seem surprising. But, in a maneuver not without its appealing and elegant dialectical finesse, Bennett turns this wild anthropomorphizing into an auto-deconstructing anthropomorphism through emphasizing that seeing the human in the non-human also immediately entails reciprocally seeing the non-human in the human (i.e., anthropomorphizing nature brings about naturalizing humans in fashions that problematize familiar representations of humanity).[66] When she admits that "anthropomorphizing has . . . its virtues,"[67] this admission must be understood as tied to her proposal that "We need to cultivate a bit of anthropomorphism – the idea that human agency has some echoes in nonhuman nature – to counter the narcissism of humans in charge of the world."[68] Resorting to an analogy Bennett no doubt would appreciate, the strategy here is analogous to a vaccine's employment of a small quantity of a particular pathogen so as to immunize the vaccinated organism against the pathology caused by that pathogen. She feels the dangers of flirting with childhood animism and crude vitalisms are worth facing for the sake of trying to cultivate a human sensibility more humbly attuned to non-human realities.[69]

Like a previously quoted Connolly ("If thinking is part of nature ... *other* aspects of nature may have variable capacities for creative production as well"), Bennett strips humanity of an exceptional privileged status in the overall order of things by projecting human features and traits onto the non-human world (as does the animistic child), thereby blurring the boundaries between the human and the non-human.[70] Also like Connolly, she refers to neurology, with its supposed emphasis that the seat of subjectivity ultimately consists at base of a swarming multitude of impersonal molecules, chemicals, currents, and minute bodies.[71] Furthermore, against the alleged anthropocentrism of, for example, historical materialism,[72] Bennett pleads for a new materialist political ecology with positive implications for green/ecological thinking – more precisely, a vital materialism fostering human beings' awareness that they are a part of and continuous with nature as a seamless web of cross-resonating agents, affects, and assemblages (a very Spinozistic-Deleuzian vision also promoted by Connolly's immanent naturalism).[73]

But, referring back to Marx's 1845 "Theses on Feuerbach," this text being one of the founding documents of the historical materialist tradition Bennett sidelines for its anthropocentrism, both Connolly and Bennett look to be guilty of advocating merely contemplative materialisms. The first sentence of "Thesis I" famously declares, "The chief defect of all hitherto existing materialism ... is that the thing, reality, sensuousness, is conceived only in the form of the object or of contemplation, but not as sensuous human activity, practice, not subjectively."[74] Of course, Spinoza, whose seventeenth-century ontology forms the foundational historical backdrop for Connollian immanent naturalism and Bennettian vital materialism alike (as well as for an eighteenth-century French materialism which Marx has in mind in this context as a forerunner of Feuerbach), certainly falls under the heading of this nineteenth-century "hitherto." Before Marx, Schelling and Hegel, as I observed earlier (both in this chapter and in Chapter 2), criticize Spinoza's metaphysics for, among other defects, failing to account (ontologically) for the (epistemological) position of contemplative reflection and enunciation from which this metaphysics is constructed and articulated. If Spinoza-the-philosopher is himself immanent to, as a finite fold or inflection, the One-All of God-as-substance, then, as Hegel puts it, his ontology is unsatisfying in that it offers nothing by way of explanation for how and why substance becomes subject – that is to say, for how and why the wholistic totality of an organically homogeneous substantial being shatters itself into a fragmented plethora of multiple attributes and modes, including those exceptional ensembles of attributes and modes through which substance achieves a self-reflective/reflexive consciousness of itself (i.e., subjects such as Spinoza who contemplate the infinite substance of which they are [apparently] finite parts). In a Marxian rephrasing of the sort of blind spot diagnosed by Schelling and Hegel with respect to Spinoza, a materialist ontology remains contemplative so long as it does not provide a theory, formulated within its own theoretical framework, for its very existence as a theory (see Chapter 2).

A brief turn to Žižek's discussions of ecology (influenced by the views of Jean-Pierre Dupuy as expressed in such books as *Pour un catastrophisme éclairé* [2002] and *Petite métaphysique des tsunamis* [2005]) clarifies how much is at stake in the differences between, on the one hand, Connolly's naturalism and Bennett's materialism, and, on the other hand, materialist approaches avowedly indebted to historical and dialectical materialisms (specifically, approaches which have it that subjects, although emerging from substance[s], come to be radically different from the "natural" ontological grounds from which they arise and within which they continue to operate). Summarizing his stance very quickly, Žižek concludes that the quotidian, spontaneous phenomenological sense of being immersed in oneness with the surrounding life-world habitats of "nature" is complicit in contributing to complacent inaction in the face of scientific knowledge of the threat of looming environmental catastrophes and collapse. When one walks out one's front door and sees the blue sky, hears the birds singing, feels the wind against one's cheek, and is aware of the surrounding trees, one's phenomenal sense of at-home oneness with all of this makes it extremely difficult to imagine and authentically believe that the entire horizon of this world is in alarming jeopardy. Hence, one can "know" as intellectually accept the imminence of environmental crisis without "believing" as feeling a tangible, gut-level conviction in its near-term inevitability.[75]

Whereas Connolly and Bennett, like many others, are convinced that human beings need to see themselves as inseparably woven into the relatively even and tightly sewn-together fabric of a greater tapestry of being, Žižek, by sharp contrast, maintains both that this already is engrained into humans' everyday horizon of experience as well as that this experiential disposition mitigates against a sense of urgency that otherwise would catapult people into action in light of an intellectual acceptance of the rapidly worsening precariousness of the present ecological circumstances. In diametrical opposition to the now well-worn narrative dear to most ecologically minded thinkers (Connolly and Bennett included), it is not less modern philosophical-scientific rationality, with its *Cogito*-like subjectivity subtracted from its enveloping environs, that is needed; it is more. Even if post-Cartesian modernity has been complicit in contributing to the dire state of the earth's ecosystems nowadays, Žižek, with his Marxist dialectical tendencies (and Wagnerian sensibilities), insists that, as he would put it, the wound can be healed only by the spear that smote it. In other words, further rational-technological manipulation is needed to get humanity out of the mess that prior rational-technological manipulation helped get it into. From a Žižekian perspective, Connollian naturalism and Bennettian materialism both fall into propping up a phenomenology whose descriptive narratives lean toward soothing subjects into inaction by mitigating against the affective registration of the science-derived knowledge of ecological dangers.

For Žižek, instead of contemplating one's immersion in Spinozistic versions of the immediacy of a given "great chain of being" (versions that would include immanent naturalism and vital materialism with their anti-anthropocentric humility resigned to a modest micropolitics of incremental nudges and tinkerings), a materialism indebted to Hegel, Schelling, and Marx (among others) surprisingly assumes the sacrilegious, atheistic mandate of, as it were, being oneself God and acting accordingly. How so? What does this even mean? Bennett refers to notions of God several times. For instance, in the prefatory remarks to *Vibrant Matter*, she contentiously proclaims:

> To attempt, as I do, to present human and nonhuman actants on a less vertical plane than is common is to bracket the question of the human and to elide the rich and diverse literature on subjectivity

and its genesis, its conditions of possibility, and its boundaries. The philosophical project of naming where subjectivity begins and ends is too often bound up with fantasies of a human uniqueness in the eyes of God, of escape from materiality, or of mastery of nature; and even where it is not, it remains an aporetic or quixotic endeavor.[76]

Much later, in the final chapter of her book and speaking of her strategy of deploying a self-deconstructing anthropomorphism, she proposes:

Maybe it is worth running the risks associated with anthropomorphizing (superstition, the divinization of nature, romanticism) because it, oddly enough, works against anthropocentrism: a chord is struck between person and thing, and I am no longer above or outside a nonhuman 'environment.' Too often the philosophical rejection of anthropomorphism is bound up with a hubristic demand that only humans and God can bear any traces of creative agency. To qualify and attenuate this desire is to make it possible to discern a kind of life irreducible to the activities of humans or gods. This material vitality is me, it predates me, it exceeds me, it postdates me.[77]

In view of Žižek's handling of ecology, the last sentence of this second block quotation (as well as statements such as "In emphasizing the ensemble nature of action and the interconnections between persons and things, a theory of vibrant matter presents individuals as simply incapable of bearing *full* responsibility for their effects"[78]) inadvertently hints at reassuring, complacency-cementing notions that might work to assuage/stifle the acute negative affects that otherwise would galvanize into frantic action those who intellectually accept the findings of environmental science (although who do not act as would seem fitting and appropriate on the basis of this knowledge-level acceptance-without-true-belief). But, this aside, if individuals acknowledge that they are immanent moments of being/substance when and where being/substance achieves (through auto-disruptively sundering itself) a self-reflective/reflexive conscious awareness of itself without any redoubled, transcendent big Other (God, Nature, etc.) being posited simultaneously alongside this, then they must confront the anxiety-inducing vortex of a groundless ground – namely, an "abyss of freedom" wherein, in the absence of a deterministic divine Other standing apart from the maelstrom of imminent materiality as an organizing authority over nature and/or mind, the subjects of a self-shattering substance are saddled with the weight of being, so to speak, God-without-God. Such subjects are left being their own horribly, monstrously free creators weighed down with the heavy burdens of the attendant responsibilities and anguish (with such burdens far outweighing whatever narcissistic gains Bennett finds offputting in most philosophical theories of subjectivity). Against the comfortingly humble (and ultimately religious) "fantasies" (to use a word Bennett uses above) of the Spinozistic ontological visions of Connolly's immanent naturalism and Bennett's vital materialism, the (apparent) "hubris" of this post-Hegelian materialism packs, as a disquieting political punch, the pointed message that "There is nothing and nobody to save you except yourselves! Substance itself has forsaken you!" Or, as Žižek might word it in response to Bennett (combining her Latourian language with his Lacanese), "Do not expectantly await any acts from actants other than ourselves!"

I have chosen to focus in this closing chapter on Connolly and Bennett specifically because their respective immanent naturalism and vital materialism are, in certain fashions, uncannily proximate to my transcendental materialism (in the same way that Spinoza and Hegel are uncannily proximate, with the latter being an immanent, rather than external, critic of the former). However, as I hope the preceding assessments of Connolly's and Bennett's positions make sharply evident, this proximity nevertheless is riven and marked by an unbridgeable divide. This chasm is nothing other than the gap between, on the one side, the (neo-)Spinozism of immanent naturalism and/or vital materialism and, on the other side, the (neo-)Hegelianism of transcendental materialism (see Chapter 3). The present chapter is an effort to begin rendering clear and tangible just how significant a difference this sort of philosophical gap makes to the theory and practice of concrete politics.

Despite these tensions between my materialism/naturalism and those of Connolly and Bennett, the three of us seem to concur as regards the urgency and importance, both intellectual and practical, of rethinking the standing and implications of the natural sciences in relation to the theoretical humanities (especially philosophy and political theory). In particular, we all reject the notion that these sciences are wholly and essentially mechanistic, reductive, or eliminative; we therefore also repudiate the assumption

that any materialism/naturalism informed by the sciences ultimately and necessarily would be, by extension, mechanistic,
reductive, or eliminative too. Hence, immanent naturalism, vital
materialism, and transcendental materialism share in common
an ability to pursue engagements with modern science without,
for all that, being driven into such dead-ends as determinism and
nihilism, both of which threaten, among other things, debilitating
political paralysis.

Finally, to circle from politics back to the neurosciences, a concluding reference to Malabou's groundbreaking 2004 book *Que
faire de notre cerveau?* (*What Should We Do with Our Brain?*)
is appropriate. One of the many strokes of genius contained in
this compact text is Malabou's move, announced in her book's
opening paragraph,[79] of extending Marx's historical materialist
insistence that humanity produces itself and its history (even when
not conscious of doing so) to the "nature" of the human brain –
and this via theoretical considerations bearing upon the profound,
far-reaching implications of neuroplasticity. However, as novel
as this move appears to be (and, indeed, genuinely is), some of
Marx's first collaborators, especially Joseph Dietzgen, Engels, and
Lenin, herald the possibility and productivity of a project such
as Malabou's (in which a more-than-contemplative, post-1845
materialism engages with modernity's sciences of nature). Taking
into account a line of thought that runs from Hegel and Marx
through Žižek and Malabou, it can be said that the substance-
as-subject *qua* the plastic, auto-affecting, self-sculpting living
brain prescribes itself as it describes itself and, hence, cannot be
captured on the basis of the unexplained "view from nowhere,"
the intellectual intuition, of any and every purely contemplative
materialism. With respect to Connolly and Bennett, Malabou's
bringing to fruition of a Marxist neuropolitics involves showing
that there is no immediate and natural givenness, no entirely fixed
essence-before-existence, borne witness to by life-scientific studies
of human beings and unambiguously signaling the superiority of
the ontologies of immanent naturalism and/or vital materialism.
Multiple Marx-inspired materialist appropriations of the sciences
of the brain (starting with Dietzgen's *The Nature of Human Brain
Work*, Engels' *Dialectics of Nature*, and Lenin's *Materialism and
Empirio-Criticism*) provide evidence that a neuropolitics need not
necessarily be a shame-tinged, self-effacing micropolitics.

If anything, the Marxist picture of "human nature" is precisely what really gets vindicated after-the-fact by today's life-scientific studies of human beings. Hence, thanks to these sciences, there is now even less tacit support, via long-standing and deeply entrenched liberal ideologies/philosophies of human nature, for the "small" politics (i.e., that of non-revolutionary Western-style democracy) Connolly, following Foucault et al., presumes in his immanent naturalist "neuropolitics" is superior to the grand politics of the revolutionary Marxist tradition. The time has arrived for a properly post-Hegelian neuropolitics willing and able to think big.

Notes

1. Johnston 2013a: 127–8.
2. Connolly 2002: 7–8.
3. Bennett 2010: 116–17.
4. Connolly 2002: 20–1, 108.
5. Foucault 2003: 261–2; Foucault 2007: 200–1, 215–16, 355–6; Foucault 2008: 70, 92, 94, 162–5, 190–2.
6. Connolly 2002: 101–3.
7. Connolly 2011: 115–16.
8. Connolly 2002: 103.
9. Johnston 2009c: 55–78.
10. Bennett 2010: 84.
11. Connolly 2002: xiii.
12. Connolly 2011: 44, 83.
13. Bennett 2010: 91.
14. Connolly 2002: xiii, 3–4, 9; Connolly 2011: 21.
15. Malabou 2009b: 215.
16. Connolly 2002: 46.
17. Johnston 2013i.
18. Connolly 2002: 4.
19. Ibid.: 51, 61.
20. Ibid.: 61.
21. Ibid.: 61–4.
22. Ibid.: 66.
23. Bennett 2010: 108–9.
24. Connolly 2011: 179.
25. Ibid.: 74.
26. Connolly 2002: 85.
27. Ibid.: 91.

28. Ibid.: 85–6.
29. Ibid.: 110–11, 113.
30. Ibid.: 88.
31. Johnston 2011c: 141–82.
32. Connolly 2002: 64; Bennett 2010: 5, 29–30, 129, 154.
33. Varela, Thompson, and Rosch 1991: xv–xvi, 149.
34. Connolly 2002: 92, 106–7.
35. Varela, Thompson, and Rosch 1991: 139–40.
36. Connolly 2011: 43–4, 71.
37. Maturana and Varela 1980: 94; Maturana and Varela 1987: 47–52.
38. Kant 1951: §64–5 [216–22].
39. Hegel 1955: 471–2.
40. Hegel 1977c: 154, 159–60, 162, 165–6, 168–71, 175.
41. Hegel 1970b: §337 [274–5, 277], §350 [351–2], §356 [377], §365 [406].
42. Connolly 2011: 23, 71–2, 81–3, 151, 171, 174.
43. Ibid.: 127.
44. Spinoza 1949: Part One, propositions XXVI through XXXII [63–8], Appendix [72–3], Part Two, proposition XXXV [108], propositions XLVIII through XLIX [119–25].
45. Hegel 1977c: 10.
46. Hegel 2002a: 110.
47. Ibid.: 110.
48. Hegel 1956: 416–17, 422–3, 435, 441–3, 446–7, 449.
49. Ibid.: 453.
50. Hegel 2008: 53–4.
51. Johnston 2008d: 202–9, 241.
52. Hegel 1971a: 234.
53. Schelling and Hegel 2002: 214–16; Hegel 2002b: 231; Hegel 1977a: 90, 95–6, 158–9; Hegel 1977b: 107–8, 112–13.
54. Hegel 1969a: 134–5, 145–6, 148–50, 153–5; Hegel 1991c: §92 [148–9].
55. Hegel 1986: 35.
56. Hegel 1971a: 234.
57. Hegel 1955: 257.
58. Ibid.: 454–5.
59. Pascal 1966: 59.
60. Žižek 1999a: 376.
61. Connolly 2002: 61–2.
62. Bennett 2010: 108–9.
63. Ibid.: x, viii, xiii, 5, 12, 21–3, 62, 116–18.

64. Ibid.: vii–viii.
65. Ibid.: 20.
66. Ibid.: 98–9.
67. Ibid.: 25.
68. Ibid.: xvi.
69. Ibid.: 18.
70. Ibid.: 31.
71. Ibid.: 10, 12–13.
72. Ibid.: xvi.
73. Ibid.: ix–x.
74. Marx 1977: 156.
75. Žižek 2008b: 420–61; Žižek 2010a: 327–52; Žižek 2009a: 155–83.
76. Bennett 2010: ix.
77. Ibid.: 120.
78. Ibid.: 37.
79. Malabou 2008: 1.

Bibliography

There are two sets of abbreviations I use when citing certain works. All citations of Freud, in reference to the *Standard Edition*, are formatted as *SE*, followed by the volume number and the page number (e.g., *SE* 21: 154). The abbreviation system for Lacan's seminars is a little more complicated. All seminars are abbreviated *S*, followed by the Roman numeral of the volume number. For those seminars available in English (seminars 1, 2, 3, 7, 11, 17, and 20), I simply give the page numbers of the volumes as published by W.W. Norton and Company (e.g., *SXI*: 256). In a few instances, I refer to the original French editions of these translated seminars; when I do so, I indicate this in brackets as [Fr.]. For those seminars published in French in book form (as of the writing of the chapters composing *Adventures in Transcendental Materialism*) but not translated into English (seminars 4, 5, 8, 10, 16, 18, and 23), the listed page numbers refer to the French editions published by Éditions du Seuil (e.g., *SX*: 52). As for the rest of the seminars, the dates of the seminar sessions (month/day/year) are listed in place of page numbers (e.g., *SXV*: 12/6/67).

Agamben, Giorgio (2004), *The Open: Man and Animal*, trans. Kevin Attell, Stanford: Stanford University Press.

Althusser, Louis (1976), "Elements of Self-Criticism," in Louis Althusser, *Essays in Self-Criticism*, trans. Grahame Lock, London: New Left Books, pp. 101–61.

—(1996), "Louis Althusser to Jacques Lacan, Paris, November 7, 1966," in Louis Althusser, *Writings on Psychoanalysis: Freud and Lacan*, trans. Jeffrey Mehlman, New York: Columbia University Press, pp. 170–2.

—(2003), "The Historical Task of Marxist Philosophy," in Louis Althusser, *The Humanist Controversy and Other Writings (1966–1967)*, ed. François Matheron, trans. G.M. Goshgarian, London: Verso, pp. 155–220.

—(2005a), "To My English Readers," in Louis Althusser, *For Marx*, trans. Ben Brewster, London: Verso, pp. 9–15.

—(2005b), "On the Materialist Dialectic: On the Unevenness of Origins," in Louis Althusser, *For Marx*, trans. Ben Brewster, London: Verso, pp. 161–218.

—(2006), "The Underground Current of the Materialism of the Encounter," in Louis Althusser, *Philosophy of the Encounter: Later Writings, 1978–1987*, ed. François Matheron and Oliver Corpet, trans. G.M. Goshgarian, London: Verso, pp. 163–207.

—(2009a), "From *Capital* to Marx's Philosophy," in Louis Althusser and Étienne Balibar, *Reading Capital*, trans. Ben Brewster, London: Verso, pp. 11–75.

—(2009b), "The Object of *Capital*," in Louis Althusser and Étienne Balibar, *Reading Capital*, trans. Ben Brewster, London: Verso, pp. 77–220.

Ansermet, François (2002), "*Des neurosciences aux logosciences*," in Nathalie Georges, Jacques-Alain Miller, and Nathalie Marchaison (eds.), *Qui sont vos psychanalystes?*, Paris: Éditions du Seuil, pp. 376–84.

Ansermet, François and Pierre Magistretti (2007), *Biology of Freedom: Neural Plasticity, Experience, and the Unconscious*, trans. Susan Fairfield, New York: Other Press.

Bacon, Francis (2000), *The New Organon*, ed. Lisa Jardine and Michael Silverthorne, Cambridge: Cambridge University Press.

Badiou, Alain (1976), *Théorie de la contradiction*, Paris: François Maspero.

—(1982), *Théorie du sujet*, Paris: Éditions du Seuil.

—(1989), "*La psychanalyse a-t-elle des fondements philosophiques?*," <http://www.entretemps.asso.fr/Badiou/Chexbres.htm> (last accessed 2 June 2013).

—(1991), "*Lacan et Platon: Le mathème est-il une idée?*," in Collège international de philosophie (ed.), *Lacan avec les philosophes*, Paris: Éditions Albin Michel, pp. 135–54.

—(1994–95), *Le antiphilosophie de Lacan: Séminaire 1994–1995*, unpublished typescript, <http://www.entretemps.asso.fr/Badiou/94–95.htm> (last accessed 1 June 2013).

—(1999), *Manifesto for Philosophy*, trans. Norman Madarasz, Albany: State University of New York Press.

—(2005), *Being and Event*, trans. Oliver Feltham, London: Continuum.

—(2006a), "The Formulas of *L'Étourdit*," trans. Scott Savaiano, *Lacanian Ink*, no. 27, Spring, pp. 80–95.

—(2006b), "Lacan and the Pre-Socratics," in Slavoj Žižek (ed.), *Lacan: The Silent Partners*, London: Verso, pp. 7–16.

—(2006c), "Matters of Appearance: An Interview with Alain Badiou [with Lauren Sedofsky]," *Artforum International*, vol. 45, no. 3, November, pp. 246–53, 322.

—(2007), *The Century*, trans. Alberto Toscano, Cambridge: Polity Press.

—(2008), "What is a Philosophical Institution? Or Address, Transmission, Inscription," in Alain Badiou, *Conditions*, trans. Steven Corcoran, London: Continuum, pp. 26–32.

—(2009a), *L'antiphilosophie de Wittgenstein*, Caen, France: Nous.

—(2009b), *Logics of Worlds: Being and Event, 2*, trans. Alberto Toscano, London: Continuum.

—(2009c), "Jacques Lacan (1901–1981)," in Alain Badiou, *Pocket Pantheon: Figures in Postwar Philosophy*, trans. David Macey, London: Verso, pp. 1–4.

—(2009d), "Louis Althusser (1918–1990)," in Alain Badiou, *Pocket Pantheon: Figures in Postwar Philosophy*, trans. David Macey, London: Verso, pp. 54–89.

—(2009e), *Theory of the Subject*, trans. Bruno Bosteels, London: Continuum.

—(2010), "*Formules de «l'Étourdit»*," in Alain Badiou and Barbara Cassin, *Il n'y a pas de rapport sexuel: Deux leçon sur «l'Étourdit» de Lacan*, Paris: Librairie Arthème Fayard, pp. 101–37.

Badiou, Alain, Joël Bellassen, and Louis Mossot (1978), *Le noyau rationnel de la dialectique hégélienne: Traductions, introductions et commentaires autour d'un texte de Zhang Shiying*, Paris: François Maspero.

Balmès, François (1999), *Ce que Lacan dit de l'être (1953–1960)*, Paris: Presses Universitaires de France.

—(2007), *Dieu, le sexe, la vérité*, Ramonville Saint-Agne, France: Éditions érès.

Becker, Ernest (1973), *The Denial of Death*, New York: The Free Press.

Beiser, Frederick C. (2002), *German Idealism: The Struggle Against Subjectivism, 1781–1801*, Cambridge, MA: Harvard University Press.

—(2005), *Hegel*, New York: Routledge.

Benjamin, Walter (1969), "Theses on the Philosophy of History," in Walter Benjamin, *Illuminations: Essays and Reflections*, ed. Hannah Arendt, trans. Harry Zohn, New York: Schocken Books, pp. 253–64.

Bennett, Jane (2010), *Vibrant Matter: A Political Ecology of Things*, Durham, NC: Duke University Press.

Benveniste, Emile (1971), "Subjectivity in Language," in Emile Benveniste,

Problems in General Linguistics, trans. Mary Elizabeth Meek, Coral Gables: University of Miami Press, pp. 223–30.

Blackmore, Susan (1999), *The Meme Machine*, Oxford: Oxford University Press.

Blanchot, Maurice (1992), *The Step Not Beyond*, trans. Lycette Nelson, Albany: State University of New York Press.

—(1993), *The Infinite Conversation*, trans. Susan Hanson, Minneapolis: University of Minnesota Press.

Bosteels, Bruno (2008), "Radical Antiphilosophy," *Filozofski Vestnik*, special issue: *Radical Philosophy?*, ed. Peter Klepec, vol. 29, no. 2, pp. 155–87.

Brown, Norman O. (1959), *Life Against Death: The Psychoanalytical Meaning of History*, Hanover, NH: Wesleyan University Press.

Butler, Judith (1990), "The Pleasures of Repetition," in Robert A. Glick and Stanley Bone (eds.), *Pleasure Beyond the Pleasure Principle: The Role of Affect in Motivation, Development, and Adaptation*, New Haven, CT: Yale University Press, pp. 259–75.

Changeux, Jean-Pierre (2004), *The Physiology of Truth: Neuroscience and Human Knowledge*, trans. M.B. DeBevoise, Cambridge, MA: Harvard University Press.

Chiesa, Lorenzo and Alberto Toscano (2005), "Ethics and Capital, *Ex Nihilo*," *Umbr(a): A Journal of the Unconscious – The Dark God*, ed. Andrew Skomra, Buffalo: Center for the Study of Psychoanalysis and Culture, State University of New York at Buffalo, pp. 9–25.

Colletti, Lucio (1979), *Marxism and Hegel*, trans. Lawrence Garner, London: Verso.

Connolly, William E. (2002), *Neuropolitics: Thinking, Culture, Speed*, Minneapolis: University of Minnesota Press.

—(2011), *A World of Becoming*, Durham, NC: Duke University Press.

Damasio, Antonio (1994), *Descartes' Error: Emotion, Reason, and the Human Brain*, New York: Avon Books.

—(1999), *The Feeling of What Happens: Body and Emotion in the Making of Consciousness*, New York: Harcourt.

—(2003), *Looking for Spinoza: Joy, Sorrow and the Feeling Brain*, New York: Harcourt.

—(2010), *Self Comes to Mind: Constructing the Conscious Brain*, New York: Pantheon.

Dawkins, Richard (1976), *The Selfish Gene*, Oxford: Oxford University Press.

Deacon, Terrence W. (2012), *Incomplete Nature: How Mind Emerged from Matter*, New York: W.W. Norton and Company.

Deleuze, Gilles (1997), "Appendix: Review of Jean Hyppolite, *Logique et existence*," in Jean Hyppolite, *Logic and Existence*, trans. Leonard Lawlor and Amit Sen, Albany: State University of New York Press, pp. 191–5.

Della Rocca, Michael (2012), "Rationalism, Idealims, Monism, and Beyond," in Eckart Förster and Yitzhak Y. Melamed (eds.), *Spinoza and German Idealism*, Cambridge: Cambridge University Press, pp. 7–26.

Dennett, Daniel C. (2003), *Freedom Evolves*, New York: Viking.

Derrida, Jacques (1993), *Aporias*, trans. Thomas Dutoit, Stanford: Stanford University Press.

—(1994), *Specters of Marx: The State of Debt, the Work of Mourning, and the New International*, trans. Peggy Kamuf, New York: Routledge.

Descartes, René (1993), *Meditations on First Philosophy*, trans. Donald A. Cress, Indianapolis: Hackett.

Dolar, Mladen (1996), "At First Sight," in Renata Salecl and Slavoj Žižek (eds.), *Gaze and Voice as Love Objects*, Durham, NC: Duke University Press, pp. 129–53.

Doz, André (1987), *La logique de Hegel et les problèmes traditionnels de l'ontologie*, Paris: Vrin.

Eldredge, Niles and Stephen Jay Gould (1972), "Punctuated Equilibria: The Tempo and Mode of Evolution Reconsidered," in Thomas J.M. Schopf (ed.), *Models in Paleobiology*, San Francisco: Freeman Cooper and Company, pp. 82–115.

Engels, Friedrich (1940), *Dialectics of Nature*, trans. C.P. Dutt, New York: International Publishers.

—(1941), *Ludwig Feuerbach and the Outcome of Classical German Philosophy*, New York: International Publishers.

—(1959), *Anti-Dühring: Herr Eugen Dühring's Revolution in Science*, 2nd edn, Moscow: Foreign Languages Publishing House.

Fichte, J.G. (1976), *Die Wissenschaftslehre in ihrem allgemeinen Umriß (1810)*, Frankfurt am Main: Vittorio Klostermann.

—(2005), *The Science of Knowing: J.G. Fichte's 1804 Lectures on the Wissenschaftslehre*, trans. Walter E. Wright, Albany: State University of New York Press.

Fink, Bruce (1996), "The Nature of Unconscious Thought or Why No One Ever Reads Lacan's Postface to the 'Seminar on 'The Purloined Letter,'"" in Richard Feldstein, Bruce Fink, and Maire Jaanus (eds.), *Reading Seminars I and II: Lacan's Return to Freud*, Albany: State University of New York Press, pp. 173–91.

Fink, Eugen (1970), "Appendix VIII: Fink's Appendix on the Problem of the 'Unconscious,'" in Edmund Husserl, *The Crisis of the European Sciences and Transcendental Phenomenology: An Introduction to Phenomenological Philosophy*, trans. David Carr, Evanston: Northwestern University Press, pp. 385–7.

Foucault, Michel (2003), *"Society Must be Defended": Lectures at the Collège de France, 1975–1976*, ed. Mauro Bertani and Alessandro Fontana, trans. David Macey, New York: Picador.

—(2007), *Security, Territory, Population: Lectures at the Collège de France, 1977–1978*, ed. Michel Senellart, trans. Graham Burchell, New York: Picador.

—(2008), *The Birth of Biopolitics: Lectures at the Collège de France, 1978–1979*, ed. Michel Senellart, trans. Graham Burchell, Basingstoke: Palgrave Macmillan.

Freud, Sigmund (1953–74), *The Standard Edition of the Complete Psychological Works of Sigmund Freud*, 24 volumes, ed. and trans. James Strachey, in collaboration with Anna Freud, assisted by Alix Strachey and Alan Tyson, London: Hogarth Press and the Institute of Psycho-Analysis:

—"Extracts from the Fliess Papers," *SE* 1: 173–280.

—*Project for a Scientific Psychology*, *SE* 1: 281–397.

—"The Aetiology of Hysteria," *SE* 3: 187–221.

—"Abstracts of the Scientific Writings of Dr. Sigm. Freud," *SE* 3: 223–57.

—*The Interpretation of Dreams*, *SE* 4–5

—"Fragment of an Analysis of a Case of Hysteria," *SE* 7: 1–122.

—*Three Essays on the Theory of Sexuality*, *SE* 7: 123–245.

—*Totem and Taboo*, *SE* 13: 1–162.

—"On Narcissism: An Introduction," *SE* 14: 67–102.

—"Instincts and Their Vicissitudes," *SE* 14: 109–40.

—"The Unconscious," *SE* 14: 159–215.

—"Mourning and Melancholia," *SE* 14: 237–58.

—"Thoughts for the Times on War and Death," *SE* 14: 273–302.

—"On Transience," *SE* 14: 303–7.

—"The Uncanny," *SE* 17: 217–56.

—*Beyond the Pleasure Principle*, *SE* 18: 1–64.

—*The Future of an Illusion*, *SE* 21: 1–56.

—*New Introductory Lectures on Psycho-Analysis*, *SE* 22: 1–182.

—(1987), "Overview of the Transference Neuroses," in Sigmund Freud, *A Phylogenetic Fantasy: Overview of the Transference Neuroses*, ed. Ilse Grubrich-Simitis, trans. Axel Hoffer and Peter T. Hoffer, Cambridge, MA: Harvard University Press, pp. 5–20.

Gabriel, Markus (2011), *Transcendental Ontology: Essays in German Idealism*, London: Continuum.

Gabriel, Markus and Slavoj Žižek (2009), "Introduction: A Plea for a Return to Post-Kantian Idealism," in Markus Gabriel and Slavoj Žižek, *Mythology, Madness and Laughter: Subjectivity in German Idealism*, London: Continuum, pp. 1–14.

Grant, Iain Hamilton (2008), *Philosophies of Nature After Schelling*, paperback edition, London: Continuum.

Green, André (2000), "*L'originaire dans la psychanalyse*," in André Green, *La diachronie en psychanalyse*, Paris: Les Éditions de Minuit, pp. 41–85.

Hägglund, Martin (2008), *Radical Atheism: Derrida and the Time of Life*, Stanford: Stanford University Press.

—(2009a), "Chronolibidinal Reading: Deconstruction and Psychoanalysis," *New Centennial Review*, special issue: "Living On: Of Martin Hägglund," ed. David E. Johnson, vol. 9, no. 1, Spring, pp. 1–43.

—(2009b), "The Challenge of Radical Atheism: A Response," *New Centennial Review*, special issue: "Living On: Of Martin Hägglund," ed. David E. Johnson, vol. 9, no. 1, Spring, pp. 227–52.

—(2011), "Radical Atheist Materialism: A Critique of Meillassoux," in Levi Bryant, Nick Srnicek, and Graham Harman (eds.), *The Speculative Turn: Continental Materialism and Realism*, Melbourne: Re.press, pp. 114–29.

—(2012), *Dying for Time: Proust, Woolf, Nabokov*, Cambridge, MA: Harvard University Press.

Hägglund, Martin, Adrian Johnston, and Slavoj Žižek (2012), "Conditions of Possibility," Graduate Center, City University of New York, October 19, <http://videostreaming.gc.cuny.edu/videos/video/331/> (last accessed 25 March 2013).

Hebb, Donald O. (1949), *The Organization of Behavior: A Neuropsychological Theory*, New York: Wiley.

Hegel, G.W.F. (1955), *Lectures on the History of Philosophy, Volume Three*, trans. E.S. Haldane and Frances H. Simson, New York: Humanities Press.

—(1956), *The Philosophy of History*, trans. J. Sibree, New York: Dover Publications.

—(1969a), *Science of Logic*, trans. A.V. Miller, London: George Allen & Unwin.

—(1969b), *Wissenschaft der Logik, I, Werke in zwanzig Bänden, 5*, ed. Eva Moldenhauer and Karl Markus Michel, Frankfurt am Main: Suhrkamp.

—(1969c), *Wissenschaft der Logik, II, Werke in zwanzig Bänden, 6*, ed. Eva Moldenhauer and Karl Markus Michel, Frankfurt am Main: Suhrkamp.

—(1970a), *Phänomenologie des Geistes, Werke in zwanzig Bänden, 3*, ed. Eva Moldenhauer and Karl Markus Michel, Frankfurt am Main: Suhrkamp.

—(1970b), *Philosophy of Nature: Part Two of the Encyclopedia of the Philosophical Sciences*, trans. A.V. Miller, Oxford: Oxford University Press.

—(1970c), *Vorlesungen über die Philosophie der Geschichte, Werke in zwanzig Bänden, 12*, ed. Eva Moldenhauer and Karl Markus Michel, Frankfurt am Main: Suhrkamp.

—(1971a), "*Das älteste Systemprogramm des deutschen Idealismus*," in *Werke in zwanzig Bänden, 1: Frühe Schriften*, ed. Eva Moldenhauer and Karl Markus Michel, Frankfurt am Main: Suhrkamp, pp. 234–6.

—(1971b), *Philosophy of Mind: Part Three of the Encyclopedia of the Philosophical Sciences*, trans. William Wallace, Oxford: Oxford University Press.

—(1977a), *The Difference Between Fichte's and Schelling's System of Philosophy*, trans. H.S. Harris and Walter Cerf, Albany: State University of New York Press.

—(1977b), *Faith and Knowledge*, trans. Walter Cerf and H.S. Harris, Albany: State University of New York Press.

—(1977c), *Phenomenology of Spirit*, trans. A.V. Miller, Oxford: Oxford University Press.

—(1984a), *Lectures on the Philosophy of Religion, Volume One: Introduction and the Concept of Religion*, ed. Peter C. Hodgson, trans. R.F. Brown, P.C. Hodgson, J.M. Stewart, J.P. Fitzer, and H.S. Harris, Berkeley: University of California Press.

—(1984b), "Hegel to Niethammer: Bamberg, November 22, 1808," in G.W.F. Hegel, *Hegel: The Letters*, trans. Clark Butler and Christiane Seiler, Bloomington: Indiana University Press, pp. 180–2.

—(1984c), "Hegel to Niethammer: Nuremberg, October 23, 1812," in G.W.F. Hegel, *Hegel: The Letters*, trans. Clark Butler and Christiane Seiler, Bloomington: Indiana University Press, pp. 275–82.

—(1984d), "Hegel to Duboc: Berlin, April 29, 1823," in G.W.F. Hegel, *Hegel: The Letters*, trans. Clark Butler and Christiane Seiler, Bloomington: Indiana University Press, pp. 498–500.

—(1986), *The Jena System, 1804–5: Logic and Metaphysics*, ed. John W. Burbidge and George di Giovanni, Montreal and Kingston: McGill-Queen's University Press.

—(1987), *Lectures on the Philosophy of Religion, Volume Two: Determinate Religion*, ed. Peter C. Hodgson, trans. R.F. Brown, P.C. Hodgson, J.M. Stewart, and H.S. Harris, Berkeley: University of California Press.

—(1990), *Encyclopedia of the Philosophical Sciences in Outline and Critical Writings*, ed. Ernst Behler, New York: Continuum.

—(1991a), *Elements of the Philosophy of Right*, ed. Allen W. Wood, trans. H.B. Nisbet, Cambridge: Cambridge University Press.

—(1991b), "Preface to the Second Edition (1827)," in G.W.F. Hegel, *The Encyclopedia Logic: Part I of the Encyclopedia of Philosophical Sciences with the Zusätze*, trans. T.F. Geraets, W.A. Suchting, and H.S. Harris, Indianapolis: Hackett, pp. 4–17.

—(1991c), *The Encyclopedia Logic: Part I of the Encyclopedia of Philosophical Sciences with the Zusätze*, trans. T.F. Geraets, W.A. Suchting, and H.S. Harris, Indianapolis: Hackett.

—(2002a), "The Earliest System-Program of German Idealism," trans. H.S. Harris, in G.W.F. Hegel, *Miscellaneous Writings of G.W.F. Hegel*, ed. Jon Stewart, Evanston: Northwestern University Press, pp. 110–12.

—(2002b), "How the Ordinary Human Understanding Takes Philosophy (as Displayed in the Works of Mr. Krug)," trans. H.S. Harris, in G.W.F. Hegel, *Miscellaneous Writings of G.W.F. Hegel*, ed. Jon Stewart, Evanston: Northwestern University Press, pp. 226–44.

—(2008), *Lectures on Logic: Berlin, 1831*, trans. Clark Butler, Bloomington: Indiana University Press.

Heidegger, Martin (1962), *Being and Time*, trans. John Macquarrie and Edward Robinson, New York: Harper & Row.

—(1993), "Modern Science, Metaphysics, and Mathematics," trans. W.B. Barton, Jr. and Vera Deutsch, in Martin Heidegger, *Basic Writings*, ed. David Farrell Krell, New York: HarperCollins, pp. 267–305.

Henrich, Dieter (2003), *Between Kant and Hegel: Lectures on German Idealism*, ed. David S. Pacini, Cambridge, MA: Harvard University Press.

—(2010a), "*Hegels Logik der Reflexion,*" in Dieter Henrich, *Hegel im Kontext*, Frankfurt am Main: Suhrkamp, pp. 95–157.

—(2010b), "*Nachwort zur fünften Auflage,*" in Dieter Henrich, *Hegel im Kontext*, Frankfurt am Main: Suhrkamp, pp. 217–26.

Hindrichs, Gunnar (2012), "Two Models of Metaphysical Inferentialism:

Spinoza and Hegel," in Eckart Förster and Yitzhak Y. Melamed (eds.), *Spinoza and German Idealism*, Cambridge: Cambridge University Press, pp. 214–31.

Hobbes, Thomas (1985), *Leviathan*, ed. C.B. Macpherson. New York: Penguin.

Hölderlin, Friedrich (1972), *"Über Urtheil und Seyn,"* trans. H.S. Harris, in H.S. Harris, *Hegel's Development: Toward the Sunlight, 1770–1801*, Oxford: Oxford University Press, pp. 515–16.

Houlgate, Stephen (2006), *The Opening of Hegel's Logic: From Being to Infinity*, West Lafayette: Purdue University Press.

Hume, David (1969), *A Treatise of Human Nature*, ed. Ernest C. Mossner, New York: Penguin.

Husserl, Edmund (1964), *The Phenomenology of Internal Time-Consciousness*, ed. Martin Heidegger, trans. James S. Churchill, Bloomington: Indiana University Press.

Hyppolite, Jean (1997), *Logic and Existence*, trans. Leonard Lawlor and Amit Sen, Albany: State University of New York Press.

Jablonka, Eva and Marion J. Lamb (2005), *Evolution in Four Dimensions: Genetic, Epigenetic, Behavioral, and Symbolic Variation in the History of Life*, Cambridge, MA: MIT Press.

Jacobi, Friedrich Heinrich (1994), *David Hume on Faith, or Idealism and Realism: A Dialogue*, in Friedrich Heinrich Jacobi, *The Main Philosophical Writings and the Novel Allwill*, ed. and trans. George di Giovanni, Montreal and Kingston: McGill-Queen's University Press, pp. 253–338.

Johnston, Adrian (2001), "The Vicious Circle of the Super-Ego: The Pathological Trap of Guilt and the Beginning of Ethics," *Psychoanalytic Studies*, vol. 3, no. 3/4, September-December, pp. 411–24.

—(2005a), "Intimations of Freudian Mortality: The Enigma of Sexuality and the Constitutive Blind Spots of Freud's Self-Analysis," *Journal for Lacanian Studies*, vol. 3, no. 2, pp. 222–46.

—(2005b), "Nothing is Not Always No-one: (a)Voiding Love," *Filozofski Vestnik*, special issue: "The Nothing(ness)/Le rien/Das Nichts," ed. Alenka Zupančič. vol. 26, no. 2. pp. 67–81.

—(2005c), *Time Driven: Metapsychology and the Splitting of the Drive*, Evanston: Northwestern University Press.

—(2006), "Ghosts of Substance Past: Schelling, Lacan, and the Denaturalization of Nature," in Slavoj Žižek (ed.), *Lacan: The Silent Partners*, London: Verso, pp. 34–55.

—(2007a), "Lightening Ontology: Slavoj Žižek and the Unbearable Lightness of Being Free," *Lacanian Ink: The Symptom*, no. 8, Spring,

<http://www.lacan.com/symptom8_articles/johnston8.html> (last accessed 14 April 2013).

—(2007b), "Slavoj Žižek's Hegelian Reformation: Giving a Hearing to *The Parallax View*," *Diacritics: A Review of Contemporary Criticism*, vol. 37, no. 1, Spring, pp. 3–20.

—(2008a), "A Blast from the Future: Freud, Lacan, Marcuse, and Snapping the Threads of the Past," *Umbr(a) – A Journal of the Unconscious: Utopia*, ed. Ryan Anthony Hatch, Buffalo: Center for the Study of Psychoanalysis and Culture, State University of New York at Buffalo, pp. 67–84.

—(2008b), "Conflicted Matter: Jacques Lacan and the Challenge of Secularizing Materialism," *Pli: The Warwick Journal of Philosophy*, no. 19, Spring, pp. 166–88.

—(2008c), "What Matter(s) in Ontology: Alain Badiou, the Hebb-Event, and Materialism Split from Within," *Angelaki: Journal of the Theoretical Humanities*, vol. 13, no. 1, April, pp. 27–49.

—(2008d), *Žižek's Ontology: A Transcendental Materialist Theory of Subjectivity*, Evanston: Northwestern University Press.

—(2009a), *Badiou, Žižek, and Political Transformations: The Cadence of Change*, Evanston: Northwestern University Press.

—(2009b), "Life Terminable and Interminable: The Undead and the Afterlife of the Afterlife – A Friendly Disagreement with Martin Hägglund," *New Centennial Review*, special issue: "Living On: Of Martin Hägglund," ed. David E. Johnson, vol. 9, no. 1, Spring, pp. 147–89.

—(2009c), "The Right Left: Alain Badiou and the Disruption of Political Identities," *Yale French Studies*, special issue: "Turns to the Right?," ed. Lawrence Schehr and Michael Johnson, no. 116/117, pp. 55–78.

—(2010a), "Freud and Continental Philosophy," in Alan D. Schrift (ed.), *The History of Continental Philosophy*, eight volumes, *Volume III: The New Century – Bergsonism, Phenomenology, and Responses to Modern Science*, ed. Keith Ansell Pearson and Alan D. Schrift, Durham: Acumen, pp. 319–46.

—(2010b), "The Misfeeling of What Happens: Slavoj Žižek, Antonio Damasio, and a Materialist Account of Affects," *Subjectivity*, special issue: "Žižek and Political Subjectivity," ed. Derek Hook and Calum Neill, vol. 3, no. 1, April, pp. 76–100.

—(2010c), "Sextimacy: Freud, Mortality, and a Reconsideration of the Role of Sexuality in Psychoanalysis" in Jens De Vleminck and Eran Dorfman (eds.), *Sexuality and Psychoanalysis: Philosophical Criticisms*, Leuven: Leuven University Press, pp. 35–59.

—(2011a), "From Scientific Socialism to Socialist Science: *Naturdialektik* Then and Now," *Communism: A New Beginning?*, New York, New York, October 15, <https://www.youtube.com/watch?v=VOLTlKpzdho> (last accessed 25 March 2013).

—(2011b), "Hume's Revenge: *À Dieu*, Meillassoux?," in Levi Bryant, Nick Srnicek, and Graham Harman (eds.), *The Speculative Turn: Continental Materialism and Realism*, Melbourne: Re.press, pp. 92–113.

—(2011c), "Repeating Engels: Renewing the Cause of the Materialist Wager for the Twenty-First Century," *Theory @ Buffalo*, special issue: "animal.machine.sovereign," 15, pp. 141–82.

—(2011d), "Second Natures in Dappled Worlds: John McDowell, Nancy Cartwright, and Hegelian-Lacanian Materialism," *Umbr(a): A Journal of the Unconscious – The Worst*, ed. Matthew Rigilano and Kyle Fetter, Buffalo: Center for the Study of Psychoanalysis and Culture (State University of New York at Buffalo), pp. 71–91.

—(2011e), "The Weakness of Nature: Hegel, Freud, Lacan, and Negativity Materialized," in Slavoj Žižek, Clayton Crockett, and Creston Davis (eds.), *Hegel and the Infinite: Religion, Politics, and Dialectic*, New York: Columbia University Press, pp. 159–79.

—(2012a), "Reflections of a Rotten Nature: Hegel, Lacan, and Material Negativity," *Filozofski Vestnik*, special issue: "Science and Thought," ed. Frank Ruda and Jan Voelker, vol. 33, no. 2, pp. 23–52.

—(2012b), "Turning the Sciences Inside Out: Revisiting Lacan's 'Science and Truth,'" in Peter Hallward and Knox Peden (eds), *Concept and Form, Volume Two: Interviews and Essays on the Cahiers pour l'Analyse*, London: Verso, pp. 105–21.

—(2012c), "The Voiding of Weak Nature: The Transcendental Materialist Kernels of Hegel's *Naturphilosophie*," *Graduate Faculty Philosophy Journal*, vol. 33, no. 1, Spring, pp. 103–57.

—(2013a), "From Scientific Socialism to Socialist Science: *Naturdialektik* Then and Now," *The Idea of Communism 2: The New York Conference*, ed. Slavoj Žižek, London: Verso, pp. 103–36.

—(2013b), "Jacques Lacan (1901–1981)," *Stanford Encyclopedia of Philosophy*, <http://plato.stanford.edu/entries/lacan> (last accessed 29 May 2013).

—(2013c), "Preface: From Nonfeeling to Misfeeling – Affects Between Trauma and the Unconscious," in Adrian Johnston and Catherine Malabou, *Self and Emotional Life: Philosophy, Psychoanalysis, and Neuroscience*, New York: Columbia University Press, pp. ix–xviii.

—(2013d), "Misfelt Feelings: Unconscious Affect Between Psychoanalysis,

Neuroscience, and Philosophy," in Adrian Johnston and Catherine Malabou, *Self and Emotional Life: Philosophy, Psychoanalysis, and Neuroscience*, New York: Columbia University Press, pp. 73–210.

—(2013e), "Drive Between Brain and Subject: An Immanent Critique of Lacanian Neuro-psychoanalysis," *Southern Journal of Philosophy*, special issue: "Annual Murray Spindel Conference: Freudian Future(s)" (forthcoming).

—(2013f), "Lacking Causes: Privative Causality from Locke and Kant to Lacan and Deacon," *Speculations: A Journal of Speculative Realism* (forthcoming).

—(2013g), "The Object in the Mirror of Genetic Transcendentalism: Lacan's *Objet petit a* Between Visibility and Invisibility," *Continental Philosophy Review*, special issue: "Reading *Seminar XIII: The Object of Psychoanalysis*," ed. Thomas Brockelman and Dominiek Hoens (forthcoming).

—(2013h), "Points of Forced Freedom: Eleven (More) Theses on Materialism," *Speculations: A Journal of Speculative Realism* (forthcoming).

—(2013i), *Prolegomena to Any Future Materialism, Volume One: The Outcome of Contemporary French Philosophy*, Evanston: Northwestern University Press (forthcoming).

—(2013j), "Slavoj Žižek," in William Schroeder (ed.), *The Blackwell Companion to Continental Philosophy*, 2nd edn, Oxford: Blackwell (forthcoming).

—(2013k), "This *is* Orthodox Marxism: The Shared Materialist *Weltanschauung* of Marx and Engels," *Quaderni materialisti*, special issue: "On Sebastiano Timpanaro" (forthcoming).

—(2014), *Prolegomena to Any Future Materialism, Volume Two: A Weak Nature Alone*, Evanston: Northwestern University Press (under review).

—(2015), *Prolegomena to Any Future Materialism, Volume Three: Substance Also as Subject*, Evanston: Northwestern University Press (under review).

Kandel, Eric R. (2005a), "Psychotherapy and the Single Synapse: The Impact of Psychiatric Thought on Neurobiologic Research," in Eric R. Kandel, *Psychiatry, Psychoanalysis, and the New Biology of Mind*, Washington, DC: American Psychiatric Publishing, pp. 5–26.

—(2005b), "A New Intellectual Framework for Psychiatry," in Eric R. Kandel, *Psychiatry, Psychoanalysis, and the New Biology of Mind*, Washington, DC: American Psychiatric Publishing, pp. 27–58.

—(2005c), "From Metapsychology to Molecular Biology: Explorations Into the Nature of Anxiety," in Eric R. Kandel, *Psychiatry, Psychoanalysis, and the New Biology of Mind*, Washington, DC: American Psychiatric Publishing, pp. 117–56.

Kant, Immanuel (1917), *Anthropologie in pragmatischer Hinsicht*, in Immanuel Kant, *Kant's gesammelte Schriften: Band VII*, Berlin: Georg Reimer, 1917.

—(1951), *Critique of Judgment*, trans. J.H. Bernard, New York: Hafner.

—(1965), *Critique of Pure Reason*, trans. Norman Kemp Smith, New York: Saint Martin's Press.

—(1978), *Anthropology from a Pragmatic Point of View*, trans. Victor Lyle Dowdell, Carbondale: Southern Illinois University Press.

—(1983), "Speculative Beginning of Human History," in Immanuel Kant, *Perpetual Peace and Other Essays*, trans. Ted Humphrey, Indianapolis: Hackett, pp. 49–60.

Koyré, Alexandre (1958), *From the Closed World to the Infinite Universe*, New York: Harper Torchbooks.

Kripke, Saul A. (1972), *Naming and Necessity*, Cambridge, MA: Harvard University Press.

Lacan, Jacques (1966a), "*Du sujet enfin en question*," in Jacques Lacan, *Écrits*, Paris: Éditions du Seuil, pp. 229–36.

—(1966b), "*La science et la vérité*," in Jacques Lacan, *Écrits*, Paris: Éditions du Seuil, pp. 855–77.

—(1970), "Of Structure as an Inmixing of an Otherness Prerequisite to Any Subject Whatever," in Richard Macksey and Eugenio Donato (eds.), *The Structuralist Controversy: The Languages of Criticism and the Sciences of Man*, Baltimore: Johns Hopkins University Press, pp. 186–200.

—(1973), *Télévision*, Paris: Éditions du Seuil.

—(1977), "Desire and the Interpretation of Desire in *Hamlet*," ed. Jacques-Alain Miller, trans. James Hulbert, *Yale French Studies*, special issue: "Literature and Psychoanalysis – The Question of Reading: Otherwise," no. 55/56, pp. 11–52.

—(1980), "*Monsieur A.*," *Ornicar?*, no. 21–22, Summer, pp. 17–20.

—(1990a), "Television," trans. Denis Hollier, Rosalind Krauss, and Annette Michelson, in Jacques Lacan, *Television/A Challenge to the Psychoanalytic Establishment*, ed. Joan Copjec, New York: W.W. Norton and Company, pp. 1–46.

—(1990b), "Introduction to the Names-of-the-Father Seminar," trans. Jeffrey Mehlman, in Jacques Lacan, *Television/A Challenge to the*

Psychoanalytic Establishment, ed. Joan Copjec, New York: W.W. Norton and Company, pp. 81–95.

—(1990c), "Responses to Students of Philosophy Concerning the Object of Psychoanalysis," trans. Jeffrey Mehlman, in Jacques Lacan, *Television/A Challenge to the Psychoanalytic Establishment*, ed. Joan Copjec, New York: W.W. Norton and Company, pp. 107–14.

—(1990d), "Letter of Dissolution," trans. Jeffrey Mehlman, in Jacques Lacan, *Television/A Challenge to the Psychoanalytic Establishment*, ed. Joan Copjec, New York: W.W. Norton and Company, pp. 129–31.

—(2001a), "*Discours de Rome*," in Jacques Lacan, *Autres écrits*, ed. Jacques-Alain Miller, Paris: Éditions du Seuil, pp. 133–64.

—(2001b), "*Problèmes cruciaux pour la psychanalyse: Compte rendu du Séminaire 1964–1965*," in Jacques Lacan, *Autres écrits*, ed. Jacques-Alain Miller, Paris: Éditions du Seuil, pp. 199–202.

—(2001c), "*Reponses à des étudiants en philosophie*," in Jacques Lacan, *Autres écrits*, ed. Jacques-Alain Miller, Paris: Éditions du Seuil, pp. 203–11.

—(2001d), "*Petit discours à l'ORTF*," in Jacques Lacan, *Autres écrits*, ed. Jacques-Alain Miller, Paris: Éditions du Seuil, pp. 221–6.

—(2001e), "*Peut-être à Vincennes* ," in Jacques Lacan, *Autres écrits*, ed. Jacques-Alain Miller, Paris: Éditions du Seuil, pp. 313–15.

—(2001f), "*La méprise du sujet supposé savoir*," in Jacques Lacan, *Autres écrits*, ed. Jacques-Alain Miller, Paris: Éditions du Seuil, pp. 329–39.

—(2001g), "*L'acte psychanalytique: Compte rendu du Séminaire 1967–1968*," in Jacques Lacan, *Autres écrits*, ed. Jacques-Alain Miller, Paris: Éditions du Seuil, pp. 375–83.

—(2001h), "*Radiophonie*," in Jacques Lacan, *Autres écrits*, ed. Jacques-Alain Miller, Paris: Éditions du Seuil, pp. 403–47.

—(2001i), "*L'étourdit*," in Jacques Lacan, *Autres écrits*, ed. Jacques-Alain Miller, Paris: Éditions du Seuil, pp. 449–95.

—(2005a), "*Le symbolique, l'imaginaire et le réel*," in Jacques Lacan, *Des noms-du-père*, ed. Jacques-Alain Miller, Paris: Éditions du Seuil, pp. 9–63.

—(2005b), "*Introduction aux Noms-du-Père*," in Jacques Lacan, *Des Noms-du-Père*, ed. Jacques-Alain Miller, Paris: Éditions du Seuil, pp. 65–104.

—(2005c), "*Le triomphe de la religion*," in Jacques Lacan, *Le triomphe de la religion, précédé de Discours aux catholiques*, ed. Jacques-Alain Miller, Paris: Éditions du Seuil, pp. 67–102.

—(2006a), "Aristotle's Dream," trans. Lorenzo Chiesa, *Angelaki: Journal of the Theoretical Humanities*, vol. 11, no. 3, December, pp. 83–4.

—(2006b), "Seminar on 'The Purloined Letter,'" in Jacques Lacan, *Écrits: The First Complete Edition in English*, trans. Bruce Fink, New York: W.W. Norton and Company, pp. 6–48.

—(2006c), "The Mirror Stage as Formative of the *I* Function as Revealed in Psychoanalytic Experience," in Jacques Lacan, *Écrits: The First Complete Edition in English*, trans. Bruce Fink, New York: W.W. Norton and Company, pp. 75–81.

—(2006d), "Aggressiveness in Psychoanalysis," in Jacques Lacan, *Écrits: The First Complete Edition in English*, trans. Bruce Fink, New York: W.W. Norton and Company, pp. 82–101.

—(2006e), "Presentation on Psychical Causality," in Jacques Lacan, *Écrits: The First Complete Edition in English*, trans. Bruce Fink, New York: W.W. Norton and Company, pp. 123–58.

—(2006f), "On the Subject Who Is Finally in Question," in Jacques Lacan, *Écrits: The First Complete Edition in English*, trans. Bruce Fink, New York: W.W. Norton and Company, pp. 189–96.

—(2006g), "The Function and Field of Speech and Language in Psychoanalysis," in Jacques Lacan, *Écrits: The First Complete Edition in English*, trans. Bruce Fink, New York: W.W. Norton and Company, pp. 197–268.

—(2006h), "Variations on the Standard Treatment," in Jacques Lacan, *Écrits: The First Complete Edition in English*, trans. Bruce Fink, New York: W.W. Norton and Company, pp. 269–302.

—(2006i), "The Freudian Thing, or, the Meaning of the Return to Freud in Psychoanalysis," in Jacques Lacan, *Écrits: The First Complete Edition in English*, trans. Bruce Fink, New York: W.W. Norton and Company, pp. 334–63.

—(2006j), "Psychoanalysis and Its Teaching," in Jacques Lacan, *Écrits: The First Complete Edition in English*, trans. Bruce Fink, New York: W.W. Norton and Company, pp. 364–83.

—(2006k), "On a Question Prior to Any Possible Treatment of Psychosis," in Jacques Lacan, *Écrits: The First Complete Edition in English*, trans. Bruce Fink, New York: W.W. Norton and Company, pp. 445–88.

—(2006l), "The Direction of the Treatment and the Principles of Its Power," in Jacques Lacan, *Écrits: The First Complete Edition in English*, trans. Bruce Fink, New York: W.W. Norton and Company, pp. 489–542.

—(2006m), "The Signification of the Phallus," in Jacques Lacan, *Écrits:*

The First Complete Edition in English, trans. Bruce Fink, New York: W.W. Norton and Company, pp. 575–84.

—(2006n), "On an Ex Post Facto Syllabary," in Jacques Lacan, *Écrits: The First Complete Edition in English*, trans. Bruce Fink, New York: W.W. Norton and Company, pp. 602–9.

—(2006o), "The Subversion of the Subject and the Dialectic of Desire in the Freudian Unconscious," in Jacques Lacan, *Écrits: The First Complete Edition in English*, trans. Bruce Fink, New York: W.W. Norton and Company, pp. 671–702.

—(2006p), "Position of the Unconscious," in Jacques Lacan, *Écrits: The First Complete Edition in English*, trans. Bruce Fink, New York: W.W. Norton and Company, pp. 703–21.

—(2006q), "Science and Truth," in Jacques Lacan, *Écrits: The First Complete Edition in English*, trans. Bruce Fink, New York: W.W. Norton and Company, pp. 726–45.

Lacan, Jacques, The Seminars:

—(1988), *The Seminar of Jacques Lacan, Book I: Freud's Papers on Technique, 1953–1954*, ed. Jacques-Alain Miller, trans. John Forrester, New York: W.W. Norton and Company.

—(1988), *The Seminar of Jacques Lacan, Book II: The Ego in Freud's Theory and in the Technique of Psychoanalysis, 1954–1955*, ed. Jacques-Alain Miller, trans. Sylvana Tomaselli, New York: W.W. Norton and Company.

—(1993), *The Seminar of Jacques Lacan, Book III: The Psychoses, 1955–1956*, ed. Jacques-Alain Miller, trans. Russell Grigg, New York: W.W. Norton and Company.

—(1994), *Le Séminaire de Jacques Lacan, Livre IV: La relation d'objet, 1956–1957*, ed. Jacques-Alain Miller, Paris: Éditions du Seuil.

—(1998), *Le Séminaire de Jacques Lacan, Livre V: Les formations de l'inconscient, 1957–1958*, ed. Jacques-Alain Miller, Paris: Éditions du Seuil.

—(1958–59), *Le Séminaire de Jacques Lacan, Livre VI: Le désir et son interprétation, 1958–1959*, unpublished typescript.

—(1992), *The Seminar of Jacques Lacan, Book VII: The Ethics of Psychoanalysis, 1959–1960*, ed. Jacques-Alain Miller, trans. Dennis Porter, New York: W.W. Norton and Company.

—(2001), *Le Séminaire de Jacques Lacan, Livre VIII: Le transfert, 1960–1961*, seconde édition corrigée, ed. Jacques-Alain Miller, Paris: Éditions du Seuil.

—(1961–62), *Le Séminaire de Jacques Lacan, Livre IX: L'identification, 1961–1962*, unpublished typescript.

—(2004), *Le Séminaire de Jacques Lacan, Livre X: L'angoisse, 1962–1963*, ed. Jacques-Alain Miller, Paris: Éditions du Seuil.

—(1973), *Le Séminaire de Jacques Lacan, Livre XI: Les quatre concepts fondamentaux de la psychanalyse, 1964*, ed. Jacques-Alain Miller, Paris: Éditions du Seuil.

—(1977), *The Seminar of Jacques Lacan, Book XI: The Four Fundamental Concepts of Psychoanalysis, 1964*, ed. Jacques-Alain Miller, trans. Alan Sheridan, New York: W.W. Norton and Company.

—(1965–66), *Le Séminaire de Jacques Lacan, Livre XIII: L'objet de la psychanalyse, 1965–1966*, unpublished typescript.

—(1966–67), *Le Séminaire de Jacques Lacan, Livre XIV: La logique du fantasme, 1966–1967*, unpublished typescript.

—(1967–68), *Le Séminaire de Jacques Lacan, Livre XV: L'acte psychanalytique, 1967–1968*, unpublished typescript.

—(2006), *Le Séminaire de Jacques Lacan, Livre XVI: D'un Autre à l'autre, 1968–1969*, ed. Jacques-Alain Miller, Paris: Éditions du Seuil.

—(1991), *Le Séminaire de Jacques Lacan, Livre XVII: L'envers de la psychanalyse, 1969–1970*, ed. Jacques-Alain Miller, Paris: Éditions du Seuil.

—(2007), *The Seminar of Jacques Lacan, Book XVII: The Other Side of Psychoanalysis, 1969–1970*, ed. Jacques-Alain Miller, trans. Russell Grigg, New York: W.W. Norton and Company.

—(2006), *Le Séminaire de Jacques Lacan, Livre XVIII: D'un discours qui ne serait pas du semblant, 1971*, ed. Jacques-Alain Miller, Paris: Éditions du Seuil.

—(2011), *Le Séminaire de Jacques Lacan, Livre XIX: ... ou pire, 1971–1972*, ed. Jacques-Alain Miller, Paris: Éditions du Seuil.

—(1971–72), *Le Séminaire de Jacques Lacan, Livre XIX: Le savoir du psychanalyste, 1971–1972*, unpublished typescript.

—(1998), *The Seminar of Jacques Lacan, Book XX: Encore, 1972–1973*, ed. Jacques-Alain Miller, trans. Bruce Fink, New York: W.W. Norton and Company.

—(1973–74), *Le Séminaire de Jacques Lacan, Livre XXI: Les non-dupes errent, 1973–1974*, unpublished typescript.

—(1975), *Le Séminaire de Jacques Lacan, Livre XXII: R.S.I., 1974–1975*, ed. Jacques-Alain Miller, *Ornicar?*, nos. 2, 3, 4, 5.

—(2005), *Le Séminaire de Jacques Lacan, Livre XXIII: Le sinthome, 1975–1976*, ed. Jacques-Alain Miller, Paris: Éditions du Seuil.

—(1977–79), *Le Séminaire de Jacques Lacan, Livre XXIV: L'insu que sait de l'une-bévue, s'aile à mourre, 1976–1977*, ed. Jacques-Alain Miller, *Ornicar?*, nos. 12/13, 14, 15, 16, 17/18.

—(1977–78), *Le Séminaire de Jacques Lacan, Livre XXV: Le moment de conclure, 1977–1978*, unpublished typescript.

—(1980), *Le Séminaire de Jacques Lacan, Livre XXVII: Dissolution, 1980*, unpublished typescript.

Laplanche, Jean and Jean-Bertrand Pontalis (1973), *The Language of Psycho-Analysis*, trans. Donald Nicholson-Smith, New York: W.W. Norton and Company.

—(1986), "Fantasy and the Origins of Sexuality," in Victor Burgin, James Donald, and Cora Kaplan (eds.), *Formations of Fantasy*, New York: Methuen, pp. 5–34.

La Rochefoucauld, François duc de (1959), *Maxims*, trans. Leonard Tancock, New York: Penguin.

Lear, Jonathan (1990), *Love and Its Place in Nature: A Philosophical Interpretation of Freudian Psychoanalysis*, New Haven, CT: Yale University Press.

—(2000), *Happiness, Death, and the Remainder of Life*, Cambridge, MA: Harvard University Press.

—(2005), *Freud*, New York: Routledge.

Lebrun, Gérard (1972), *La patience du Concept: Essai sur le Discours hégélien*, Paris: Gallimard.

LeDoux, Joseph (1996), *The Emotional Brain: The Mysterious Underpinnings of Emotional Life*, New York: Simon & Schuster.

—(2002), *Synaptic Self: How Our Brains Become Who We Are*, New York: Penguin Books.

Lenin, V.I. (1972), *Materialism and Empirio-Criticism*, Beijing: Foreign Languages Press.

—(1975), "The Three Sources and Three Component Parts of Marxism," in V.I. Lenin, *The Lenin Anthology*, ed. Robert C. Tucker, New York: W.W. Norton and Company, pp. 640–4.

Libet, Benjamin (2004), *Mind Time: The Temporal Factor in Consciousness*, Cambridge, MA: Harvard University Press.

Linden, David J. (2007), *The Accidental Mind: How Brain Evolution Has Given Us Love, Memory, Dreams, and God*, Cambridge, MA: Harvard University Press.

Longuenesse, Béatrice (1981), *Hegel et la critique de la métaphysique*, Paris: Vrin.

Lukács, Georg (1971), "What is Orthodox Marxism?," in Georg Lukács, *History and Class Consciousness*, trans. Rodney Livingstone, Cambridge, MA: MIT Press, pp. 1–26.

—(1978a), *The Ontology of Social Being: 1. Hegel*, trans. David Fernbach, London: Merlin Press.

—(1978b), *The Ontology of Social Being: 2. Marx*, trans. David Fernbach, London: Merlin Press.

—(1980), *The Ontology of Social Being: 3. Labour*, trans. David Fernbach, London: Merlin Press.

McGinn, Colin (1999), *The Mysterious Flame: Conscious Minds in a Material World*, New York: Basic Books.

Macherey, Pierre (1990), *Hegel ou Spinoza*, 2nd edn, Paris: Éditions la Découverte.

Maimon, Salomon (2010), *Essay on Transcendental Philosophy*, trans. Nick Midgley, Henry Somers-Hall, Alistair Welchman, and Merten Reglitz, London: Continuum.

Maker, William (1998), "The Very Idea of the Idea of Nature, or Why Hegel Is Not an Idealist," in Stephen Houlgate (ed.), *Hegel and the Philosophy of Nature*, Albany: State University of New York Press, pp. 1–27.

Malabou, Catherine (2004), *Que faire de notre cerveau?*, Paris: Bayard.

—(2005), *The Future of Hegel: Plasticity, Temporality and Dialectic*, trans. Lisabeth During, New York: Routledge.

—(2007), *Les nouveaux blessés: De Freud à la neurologie, penser les traumatismes contemporains*, Paris: Bayard.

—(2008), *What Should We Do with Our Brain?*, trans. Sebastian Rand, New York: Fordham University Press.

—(2009a), "*Préface*," in Catherine Malabou, *La chambre du milieu: De Hegel aux neurosciences*, Paris: Hermann, pp. 7–10.

—(2009b), "*Les enjeux idéologiques de la plasticité neuronale*," in Catherine Malabou, *La chambre du milieu: De Hegel aux neurosciences*, Paris: Hermann, pp. 213–28.

—(2009c), "*Pour une critique de la raison neurobiologique: À propos de Jean-Pierre Changeux, Du Vrai, du Beau, du Bien, Une nouvelle approche neuronale*," in Catherine Malabou, *La chambre du milieu: De Hegel aux neurosciences*, Paris: Hermann, pp. 229–37.

—(2009d), *Ontologie de l'accident: Essai sur la plasticité destructrice*, Paris: Éditions Léo Scheer.

—(2010), *Plasticity at the Dusk of Writing: Dialectic, Destruction, Deconstruction*, trans. Carolyn Shread, New York: Columbia University Press.

—(2013a), "Go Wonder: Subjectivity and Affects in Neurobiological Times," in Adrian Johnston and Catherine Malabou, *Self and Emotional Life: Philosophy, Psychoanalysis, and Neuroscience*, New York: Columbia University Press, pp. 1–72.

—(2013b), "Postface: The Paradoxes of the Principle of Constancy," in

Adrian Johnston and Catherine Malabou, *Self and Emotional Life: Philosophy, Psychoanalysis, and Neuroscience*, New York: Columbia University Press, pp. 211–24.

Mao Tse-Tung (2007), "On Contradiction," in Mao Tse-Tung, *On Practice and Contradiction*, ed. Slavoj Žižek, London: Verso, pp. 67–102.

Marcus, Gary (2008), *Kludge: The Haphazard Evolution of the Human Mind*, New York: Houghton Mifflin Harcourt.

Marx, Karl (1977), "Theses on Feuerbach," trans. S. Ryazanskaya, in David McLellan (ed.), *Karl Marx: Selected Writings*, Oxford: Oxford University Press, 1977, pp. 156–8.

—(1990), *Capital: Volume One*, trans. Ben Fowkes, New York: Penguin.

—(1993), *Grundrisse: Foundations of the Critique of Political Economy (Rough Draft)*, trans. Martin Nicolaus, New York: Penguin.

Maturana, Humberto R. and Francisco J. Varela (1980), *Autopoiesis and Cognition: The Realization of the Living*, Dordrecht: D. Reidel.

—(1987), *The Tree of Knowledge: The Biological Roots of Human Understanding*, Boston: New Science Library.

Metzinger, Thomas (2009), *The Ego Tunnel: The Science of the Mind and the Myth of the Self*, New York: Basic Books.

Miller, Jacques-Alain (1977/1978), "Suture (elements of the logic of the signifier)," trans. Jacqueline Rose, *Screen*, vol. 18, no. 4, Winter, pp. 24–34.

Milner, Jean-Claude (1991), "*Lacan et la science moderne*," in Collège international de philosophie (ed.), *Lacan avec les philosophes*, Paris: Éditions Albin Michel, pp. 335–51.

—(1995), *L'Œvre claire: Lacan, la science, la philosophie*, Paris: Éditions du Seuil.

—(2000), "*De la linguistique à la linguisterie*," in l'École de la Cause freudienne (ed.), *Lacan, l'écrit, l'image*, Paris: Flammarion, pp. 7–25.

—(2002), *Le périple structural: Figures et paradigme*, Paris: Éditions du Seuil.

—(2012), "The Force of Minimalism: An Interview with Jean-Claude Milner (with Knox Peden)," trans. Tzuchien Tho, in Peter Hallward and Knox Peden (eds.), *Concept and Form, Volume Two: Interviews and Essays on the Cahiers pour l'Analyse*, London: Verso, pp. 229–44.

Moder, Gregor (2013), *Hegel und Spinoza: Negativität in der gegenwärtigen Philosophie*, trans. Alfred Leskovec, Vienna: Turia & Kant.

Moyar, Dean (2012), "Thought and Metaphysics: Hegel's Critical Reception of Spinoza," in Eckart Förster and Yitzhak Y. Melamed (eds.), *Spinoza and German Idealism*, Cambridge: Cambridge University Press, pp. 197–213.

Muller, John P. (1980), "Psychosis and Mourning in Lacan's *Hamlet*," *New Literary History*, vol. 12, no. 1, Autumn, pp. 147–65.

Panksepp, Jaak (1998), *Affective Neuroscience: The Foundations of Human and Animal Emotions*, Oxford: Oxford University Press.

Pascal, Blaise (1966), *Pensées*, trans. A.J. Krailsheimer, New York: Penguin.

Pfister, Oskar (1993), "The Illusion of a Future: A Friendly Disagreement with Prof. Sigmund Freud," ed. Paul Roazen, trans. Susan Abrams, *International Journal of Psycho-Analysis*, vol. 74, no. 3. pp. 557–79.

Pico della Mirandola, Giovanni (1998), "On the Dignity of Man," in Giovanni Pico della Mirandola, *On the Dignity of Man*, trans. Charles Glenn Wallis, Paul J.W. Miller, and Douglas Carmichael, Indianapolis: Hackett, pp. 1–34.

Pippin, Robert B. (1989), *Hegel's Idealism: The Satisfactions of Self-Consciousness*, Cambridge: Cambridge University Press.

—(2008), *Hegel's Practical Philosophy: Rational Agency as Ethical Life*, Cambridge: Cambridge University Press.

Rank, Otto (1958), *Beyond Psychology*, New York: Dover.

—(1993), *The Trauma of Birth*, New York: Dover.

Regnault, François (1997), "*L'antiphilosophie selon Lacan*," *Conférences d'esthétique lacanienne*, Paris: Agalma, 1997, pp. 57–80.

Rogers, Lesley (2001), *Sexing the Brain*, New York: Columbia University Press.

Safouan, Moustapha (1983), *Pleasure and Being: Hedonism from a Psychoanalytic Point of View*, trans. Martin Thom, New York: Saint Martin's Press.

Sartre, Jean-Paul (1948), *Existentialism and Humanism*, trans. Philip Mairet, London: Methuen.

Schelling, F.W.J. (1936), *Philosophical Inquiries into the Nature of Human Freedom, and matters connected therewith*, trans. James Gutmann, Chicago: Open Court Publishing Company.

—(1966), *On University Studies*, trans. E.S. Morgan, Athens, OH: Ohio University Press.

—(1978), *System of Transcendental Idealism*, trans. Peter Heath and Michael Vater, Charlottesville: University Press of Virginia.

—(1980), "Philosophical Letters on Dogmatism and Criticism," in F.W.J. Schelling, *The Unconditional in Human Knowledge: Four Early Essays (1794–1796)*, trans. Fritz Marti, Lewisburg: Bucknell University Press, pp. 156–218.

—(1984), *Bruno, or On the Natural and the Divine Principle of Things*, trans. Michael G. Vater, Albany: State University of New York Press.

—(1988), *Ideas for a Philosophy of Nature as Introduction to the Study of This Science*, trans. Errol E. Harris and Peter Heath, Cambridge: Cambridge University Press.

—(1994a), *On the History of Modern Philosophy*, trans. Andrew Bowie, Cambridge: Cambridge University Press.

—(1994b), "System of Philosophy in General and of the Philosophy of Nature in Particular," in F.W.J. Schelling, *Idealism and the Endgame of Theory: Three Essays by F.W.J. Schelling*, trans. Thomas Pfau, Albany: State University of New York Press, pp. 139–94.

—(1994c), "Stuttgart Seminars," in F.W.J. Schelling, *Idealism and the Endgame of Theory: Three Essays by F.W.J. Schelling*, trans. Thomas Pfau, Albany: State University of New York Press, pp. 195–268.

—(2000), *The Ages of the World: Third Version (c. 1815)*, trans. Jason M. Wirth, Albany: State University of New York Press.

—(2002), *Clara – or, On Nature's Connection to the Spirit World*, trans. Fiona Steinkamp, Albany: State University of New York Press.

—(2004), *First Outline of a System of the Philosophy of Nature*, trans. Keith R. Peterson, Albany: State University of New York Press.

—(2007), *The Grounding of the Positive Philosophy*, trans. Bruce Matthews, Albany: State University of New York Press.

Schelling, F.W.J. and G.W.F. Hegel (2002), "Introduction for the *Critical Journal of Philosophy*: On the Essence of Philosophical Criticism Generally, and Its Relationship to the Present State of Philosophy in Particular," trans. H.S. Harris, in G.W.F. Hegel, *Miscellaneous Writings of G.W.F. Hegel*, ed. Jon Stewart, Evanston: Northwestern University Press, pp. 207–25.

Soler, Colette (2006), "*Lacan en antiphilosophie*," *Filozofski Vestnik*, special issue: "*Philosophie, psychanalyse: alliance ou mésalliance?*," ed. Jelica Šumič-Riha, vol. 27, no. 2, pp. 121–44.

—(2009), *Lacan, l'inconscient réinventé*, Paris: Presses Universitaires de France.

—(2011), *Les affects lacaniens*, Paris: Presses Universitaires de France.

Solms, Mark and Oliver Turnbull (2002), *The Brain and the Inner World: An Introduction to the Neuroscience of Subjective Experience*, New York: Other Press.

Spinoza, Baruch (1949), *Ethics*, ed. James Gutmann, New York: Hafner.

Stalin, J.V. (1940), *Dialectical and Historical Materialism*, New York: International Publishers.

—(1972a), "Concerning Marxism in Linguistics," in J.V. Stalin, *Marxism and Problems of Linguistics*, Peking: Foreign Languages Press, pp. 3–32.

—(1972b), "Concerning Certain Problems of Linguistics," in J.V. Stalin, *Marxism and Problems of Linguistics*, Peking: Foreign Languages Press, pp. 33–40.

Stanovich, Keith E. (2004), *The Robot's Rebellion: Finding Meaning in the Age of Darwin*, Chicago: University of Chicago Press.

Theunissen, Michael (1980), *Sein und Schein: Die kritische Funktion der Hegelschen Logik*, Frankfurt am Main: Suhrkamp.

Varela, Francisco J., Evan Thompson, and Eleanor Rosch (1991), *The Embodied Mind: Cognitive Science and Human Experience*, Cambridge, MA: MIT Press.

Vater, Michael (2012), "Schelling's Philosophy of Identity and Spinoza's *Ethica more geometrico*," in Eckart Förster and Yitzhak Y. Melamed (eds.), *Spinoza and German Idealism*, Cambridge: Cambridge University Press, pp. 156–74.

Vaysse, Jean-Marie (1994), *Totalité et subjectivité: Spinoza dans l'idéalisme allemand*, Paris: Vrin.

Westphal, Kenneth R. (1989), *Hegel's Epistemological Realism*, Dordrecht, Netherlands: Kluwer Academic Publishers.

Wittgenstein, Ludwig (1961), *Tractatus Logico-Philosophicus*, trans. D.F. Pears and B.F. McGuinness, London: Routledge & Kegan Paul.

Žižek, Slavoj (1988), *Le plus sublime des hystériques: Hegel passe*. Paris: Points Hors Ligne.

—(1989), *The Sublime Object of Ideology*, London: Verso.

—(1993), *Tarrying with the Negative: Kant, Hegel, and the Critique of Ideology*, Durham, NC: Duke University Press.

—(1994a), "Kant as a Theoretician of Vampirism," *Lacanian Ink*, no. 8, Spring, pp. 19–33.

—(1994b), *The Metastases of Enjoyment: Six Essays on Woman and Causality*, London: Verso.

—(1996a), "'I Hear You with My Eyes'; or, The Invisible Master," in Renata Salecl and Slavoj Žižek (eds.), *Gaze and Voice as Love Objects*, Durham, NC: Duke University Press, pp. 90–126.

—(1996b), *The Indivisible Remainder: An Essay on Schelling and Related Matters*, London: Verso.

—(1997a), "The Abyss of Freedom," in F.W.J. von Schelling and Slavoj Žižek, *The Abyss of Freedom/Ages of the World*, Ann Arbor: University of Michigan Press, pp. 1–104.

—(1997b), "Interview – with Andrew Long and Tara McGann," *JPCS:*

Journal for the Psychoanalysis of Culture and Society, vol. 2, no. 1, Spring, pp. 133–7.

—(1997c), *The Plague of Fantasies*, London: Verso.

—(1998), "Introduction: Cogito as a Shibboleth," in Slavoj Žižek (ed.), *Cogito and the Unconscious*, Durham, NC: Duke University Press, pp. 1–8.

—(1999a), *The Ticklish Subject: The Absent Centre of Political Ontology*, London: Verso.

—(1999b), "The Spectre of Ideology," in Elizabeth Wright and Edmond Wright (eds.), *The Žižek Reader*, Oxford: Blackwell, pp. 53–86.

—(1999c), "Death and the Maiden," in Elizabeth Wright and Edmond Wright (eds.), *The Žižek Reader*, Oxford: Blackwell, pp. 206–22.

—(2000), "*Da Capo senza Fine*," in Judith Butler, Ernesto Laclau, and Slavoj Žižek, *Contingency, Hegemony, Universality: Contemporary Dialogues on the Left*, London: Verso, pp. 213–62.

—(2001a), *The Fright of Real Tears: Krzysztof Kieślowski Between Theory and Post-Theory*, London: British Film Institute.

—(2001b), *On Belief*, New York: Routledge.

—(2002a), *For They Know Not What They Do: Enjoyment as a Political Factor*, 2nd edn, London: Verso.

—(2002b), "'I Do Not Order My Dreams,'" in Slavoj Žižek and Mladen Dolar, *Opera's Second Death*, New York: Routledge, pp. 103–225.

—(2003), *The Puppet and the Dwarf: The Perverse Core of Christianity*, Cambridge, MA: MIT Press.

—(2004a), *Iraq: The Borrowed Kettle*, London: Verso.

—(2004b), *Organs without Bodies: On Deleuze and Consequences*, New York: Routledge.

—(2005), "Lacan – At What Point is he Hegelian?," trans. Rex Butler and Scott Stephens, in Slavoj Žižek, *Interrogating the Real*, ed. Rex Butler and Scott Stephens, London: Continuum, pp. 26–37.

—(2006a), *The Parallax View*, Cambridge, MA: MIT Press.

—(2006b), Slavoj Žižek, "*Philosophie en situations: La pensée de Slavoj Žižek – Pop Philosophie: Audio Lecture-France Culture*," May 26, 2006, <http://www.lacan.com/zizekone.htm> (last accessed 14 April 2013).

—(2007a), "From *objet a* to Subtraction," *Lacanian Ink*, no. 30, Fall, pp. 131–41.

—(2007b), "Why Only an Atheist Can Believe: Politics on the Edge of Fear and Trembling," *International Journal of Žižek Studies*, vol. 1, no. 0, <http://zizekstudies.org/index.php/ijzs/article/view/7/36> (last accessed 14 April 2013).

—(2008a), "Descartes and the Post-Traumatic Subject," *Filozofski Vestnik*, special issue: "Radical Philosophy?," ed. Peter Klepec, vol. 29, no. 2, pp. 9–29.

—(2008b), *In Defense of Lost Causes*, London: Verso.

—(2009a), "Ecology," in Astra Taylor (ed.), *The Examined Life: Excursions with Contemporary Thinkers*, New York: The New Press, pp. 155–83.

—(2009b), "The Fear of Four Words: A Modest Plea for the Hegelian Reading of Christianity," in Slavoj Žižek and John Milbank, *The Monstrosity of Christ: Paradox or Dialectic?*, ed. Creston Davis, Cambridge, MA: MIT Press, pp. 24–109.

—(2009c), "Dialectical Clarity Versus the Misty Conceit of Paradox," in Slavoj Žižek and John Milbank, *The Monstrosity of Christ: Paradox or Dialectic?*, ed. Creston Davis, Cambridge, MA: MIT Press, pp. 234–306.

—(2009d), "Discipline Between Two Freedoms – Madness and Habit in German Idealism," in Markus Gabriel and Slavoj Žižek, *Mythology, Madness and Laughter: Subjectivity in German Idealism*, London: Continuum, pp. 95–121.

—(2009e), "Fichte's Laughter," in Markus Gabriel and Slavoj Žižek, *Mythology, Madness and Laughter: Subjectivity in German Idealism*, London: Continuum, pp. 122–67.

—(2010a), *Living in the End Times*, London: Verso.

—(2010b), "Some Concluding Notes on Violence, Ideology, and Communist Culture," *Subjectivity*, special issue: "Žižek and Political Subjectivity," ed. Derek Hook and Calum Neill, vol. 3, no. 1, April, pp. 101–16.

—(2010c), *À travers le réel: Entretiens avec Fabien Tarby*, Paris: Nouvelle Éditions Lignes.

—(2011a), Private Communication with Author.

—(2011b), "Is it Still Possible to be a Hegelian Today?," in Levi Bryant, Nick Srnicek, and Graham Harman (eds.), *The Speculative Turn: Continental Materialism and Realism*, Melbourne: Re.press, pp. 202–23.

—(2011c), "Interview [with Ben Woodward]," in Levi Bryant, Nick Srnicek, and Graham Harman (eds.), *The Speculative Turn: Continental Materialism and Realism*, Melbourne: Re.press, pp. 406–15.

—(2012), *Less Than Nothing: Hegel and the Shadow of Dialectical Materialism*, London: Verso.

Zupančič, Alenka (1996), "Philosophers' Blind Man's Buff," in Renata Salecl and Slavoj Žižek (eds.), *Gaze and Voice as Love Objects*, Durham, NC: Duke University Press, pp. 32–58.

—(2001), *Das Reale einer Illusion: Kant und Lacan*, trans. Reiner Ansén, Frankfurt am Main: Suhrkamp.

—(2002), *Esthétique du désir, éthique de la jouissance*, Paris: Théétète éditions.

—(2008), *The Odd One In: On Comedy*, Cambridge, MA: MIT Press.

—(2011), "Realism in Psychoanalysis," *Journal of European Psychoanalysis*, special issue: "Lacan and Philosophy: The New Generation," ed. Lorenzo Chiesa, no. 32, pp. 29–48.

Index

351